Silverlight™ 2 Bible

Brad Dayley and Lisa DaNae Dayley

WILEY

Wiley Publishing, Inc.

Silverlight™ 2 Bible

Published by
Wiley Publishing, Inc.
10475 Crosspoint Boulevard
Indianapolis, IN 46256
www.wiley.com

Published by Wiley Publishing, Inc., Indianapolis, Indiana

Published simultaneously in Canada

ISBN: 978-0-470-37500-6

Manufactured in the United States of America

10 9 8 7 6 5 4 3 2 1

For general information on our other products and services or to obtain technical support, please contact our Customer Care Department within the U.S. at (800) 762-2974, outside the U.S. at (317) 572-3993 or fax (317) 572-4002.

Library of Congress Control Number: 2008935813

About the Authors

Brad Dayley is a senior software engineer with 17 years of experience designing, developing, and implementing software from the kernel level up through Web development. He is the author of several books on server and network management, the Python language, and Web frameworks. When he is not developing software or writing books, he can be found biking, hiking, and/or Jeeping somewhere in the remote regions of the western U.S. with his wife, DaNae, and four sons.

Lisa DaNae Dayley's two great loves are writing and computers. With a degree in Advertising from Brigham Young University, DaNae has owned and operated a media creation business for 14 years incorporating writing, graphic design, and video editing over the years. She has coauthored several books with her husband, Brad, and is the author of Roxio Easy Media Creator 8 in a Snap and PhotoShop CS3 Extended Video and 3D Bible. When she's not at her computer, she can be found in the great outdoors, preferably in a Jeep.

Credits

Acquisitions Editor
Courtney Allen

Project Editor
Jama Carter

Technical Editor
Ed Blankenship

Copy Editor
Kim Heusel

Editorial Manager
Robyn Siesky

Business Manager
Amy Knies

Sr. Marketing Manager
Sandy Smith

**Vice President and Executive Group
Publisher**
Richard Swadley

Vice President and Executive Publisher
Bob Ipsen

Vice President and Publisher
Barry Pruett

Project Coordinator
Erin Smith

Graphics and Production Specialists
Nikki Gately, Jennifer Henry,
Christine Williams

Quality Control Technician
John Greenough

Proofreading
Nancy Rappoport

Indexing
Potomac Indexing, LLC

Contents

Contents

Contents

Contents

Preface

For years Adobe Flash has dominated the realm of rich media content for Web pages using their browser plug-in. Adobe has put a lot of effort into providing a good platform for developers to implement the functionality necessary to deliver next generation Web pages. Microsoft has a history of delivering great development platforms that are supported by industry leading tools and development support. With Silverlight, Microsoft has captured a truly great vision of the next generation of Web services.

Microsoft's first attempt was Silverlight 1.0, a cross-browser, cross-platform browser plug-in for client side Web application. Silverlight 1.0 included a media pipeline that allowed designers and developers the ability to deliver a media-rich UI with high quality audio, video, and images.

The Silverlight 1.0 architecture provided a browser plug-in and JavaScript libraries that enabled developers to implement a subset of the already proven architecture Windows Presentation Foundation (WPF) as the UI interface and a JavaScript back end for client-side Web applications.

Silverlight 1.0 was a fair first attempt and showed some good promise; however, it fell far short of being the "Flash Killer" that it was originally nicknamed by developers. Developers were still pretty limited in what they could really do with unmanaged JavaScript applications, and the WPF style controls were very limited.

Silverlight 2 is a completely different story. Microsoft actually listened pretty well to the complaints coming from developers and the criticism that Silverlight 1.0 received. Silverlight 2 adds support for the .NET platform as well as Dynamic Language Runtime (DLR) support allowing developers to write their Silverlight applications in Visual C#, Visual Basic, AJAX, JavaScript, Ruby, and Python. Silverlight 2 also provides some great interaction with ASP.NET AJAX on both the client and server side.

Opening up the .NET platform to Silverlight developers now provides an extremely robust backend platform that allows developers to write rich interactive applications that are able to easily integrate with existing Web services and technologies.

Silverlight 2 also provides a much greater set of XAML controls from WPF, including things such as data grids, calendars, buttons, and list boxes. Using Silverlight 2 XAML, developers and designers can implement rich UIs with 2-D animations, vector graphics, and interactive media content.

As part of the Silverlight 2 offering, Microsoft also provides extremely useful support in the Visual Studio development tools for developers. For designers, Microsoft provides support in the Expression Studio Suite allowing designers to quickly deliver Silverlight-ready UI, images, and media.

Acknowledgments

Our sincere gratitude goes out to the following persons, without whom this book could not have happened:

Our friends and family who force us to be more intelligent and creative than we necessarily would like to be.

Thanks to Scott Guthrie, Jesse Liberty, Tim Heuer, and ALL (please don't be offended if I left your name out, my appreciation goes to everyone) the other folks at Microsoft who are so diligent about posting updates and examples and answering questions.

To our editors who made the book readable, technically accurate, and kept us on track, you really rock. Thanks to Courtney Allen for keeping us on track and getting the project moving in the right direction. Thanks to Jama Carter for all your hard work and making sure that the end result was the highest standard. Thanks to Kim Heusel for interpreting the ramblings of our minds into legible English. And thanks to Ed Blankenship for making certain all the concepts in this book are technically accurate and that the code examples really work.

Also, thanks to everyone else at Wiley who helped get this project out the door.

Who Should Read This Book

Silverlight 2 is intended for two groups of people, designers and Web developers. In Web development there is an inherent need to separate content from presentation. Microsoft has really kept that in mind in designing the Silverlight platform. I've also kept that in mind while writing this book, and it is intended for both designers and developers. The design and development sections are separated.

The design sections of this book are written with the assumption that you are at least somewhat familiar with HTML Web page design. If you are designing Web pages, then this book will help you understand the advantages of incorporating Silverlight applications to provide a rich UI.

If you are writing any kind of Web application or service, you should really consider the Silverlight platform for the Web client. Silverlight applications can easily plug into existing environments that deliver Web services over most technologies.

The development sections of this book are written for developers that have some experience with .NET programming. The book will take you through the process of creating Silverlight applications using the .NET languages from that perspective.

How This Book Is Organized

I've tried to organize the book to flow from one topic to the next. Part I gives you the background and helps you get your environment set up. Part II covers building the UI for Silverlight applications. Part III discusses developing the functionality for the UI. Part IV covers some additional development concepts that were not covered in Part III.

Part I: Silverlight Basics

Part I of the book focuses on introducing you to the Silverlight platform and helping you understand the architecture. If you are already familiar with the Silverlight 1.0 architecture, you should still read this part. There have been so many changes between 1.0 and 2 that it is really a completely new platform.

Part I also covers how to get started developing Silverlight applications by setting up an appropriate development environment. I also discuss some of the tools that are available to designers and developers when developing Silverlight applications.

Part II: Silverlight Design Fundamentals

Part II of this book focuses on the design side of Silverlight applications. Chapter 3 gives a brief overview of the XAML that is used in Silverlight. I discuss the controls and how to implement layout, animations, transforms, and so on. Chapter 4 and Chapter 5 discuss some of the design tools that designers can use to build rich, stylish, and interactive UI components for Silverlight applications.

Even if you are a developer, you should read this section. As a developer it will help you understand how the UI components are put together, and it will also help you understand how to interact with the XAML controls in your code.

Part III: Programming Silverlight Applications

Part III of this book is designed to give you an introduction into programming Silverlight applications. It covers the basics of creating Silverlight applications in Visual Studio and how to build and deploy Silverlight applications.

Part III also discusses how to develop Silverlight applications using the .NET language, DLR languages, ASP.NET AJAX, and unmanaged JavaScript. Part III is designed to help you understand the options available to you when writing Silverlight applications.

Part IV: Understanding Silverlight Frameworks

Part IV of this book is designed to give you a breakdown of the three major frameworks Silverlight 2 provides. Much of the presentation framework will already have been covered in Chapter 3 and Part III of the book; however, Chapter 13 will discuss some of the more important parts that were missed.

Chapter 14 discusses the Silverlight communication framework including Web clients, sockets, and Web requests. This chapter is designed to give you the necessary tools for your Silverlight applications to interact with existing Web services.

Chapter 15 discusses the Silverlight data framework including XML reading and writing, data binding, and LINQ. This chapter is designed to give you the necessary tools for your Silverlight applications to manage data internally and interact with data coming from and going to existing Web services.

Part V: Appendixes

Part V is where you find links to helpful resources as you learn and apply Silverlight applications (Appendix A) and a listing of available methods, properties, and events for commonly used Silverlight controls (Appendix B).

How to Get the Most out of This Book

The following are some suggestions on how to get the most out of this book:

Read each chapter in order. I've tried to organize the book to flow from one topic to the next. Along the way I've included example code in Listings that show both the XAML and managed code necessary to implement the concept. I've tried not to cover the same things more than once, and if you skip around you may miss something. For example, I cover accessing a WSDL Web service in Chapter 10 when discussing ASP.NET, but not in Chapter 14 when discussing the communication framework.

Experiment with the code. Because Silverlight interacts with so many different frameworks, there are usually several different methods that can be employed for any given problem. I would suggest spending some time playing around after reading each chapter, especially the chapters in Part III. Use the example code as a base and then implement your own additional features. The code examples are fairly simple intentionally. Silverlight applications inherently take a lot of lines of code, especially if you are implementing very many graphic elements. I hate reading books and having to wade through page after page of code with most of the code not relevant to the current topic. However, the examples are complete and stick to the topic with little or no extraneous code.

Read the icons. The book is interlaced with several different icons such as Tip, Note, Caution, and Cross-Reference. The icons include important and useful points that I wanted to highlight.

Read additional materials. This book is designed to give you a good understanding of the Silverlight platform. I was not able to cover all the capabilities of the various technologies that integrate with Silverlight such as .NET, WPF, WCF, DLR languages, and LINQ. To really get the most out of Silverlight, you should study up on the external topics and then read/review those sections of the book.

Part I

Silverlight Basics

Chapter 1

Getting to Know Silverlight

S ilverlight is Microsoft's implementation of a cross-browser, cross-platform client framework that allows designers and developers to deliver Rich Internet Applications (RIA) embedded in Web pages. Silverlight is fitted with a flexible media pipeline that makes it extremely easy to implement media-rich controls in your Web applications.

This chapter gives you a brief introduction to the Silverlight framework. The following sections discuss what Silverlight is and why you would want to use it to develop Web-based applications. They also define the architecture behind the Silverlight framework and Silverlight applications to help you understand how Silverlight fits into the Web services picture.

What Is Silverlight?

You can look at the Silverlight framework as a combination of three very different architectures: the browser plug-in, presentation framework, and .NET framework. The culmination of these frameworks allows Silverlight to bridge the gap between presentation user interface (UI) using declarative languages and functional programming using a subset of the .NET framework.

The lightweight browser plug-in provides the necessary interaction with the browser enabling the same Silverlight application to run on multiple platforms. The plug-in must be installed by the user before Silverlight applications can be viewed in the browser.

Silverlight applications are implemented as embedded objects in Web pages. When the browser encounters a Silverlight object in the Web page, the plug-in downloads an XAP package from the Web server that contains the binaries and resources for the Silverlight application and then begins code execution inside the Web page.

IN THIS CHAPTER

What is Silverlight?

Benefits of using Silverlight

Limitations of using Silverlight

Understanding the components of the Silverlight framework

Understanding the components of Silverlight applications

Silverlight applications are run as client-side applications without the need to refresh the browser to update the UI. However, because of the built-in .NET framework, Silverlight applications can easily integrate with server-side controls and services. Using Silverlight's implementation of the .NET framework, developers can easily integrate existing libraries and code into Silverlight applications.

Silverlight's presentation framework is a subset of the Window Presentation Foundation (WPF), which is based on the eXtensible Application Markup Language (XAML) programming language. The XAML language is simply based on the XML language with application elements that map to objects and properties in the .NET framework. Because it is based on the XML language format it can be easily parsed and integrated with many technologies.

The XAML language lends itself to the UI design side of Silverlight because it is simple to implement and understand. All of the UI generated by XAML is vector based, allowing it to be dynamically reshaped and resized easily while maintaining a crisp visual effect.

Silverlight's implementation of WPF provides a rich set of controls such as buttons, calendars, text boxes, scroll viewers, a data grid, and much more. These controls are easy to implement in the XAML language as well as easy to access from .NET managed code.

Silverlight's media pipeline makes it simple to stream media such as WMV, MP3, and JPEG files to your application UI. This allows you to add rich UI elements that can give users a true Web experience.

Why Use Silverlight?

The biggest reason to use Silverlight is that it seamlessly integrates the XAML declarative language with the .NET framework. XAML adoption is growing rapidly because of how easy it is to implement amazing UI interfaces. Many developers already have applications and libraries written in .NET. That code can usually be easily modified to fit Silverlight applications.

The Silverlight platform appeals to both designers and to developers because it provides a dynamic platform that makes it easy to develop powerful Web applications that incorporate rich graphics, audio, and video. There is a distinct division between the declarative XAML designers use and the .NET managed code that developers use, allowing each side to implement its piece and easily integrate the two.

Another reason Silverlight appeals to both designers and developers is that Microsoft offers powerful tools that make it easy to implement Silverlight applications. Microsoft's Expression Suite provides useful tools to implement Silverlight UI and encode media. Microsoft's Visual Studio provides a dynamic development interface with tools that speed up and increase productivity.

Some other reasons to use Silverlight are listed here:

- **It is a cross-browser, cross-platform technology, which provides a consistent user experience everywhere it runs.**
- **The Silverlight plug-in installs in seconds and leaves a very small footprint.**

■ **After you install the plug-in, users no longer need to install anything on their workstations to run Silverlight applications.** The applications are available to them from whatever browser they are accessing.

■ **It runs a client-side application that can read data and update the UI without interrupting the user by refreshing the whole page.**

■ **It can run asynchronous communications with the server allowing the UI to continue to function while waiting for the server response.**

■ **It delivers rich video, audio, and graphics.**

There are some disadvantages to implementing Silverlight applications as opposed to traditional client applications. It is important that you understand those limitations when deciding to use Silverlight.

The following is a list of Silverlight limitations that may impact your applications:

■ **The user must have access to the Internet for Silverlight applications to run.** Also, if your Silverlight applications have a lot of media that is bandwidth intensive, slow Internet connections can impact the user experience.

■ **Limited access to the file system.** Browser-based applications are limited in their access to the files system. However, you can ask the user to access the local file system to read files and there is an isolated local storage that you can use for small amounts of persistent data.

■ **Browser settings may limit Silverlight applications.** Users have the ability to disable scripting and controls in their browsers. These settings may limit or inhibit running Silverlight applications.

■ **The data that is dynamically implemented in Silverlight applications is not visible to search engines.** If you have data that needs to be visible to search engines to give your Web site exposure, you need to find some way to expose that data outside of Silverlight.

Comparing Silverlight 1.0 and 2

The difference between Silverlight 1.0 and 2 is very significant. The biggest change is the implementation of the .NET framework. If you are familiar with Silverlight 1.0 then you will be used to coding the application functionality in JavaScript. You still can implement functionality using JavaScript; however, you can now also implement functionality using C#, Visual Basic, Python, Ruby, and managed JavaScript.

Another major change is the introduction of the XAP package. In Silverlight 1.0, the XAML code was referenced directly by the Silverlight object embedded in the browser. In Silverlight 2, however, the embedded object references an XAP package that contains the XAP file, assemblies, and resources necessary to run the Silverlight application.

NOTE Because of the number of changes from Silverlight 1.0 to Silverlight 2, there are several code-breaking changes. Visit Microsoft's Web site at `http://msdn.microsoft.com/en-us/library/cc189007(VS.95).aspx` to see a list of code breakers that may apply to your Silverlight 1.0 applications.

To help you get a feel for the changes between Silverlight 1.0 and 2, Table 1.1 provides a list of features implemented in Silverlight 2 versus what was implemented in Silverlight 1.0 that was collected from the MSDN documentation.

TABLE 1.1

Silverlight 1.0 versus 2 Feature Comparison

Features	Silverlight 1.0	Silverlight 2
2D Vector Animation/Graphics	YES	YES
AJAX Support	YES	YES
Cross-Browser (Firefox, IE, Safari)	YES	YES
Cross-Platform (Windows, Mac)	YES	YES
Framework Languages (Visual Basic, Visual C#, IronRuby, IronPython)	NO	YES
HTML DOM Integration	YES	YES
HTTP Networking	YES	YES
Isolated Storage	NO	YES
JavaScript Support	YES	YES
JSON, REST, SOAP/WS-*, POX, and RSS Web Services (as well as support for Sockets)	NO	YES
Cross Domain Network Access	NO	YES
LINQ to Objects	NO	YES
Canvas Layout Support	YES	YES
StackPanel, Grid, and Panel Layout Support	NO	YES
Managed Control Framework	NO	YES
Full suite of Controls (`TextBox`, `RadioButton`, `Slider`, `Calendar`, `DatePicker`, `DataGrid`, `ListBox`, and others)	NO	YES
Deep Zoom Technology	NO	YES
Managed HTML Bridge	NO	YES
Managed Exception Handling	NO	YES
Media — Content Protection	NO	YES
Media — 720P High Definition (HD) Video	YES	YES
Media — Audio/Video Support (VC-1, WMV,WMA, MP3)	YES	YES

Features	Silverlight 1.0	Silverlight 2
Media — Image Support (JPEG, PNG)	YES	YES
Media Markers	YES	YES
Rich Core Framework (for example, Generics, collections)	NO	YES
Security Enforcement	NO	YES
Silverlight ASP.NET Controls (asp:media, asp:xaml)	YES	YES
Type Safety Verification	NO	YES
Windows Media Server Support	YES	YES
XAML Parser (based on WPF)	YES	YES
XMLReader/Writer	NO	YES

Silverlight Framework Architecture

One of the most appealing features of Silverlight is its ability to easily integrate into several different architectures. The Silverlight framework allows applications to access Web services, databases, Web servers, and other data sources to acquire data that is displayed in the UI. It also allows the application to integrate with the Web page DOM as well as AJAX and JavaScript to enhance the functionality of the Web page.

Figure 1.1 outlines a basic architecture of the Silverlight framework and how it fits into the full stack from the Web browser to Web servers and other services.

Notice in Figure 1.1 that the Silverlight framework sits in between the Web browser DOM and the Web services. JavaScript and AJAX flow up the stack and can be integrated and accessed from all layers of the Silverlight framework.

Figure 1.1 shows the Silverlight framework broken down into the Silverlight Plug-in, Core Presentation Framework, and NET Silverlight Framework. The following sections discuss each layer of the Silverlight architecture.

The Silverlight plug-in

The Silverlight plug-in is a very lightweight component that is necessary for users to access Silverlight applications. The plug-in download and install take only a few moments and do not take up much hard drive space.

> **NOTE** When a Web page containing a Silverlight application is displayed, the user should be given a link to download the plug-in from Microsoft if the plug-in is not already installed.

The Silverlight plug-in is responsible for accessing the Silverlight object in the Web page, downloading and accessing the XAP package, setting up the program environment, and beginning execution of the application.

FIGURE 1.1

Silverlight framework architecture diagram

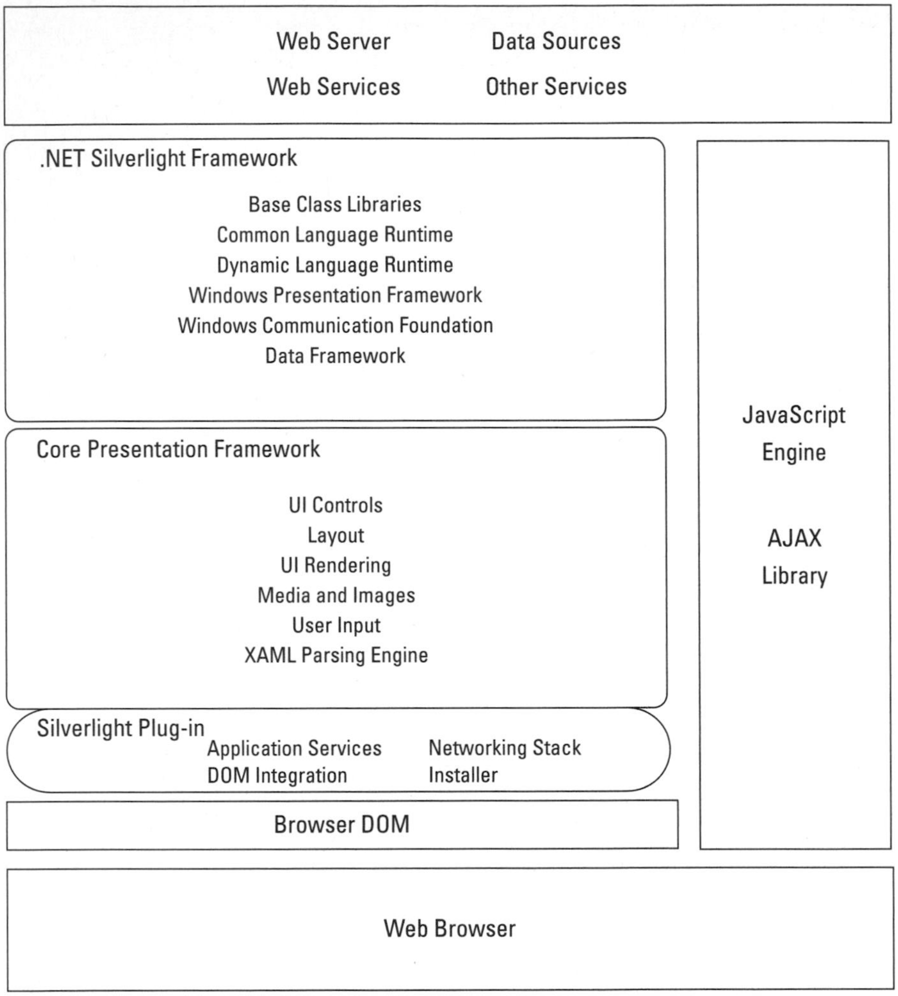

Web Server	Data Sources
Web Services	Other Services

.NET Silverlight Framework

Base Class Libraries
Common Language Runtime
Dynamic Language Runtime
Windows Presentation Framework
Windows Communication Foundation
Data Framework

Core Presentation Framework

UI Controls
Layout
UI Rendering
Media and Images
User Input
XAML Parsing Engine

JavaScript
Engine

AJAX
Library

Silverlight Plug-in

Application Services	Networking Stack
DOM Integration	Installer

Browser DOM

Web Browser

The Silverlight core presentation framework

The Silverlight core presentation framework is a subset of the Windows Presentation Foundation language. The core presentation framework provides the libraries and utilities necessary to parse the Silverlight XAML files, present the UI to the browser, and handle interaction from the user.

The following is a list of components that are included with the core presentation framework listed in Figure 1.1:

- **XAML parser:** Parses the XAML files into objects.
- **UI renderer:** Handles rendering of XAML objects, such as vector/bitmap graphics, animation, and text, into UI elements that are displayed in the applications.
- **Layout:** Utilizes canvas, grid, and other controls to dynamically position and size UI elements.
- **Controls:** Implements extensible controls, such as buttons, sliders, calendars, and text boxes, which provide customizable functionality to applications.
- **Media pipeline:** Provides streaming of audio and video files as well as playback and other management.
- **Data binding:** Enables data objects to be directly linked to UI elements in a one-way or two-way relationship. Changes to values can then be reflected automatically using the link.
- **Input:** Handles the input from user input devices such as a mouse, keyboard, and other input requests.
- **DRM:** Implements digital rights management to protect media files in Web applications.

The .NET Silverlight framework

The .NET Silverlight framework is a subset of the .NET programming platform. Silverlight uses much of the .NET framework and enhances some of the libraries to provide additional functionality necessary for Silverlight applications.

The .NET Silverlight framework provides the libraries and utilities necessary to implement managed code that accesses remote services and data, interacts with code from the core presentation framework, accesses SQL and other data sources, and provides the functionality to your Silverlight applications.

The following is a list of components that are included with the .NET Silverlight framework listed in Figure 1.1:

- **Common Language Runtime (CLR):** Provides the memory management, type checking, exception handling, and garbage collection for Silverlight applications
- **Base Class Libraries:** Provides the base set of .NET libraries that handle basic programming functionality such as string handling, regular expressions, collections, and input/ output
- **Dynamic Language Runtime (DLR):** Provides the framework to dynamically compile and execute JavaScript, IronPython, and IronRuby managed code in Silverlight applications
- **Windows Presentation Foundation (WPF):** Provides libraries to parse, access, and modify controls defined in XAML files as well as create and dynamically add new ones

■ **Windows Communication Foundation (WCF):** Provides libraries to interface with remote services, such as Web servers, RSS feeds, and other Web services

■ **Data Framework:** Provides a set of libraries to parse and serialize XML data as well as support for Language Integrated Query (LINQ) requests to XML sources and SQL databases

Silverlight application architecture

Silverlight applications can be broken down into three distinct components, each of which is written in a different language. Figure 1.2 shows a diagram of these components as well as some of their uses. These components directly map to the components of the Silverlight framework architecture that are described in following chapters.

FIGURE 1.2

Silverlight application architecture diagram

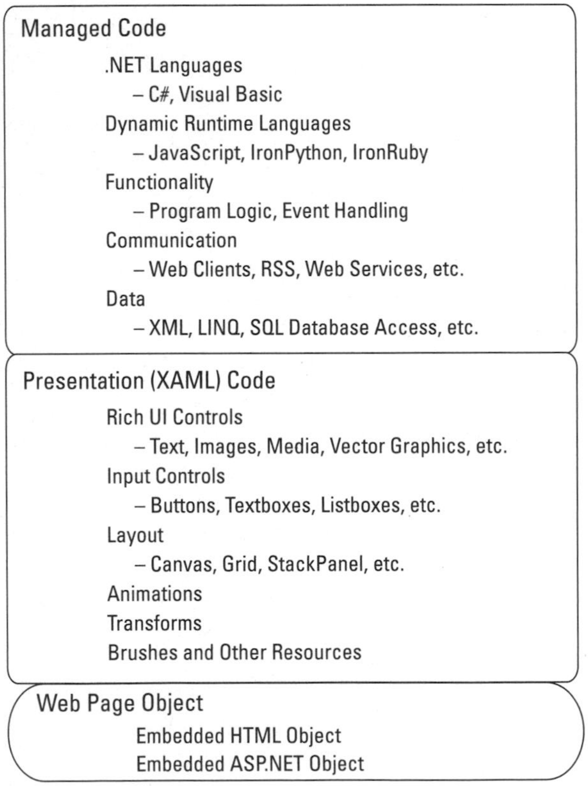

```
Managed Code
        .NET Languages
            – C#, Visual Basic
        Dynamic Runtime Languages
            – JavaScript, IronPython, IronRuby
        Functionality
            – Program Logic, Event Handling
        Communication
            – Web Clients, RSS, Web Services, etc.
        Data
            – XML, LINQ, SQL Database Access, etc.

Presentation (XAML) Code
        Rich UI Controls
            – Text, Images, Media, Vector Graphics, etc.
        Input Controls
            – Buttons, Textboxes, Listboxes, etc.
        Layout
            – Canvas, Grid, StackPanel, etc.
        Animations
        Transforms
        Brushes and Other Resources

Web Page Object
        Embedded HTML Object
        Embedded ASP.NET Object
```

The bottom layer in Figure 1.2 is the Web Page Object. This is an HTML element or ASP.NET control that tells the browser to use the Silverlight plug-in to load a Silverlight application.

The middle layer in Figure 1.2 is the Presentation Code. This is one or more XAML files that define the UI elements, user input controls, transformations, and animations that will be implemented in the Silverlight application. Most of the UI will be written in XAML because it is simple to implement especially with the aid of applications such as Microsoft's Expression Blend.

The top layer in Figure 1.2 is the Managed Code. These are .NET code-behind files that are actually part of the same class as the XAML files. This provides the managed code with the ability to access and modify the UI elements defined in the XAML file to implement functionality in Silverlight applications. These files can be written in C#, Visual Basic, JavaScript, IronPython, and IronRuby. Using Silverlight implementation of the .NET framework, managed code is able to implement data access and communication to a variety of services.

Summary

Silverlight is a cross-browser, cross-platform client framework that allows designers and developers to deliver rich Internet applications embedded in Web pages. Silverlight is fitted with a flexible media pipeline that makes it extremely easy to implement media-rich controls in your Web applications.

The Silverlight framework is made up of three main components: the browser plug-in, core presentation framework, and .NET Silverlight framework. This framework is based on a subset of other well-established frameworks such as the .NET platform and the WPF framework.

Silverlight applications are also made up of three distinct components that correspond to each aspect of the framework. Silverlight objects are embedded in Web pages. The UI elements of Silverlight applications are defined in XAML files that are parsed and rendered using the core presentation framework. The functionality of Silverlight applications is implemented using managed .NET code-behind files that share the same class with the XAML file.

In this chapter, you learned:

- What Silverlight is
- How Silverlight fits in the Web services and applications picture
- The advantages of using Silverlight
- Silverlight's limitations
- What components make up the Silverlight framework
- How the components of the Silverlight framework relate to each other
- How the components of the Silverlight framework relate to the components of Silverlight applications

Chapter 2

Getting Started with Silverlight

The best way to learn Silverlight is to jump right in and start playing. Silverlight is really designed for two different worlds: designers and developers. The environment that each wants will be a bit different.

As a developer, you need to set up a development environment that you can use to create and test Silverlight applications. You need to have an editor to create and edit the XAML and managed code, a browser with the Silverlight plug-in installed to test the applications, and the Silverlight Software Development Kit (SDK).

As a designer, you should at least consider installing the development tools. In addition, you will likely want to install some of the design tools available to work with XAML objects. Even as a developer, the design tools make your life easier and speed up your product development.

This chapter discusses the process of setting up a development environment to develop Silverlight applications. It also describes some additional development tools that are extremely useful when designing Silverlight UI and encoding media for use in Silverlight applications.

Implementing the Silverlight Development Environment

In this section, we discuss the basics of setting up a development environment for Silverlight. This is a little bit different for Silverlight 2 than for Silverlight 1.0.

TIP The best place to go to get information about setting up your development environment for Silverlight is the www.silverlight.net/GetStarted Web site. That Web site is constantly updated with news and current information about drivers that need to be downloaded.

With Silverlight 1.0 all you needed to do was to create an HTML file that hosted the Silverlight object and contained any JavaScript functionality, create an XAML file that defined the UI interface, and then include the Silverlight.js JavaScript library. That method is discussed in more detail in Chapter 9.

With Silverlight 2, in addition to the HTML and XAML files, you also need to create assemblies containing your compiled managed code, library assemblies, resources, a manifest, and other items in an XAP package. This can get somewhat complex if you are trying to do it all manually. This is discussed in more detail in Chapter 7 and Chapter 11 when we talk about creating Silverlight applications and using the DLR.

All of the linking and packaging is handled for you if you are using Visual Studio 2008 to develop your Silverlight 2 applications. If you are new to Silverlight, you will want to use Visual Studio until you get a better feel for what needs to be included in the package.

With that in mind, the basic needs for starting a Silverlight development environment are Visual Studio 2008, the Silverlight plug-in, the Silverlight tools for Visual Studio, and the Silverlight SDK.

Installing Visual Studio 2008

The first step in creating a development environment for Silverlight is to install Visual Studio 2008. Because everyone seems to have his or her own preferences and there is plenty of documentation on the Web of how to do this, we won't discuss the process of installing Visual Studio in this book.

However, there is one requirement for Silverlight that you should note when installing Visual Studio. Make sure that you install the Visual Web Developer feature during the install. That is necessary to install the Silverlight tools for Visual Studio later.

Installing the Silverlight plug-in

If you have been looking at Silverlight at all, you probably have already installed the Silverlight 2 plug-in. If not, when you go to www.microsoft.com/silverlight, you see a link similar to the one in Figure 2.1 that asks if you want to install Microsoft Silverlight. That means you haven't installed the plug-in.

CAUTION If you have already installed the Silverlight 1.0, 1.1, or a 2 plug-in, you need to uninstall that plug-in before installing the latest plug-in. That can be done using the Add/ Remove Programs option in the Control Panel.

FIGURE 2.1

Example of a Silverlight plug-in download link

The Silverlight 2 plug-in can be installed in a couple of ways. You can click the link to the Silverlight 2 plug-in shown in Figure 1.1, or you can install the plug-in with the Microsoft Silverlight Tools for Visual Studio download discussed in the next section.

Installing the Silverlight plug-in allows you to run Silverlight applications in your Web browser, a must for debugging. The download only takes a few seconds and requires only about 5MB of space on your hard drive.

Installing the Silverlight SDK

There are two options to install the Silverlight SDK, both of which can be found at www.silverlight.net/GetStarted.

The first option is to install the Silverlight Tools for Visual Studio. If you are using Visual Studio you will want to use this option because it installs helpful tools and templates directly into Visual Studio. The following is a list of things that are installed with this toolkit:

- Silverlight 2 plug-in
- Silverlight SDK

- Visual Basic and C# project templates
- Intellisense and code generators for XAML
- Debugging for Silverlight applications
- Integration with Expression Blend

The second option is to only install the Silverlight SDK. If you are not using Visual Studio, choose this option. To download and install, follow these steps:

1. Open the `www.silverlight.net/GetStarted` **Web page in a browser.**
2. **Click the Install Silverlight Tools for Visual Studio link shown in Figure 2.2. The download page appears.**
3. **Review the System Requirements and Installation sections of the download page.**
4. **Click Download and specify a location to save the file.**
5. **When the file is downloaded, double-click it in Windows Explorer to install the tools and the SDK.**

FIGURE 2.2

Getting Started Web Page at the Silverlight.net Web site showing the download link to the Silverlight Tools for Visual Studio

The Silverlight Tools for Visual Studio installer adds some templates and settings to Visual Studio and adds some additional tools and resources to the Microsoft SDK's folder, typically at `C:\Program Files\Microsoft SDKs`. Figure 2.3 shows the directory structure of the Silverlight SDK. You need to know the location of that SDK directory later in this book.

FIGURE 2.3

Directory structure created when the Silverlight SDK is installed

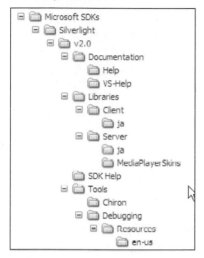

Implementing Silverlight applications on the Linux platform

The team responsible for the Mono project at Novell has created a version of Silverlight called Moonlight for the Linux platform. The Moonlight project provides a plug-in for Linux browsers and an SDK to develop Silverlight applications on the Linux platform.

The Moonlight plug-in can be downloaded from `www.go-mon.com/moonlight`.

You can also access the Moonlight IDE called lunareclipse for designing the XAML elements of the Silverlight application. The lunareclipse module is available from the Mono SVN site at `http://anonsvn.mono-project.com/source/trunk/lunareclipse`.

The Moonlight project is still changing. For information about the Moonlight SDK and how to set up the development environment on Linux, go to the Moonlight project page at `www.mono-project.com/Moonlight` and the development notes at `www.mono-project.com/MoonlightNotes`.

Understanding Silverlight Development Tools

One of the biggest advantages of Silverlight is that it is being developed by Microsoft. That means that there is a rich set of tools that makes design and development much easier and efficient. The previous section only discusses using Visual Studio; however, there are other applications that make designing content and developing Silverlight applications much easier.

The purpose of this section is to briefly discuss some of the tools that can help you as you design and develop Silverlight applications.

Using Silverlight in Visual Studio 2008

The main focal point of Silverlight development will likely originate in Visual Studio. Visual Studio provides a limited ability to design XAML elements, write supporting code, compile and package the application, and debug.

NOTE **If you are running Visual Studio on Vista, you may want to launch it as administrator so that you can debug your applications. To do this, right-click on the link in the Start menu and select Run as administrator from the pop-up menu.**

If you installed the plug-in for Visual Studio, then when you choose File ➪ New ➪ Project from the main menu in Visual Studio, a Silverlight link in the Project types list appears that contains a Silverlight Application template and a Silverlight Class Library template, as shown in Figure 2.4.

FIGURE 2.4

Silverlight project types added to Visual Studio by the Silverlight Tools for Visual Studio install

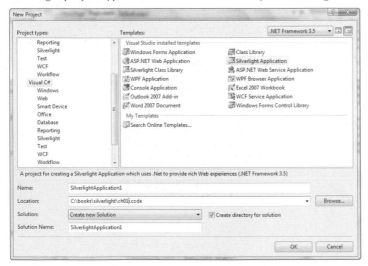

CROSS-REF There is a more in-depth discussion of Visual Studio in Chapter 6.

Designing Silverlight applications and elements in Expression Blend

While Visual Studio is great for programming, compiling, and testing the .NET side of Silverlight applications, it is not very effective in working with the XAML controls. Expression Blend is designed specifically to provide application interface that is more familiar to designers.

This allows designers to use an application they are familiar with when working with XAML files. As the elements in the design view are changed, the XAML code is updated to reflect the changes. Figure 2.5 shows Expression Blend in split view showing both design elements and their corresponding XAML code.

FIGURE 2.5

Silverlight project in Expression Blend showing the split design/XAML view

CROSS-REF   Expression Blend is discussed in much more detail in Chapter 4.

NOTE   Expression Blend is part of Microsoft's Expression Studio and can be downloaded as a trial version at www.microsoft.com/expression. You need Expression Blend 2.5 or later for Silverlight applications.

Encoding Silverlight media elements in Expression Encoder

Another very useful tool if you plan to add video or audio to your Web site is Expression Encoder. Expression Encoder, shown in Figure 2.6, is a graphical application that allows designers and developers to take audio and video from a variety of sources and encode it into a form that can be implemented in Silverlight applications.

CROSS-REF   Expression Encoder is discussed in much more detail in Chapter 5.

Expression Encoder provides the following major features useful when adding audio and video to Silverlight applications:

- **Import audio and video files from a wide range of file types.** This means that files can be delivered in almost any format and you can quickly encode them to be consumed by Silverlight applications.

- **Set the output size, quality, and volume level to conform to your Web site needs** allowing you to encode files for specific bandwidths available to your users.

- **Add programmable scripting, chapters, and other elements that allow Silverlight applications to interact with the audio and video streams.**

NOTE   Expression Encoder is part of Microsoft's Expression Studio and can be downloaded as a trial version at www.microsoft.com/expression. You need Expression Encoder 2.0 or later for Silverlight applications.

Outputting vector images as XAML using Expression Design

Most Silverlight controls are based on vector graphics. This allows them to be crisp even when resized. The vector graphics for the controls are defined as XAML elements in Silverlight applications. This means that just about any vector graphic image can be converted to XAML and displayed, resized, and transformed in Silverlight applications.

FIGURE 2.6

Video project in Expression Encoder encoding video for a Silverlight application

The easiest way to do this is to create or import vector art into Expression Design and then export it as XAML. Expression Design, shown in Figure 2.7, is another application that provides an interface familiar to designers to create and edit vector images.

This allows designers to create custom art that can easily be integrated into your Web applications. This process is discussed in more detail in Chapter 4.

NOTE   Expression Design is part of Microsoft's Expression Studio and can be downloaded as a trial version from www.microsoft.com/expression. You need Expression Design 2.0 or later for Silverlight applications.

FIGURE 2.7

Exporting a vector art project in Expression Design to XAML that can be used in a Silverlight application

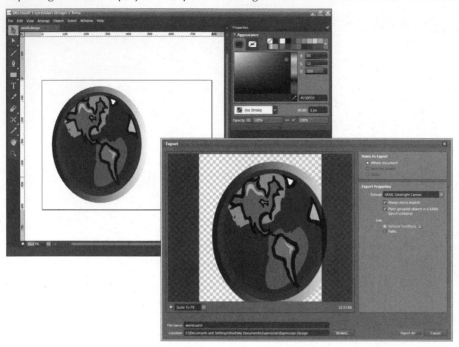

Encoding Multiscale Images Using Deep Zoom Composer

Silverlight includes a `MultiScaleImage` control that allows you to implement multiscale images in your Silverlight applications. Deep Zoom Composer is a great tool to use when creating multi-scale images that can be used by the `MultiScaleImage` control. Deep Zoom Composer provides a nice user interface that allows you to quickly create multiscale images.

Deep Zoom Composer lets you import image files and arrange them as a high-resolution image. The high-resolution image can then be exported as a multiscale image that can be implemented in Silverlight applications.

Building Your First Silverlight Application

Now that you have the Silverlight development environment set up, you will likely want to jump right in and create a Silverlight application. This section takes you through a step-by-step process of creating a very simple Visual Basic Silverlight application.

The purpose of this section is to quickly familiarize you with the basics of adding an XAML control to the `Page.xaml` file that is created when you create a Silverlight application project in Visual Studio. This gives you the basics you need as you learn about some of the Silverlight controls in Chapter 3. Chapter 6 covers a more detailed example of creating a similar project using Visual C#.

Use the following steps to create a simple Visual Basic Silverlight application:

1. **Choose File ➪ New ➪ Project from the main menu in Visual Studio.**
2. **Select Visual Basic from the Project Types list shown in Figure 2.8.**

FIGURE 2.8

New Project creation window in Visual Studio with the Visual Basic Silverlight Application template selected

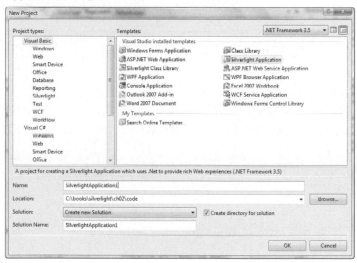

3. Select the Silverlight Application template from the Templates list.

4. Type the name of the project and set the location to create the new project.

5. Click OK to begin creating the project.

6. Select the Generate an HTML test page to host Silverlight within this project option, as shown in Figure 2.9.

7. Click OK to create the project.

FIGURE 2.9

New Project application window in Visual Studio with the Generate an HTML test page to host Silverlight within this project option selected

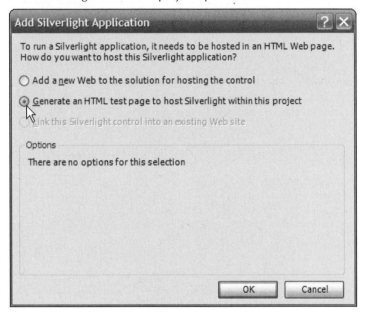

8. The `Page.xaml` **file appears in a split Design/XAML view, as shown in Figure 2.10.** Open the Toolbox if it is not already open by choosing View ⇨ Toolbox in the main menu.

9. **Click and drag a Button control from the Silverlight Controls list in the Toolbox to the XAML pane of** `Page.xaml`, **as shown in Figure 2.10.**

FIGURE 2.10

Dragging a `Button` control from the Toolbox to the XAML pane

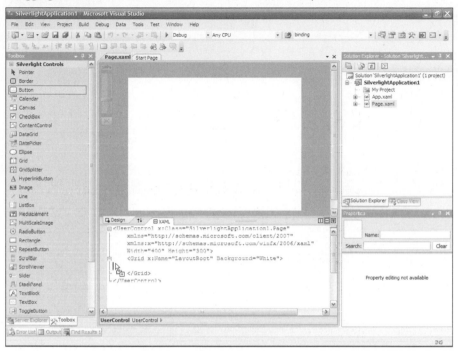

10. Modify the `Button` control in the XAML pane with the following code, as shown in Figure 2.11:

```
<Button x:Name="myButton"
        Content="Click Me"
        Height="50"
        Width="200">
</Button>
```

11. Save the `Page.xaml` file.

12. Expand the `Page.xaml` link in the Solution Explorer, as shown in Figure 2.12, to reveal the `Page.xaml.vb` code-behind file.

FIGURE 2.11

Defining the Name, Content, Height, and Width of a Button control to the XAML pane

FIGURE 2.12

Opening the Page.xaml.vb code-behind file in Visual Studio

13. Double-click on the `Page.xaml.vb` code-behind file to open it in the file.

14. Add the following line of code to the `New()` function in the `Page.xaml.vb` file, as shown in Figure 2.13, to attach a `Click` event handler to the `Button` control:

```
AddHandler myButton.Click, AddressOf myButton_Click
```

15. Add the following `myButton_Click()` function to the `Page.xaml.vb`, file as shown in Figure 2.13, to change the `Button Content` when it is clicked. If you are not familiar with Visual Basic, the `<space><underscore>` " _ " character sequence at the end of the line tells the compiler that the next line should be treated as part of this line:

```
Private Sub myButton_Click _
                    (ByVal sender As System.Object, _
                    ByVal e As System.Windows.
    RoutedEventArgs)
      myButton.Content = "My First Silverlight"
End Sub
```

FIGURE 2.13

Visual Basic code that attaches an event handler to the `Button` control to modify the button content

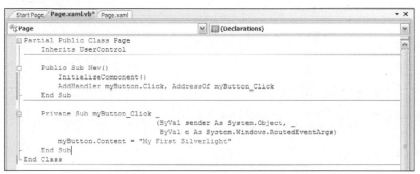

16. Press Ctrl+F5 to launch the application in a Web browser.

17. When you click the button, the text changes, as shown in Figure 2.14.

NOTE As you go through Chapter 3, you can use the same process to add Silverlight controls to your project as you did in steps 1 through 11 and then test them using the Ctrl+F5 key sequence.

FIGURE 2.14

Testing the new Silverlight application. When the button is clicked, the content changes to a new string.

 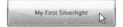

Summary

To develop Silverlight applications, you need to set up a development environment that they can use to create and test Silverlight applications. The most powerful and simplest to implement is Visual Studio with the Silverlight Toolkit for Visual Studio.

There are also many design applications that can help when creating Silverlight applications. Expression Blend is a great graphical interface to create the layout of the UI in XAML. Expression Encoder helps you encode audio and video for your Silverlight applications. Expression Design is helpful to edit vector art and export it into XAML for your Silverlight applications.

This chapter also gave you a quick look at the steps to create a Silverlight application, add Silverlight controls, and implement an event handler.

In this chapter, you learned:

- What is necessary to begin developing Silverlight applications
- How to download and install the Silverlight SDK and other tools
- What design tools are available to design a Silverlight application UI
- How to create a Silverlight project in Visual Studio
- How to add Silverlight controls to a Silverlight application
- How to test a Silverlight application in Visual Studio

Part II

Silverlight Design Fundamentals

Chapter 3

Using XAML to Build Declarative Silverlight Applications

X AML (eXtensible Application Markup Language) is a declarative language used to define the graphical design of applications. Silverlight] contains a subset of the full XAML language implemented in Windows Presentation Foundation (WPF). Silverlight applications use XAML code to create and lay out the UI elements.

Silverlight 1.0 had only a small subset of the WPF controls. Silverlight 2 expands that subset substantially by adding several new Silverlight controls. This chapter is designed to quickly bring you up to speed on the basics of XAML in Silverlight.

The following sections discuss various aspects of Silverlight's implementation of XAML. They also discuss the various controls and how to use them to lay out applications and implement functionality such as forms and animations.

Understanding the Silverlight/ XAML Relationship

Silverlight applications are built from two code bases — XAML and managed code. The managed code can be written in C#, Visual Basic, JavaScript, or any of the Dynamic Language Runtime (DLR) languages. The common code in all Silverlight applications is XAML.

You use XAML code in Silverlight to create the visual elements that make up the UI. XAML provides a robust set of controls that allow you to create rich, professional-looking UI very rapidly.

CROSS-REF **Chapters 6, 7, and 8 provide more detailed information about the relationship between code-behind pages and XAML.**

Understanding XML Namespaces

A very important aspect of XAML that you need to be familiar with is the concept of namespaces. An XML namespace is a method to avoid element name conflicts when using multiple libraries.

XML namespaces are implemented in Silverlight XAML files by adding an `xmlns="URI"` attribute to the root `UserControl` element for each library that you are using in the file. For example, the following line of code adds the XAML presentation namespace to an XAML file:

```
xmlns="http://schemas.microsoft.com/winfx/2006/xaml/presentation"
```

When using multiple Silverlight namespaces in the same XAML file, you will need to distinguish them from each other by specifying a prefix using the `xmlns:prefix="clr-namespace:nam espace;assembly=library assembly"`. For example, to add the `System.Windows. Controls` namespace along with the presentation namespace, you could use the following lines of code:

```
xmlns="http://schemas.microsoft.com/winfx/2006/xaml/presentation"
xmlns:ex="clr-namespace:System.Windows.Controls;assembly=System.
    Windows.Controls.Extended"
```

To access an element in a specific namespace, the prefix is added to the element name. For example, to create a `Calendar` control located in the `System.Windows.Controls` namespace, you would use the following code:

```
<ex:Calendar></ex:Calendar>
```

Another common namespace declaration is for the XAML namespace. The XAML namespace is used to define the `Class` and `Name` attributes of Silverlight controls. The XAML namespace is typically given the x: prefix, for example:

```
xmlns:x="http://schemas.microsoft.com/winfx/2006/xaml"
```

Most of the Silverlight controls can be accessed using the presentation namespace previously defined. Most of the rest of the Silverlight controls, such as `Calendar` and `TabControl`, are accessed using the `SystemWindows.Controls.Extended` namespace also previously described. Some others can be accessed using the `System.Windows.Controls.Primitives` namespace.

The following code shows an example `UserControl` statement that defines all of these namespaces:

```
<UserControl
    xmlns:prim="clr-namespace:System.Windows.Controls.
    Primitives;assembly=System.Windows.Controls.Extended"

xmlns:ex="clr-namespace:System.Windows.
Controls;assembly=System.Windows.Controls.Extended"
 x:Class="SilverlightApplication1.Page"
 xmlns="http://schemas.microsoft.com/winfx/2006/xaml/
presentation"
 xmlns:x="http://schemas.microsoft.com/winfx/2006/xaml">
```

Creating Silverlight Controls

Silverlight 2 provides a fairly robust set of controls that enable you to quickly add rich UI elements to your applications. The purpose of this section is to familiarize you with some of the different Silverlight controls that are used to render UI elements to Silverlight applications.

This section discusses some of the common properties that allow you to affect the look and feel of the controls and how to implement these controls in XAML.

Creating a Button

The `Button` control in Silverlight creates a standard rectangle button. The size of the button is determined by the `Height` and `Width` properties. Text can be added to the button by setting the `Content` property. For example, the following code creates a `Button` control that reads Click Me and is 100 pixels wide and 50 pixels high:

```
<Button Content="Click Me"
    Height="50"
    Width="150" />
```

> **TIP** You can use a `RepeatButton` control in place of a `Button` control. The only difference is that the `RepeatButton` repeatedly raises the `Click` event as long as the button is clicked and the mouse button held down. This can be useful if you want the button to adjust a value incrementally. The user can just hold down a `RepeatButton` whereas a `Button` control needs to be clicked each time.

Like most Silverlight controls, `Button` controls provide several properties that can be set to customize the look and feel of the control. For example, the following code defines the same button but changes the `FontFamily`, `FontSize`, `FontWeight`, `FontStyle`, `Foreground`, and `Background` properties to change the appearance:

```
<Button Content="Click Me"
    Height="50"
    Width="150"
    FontFamily="Trebuchet"
    FontSize="24"
    FontWeight="Bold"
    FontStyle="Italic"
    Foreground="Red"
    Background="Blue"/>
```

Figure 3.1 shows an example of the simple Button control and the more stylish Button control.

FIGURE 3.1

Rendered Button controls

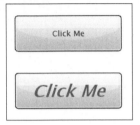

Creating a Calendar

The Calendar control in Silverlight is used to render a calendar in the application that can be used to simply view dates, or it can be used to select dates. The size of the calendar is determined by the Height and Width properties.

Most of the work with calendars is done programmatically; however, you can set some layout properties such as the FirstDayOfWeek and IsTodayHighlighted properties.

You can also control some of the behavior such as setting the AreDatesInPastSelectable property to inhibit past dates from being selected in the Calendar control, as shown in the following code:

```
<Calendar FirstDayOfWeek="Monday"
        IsTodayHighlighted="True"
        AreDatesInPastSelectable="True"
        Height="200" Width="200"/>
```

Figure 3.2 shows an example of the simple Calendar control.

FIGURE 3.2

Rendered `Calendar` control

Creating a CheckBox

`CheckBox` controls are very similar to `Button` controls and inherit most of the `Button` controls' properties and events. A `CheckBox` control allows you to create a check box element that can be toggled on or off by clicking it with the mouse. The `CheckBox` control defaults to unchecked; however, you can define it as being set initially in XAML using the `IsChecked` property. A basic check box can be created with the following code:

```
<CheckBox Content="Set Me"
          Height="50" Width="100"
          IsChecked="True" />
```

`CheckBox` controls can be declared in XAML with several different properties that enhance their look and feel. For example, the following code declares a `CheckBox` control with a nested `Content` property element that includes an `Image` element.

```
<CheckBox Height="50" Width="100"
          IsChecked="True">
    <CheckBox.Content>
        <Image Source="image.jpg"
               Height="50" Width="75" />
    </CheckBox.Content>
</CheckBox>
```

Figure 3.3 shows the rendered results of both `CheckBox` controls.

FIGURE 3.3

Rendered `CheckBox` controls

Creating a DatePicker

The `DatePicker` control is very similar to the `Calendar` control. The main component in the `DatePicker` control is a text box that allows the user to see and set a textual representation of the date. To the right of the control, as shown in Figure 3.4, is a button that displays an accompanying `Calendar` control to make date selection easier.

FIGURE 3.4

Rendered `DatePicker` control

The `DatePicker` control has most of the same properties as the `Calendar` control; for example, the following code defines a `DatePicker` with the `IsTodayHighlighted` property set to `True`:

```
<DatePicker IsTodayHighlighted="True"
            Height="100" Width="100"/>
```

Creating a HyperlinkButton

The `HyperlinkButton` control is kind of a hybrid cross between a button and text. The control appears similar to a `TextBlock`; however, it has mouse clicking functionality of a `Button` control built into it.

What makes the `HyperlinkButton` control unique is the `NavigateUri` property. You can set the `NavigateUri` property to any URI, as shown in the following code. When the `HyperlinkButton` is clicked, the browser navigates to that URI:

```
<HyperlinkButton Content="Silverlight Link"
                 NavigateUri="http://www.silverlight.net"
                 Height="50" Width="150" FontSize="20"
                 Margin="0,0,0,0"/>
<HyperlinkButton Content="MicroSoft Link"
                 NavigateUri="http://www.microsoft.com"
                 Height="50" Width="150" FontSize="20"
                 Margin="00,50,0,0" />
```

Figure 3.5 shows the rendered `HyperlinkButton` controls.

FIGURE 3.5

Rendered `HyperlinkButton` controls

Creating an Image

One of the most useful Silverlight controls in adding a professional look to applications is the `Image` control. The `Image` control allows you to add images to your applications as a code-manageable control by simply referencing their URI in the `Source` property.

The `Height` and `Width` properties allow you to set the size of the `Image` control and the `Stretch` property defines how the image file fills that space. As shown in the following code, the `Stretch` property can be set to `None` (default), `Fill`, `Uniform`, and `UniformToFill`:

```
<Image Source="image2.jpg"
       Height="100" Width="100"
       Margin="10,0,0,0" HorizontalAlignment="Left"/>
<Image Source="image2.jpg"
       Stretch="Fill"
       Height="100" Width="100"
       Margin="120,0,0,0" HorizontalAlignment="Left"/>
<Image Source="image2.jpg"
       Stretch="Uniform"
       Height="100" Width="100"
       Margin="230,0,0,0" HorizontalAlignment="Left"/>
<Image Source="image2.jpg"
       Stretch="UniformToFill"
       Height="100" Width="100"
       Margin="340,0,0,0" HorizontalAlignment="Left"/>
```

Figure 3.6 shows the rendered `Image` controls from the previous code. Even though it is the same image, the `Stretch` property changes how the image actually is rendered. `None` and `Uniform` settings simply display the image uniformly in the space provided by the `Height` and `Width` settings. `Fill` stretches the image to fill the space. `UniformToFill` keeps the image uniform but clips it so that it fills the entire space specified by `Height` and `Width`.

FIGURE 3.6

Rendered `Image` controls

Creating a ListBox

The `ListBox` control is a container for several child elements. The `ListBox` control allows you to create a selectable list of one or more items. Items in the list are defined by `ListBoxItem` tags. For example, the following code defines a list with four items:

```
<ListBox Width="100">
    <ListBoxItem Content="Option 1" />
    <ListBoxItem Content="Option 2" />
    <ListBoxItem Content="Option 3" />
    <ListBoxItem Content="Option 4" />
</ListBox>
```

Typically the `ListBox` child elements are simple `ListBoxItem` controls or `TextBlock` controls. However, they can be almost any Silverlight control. For example, the following code shows you three different ways to add a child element. The first item is a simple `ListBoxItem`, the second is a `TextBlock` inside a `ListBoxItem`, and the third is a `StackPanel` containing an `Image` and `TextBlock` control inside the `ListBoxItem`:

```
<ListBox  Width="200" Height="120">
    <ListBoxItem Height="30"
                 Content="Jeeping"/>
    <ListBoxItem Height="30">
        <TextBlock Text="Hiking"/>
    </ListBoxItem>
    <ListBoxItem>
        <StackPanel Orientation="Horizontal">
            <Image Height="30" Width="50" Source="i3.jpg" />
            <TextBlock Text="Desert Sunsets"/>
        </StackPanel>
    </ListBoxItem>
</ListBox>
```

Figure 3.7 shows the rendered `ListBox` controls from the previous code.

FIGURE 3.7

Rendered `ListBox` controls

Creating a MediaElement

Another useful Silverlight control for adding a professional look to applications is the `MediaElement` control. Just as with the `Image` control, the `MediaElement` control allows you to add audio and video to your applications as a code-manageable control by simply referencing their URI in the `Source` property.

The `Height` and `Width` properties allow you to set the size of the `MediaElement` control, and the `Stretch` property works the same as with `Image` controls. Much of the work with `MediaElement` controls is done programmatically. However, you can set the `Volume` and `Balance` audio settings in XAML. You can also set `AutoPlay` to `True` if you want the media to start playing after it is rendered. Another useful property that can be set in XAML is the `AudioStreamIndex` that allows you to set the time index in seconds to begin playing the media:

```
<MediaElement Source="video.wmv"
              AutoPlay="True"
              AudioStreamIndex="2"
              Volume="10" Balance="-2"
              Height="200" Width="300" />
```

Figure 3.8 shows the rendered XAML from the previous code playing a video file.

Rendered `MediaElement` control

Creating a RadioButton

`RadioButton` controls are very similar to `CheckBox` controls and also inherit most of the `Button` controls' properties and events. A `RadioButton` control allows you to create a radio button element that can be toggled on or off by clicking it with the mouse.

The `RadioButton` control also defaults to unchecked; however, you can define it as being set initially in XAML using the `IsChecked` property. Another interesting property of the `RadioButton` control is the `ClickMode`. You can set the `ClickMode` property to set the radio button on mouse `Hover`, `Press`, or `Release`; for example:

```
<RadioButton Content="Our Option"
          Height="50" Width="100"
          ClickMode="Hover" />
```

`RadioButton` controls also implement the `Content` property to display some kind of identification with the radio button. Just as with other Silverlight controls, you can nest the `Content` property and add additional controls as children. For example, the following code declares a `RadioButton` control with a nested `Content` property element that includes a `TextBlock` element allowing users to input their own option:

```
<RadioButton Height="50" Width="150"
          IsChecked="True">
    <RadioButton.Content>
        <TextBox Text="Your Option"
        Height="30" Width="100" />
    </RadioButton.Content>
</RadioButton>
```

Figure 3.9 shows the rendered results of both `RadioButton` controls.

FIGURE 3.9

Rendered `RadioButton` controls

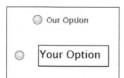

Creating a ScrollBar

A scroll bar can be created with the `ScrollBar` control. The `ScrollBar` control renders a typical scroll bar in the application that can be used to allow users to input values or control other XAML elements programmatically.

The scroll bar can be set to be either vertical or horizontal by setting the `Orientation` property to `Horizontal` or `Vertical`. The maximum and minimum values of the scroll bar can be set using the `Maximum` and `Minimum` properties. The size of the slider can be set using the `ViewportSize` property. The current value of the scroll bar can be set using the `Value` property.

```
<ScrollBar Value="25"
          Orientation="Horizontal"
          Minimum="1" Maximum="100"
          ViewportSize="50"
          Height="30" Width="300"
          Cursor="Hand">
</ScrollBar>
```

It is a good idea to set the `Cursor` property of the `ScrollBar` control to `Hand` so that the mouse cursor changes into a hand when using the scroll bar to set the value. Figure 3.10 shows a rendered `ScrollBar` control.

FIGURE 3.10

Rendered `ScrollBar` control

Creating a ScrollViewer

The `ScrollViewer` control is used to implement content in an application in a place where there is not room enough to host the content. The `ScrollViewer` control implements a content area with a horizontal and/or vertical scroll bar.

The content of a `ScrollViewer` is placed in the `Content` property. Typically you want to nest the child elements of the `ScrollViewer` using the `ScrollViewer.Content` property, as shown in the following code snippet:

```
<ScrollViewer
    VerticalScrollBarVisibility="Auto"
    HorizontalScrollBarVisibility="Auto"
    Height="400" Width="400">
        <ScrollViewer.Content>
            <Grid Height="1000" Width="1000">
                <Image Source="image2.jpg" Height="400"
Width="500"
                        VerticalAlignment="Top"
                        HorizontalAlignment="Left"
                        Margin="0,0,0,0"/>
                <Image Source="image1.jpg" Height="400"
Width="500"
                        VerticalAlignment="Top"
                        HorizontalAlignment="Left"
                        Margin="300,300,0,0"/>
            </Grid>
        </ScrollViewer.Content>
    </ScrollViewer>
```

The `Content` property can contain only a single child element such as a `TextBlock` for lengthy text or an Image control containing a large image. However, you can nest several controls inside of a `Grid` or `Canvas` control as shown in the previous code.

TIP Many of the Silverlight controls have a `Content` property that can be nested as described in the `ScrollViewer` section. Using this technique allows you to add almost any content to those controls. For example, you could place an `Image` as the content for a `Button` control.

You can configure whether to show the scroll bars when the `ScrollViewer` is rendered by setting the `VerticalScrollBarVisibility` and `HorizontalScrollBarVisibility` properties. These properties can be set to `Auto`, `Disabled`, `Visible`, and `Hidden`.

Figure 3.11 shows a rendered `ScrollViewer` control that contains an image that is much larger than the space allowed for the content.

FIGURE 3.11

Rendered `ScrollViewer` control

Creating a Slider

The `Slider` control is similar the `ScrollBar` control. It has a handle that can be dragged with the mouse and can be used to indicate things such as the volume or playback position of a `MediaElement`.

The slider can be set to be either vertical or horizontal by setting the `Orientation` property to `Horizontal` or `Vertical`. The size of the slider can be set using the `Height` and `Width` properties. The maximum and minimum values of the scroll bar can be set using the `Maximum` and `Minimum` properties. The current value of the slider can be set using the `Value` property.

```
<Slider Value="25"
        Orientation="Horizontal"
        Minimum="1" Maximum="100"
        Height="30" Width="300"
        Cursor="Hand">
</Slider>
```

Just as with a `ScrollBar` control it is a good idea to set the `Cursor` property of the `Slider` control to `Hand` so that the mouse cursor changes into a hand when using the scroll bar to set the value. Figure 3.12 shows a rendered `Slider` control.

FIGURE 3.12

Rendered a `Slider` control

Creating a TextBlock

Probably the most commonly used Silverlight control is the `TextBlock`. A `TextBlock` control is a static text element that can't be changed or edited by the user of your Silverlight application.

You use `TextBlock` `controls` to create most of the textual elements in your Silverlight applications. A `TextBlock` is a very versatile control. For example, it can contain a simple word or numerous lines of wrapping text with a stylish color and font defined.

A simple `TextBlock` control can be defined by setting the `Text` control to the value of the string that is rendered in the application. For example:

```
<TextBlock Text="I think, therefore I am." />
```

You can also control the size and style of the text using the `FontFamily`, `FontSize`, `FontWeight`, `FontStyle`, and `FontStretch` properties to set the typeface, size, boldness, italics, and whether the text should be stretched to fill the size of the control defined by `Height` and `Width`.

To specify if the text should wrap to the next line if it is wider than the `Width` property, set the `TextWrapping` property to `Wrap`. You can control the justification of the text by setting the `TextAlignment` property to `Left`, `Right`, or `Center`. The following example code shows a more complex version of a `TextBlock`:

```
<TextBlock TextWrapping="Wrap"
           Text="I think, therefore I am."
           FontFamily="Comic Sans MS"
           FontSize="20" FontWeight="Bold"
           Height="150" Width="180" />
```

At times you may want to specify different properties for different sections of text in a single TextBlock. This can be done by using the Run element to encase those settings with a Text property that defines the text. The following code implements two Run elements, each with its own font size, color, and typeface:

```
<TextBlock TextWrapping="Wrap"
        HorizontalAlignment="Center"
        TextAlignment="Right">
    <Run FontFamily="Comic Sans MS"
        FontSize="20" FontWeight="Bold"
        Foreground="DarkBlue"
        Text="I think, therefore I am."/>
    <LineBreak />
    <Run FontFamily="Ariel"
        FontSize="10" FontStyle="Italic"
        Foreground="LightBlue"
        Text="-Rene Descartes"/>
</TextBlock>
```

The LineBreak element is added to the previous code to implement a line break between the two sections of text. Figure 3.13 shows each of the TextBlock examples in this section.

FIGURE 3.13

Rendered TextBlock control

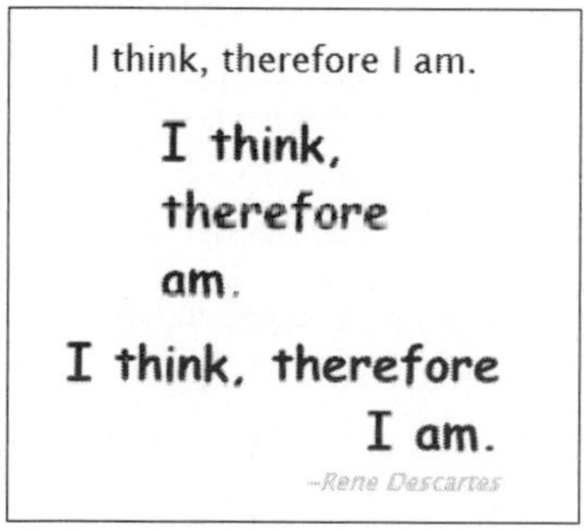

Creating a TextBox

A TextBox is a new control that allows you to implement text input from the user in your Silverlight applications. For example, you can use TextBox controls to create input areas for names, passwords, and other information that the user must provide. The TextBox implements an editable text box in the application that accepts keyboard input.

> **NOTE** If you want the user to be able to enter more than one line in a TextBox by pressing Enter, you'll want to add AcceptsReturn="True" to your code listing.

The TextBox control is very similar to the TextBlock control in that you can define all of the font style properties. For example, the following code defines a TextBox and sets the FontFamily, FontSize, and TextAlignment properties:

```
<TextBox Text="Your Input"
         Background="LightGray"
         BorderBrush="DarkGray"
         BorderThickness="2"
         TextAlignment="Center"
         FontFamily="Georgia"
         FontSize="20"
         Height="30" Width="200" />
```

You can also define the appearance of the box that surrounds the text by setting the Background, BorderBrush, and BorderThickness as shown in the previous code. Figure 3.14 shows the rendered TextBox example.

FIGURE 3.14

Rendered TextBox control

Creating a ToggleButton

ToggleButton controls are very basically a cross between a Button control and a CheckBox control. They inherit all of the Button controls' properties and events; however, they also inherit the state functionality of a CheckBox control.

When the user clicks on a ToggleButton control and releases the mouse, the ToggleButton stays in a pressed state. This allows you to implement button elements that set on or off type values. Just as with CheckBox controls, the state of the ToggleButton is determined by the IsChecked property, which defaults to False.

The following code defines a basic ToggleButton control:

```
<ToggleButton Content="ON/OFF"
              Height="40" Width="100"
              IsChecked="True" />
```

Figure 3.15 shows the rendered results of the ToggleButton control.

FIGURE 3.15

Rendered ToggleButton control

Designing the Layout of Silverlight Applications

When you create several UI Silverlight controls, they can quickly become very cumbersome and disorganized unless you implement some kind of layout. Silverlight provides several controls that enable you to lay out your applications easily and precisely.

The Canvas and Grid controls are container controls designed to hold and lay out child controls. The Canvas and Grid controls have properties that allow you to set the size and behavior of the child controls nested inside. The following sections discuss using the Canvas, Grid, StackPanel, and Border controls to lay out Silverlight applications.

Using a Canvas control

The Canvas control allows you to group several Silverlight controls into a single group of elements. The position of the child controls in a Canvas control is determined by offsets from the top-left edge of the canvas. This allows you to define the position of the controls in the canvas by simply setting the Canvas.Top and Canvas.Left properties of a control.

For example, the following code sets the position of a TextBlock control in a Canvas to 20 pixels down and 200 pixels from the top-left corner of the Canvas:

```
<Canvas Height="50" Width="400" >
    <TextBlock Text="My Text"
               Canvas.Top="20"
               Canvas.Left="200" />
</Canvas>
```

Because the position of the child controls in a Canvas is based on the top-left corner, when you reposition the Canvas in the application, all of the child controls are moved and maintain their layout.

Another nice feature of the Canvas control is the Canvas.ZIndex property. The Canvas.ZIndex property gives you the ability to set the front to back position of child controls in relationship to each other.

The `Canvas.ZIndex` is based on a number starting with 0 being the farthest back. For example, in the following code, the first `Image` control appears on top of the second `Image` control:

```
<Canvas>
    <Image Source="iamge.jpg" Canvas.ZIndex="1"
            Height="200" Width="200"
            Canvas.Top="50" Canvas.Left="50"/>
    <Image Source="iamge.jpg" Canvas.ZIndex="0"
            Height="200" Width="200"
</Canvas>
```

For complex Silverlight applications, you may need to create several `Canvas` controls that contain other controls and even nest them in other `Canvas` or `Grid` controls.

The code in Listing 3.1 shows an example of a Silverlight application that nests objects in multiple `Canvas` controls:

LISTING 3.1

Nested Canvas Controls Implementing the Layout of Silverlight Controls

```
<Canvas x:Name="LayoutRoot"
        Background="White">
    <Canvas Height="50" Width="400"
            Background="Black">
        <TextBlock Text="My Log"
                Foreground="White"
                Canvas.Left="20"
                FontSize="24" />
    </Canvas>
    <Canvas Canvas.Top="50"
            Height="250" Width="400"
            Background="#eeeeee">
        <TextBlock Text="Add an Entry"
                Canvas.Top="30" Canvas.Left="50"/>
        <TextBox Text="Add an Entry"
                Height="100" Width="200"
                Canvas.Top="70" Canvas.Left="100"/>
        <Button Content="Enter"
                Height="30" Width="80"
                Canvas.Top="200" Canvas.Left="150"/>
    </Canvas>
</Canvas>
```

In Listing 3.1, the root `Canvas` control contains two nested `Canvas` controls. The first nested `Canvas` control defines an area at the top of the application with a `TextBlock` controls position 20 pixels to the left using the `Canvas.Left` property.

The second nested `Canvas` control is positioned 50 pixels down from the top of the root `Canvas` control using the `Canvas.Top` property. Inside the second nested `Canvas` control, a `TextBlock`, `TextBox`, and `Button` control are defined and positioned using the `Canvas.Top` and `Canvas.Left` properties.

Figure 3.16 shows the rendered results from the XAML code in Listing 3.1.

FIGURE 3.16

Silverlight controls rendered in a Canvas

Using a Grid control

The `Grid` control allows you to lay out your Silverlight controls into a series of rows and columns. Then as you add additional Silverlight controls, you can specify in which row or column they should be placed. You can also set the alignment and specify margins for Silverlight controls that help you position controls inside the grid.

Using columns and rows

The first step in setting up a `Grid` control is to define the rows and columns that are implemented in the application. This is done using the `Grid.RowDefinitions` and `Grid.ColumnDefinitions` properties and then assigning `RowDefintion` and `ColumnDefinition` elements to those properties. For example, the following code defines a `Grid` with two rows and three columns:

```
<Grid Height="400", Width="400">
    <Grid.RowDefinitions>
        <RowDefinition Height="50"/>
        <RowDefinition/>
```

```
    </Grid.RowDefinitions>
    <Grid.ColumnDefinitions>
        <ColumnDefinition Width="100"/>
        <ColumnDefinition Width="10"/>
        <ColumnDefinition/>
    </Grid.ColumnDefinitions>
</Grid>
```

NOTE When defining rows and columns for a Grid, the `Height` and `Width` properties set the height of the row and the width of the column. If these values are not set, Silverlight tries to evenly use the space remaining.

To position child controls inside the `Grid`, you use the `Grid.Row` and `Grid.Column` properties to reference the row and column. The top-left corner of the grid is row 0 and column 0. For example, the following code adds two `Image` controls to a grid, one to row 1 column 0 and the second to row 2 column 0:

```
<Image Source="image.jpg"
       Grid.Row="1" Grid.Column="0"
       Height="100" Width="150" />
<Image Source="image2.jpg"
       Grid.Row="2" Grid.Column="0"
       Height="100" Width="150" />
```

TIP A very useful feature when developing Silverlight applications using `Grid` controls is to turn on the gridlines while you are developing. This is done by setting the `ShowGridLines` property of the `Grid` control to `True`.

You can span multiple grid rows and columns using the `Grid.RowSpan` and `Grid.ColumnSpan` properties. To set a Silverlight control to span multiple columns, set the `Grid.ColumnSpan` property to the number of columns that will be spanned. To set a Silverlight control to span multiple rows, set the `Grid.RowSpan` property to the number of rows that will be spanned. For example, to span two rows and two columns with an `Image` control, use the following code:

```
<Image Source="image.jpg"
       Grid.Row="1" Grid.Column="0"
       Grid.ColumnSpan="2"
       Grid.RowSpan="2"
       Height="200" Width="250" />
```

Another useful control when working with grids is the `GridSplitter` control. The `GridSplitter` control allows you to assign attributes to one or more blocks in the grid. The `GridSplitter` allows you to set the background color and size of grid block. For example, the following code defines a `GridSplitter` control that acts as a divider between column 0 and column 2 in a `Grid` control:

```
<GridSplitter Background="Black" Width="5"
              Grid.Row="0" Grid.Column="1"
              VerticalAlignment="Stretch"
              HorizontalAlignment="Center" />
```

Using Grid controls, you can quickly lay out applications that conform to a rigid structure. The code in Listing 3.2 shows an example of a Silverlight application that implements a Grid control:

LISTING 3.2

Implementing a Grid to Set the Layout of Silverlight Controls

```
<Grid x:Name="LayoutRoot"
      Background="White"
      ShowGridLines="True">
    <Grid.RowDefinitions>
        <RowDefinition Height="50"/>
        <RowDefinition/>
        <RowDefinition/>
    </Grid.RowDefinitions>
    <Grid.ColumnDefinitions>
        <ColumnDefinition Width="150"/>
        <ColumnDefinition Width="10"/>
        <ColumnDefinition/>
    </Grid.ColumnDefinitions>
    <Canvas Background="Black"
            Grid.Column="0"
            Grid.ColumnSpan="3">
        <TextBlock Text="Describe the Image"
                   FontSize="30"
                   Margin="50,5,0,0"
                   Foreground="White"/>
    </Canvas>
    <Image Source="image.jpg"
           Grid.Row="1" Grid.Column="0"
           Height="100" Width="150" />
    <Image Source="image2.jpg"
           Grid.Row="2" Grid.Column="0"
           Height="100" Width="150" />
    <TextBox BorderThickness="2"
             Grid.Row="1" Grid.Column="2"
             Height="100" Width="200" />
    <TextBox BorderThickness="2"
             Grid.Row="2" Grid.Column="2"
             Height="100" Width="200" />
</Grid>
```

In Listing 3.2, the root `Grid` control contains definitions for three rows and three columns. Figure 3.17 shows the gridlines for those rows and columns. The gridlines are turned on by setting the `ShowGridLines` property to `True`.

FIGURE 3.17

Viewing the gridlines in a `Grid` control

The code in Listing 3.2 implements a `Canvas` control with a black background that spans all three columns in the grid by setting the `Grid.ColumnSpan` property to 3. A `TextBlock` is added as a child element to the `Canvas`. Notice that the position of the `TextBlock` is adjusted using the `Margin` property.

The code adds two `Image` controls and two `TextBox` controls to the `Grid` and places them using the `Grid.Row` and `Grid.Column` properties.

Figure 3.18 shows the rendered results from the XAML code in Listing 3.2.

FIGURE 3.18

Silverlight controls rendered in a grid

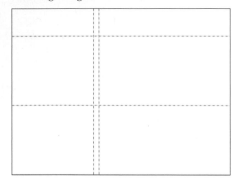

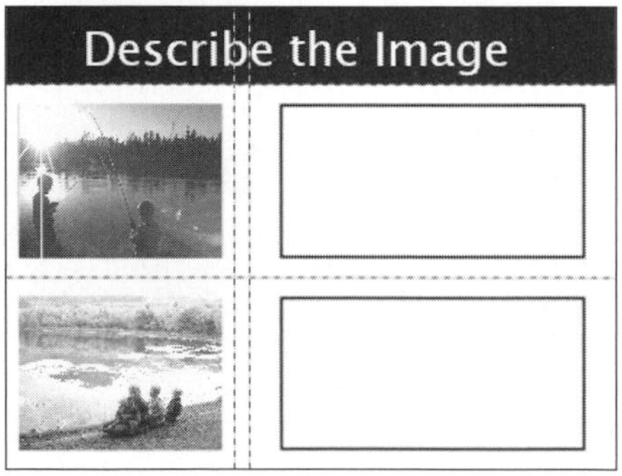

Using margins and alignment

Another useful feature of implementing grids is the ability to use the VerticalAlignment, HorizontalAlignment, and Margin properties to quickly set the left, right, top, and bottom position for Silverlight controls. Often, you can implement Silverlight applications using a Grid by only using the VerticalAlignment, HorizontalAlignment, and Margin properties instead of configuring rows and columns.

The HorizontalAlignment property can be set to Left, Center, or Right. The VerticalAlignment property can be set to Top, Center, or Bottom. When these properties are set, the Margin property defines the offset from those alignment properties based on a string with the following format:

```
Margin="left, top, right, bottom"
```

To understand this better, consider the code in Listing 3.3. The code defines a simple Grid control with three Image controls as children. Instead of implementing rows and columns, the code simply defines the VerticalAlignment and HorizontalAlignment properties of the Image controls to point to the top left, center, and bottom right of the grid.

The code in Listing 3.3 is then able to use the Margin properties to set the offset from the edges of the grid to place the images in the appropriate layout as shown in Figure 3.19.

LISTING 3.3

XAML That Implements Alignment and Margin Settings to Layout of Silverlight Controls in a Grid

```xaml
<Grid x:Name="LayoutRoot" Background="White">
        <Image Source="image.jpg"
               Height="100" Width="150"
               VerticalAlignment="Top"
               HorizontalAlignment="Left"
               Margin="5,15,0,0"/>
        <Image Source="image2.jpg"
               Height="100" Width="150"
               VerticalAlignment="Center"
               HorizontalAlignment="Center"
               Margin="0,0,0,0"/>
        <Image Source="image3.jpg"
               Height="100" Width="150"
               VerticalAlignment="Bottom"
               HorizontalAlignment="Right"
               Margin="0,0,10,10"/>
    </Grid>
```

FIGURE 3.19

Rendered images using the `Alignment` and `Margin` properties to set their position of Silverlight controls in a grid

Using a TabControl control

One of the most useful layout controls is the `TabControl`. The `TabControl` provides a means to implement several different layers of panels that can be accessed using tabs. Using a `TabControl` will allow you the ability to quickly provide a lot more content in the Silverlight application and still have it all readily available to the user.

Using the `TabControl` to implement tabbed panels actually involves using three different levels of controls. The highest level is the `TabPanel` control. The `TabPanel` control acts as a parent panel for the `TabControl`, similar to how `Canvas` and `Grid` controls act as parents for other controls. The `TabPanel` control provides a place to set the size and other base layout attributes for the tabbed panel.

The `TabControl` is the next level in the hierarchy. The `TabControl` acts as a container for all of the tabbed content that is added to the tabbed panel. You can set the size of the control using the `Height` and `Width` attributes of the `TabControl`. You can set the behavior of the the `TabControl` by specifying the `TabSripPlacement` and `TabNavigation` properties. The `TabStripPlacement` property specifies whether the tabs should be placed on the `Top`, `Left`,

Right, or Bottom of the control. The TabNavigation specifies whether tab navigation should Cycle, be Local, or only apply Once to the control.

The lowest level is the TabItem control. The TabItem control is used as a container for the actual content that is displayed in a single tab. The most important attributes of the TabItem are the Header and Content attributes. The Header attribute specifies what content is displayed in the tab and the Content attribute specifies what content is displayed in the tabbed panel.

The code in Listing 3.4 shows an implementation of a TabControl to illustrate how tabbed panels are implemented in Silverlight.

The code in Listing 3.4 first defines a TabPanel control and sets the HorizontalAlignment and VerticalAlignment attributes to place the control in the center of the Grid. The Background property of the control is set to LightGray.

The code in Listing 3.4 then defines a TabControl control and sets the Height and Width properties to define the size of the control. The TabStripPlacement control is set to Left to place the tabs on the left hand side of the control.

Next, the code defines three TabItem controls. The first TabItem control defines the Header attribute in the TabItem statement. The second TabItem control defines the Header as a TextBlock control using the TabItem.Header statement. The third TabItem control defines the Header as an Image control using the TabItem.Header statement.

The content of the first two TabItem controls is defined as TextBlock controls. The content of the third TabItem control is defined as an Image control.

LISTING 3.4

XAML That Implements a Tabbed Panel Using the TabControl Control

```
<UserControl
    xmlns:prim="clr-namespace:System.Windows.Controls.
    Primitives;assembly=System.Windows.Controls.Extended"
    xmlns:ex="clr-namespace:System.Windows.Controls;assembly=System.
Windows.Controls.Extended"
    x:Class="tabpanel.Page"
    xmlns="http://schemas.microsoft.com/winfx/2006/xaml/presentation"
    xmlns:x="http://schemas.microsoft.com/winfx/2006/xaml"
    Width="400" Height="400">
    <Grid x:Name="LayoutRoot" Background="White">
      <prim:TabPanel VerticalAlignment="Center"
                HorizontalAlignment="Center"
                Background="LightGray">
        <ex:TabControl TabStripPlacement="Left"
                   Height="200" Width="300" >
          <ex:TabItem Header="Animal">
```

```
                <TextBlock Text="American Bison"
                           FontSize="30"
                           HorizontalAlignment="Center"/>
            </ex:TabItem>
            <ex:TabItem>
                <ex:TabItem.Header>
                    <TextBlock FontSize="15"
                               FontFamily="Times New Roman"
                               Text="Location"/>
                </ex:TabItem.Header>
                <ex:TabItem.Content>
                    <TextBlock Text="YellowStone National Park"
                               HorizontalAlignment="Center"/>
                </ex:TabItem.Content>
            </ex:TabItem>
            <ex:TabItem>
                <ex:TabItem.Header>
                    <Image Source="image.jpg" Width="50" />
                </ex:TabItem.Header>
                <Image Source="image.jpg" Width="200" />
            </ex:TabItem>
        </ex:TabControl>
      </prim:TabPanel>
    </Grid>
  </UserControl>
```

The result of the code in Listing 3.4 is displayed in Figure 3.20. A tabbed panel with three tabs is rendered. When each of the tabs is selected, different content is displayed in the panel.

FIGURE 3.20

Rendered tabbed panel displaying three tabs that display different content

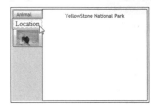

Using a StackPanel control

The StackPanel control is a container control that allows you to add child controls similar to the Canvas and Grid controls. The StackPanel automatically lays out controls evenly either horizontally or vertically. The orientation of the StackPanel is configured by setting the Orientation property to either Vertical or Horizontal.

Typically, StackPanel controls are used to lay out a group of controls in a Grid or Canvas. For example, the following code implements a StackPanel to line up a group of RadioButton controls in a Canvas:

```
<Canvas x:Name="LayoutRoot" Background="LightGray">
    <StackPanel Background="White"
                Orientation="Vertical"
                Canvas.Top="50" Canvas.Left="50"
                Height="100" Width="100">
        <RadioButton Content="Option A"
                     HorizontalAlignment="Center"/>
        <RadioButton Content="Option B"
                     HorizontalAlignment="Center"/>
        <RadioButton Content="Option C"
                     HorizontalAlignment="Center"/>
        <RadioButton Content="Option D"
                     HorizontalAlignment="Center"/>
    </StackPanel>
</Canvas>
```

The RadioButton controls are lined up vertically, as shown in Figure 3.21. The position of the StackPanel can be altered by changing the Canvas.Top and Canvas.Left properties. However, the layout of the RadioButton controls inside the StackPanel remains consistent.

FIGURE 3.21

Rendered RadioButton controls in a StackPanel

Using a Border control

The Border control is used to create some sort of spacing or border around other Silverlight controls. Border controls allow you to set options that place a border around an element that is defined as a child. For example, the following code defines a border around a single Button control setting the BorderThickness and BorderBrush properties:

```
<Border BorderThickness="5"
        BorderBrush="Blue" Background="LightGray"
        Height="100" Width="250">
    <Button Content="Bordered Button"
        Height="50" Width="200" />
</Border>
```

Border controls can contain only one child element; however, you can encase several controls in a container element such as a StackPanel control. For example, the following example placed a border around several Button controls contained in a StackPanel:

```
<Border BorderThickness="5"
        BorderBrush="Blue"
        Height="160" Width="120">
    <StackPanel>
        <RadioButton Content="Option 1"
            Height="50" Width="200"
            Margin="20,0,0,0"/>
        <RadioButton Content="Option 2"
            Height="50" Width="200"
            Margin="20,0,0,0" />
        <RadioButton Content="Option 3"
            Height="50" Width="200"
            Margin="20,0,0,0" />
    </StackPanel>
</Border>
```

Figure 3.22 shows an example of each of the code examples.

FIGURE 3.22

Rendered StackPanel inside of a border displays the radio buttons as a group.

Using XAML Transforms

One of the coolest things about working with vector-based controls in XAML is that you can implement transformations. Using the RenderTransform property of a Silverlight control, you can easily adjust the size, location, rotation, and skew of the control.

Transformations are defined in a TransformGroup block consisting of one or more of the following: ScaleTransform, SkewTransform, RotateTransform, and TranslateTransform.

The following code shows the basic framework needed to apply transformations on an Image control:

```
<Image.RenderTransform>
    <TransformGroup>
        <ScaleTransform/>
        <SkewTransform/>
        <RotateTransform/>
        <TranslateTransform/>
    </TransformGroup>
</Image.RenderTransform>
```

The center point of the translation is based off the RenderTransformOrigin property of the control. The RenderTransformOrigin property is based on two coordinate points. To render around the center of the control, use the following setting:

```
RenderTransformOrigin="0.5,0.5"
```

> **TIP** If you apply a transform to a Canvas, Grid, or StackPanel control, then the transform applies to all children in the control. This is often a simple and effective way of resizing components in your applications.

The following sections discuss each of the transformations that can be applied to Silverlight controls.

ScaleTransform

The ScaleTransform allows you to adjust the horizontal and vertical scale of the Silverlight control. This is done by setting the ScaleX property to adjust the horizontal scale and the ScaleY property to adjust the vertical scale.

The values of ScaleX and ScaleY are based on 1 being the current size of the control. If you set the ScaleX property to .5, the control is scaled down to half the height. If you set the ScaleY property to 2, the control is scaled up to double the width.

For example, the following code scales Image control to twice the initial size:

```
<Image Source="image.jpg"
       Height="200" Width="300"
       RenderTransformOrigin="0.5,0.5" >
    <Image.RenderTransform>
       <TransformGroup>
           <ScaleTransform ScaleX="2" ScaleY="2"/>
           <SkewTransform/>
           <RotateTransform/>
           <TranslateTransform/>
       </TransformGroup>
       </Grid.RenderTransform>
</Image>
```

RotateTransform

The RotateTransform allows you to adjust the rotation of the Silverlight control. This is done by setting the Angle property to adjust the angle of rotation.

The value of Angle is based on degrees from 0 to 360. For example, the following code rotates an Image control 45 degrees clockwise:

```
<Image Source="image.jpg"
       Height="200" Width="300"
       RenderTransformOrigin="0.5,0.5" >
    <Image.RenderTransform>
       <TransformGroup>
           <ScaleTransform/>
           <SkewTransform/>
           <RotateTransform Angle="45"/>
           <TranslateTransform/>
       </TransformGroup>
    </Image.RenderTransform>
</Image>
```

You can also rotate controls counterclockwise by setting Angle to a negative value between 0 and −360. For example, the following code rotates the same image counterclockwise, as shown in Figure 3.23:

```
<Image Source="image.jpg"
       Height="200" Width="300"
       RenderTransformOrigin="0.5,0.5" >
    <Image.RenderTransform>
        <TransformGroup>
```

```
                    <ScaleTransform/>
                    <SkewTransform/>
                    <RotateTransform Angle="-45"/>
                    <TranslateTransform/>
                </TransformGroup>
            </Image.RenderTransform>
        </Image>
```

FIGURE 3.23

Rotated `Image` controls rendered using the `RotateTransform`

SkewTransform

The `SkewTransform` allows you to adjust the horizontal and vertical skew of the Silverlight control. This is done by setting the `AngleX` property to adjust the horizontal skew and the `AngleY` property to adjust the vertical skew.

The values of `AngleX` and `AngleY` are based on degrees from 0 to 360. For example, the following code skews an `Image` control 5 degrees clockwise in the X plane and 10 degrees clockwise in the Y plane, as shown in Figure 3.24:

```
<Image Source="image.jpg"
       Height="200" Width="300"
       RenderTransformOrigin="0.5,0.5" >
    <Image.RenderTransform>
        <TransformGroup>
            <ScaleTransform/>
            <SkewTransform AngleX="5" AngleY="10" />
            <RotateTransform/>
            <TranslateTransform/>
        </TransformGroup>
    </Image.RenderTransform>
</Image>
```

FIGURE 3.24

Skewed Image controls rendered using the SkewTransform

You can also skew controls counterclockwise by setting AngleX and AngleY to a negative value between 0 and –360.

TranslateTransform

The TranslateTransform allows you to adjust the horizontal and vertical position of the Silverlight control relative to its original position. This is done by setting the X property to adjust the horizontal position and the Y property to adjust the vertical position.

The values of X and Y are based on pixels. For example, the following code repositions a TextBlock control 10 pixels to the right and 20 pixels upward:

```
<TextBlock Text="Title"
       Height="50" Width="100"
       RenderTransformOrigin="0.5,0.5" >
    <Image.RenderTransform>
        <TransformGroup>
            <ScaleTransform/>
            <SkewTransform/>
            <RotateTransform/>
            <TranslateTransform X="10" Y="-20" />
        </TransformGroup>
    </Image.RenderTransform>
</Image>
```

Opacity

The Opacity property of a control is not really part of the TransformGroup; however, it is commonly used with the transforms especially when rendering animations. The Opacity property controls the transparency of the Silverlight control on a scale of 0 to 100 where 0 is invisible and 100 is fully visible.

To illustrate how opacity is used, consider the code in Listing 3.5. The code implements two Image controls. The first Image control is skewed slightly by setting AngleX to –5 and AngleY to 10.

The second Image control is skewed much more by setting AngleX to –5 and AngleY to 10. This essentialy flips the image on the X axis so that you have a mirror image.

The Opacity property of the second Image control is set to 45 to make the image appear partially transparent. The result is a reflection, as shown in Figure 3.25.

LISTING 3.5

XAML That Implements Transform and Transparency Settings to Create a Reflection of an Image

```
<Image Source="image.jpg"
       Height="100" Width="200"
       VerticalAlignment="Top"
       Margin="100,50,50,0"
       RenderTransformOrigin="0.5,0.5" >
    <Image.RenderTransform>
        <TransformGroup>
            <ScaleTransform/>
            <SkewTransform AngleX="-5" AngleY="10"/>
```

```
            <RotateTransform/>
            <TranslateTransform/>
        </TransformGroup>
    </Image.RenderTransform>
</Image>
<Image Source="image.jpg"
        Height="100" Width="200"
        RenderTransformOrigin="0.5,0.5"
        Opacity="0.45"
        Margin="0,100,30,30">
    <Image.RenderTransform>
        <TransformGroup>
            <ScaleTransform ScaleY="-0.7"/>
            <SkewTransform AngleX="-45" AngleY="10"/>
            <RotateTransform/>
            <TranslateTransform/>
        </TransformGroup>
    </Image.RenderTransform>
</Image>
```

FIGURE 3.25

Rendered reflection effect using `Transforms` and `Opacity`

Drawing

Silverlight provides some basic drawing controls that allow you to create almost any shape as vector graphics in the application. The basic drawing controls you see most often are the `Rectangle`, `Ellipse`, and `Path`.

We are not going to spend a lot of time in this section. You can really do virtually anything using these drawing controls; however, it can become very time consuming and typically it is better to import vector images created in applications such as Adobe Illustrator.

CROSS-REF For more information about how to import vector graphics from Adobe Illustrator, see Chapter 4.

Creating a Rectangle

Rectangles are created in XAML using the `Rectangle` control. You can set the color of the rectangle, color of the outline, and thickness of the outline by defining the `Fill`, `Stroke`, and `StrokeThickness` properties.

The size of the `Rectangle` control is defined by the `Height` and `Width` property. For example, the following code defines a `Rectangle` control that is 50 pixels wide and 50 pixels high:

```
<Rectangle Fill="Blue"
           Stroke="Black"
           StrokeThickness="5"
           Height="50" Width="50" />
```

Creating an Ellipse

Ellipses and circles are created in XAML using the `Ellipse` control. Just as with the `Rectangle` control, you can set the color of the rectangle, color of the outline, and thickness of the outline by defining the `Fill`, `Stroke`, and `StrokeThickness` properties.

The size of the `Ellipse` control is defined by the `Height` and `Width` property. For example, the following code defines an `Ellipse` control that is 50 pixels wide and 50 pixels high:

```
<Ellipse Fill="Blue"
         Stroke="Black"
         StrokeThickness="5"
         Height="50" Width="50" />
```

Creating a Path

`Path` controls are used for almost everything else that `Rectangle` and `Ellipse` controls cannot do. `Path` controls many of the same properties, such as the `Height`, `Width`, `Fill`, `Stroke`, and `StrokeThickness`. However, the shape of the `Path` control is determined by the value of the `Data` property.

The `Data` property of a `Path` control is actually a mini-language all in its own that allows you to input points that define the geometry of the control. For example, the following code defines a simple path with a Red fill, as shown in Figure 3.26:

```
<Path Margin="100,60,100,60" Height="50" Width="50"
    Data="M107,-10 C135,399 16,193 148,-172 C162,157 173,148
12,100"
    Fill="Red"
    Stretch="Fill"
    Stroke="Black"/>
```

FIGURE 3.26
_____

Rendered `Path` control

For more information about the language used with the `Data` property, you can look at the documentation at the following location:

```
http://msdn.microsoft.com/en-us/library/cc189041(vs.95).aspx
```

Using XAML Brushes

So far, the examples of setting the brushes used for properties such as the `Background` property of Silverlight controls has been limited to simply setting a solid color. You can do a lot of different things with the brushes used for properties such as a `Canvas Background` or a `TextBlock Foreground` property by actually defining the brush element.

The following sections discuss the different types of brush elements that can be added to properties of Silverlight controls.

Adding a SolidColorBrush

The SolidColorBrush is the most common type that you can apply to Silverlight objects. A SolidColorBrush is automatically created for you when you set the color in one of the properties of a Silverlight object. For example, the following code automatically creates a SolidColorBrush implicitly for the Background property of a Canvas control:

```
<Canvas Background="Blue"
        Height="100" Width="200" />
```

The previous code could also be written explicitly as follows:

```
<Canvas Height="100" Width="200">
    <Canvas.Background>
        <SolidColorBrush Color="Blue" />
    </Canvas.Background>
</Canvas>
```

Adding the SolidColorBrush explicitly takes considerably more code; however, you can set some additional properties of the SolidColorBrush element to enhance the look and feel of the control. For example, you can make the SolidColorBrush appear semitransparent by setting the Opacity property, as shown in the following code:

```
<Canvas Height="100" Width="200">
    <Canvas.Background>
        <SolidColorBrush Color="Blue" Opacity=".50" />
    </Canvas.Background>
</Canvas>
```

Adding a LinearGradientBrush

LinearGradientBrush elements are similar to the SolidColorBrush. They define a linear gradient that flows between two or more colors. You can apply them to the properties of Silverlight controls the same way that the SolidColorBrush is applied.

To apply a LinearGradientBrush to a Silverlight control, you need to define the LinearGradientBrush element and give it an EndPoint and a StartPoint that define the linear direction of the brush. The EndPoint and StartPoint are set on a 0 to 1 coordinate system separated by a comma.

Then you need to define two or more GradientStop elements inside the LinearGradientBrush. Each GradientStop element needs the Color property set. You can also define the offset between 0 and 1 where that color is set using the Offset property. Silverlight applies the gradient linearly along the path defined by the StartPoint and EndPoint values matching the colors at each GradientStop along the way.

The code in Listing 3.6 applies a `LinearGradientBrush` to the `Foreground` property of a `TextBlock`. The `LinearGradientBrush` applies three gradient stops that flow from blue in the beginning to white in the middle to blue at the end, as shown in Figure 3.27.

LISTING 3.6

XAML That Implements a LinearGradientBrush to a TextBlock Control

```
<TextBlock VerticalAlignment="Stretch"
        TextAlignment="Center"
        TextWrapping="Wrap"
        FontSize="48"
        FontWeight="Bold">
    <Run Text="Linear Gradient Brush">
        <Run.Foreground>
            <LinearGradientBrush EndPoint="0.5,1"
                                 StartPoint="0.5,0">
                <GradientStop Color="Blue"/>
                <GradientStop Color="White"
                              Offset=".5"/>
                <GradientStop Color="Blue"
                              Offset="1"/>
            </LinearGradientBrush>
        </Run.Foreground>
    </Run>
</TextBlock>
```

FIGURE 3.27

Rendered `LinearGradientBrush` in a `TextBlock` control

Adding a RadialGradientBrush

`RadialGradientBrush` elements are very similar to the `LinearGradientBrush`. They define a radial gradient that flows between two or more colors. You can apply them to the properties of Silverlight controls the same way that the `LinearGradientBrush` is applied.

To apply a RadialGradientBrush to a Silverlight control, you need to define the Radial-GradientBrush element. You can define the center of the gradient radius using the GradientOrigin property. The GradientOrigin is set on a 0 to 1 coordinate system separated by a comma.

You can also define the radius of the gradient in the X and Y planes using the RadiusX and RadiusY properties. These properties are set on a scale where 1 is the Height or Width of the Silverlight control.

Then you also need to define two or more GradientStop elements inside the Radial-GradientBrush. Each GradientStop element needs the Color property set. You can also define the offset between 0 and 1 where that color is set using the Offset property. Silverlight applies the gradient on a radius centered at the GradientOrigin and defined by the RadiusX and RadiusY properties matching the colors at each GradientStop along the way.

The code in Listing 3.7 applies a RadialGradientBrush to the Background property of a Rectangle. The RadialGradientBrush applies three gradient stops that flow from blue in the beginning to white in the middle to blue at the end, as shown in Figure 3.28. Notice that the RadiusX is larger than the RadiusY making the gradient elliptical, and the GradientOrigin is set toward the bottom of the Rectangle.

LISTING 3.7

XAML That Implements a RadialGradientBrush to a Rectangle Control

```
<Rectangle Height="120" Width="200">
    <Rectangle.Fill>
        <RadialGradientBrush RadiusX="0.8"
                             RadiusY="0.4"
                             GradientOrigin="0.5,0.75">
            <GradientStop Color="Blue"/>
            <GradientStop Color="White"
                          Offset="0.5"/>
            <GradientStop Color="Blue"
                          Offset="1"/>
        </RadialGradientBrush>
    </Rectangle.Fill>
</Rectangle>
```

FIGURE 3.28

Rendered `RadialGradientBrush` in a `Rectangle` control

Adding an ImageBrush

`ImageBrush` elements are similar to the `SolidColorBrush`. Instead of a solid color, they define an image that is applied as a brush. You can apply them to the properties of Silverlight controls the same way that the `SolidColorBrush` is applied.

To apply an `ImageBrush` to a Silverlight control, you need to define the `ImageBrush` element and set the `ImageSource` property to an image that has been added to the project. You will likely want to set the `Stretch` property so that the image appears appropriately in the control.

As an example, the following code applies an `ImageBrush` as the `Background` property of a `TextBox` control, as shown in Figure 3.29:

```
<TextBox Text="Image TextBox"
         Foreground="Black"
         Height="200" Width="300">
    <TextBox.Background>
        <ImageBrush ImageSource="image.jpg"
                    Stretch="Fill"/>
    </TextBox.Background>
</TextBox>
```

Adding a VideoBrush

`VideoBrush` elements are very similar to the `ImageBrush`. Instead of an image, they define a video `MediaElement` that is applied as a brush. You can apply them to the properties of Silverlight controls the same way that the `ImageBrush` is applied.

To apply a `VideoBrush` to a Silverlight control, you need to define the `VideoBrush` element just as you do with an `ImageBrush`. However, different from an `ImageBrush`, you need to set a `SourceName` property that points to the `x:Name` of the `MediaElement`. Therefore, you also need to define a `MediaElement` separate from the Silverlight control. If you do not want the video to be displayed outside of the Silverlight control, set the `Opacity` property of the `MediaElement` to 0.

FIGURE 3.29

Rendered `ImageBrush` in a `TextBox` control

You will also likely want to set the `Stretch` property so that the video appears appropriately in the control. As an example, the following code applies a `VideoBrush` as the `Fill` property of a `Path` control, as shown in Figure 3.30:

```
<MediaElement x:Name="movie"
              Source ="video.wmv"
              Opacity-"0"/>
<Path Data="M210,210 C135,399 16,193 148,62 C100,150 200,80
   210,210"
     Stroke="Black">
   <Path.Fill>
       <VideoBrush SourceName="movie"
                   Stretch="UniformToFill"/>
   </Path.Fill>
</Path>
```

FIGURE 3.30

Rendered `VideoBrush` in a `Path` control

Implementing Animations and Storyboards

Animations are implemented in Silverlight through the use of `Storyboard` controls that contain one or more child animation controls. The `Storyboard` acts similar to a `MediaElement` with the ability to play, pause, and stop the animation. When the `Storyboard` is played back, the animation controls modify the size, shape, and look of Silverlight controls.

Animations are used for a wide variety of purposes: from animating mouse actions on buttons to implementing complex games. This section introduces you to some of the basic concepts. You can use these concepts to implement some pretty cool features in your applications.

Silverlight supports the following types of animation controls for animating Silverlight controls using From/To or Key Frame methods described in the following sections:

- **Color:** The `ColorAnimation` and `ColorAnimationUsingKeyFrames` controls allow you to animate properties of Silverlight controls that are based on color; for example, a `SolidColorBrush` or `GradientStop`.
- **Double:** The `DoubleAnimation` and `DoubleAnimationUsingKeyFrames` controls allow you to animate properties of Silverlight controls that are based on integers or doubles; for example, the `Opacity`, `Height`, or `Width`.

- **Point:** The `PointAnimation` and `PointAnimationUsingKeyFrames` controls allow you to animate properties of Silverlight controls that are based on X and Y coordinate points.

- **Object:** The `ObjectAnimationUsingKeyFrames` control allows you to animate object-related properties of Silverlight controls; for example, the `Fill` property from one `LinearGradientBrush` to another.

The following sections take you through the process of implementing animations in your Silverlight applications.

Defining Storyboard controls

The `Storyboard` control acts as a container control for animation controls and allows you to set properties that apply to the animation. The most commonly used properties of the `Storyboard` control are the `AutoReverse`, `BeginTime`, `RepeatBehavior`, and `Duration`.

The `BeginTime` property specifies the time, in `hours:minutes:seconds` format, in the `Storyboard` timeline to begin playback of the animation.

If the `AutoReverse` property is set to `True`, the animation first plays forward and then immediately plays backward. This allows you to return the Silverlight controls to their original status. This is extremely useful when implementing animations that animate controls only when the mouse is over them.

The `RepeatBehavior` property allows you to specify the number of times to repeat the animation. If you want the animation to run indefinitely, you can set the `RepeatBehavior` property to `Forever`. If `AutoReverse` is set to `True`, then playing forward and backward only counts as a single iteration. For example, the following `Storyboard` code repeats the animation three times:

```
<Storyboard RepeatBehavior="3x" />
```

The `Duration` property allows you to specify the amount of time the `Storyboard` will take to play back. The value of `Duration` is based on the `hours:minutes:seconds` syntax. The `Duration` can also be specified on each animation control in the `Storyboard` instead of the `Storyboard` control.

The following code shows an example of a `Storyboard` that plays an animation forward and backward continuously for 2 seconds at a time:

```
<Storyboard AutoReverse="True"
            RepeatBehavior="Forever"
            Duration="0:0:2">
</Storyboard>
```

Starting animations upon page load

As you begin to implement animations in your Silverlight applications, you will find that some of them should be started by the managed code. However, some animations should be started as soon as the application is loaded.

Starting the animation when the page is loaded is possible by nesting the `Storyboard` control in an `EventTrigger` element for the root layout control. The following code shows an example of nesting a `Storyboard` control in an `EventTrigger` element of a `Grid` control:

```
<Grid x:Name="LayoutRoot" Background="White">
    <Grid.Triggers>
        <EventTrigger RoutedEvent="Grid.Loaded">
            <TriggerActionCollection>
                <BeginStoryboard>
                    <Storyboard BeginTime="0"
                                 Duration="Forever">
                    </Storyboard>
                </BeginStoryboard>
            </TriggerActionCollection>
        </EventTrigger>
    </Grid.Triggers>
</Grid>
```

The `EventTrigger` attaches to the `Loaded` event of the `Grid` element and then defines the `BeginStoryboard` element as part of the `TriggerActionCollection`.

CROSS-REF   **For more information about controlling animations in managed code, see Chapter 8.**

Creating From/To animations

The simplest form of animation to implement is the From/To animation. These animations are implemented by specifying a specific target property and then setting the `From` and `To` values in the animation.

From/To animations are implemented by adding `ColorAnimation`, `DoubleAnimation`, or `PointAnimation` controls to a `Storyboard`. You can add multiples of each control to the `Storyboard` and all will run when the `Storyboard` is played.

In the animation control, you need to specify a `Target` or `TargetName` property that points to a specific Silverlight control. The `TargetName` property is typically used because it is easy to reference names that have been added to the namescope using the `x:Name` property.

You also need to specify the `TargetProperty` property, which points to a specific property of the Silverlight control that is to be animated.

Just as with the `Storyboard` control, you can set the `AutoReverse`, `BeginTime`, `Repeat-Behavior`, and `Duration` properties in animation controls. These settings override the same settings in the `Storyboard` control.

To help you understand From/To animations, consider the code in Listing 3.8. The code implements a `Storyboard` in the `EventTrigger` of the `Grid` root layout control. The `Storyboard` defines two From/To animations that animate the `RadiusX` and `RadiusY` properties of a `RadialGradientBrush` that provides the `Fill` for an `Ellipse` control.

The animation identifies the target control by setting the `TargetName` property to pulse, which is assigned using the `x:Name` property of the `RadialGradientBrush`. The radius of the gradient fill is animated by setting the `TargetProperty` of the animations to `RadiusX` and `RadiusY` and then setting the `From` property to 0 and the `To` property to 1.

The `BeginTime` in the `Storyboard` is set to 0 and the `Duration` is set to `Forever` so that the `Storyboard` plays continuously. The `Duration` of the animations is set to 2 seconds and the `AutoReverse` property is set to `True` so that the animations reverse themselves.

The result of the `Storyboard` is that the gradient fill of the ellipse expands and collapses repeatedly, as shown in Figure 3.31.

FIGURE 3.31

Rendered From/To animation of a `RadialGradientBrush` in an `Ellipse` control

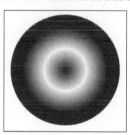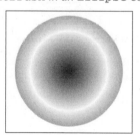

LISTING 3.8

XAML That Implements a From/To Animation to a RadialGradientBrush

```xaml
<UserControl x:Class="animation.Page"
    xmlns="http://schemas.microsoft.com/client/2007"
    xmlns:x="http://schemas.microsoft.com/winfx/2006/xaml"
    Width="400" Height="300">
<Grid x:Name="LayoutRoot" Background="White">
    <Grid.Triggers>
        <EventTrigger RoutedEvent="Grid.Loaded">
            <TriggerActionCollection>
                <BeginStoryboard>
                    <Storyboard BeginTime="0:0:0"
                                Duration="Forever">
                        <DoubleAnimation
                            Storyboard.TargetName="pulse"
                            Storyboard.TargetProperty="RadiusX"
                            From="0" To="1"
                            Duration="0:0:2"
                            AutoReverse="True" />
                        <DoubleAnimation
                            Storyboard.TargetName="pulse"
                            Storyboard.TargetProperty="RadiusY"
                            From="0" To="1"
                            Duration="0:0:2"
                            AutoReverse="True" />
                    </Storyboard>
                </BeginStoryboard>
            </TriggerActionCollection>
        </EventTrigger>
    </Grid.Triggers>
    <Ellipse Height="200" Width="200">
        <Ellipse.Fill>
            <RadialGradientBrush x:Name="pulse"
                                 RadiusX="0.0"
                                 RadiusY="0.0"
                                 GradientOrigin="0.5,0.5">
                <GradientStop Color="Blue"/>
                <GradientStop Color="White"
                              Offset="0.5"/>
                <GradientStop Color="Blue"
                              Offset="1"/>
            </RadialGradientBrush>
        </Ellipse.Fill>
    </Ellipse>
</Grid>
</UserControl>
```

Creating Key Frame animations

Key Frame animations have some similarities with From/To animations; however, instead of implementing animations by specifying a specific target property and then setting the From and To values in the animation, Key Frame animations are based on specific key frames in the animation timeline.

Key Frame animations are implemented by adding ColorAnimationUsingKeyFrames, DoubleAnimationUsingKeyFrames, UsingKeyFrames, PointAnimationUsingKeyFrames, or ObjectAnimationUsingKeyFrames controls to a Storyboard. You can add multiples of each control to the Storyboard and all runs when the Storyboard is played.

In the animation control, you need to specify a Target or TargetName property that points to a specific Silverlight control. The TargetName property is typically used because it is easy to reference names that have been added to the namescope using the x:Name property.

You also need to specify the TargetProperty property, which points to a specific property of the Silverlight control that is to be animated.

Just as with the From/To animation, you can set the AutoReverse, BeginTime, RepeatBehavior, and Duration properties in animation controls. These settings override the same settings in the Storyboard control.

The difference from From/To animations is when you define the properties that are animated. Key Frame animations not only allow you the ability to specify what properties get animated but also the specific time sequence in the timeline that they are animated. This is done by implementing a Key Frame element that specifies the animated value for each time interval.

For example, the following line of code defines a DoubleAnimationUsingKeyFrames control that implements two SplineDoubleKeyFrame elements that are animated at 1 and 2 seconds that animate the FontSize being changed to 20 at 1 second and 30 at 2 seconds.

```
<DoubleAnimationUsingKeyFrames
    Storyboard.TargetName="myText"
    Storyboard.TargetProperty="FontSize"
    BeginTime="00:00:00">
    <SplineDoubleKeyFrame KeyTime="00:00:01" Value="20"/>
    <SplineDoubleKeyFrame KeyTime="00:00:02" Value="30"/>
</DoubleAnimationUsingKeyFrames>
```

To help you understand Key Frame animations, consider the code in Listing 3.9. The code implements a Storyboard in the EventTrigger of the Grid root layout control. The Storyboard defines two DoubleAnimationUsingKeyFrames animations that animate a TranslateTransform and ScaleTransform for an Ellipse control.

We chose to use transform properties here because you likely are implementing many of your animations using transforms, and the syntax is a bit lengthy. Notice in the code that to access the `ScaleTransform` property, the `TargetProperty` setting is set as follows:

```
Storyboard.TargetProperty="(UIElement.RenderTransform).
    (TransformGroup.Children)[0].(ScaleTransform.ScaleY)"
```

The previous syntax is used to access the different properties in the `TransformGroup` for the control. The `ScaleTransform` is accessed by indexing element 0 in the `TransformGroup` using the [0] syntax. Access to the `TransformGroup` children is based on their location in the following `TransformGroup` block; `SkewTransform` is accessed by [1], `RotateTransform` is accessed by [1], and `TranslateTransform` is accessed by [3].

```
<TransformGroup>
    <ScaleTransform/>
    <SkewTransform/>
    <RotateTransform/>
    <TranslateTransform/>
</TransformGroup>
```

The first `DoubleAnimationUsingKeyFrames` control in Listing 3.9 defines four `SplineDoubleKeyFrame` elements that animate the Y property of the `TranslateTransform` of the `Ellipse`. These key frames adjust the Y position of the `Ellipse` at 1, 2, 3, and 3.5 seconds.

The second `DoubleAnimationUsingKeyFrames` control in Listing 3.9 defines two `SplineDoubleKeyFrame` elements that animate the `ScaleY` property of the `ScaleTransform` of the `Ellipse`. These key frames adjust the Y scale of the `Ellipse` at 3 and 3.5 seconds.

Only the animation that has key frames for the time sequence is implemented as the time sequence progresses. The result of the `Storyboard` is that the Ellipse appears to be a bouncing ball, as shown in Figure 3.32.

LISTING 3.9

XAML That Implements a Key Frame Animation to Animate an Ellipse into a Bouncing Ball

```xml
<UserControl x:Class="keyanimation.Page"
    xmlns="http://schemas.microsoft.com/client/2007"
    xmlns:x="http://schemas.microsoft.com/winfx/2006/xaml"
    Width="640" Height="480">
    <Grid x:Name="LayoutRoot" Background="LightGray" >
<Grid.Triggers>
<EventTrigger RoutedEvent="Grid.Loaded">
<TriggerActionCollection>
<BeginStoryboard>
```

```xaml
<Storyboard x:Name="Storyboard1"
        RepeatBehavior="Forever">
    <DoubleAnimationUsingKeyFrames AutoReverse="True"
        Storyboard.TargetName="ball"
        Storyboard.TargetProperty=
"(UIElement.RenderTransform).(TransformGroup.Children)[3].
    (TranslateTransform.Y)"
        BeginTime="00:00:00">
        <SplineDoubleKeyFrame KeyTime="00:00:01" Value="100"/>
        <SplineDoubleKeyFrame KeyTime="00:00:02" Value="200"/>
        <SplineDoubleKeyFrame KeyTime="00:00:03" Value="290"/>
        <SplineDoubleKeyFrame KeyTime="00:00:03.5" Value="306"/>
    </DoubleAnimationUsingKeyFrames>
    <DoubleAnimationUsingKeyFrames AutoReverse="True"
        Storyboard.TargetName="ball"
        Storyboard.TargetProperty=
"(UIElement.RenderTransform).(TransformGroup.Children)[0].
    (ScaleTransform.ScaleY)"
        BeginTime="00:00:00">
        <SplineDoubleKeyFrame KeyTime="00:00:03" Value="1"/>
        <SplineDoubleKeyFrame KeyTime="00:00:03.5" Value="0.5"/>
    </DoubleAnimationUsingKeyFrames>
</Storyboard>
</BeginStoryboard>
</TriggerActionCollection>
</EventTrigger>
</Grid.Triggers>
        <Ellipse x:Name="ball"
                VerticalAlignment="Top"
                Margin="0,20,0,0"
                Height="100" Width="100"
                Fill="Blue"
                RenderTransformOrigin="0.5,0.5">
            <Ellipse.RenderTransform>
                <TransformGroup>
                    <ScaleTransform/>
                    <SkewTransform/>
                    <RotateTransform/>
                    <TranslateTransform/>
                </TransformGroup>
            </Ellipse.RenderTransform>
        </Ellipse>
        <Canvas Background="DarkGray"
                VerticalAlignment="Bottom"
                Height="70" Width="640" />
    </Grid>
</UserControl>
```

FIGURE 3.32

Rendered Key Frame animation that transforms an `Ellipse` control

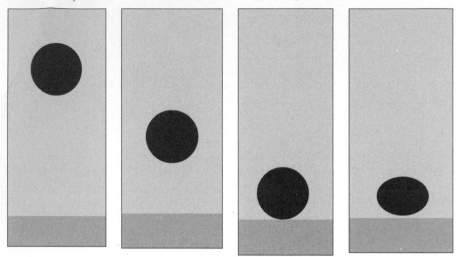

Creating animations as Resources

In the previous sections, the code implements the animations as `Storyboard` controls attached to an `EventTrigger` for a `Grid` control. This is so that the animation begins when the page loads.

If you are going to implement the functionality of starting and stopping animations in your managed code, then you want to implement the `Storyboard` as a `Resource` in your XAML file. For example, the following code defines an animation as a `UserControl.Resources` control:

```
<UserControl.Resources>
    <Storyboard x:Name="Storyboard1">
        <DoubleAnimationUsingKeyFrames
            Storyboard.TargetName="myText"
            Storyboard.TargetProperty="FontSize"
            BeginTime="00:00:00">
            <SplineDoubleKeyFrame KeyTime="00:00:01" Value="20"/>
            <SplineDoubleKeyFrame KeyTime="00:00:02" Value="30"/>
        </DoubleAnimationUsingKeyFrames>
    </Storyboard>
</UserControl.Resources>
```

Attaching Event Handlers to XAML Elements

Events can be attached to Silverlight controls either in XAML or using managed code. Most of the event handling that you implement will be in managed code. Because this chapter does not focus on managed code, we won't spend much time here.

CROSS-REF Events and event handling are discussed in much more detail in Chapter 8.

Attaching events to Silverlight controls in XAML is a simple matter of setting the event property of the control to a string representing the name of the event handler function in the managed code. For example, consider the following C# function defined in managed code:

```
private void Button_Click(object sender, RoutedEventArgs e)
{
    myButton.Content = "Clicked";
}
```

The following XAML code would attach the Click event property of the myButton control to the Button_Click event handler.

```
<Button x:Name="myButton"
        Content="Click Me"
        Height="50" Width="100"
        Click="Button_Click" />
```

Summary

This chapter introduced you to many of the aspects of the XAML programming language that are used to create and lay out the UI for most Silverlight applications. Most Silverlight applications rely on XAML to implement the right UI controls and managed code to implement the functionality.

Using XAML, you can quickly add buttons, forms, images, video, and animations to your Silverlight applications.

In this chapter, you learned how to:

- Create Silverlight controls in XAML
- Use Grid and Canvas controls to quickly and precisely lay out applications
- Transform the scale, skew, rotation, and opacity of Silverlight controls
- Implement solid color, gradient, image, and video brushes to liven up Silverlight controls
- Create and implement Storyboard animations
- Attach event handlers to Silverlight controls

Chapter 4

Using Expression Blend to Design Silverlight Applications

Using Expression Blend profoundly speeds up the implementation of the design portion of your Silverlight applications. Using Expression Blend's interface, you can quickly use the mouse to create and position Silverlight controls. Then using the Properties tab, you can quickly see and send the properties to control the look and behavior of the Silverlight controls.

Expression Blend allows you to set almost every property available without accessing the XAML code. This allows the creation of Silverlight applications to be easily divided between a design team and a development team.

This is not a comprehensive chapter on using Expression Blend. Instead, this chapter focuses on familiarizing you with some of the features necessary to design Silverlight applications in Expression Blend. The idea is to give developers enough information about the design features that they can use Expression Blend to speed up development, while at the same time giving designers enough information that they can create the design elements of a Silverlight application that can be easily consumed by developers.

IN THIS CHAPTER

Adding Silverlight controls in Expression Blend

Quickly and easily arranging Silverlight controls

Applying solid, gradient, and image brushes to controls

Animating Silverlight controls in Expression Blend using Storyboard animations

Using Expression Design to add vector graphics to Silverlight applications

> **NOTE** You will need Expression Blend 2.5 or later to create and edit Silverlight applications. At the time of this writing, Expression Blend 2.5 is available only as a preview; however, it should be released shortly.

Getting Started with Expression Blend

Expression Blend is an extremely useful tool when developing Silverlight applications. Expression Blend allows you to quickly and easily add Silverlight controls to the project, arrange them aesthetically, and then set the necessary properties that provide a rich user interface (UI).

The following sections are designed to get you up to speed quickly on creating Silverlight applications in Expression Blend, understanding the Toolbox, and using the Design and XAML views as you create Silverlight applications.

Creating a Silverlight application project in Expression Blend

Silverlight application projects in Expression Blend are actually Visual Studio Silverlight application projects. When you create a Silverlight application project, Expression Blend creates a Visual Studio SLN solution file as well as all other files typically created by Visual Studio.

CROSS-REF For more information about Visual Studio Silverlight application projects, see Chapter 6.

Included in the Silverlight application project files is a file named `Page.xaml`. This is the main file that you add Silverlight controls to in order to build the UI elements for the application.

To create a new Silverlight application project, choose File ➪ New Project from the main menu to display the New Project window, as shown in Figure 4.1.

FIGURE 4.1

Creating a new Silverlight 2 application in Expression Blend

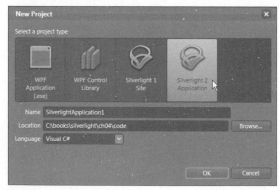

From the New Project window, select Silverlight 2 Application from the project type selections. Specify the name and location to create the project. Then specify the programming language that is used to provide functionality to the project. Currently, the options are C# and Visual Basic. Then click OK to create the new project. A new project is created and the `Page.xaml` file is displayed in the design window, as shown in Figure 4.2.

FIGURE 4.2

A new Silverlight 2 application in Expression Blend with a blank `Page.xaml` file

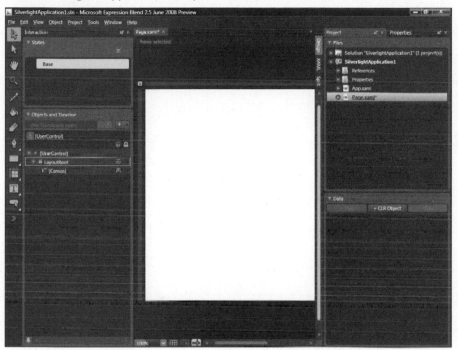

Using the Design, XAML, and Split views

Expression Blend provides three views for XAML files. The Design view shows you a graphical representation of the XAML elements similar to what is rendered in the Silverlight application. The XAML view displays the XAML code only. The Split view, shown in Figure 4.3, displays both the Design and XAML views in a split frame.

FIGURE 4.3

Split view of a Silverlight 2 application in Expression Blend

The Split view gives you the ability to modify XAML code directly and see the results without having to switch to a different view. Conversely, if you modify the Silverlight controls in the Design view of the Split view, the changes are applied to the XAML code view. There are advantages to using each of these views. The Design view provides a graphical view that makes it simple to add controls and adjust the layout. The XAML view allows the code to be changed directly. The XAML view is the best option for setting specific values of attributes. The most common method is to use the Split view so that you have access to both the Design view and the XAML code view.

Understanding the Expression Blend Toolbox

The first place to begin in using Expression Blend to design Silverlight applications is with the Toolbox located on the left side of Expression Blend. The Toolbox provides an easily accessible set of tools used to add and modify Silverlight controls in the Design view. The Toolbox is organized into several different types of tools based on the tasks they perform. The following sections discuss each of these tools.

Selection tools

The Selection tools, shown in Figure 4.4, are composed of the Selection (top) and Direct Selection (bottom) tools. The Selection tool is used to select one or more objects in the Design view. The Direct Selection tool is used to select objects that are nested inside other objects, such as a `TextBlock` control nested in a `Canvas` control.

FIGURE 4.4

The Selection tools in the Toolbox of Expression Blend

View tools

The View tools, shown in Figure 4.5, are composed of the Pan (top) and Direct Zoom (bottom) tools. The Pan tool is used to drag the center focus of the Design view, allowing you to move the entire view around the window. The Zoom tool is used to zoom in on a particular section of the Design view.

FIGURE 4.5

The View tools in the Toolbox of Expression Blend

Brush tools

The Brush tools, shown in Figure 4.6, are composed of the Eyedropper (top), Paint Bucket (middle), and Brush Transform (bottom) tools. These tools are used when modifying the brush attributes of a control. The Eyedropper tool is used to extract a specific color from an element on the screen to set the brush fill color. The Paint Bucket control is used to apply a color as a fill for an object. The Brush Transform tool is used to apply a brush transform to an object.

FIGURE 4.6

The Brush tools in the Toolbox of Expression Blend

Object tools

The Object tools are composed of the Path, Shape, Layout Panels, Text Controls, and Common Controls tools. These tools are used to add Silverlight controls to the Design view. To access the available tools, click the white arrow in the bottom right-hand corner of the control.

Path tool

The Path tool, shown in Figure 4.7, provides the Pen and Pencil tools that allow you to add paths to the Silverlight application. The Pen tool implements paths based on point to point. The parabolic arc of the line between the points can be modified by dragging the control handler of that point. The Pencil tool is completely free-form. As you drag the cursor on the Design view, a free-form line is created.

FIGURE 4.7

The Path tool in the Toolbox of Expression Blend

Shape tool

The Shape tool, shown in Figure 4.8, provides the Rectangle, Ellipse, and Line tools that allow you to add basic shapes to the Silverlight application. This tool creates a rectangle, ellipse, or line in the Design view by clicking and dragging the mouse from one point to another.

FIGURE 4.8

The Shape tool in the Toolbox of Expression Blend

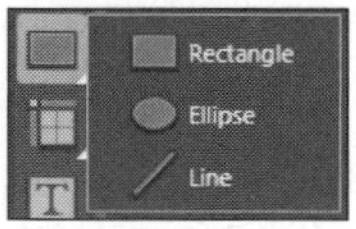

Layout Panels tool

The Layout Panels tool, shown in Figure 4.9, provides the Grid, Canvas, StackPanel, ScrollViewer, and Border tools that allow you to add Silverlight layout controls to the Design view. Using this tool, layout controls are added to the design area by clicking and dragging the mouse from one point to another.

FIGURE 4.9

The Layout Panels tool in the Toolbox of Expression Blend

Text Control tool

The Text Controls tool, shown in Figure 4.10, provides the TextBox and TextBlock tools that allow you to add text elements to your Silverlight application. Using this tool, `TextBox` and `TextBlock` controls are added to the design area by clicking and dragging the mouse from one point to another.

FIGURE 4.10

The Text Controls tool in the toolbox of Expression Blend

Common Controls tool

The Common Controls tool, shown in Figure 4.11, provides the Button, CheckBox, ListBox, RadioButton, ScrollBar, Slider, and GridSplitter tools that allow you to add common Silverlight controls to the Design view. Using this tool, Silverlight controls are added to the design area by clicking and dragging the mouse from one point to another.

FIGURE 4.11

The Common Controls tool in the Toolbox of Expression Blend

Asset tool

Asset tools provide access to most of the Silverlight controls as well as media controls and user controls. To select an asset tool, click on the double right arrow button to display the Asset Library window, as shown in Figure 4.12.

From the Asset Library window, you can click the System Controls, Media, or Custom Controls tab, and then click on one of the controls displayed. The selected control is displayed in the asset tool, and you can then add it to the Design view.

NOTE For `Image` and `MediaElement` controls to be visible in the Asset Library, you need to add them to the project. One method of doing this is by choosing Project ⇨ Add Existing Item from the main menu and then navigating to the image or media file and clicking the Open button.

FIGURE 4.12

The Asset Library tool in the Toolbox of Expression Blend

Adding Silverlight controls

Silverlight controls can be added to the project in two ways. You can type the XAML code into the XAML view, or you can select the tool from the Toolbox and then use the mouse to add the control in the Design view. As you play around with Expression Blend, you will find that it is much easier to add elements using the Design view.

For example, the Expression Blend project shown in Figure 4.13 shows a simple application that has a TextBlock, TextBox, and two Button controls added. Adding the controls was a simple process of selecting the tool on the left and then using the mouse to create the control in the Design view. The entire process only took a few seconds. As you can see, there is a large amount of XAML code generated in the XAML pane.

FIGURE 4.13

Adding Silverlight controls to the Design view of Expression Blend

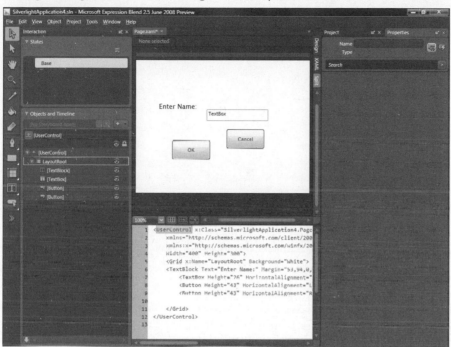

Arranging Controls in the Design View

As you begin to add more and more controls to the Design view in Expression Blend, you will notice that managing the controls can get out of hand very quickly. You need to nest your controls in layout elements such as a `Grid`, `Canvas`, or `StackPanel`. You also need to be able to align the controls so that they line up properly.

Expression Blend provides several tools that help you arrange controls so that they line up properly and are rendered in the correct location and order in the application. The following sections discuss some of the options for arranging Silverlight controls using the Design view.

Using snaplines and gridlines

The gridline and snapline feature of Expression Blend is extremely useful when trying to arrange controls so that they line up.

The gridline feature sets up a grid of evenly spaced squares. When enabled, controls that you place or move in the Design view are automatically snapped to the nearest horizontal and vertical gridline. This makes it easier to place Silverlight controls so that they line up in the application.

To view the gridline used in gridline snapping, click the Show snap grid button shown in Figure 4.14.

FIGURE 4.14

Show snap grid button in the Design view of Expression Blend

Although the horizontal and vertical gridlines are displayed, you still need to enable the gridline snapping feature by clicking the Turn on snapping to gridlines button shown in Figure 4.15. Once the gridline snapping feature is turned on, it is easy to drag an existing control in the Design view and place them in line, as shown in Figure 4.16.

FIGURE 4.15

Enabling gridline snapping in the Design view of Expression Blend

FIGURE 4.16

Aligning Silverlight controls using the gridline snapping feature of Expression Blend

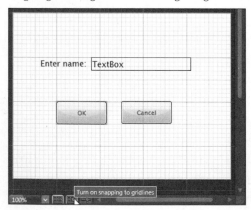

Expression Blend also provides the snapline snapping feature to align controls in the Design view. The snapline snapping feature keys off the boundaries of adjacent objects and then aligns the object being added or dragged with those adjacent objects. To enable the snapline snapping feature, click the Turn on snapping to snaplines button shown in Figure 4.17.

FIGURE 4.17

Enabling snapline snapping in the Design view of Expression Blend

After the snapline snapping feature is turned on, then it is easy to drag an existing control in the Design view and place it in line with adjacent objects. A red snapline is displayed connecting the object being dragged with the adjacent objects, as shown in Figure 4.18.

FIGURE 4.18

Aligning Silverlight controls using the snapline snapping feature of Expression Blend

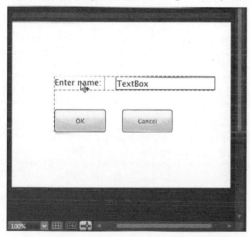

Aligning controls

Another method of arranging Silverlight controls so that they line up is using the align feature of Expression Blend. The align feature aligns two or more controls based on the left edge, horizontal center, right edge, top edge, vertical center, or bottom edge of each object.

To align two objects using the align feature, first select the control that is in the correct position, then hold the Ctrl key down and select additional controls. The align feature uses the position of the first control to change the alignment of the additional controls.

When all controls have been selected, right-click on the first control and select Align and then either Left Edges, Horizontal Centers, Right Edges, Top Edges, Vertical Centers, or Bottom Edges from the pop-up menu, as shown in Figure 4.19. The controls are aligned based on your selection as shown in Figure 4.19.

FIGURE 4.19

Aligning Silverlight controls using the align feature of Expression Blend

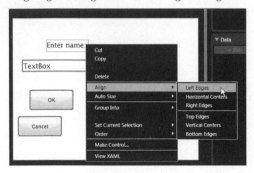
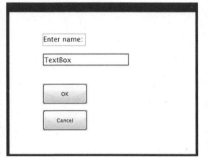

Nesting controls using layout panels

Another important aspect of arranging controls in a Silverlight application is the ability to nest several child controls into a single parent control. The most common form of this is placing UI controls inside of `Grid`, `Canvas`, or `StackPanel` controls.

Nesting controls into layout panels gives you the flexibility to control the layout of a specific set of controls based on a single parent. You can then move and adjust the parent as necessary without having to change each control in the set.

Nesting controls in Expression Blend is very simple using the Objects Interaction pane shown in Figure 4.20. Simply select the controls that you want to nest and then drag and drop them onto the parent control.

For example, Figure 4.20 shows a set of `RadioButton` controls that are nested inside a `StackPanel` control. The `StackPanel` control can be moved in the Design view without affecting the relative position of the `RadioButton` controls inside. The Interaction pane shows the

RadioButton controls nested inside the StackPanel and the XAML pane shows the RadioButton control statements nested inside the StackPanel control statement.

FIGURE 4.20

Nesting Silverlight controls in the Design view of Expression Blend

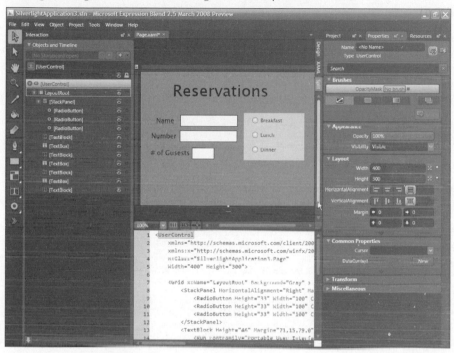

Controls can also be nested by selecting several of them in the Design view. After you select several controls, right-click on one of the controls in the selected group, select Group Into from the pop-up menu, and select the appropriate layout control. For example, Figure 4.21 shows several TextBlock and TextBox controls being grouped into a Border control.

 **TIP** You can nest controls by holding down the Alt key and then dragging them onto layout panel controls inside the Design view.

FIGURE 4.21

Grouping several Silverlight controls into a Border control using the Design view of Expression Blend

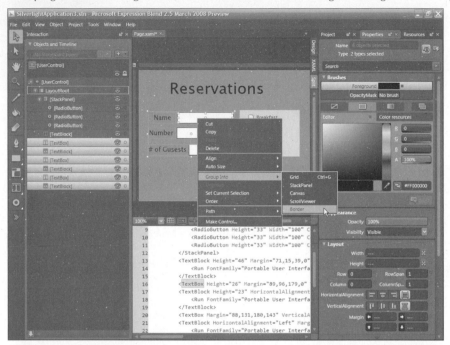

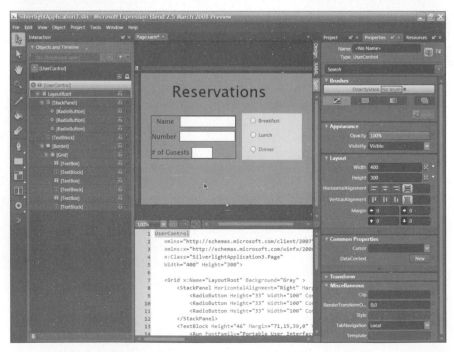

Ordering controls

When adding Silverlight controls to applications, keep in mind that the first control added is added to the parent layout panel. Subsequent controls that are added are placed on top of that control. This can be a problem if you are designing an application and want the controls to overlap.

To solve this problem, Expression Blend provides the Order feature that allows you to quickly change the order of the controls and therefore which controls are rendered on top of other controls. Using the Order feature, you can specify to change the order of a control toward the front or back either one item at a time or all the way to the front or back.

For example, Figure 4.22 shows an example of a Silverlight application that includes three Image controls and a TextBlock control. Because the TextBlock is added to the Design view first, it is partially hidden behind one of the Image controls. The text is brought forward by right-clicking on the TextBlock control and choosing Order⇨ Bring to Front from the pop-up menu, as shown in Figure 4.22. The result is that the order is changed in both the XAML code and in the Interaction pane, also shown in Figure 4.22.

Modifying the Properties of Silverlight Controls

After adding Silverlight controls to the application using the Toolbox, you can modify the properties of a selected control using the Properties tab, as shown in Figure 4.23. The Properties tab displays a series of panes that provide a graphical means of modifying the attributes of the Silverlight controls.

In Chapter 2, we showed you how to set the properties of a Silverlight control using XAML code. You will quickly see how using Expression Blend to set properties is much faster and easier for most controls. The following sections discuss the options that you have on the Properties pane to modify Silverlight controls.

FIGURE 4.22

Reordering a `TextBlock` control so that it renders on top of other controls in the Design view of Expression Blend

FIGURE 4.23

FIGURE 4.23

The control Properties tab in Expression Blend

Naming the control

The very first item that is settable from the Properties tab is the name of the Silverlight control. The name is set by typing a meaningful name into the Name text box, as shown in Figure 4.23. The name that you type is set as the `x:Name` of the object. For example, if a `TextBlock` control is selected and you type the string `myTitle`, the XAML code changes to include the `x:Name` property as shown in the following code:

```
<TextBlock x:Name="myTitle" Height="53" Margin="43,29,28,0" />
```

You should name all controls that may need to be accessed to provide functionality by the Silverlight code.

Attaching event handlers to controls

Event handlers can quickly be attached to controls from the Properties pane in Expression Blend. Clicking the Events button at the top of the Properties pane, as shown in Figure 4.24, displays the Events pane. Each event that is available for the selected control is displayed. To attach an event handler to the control, type the name of the event handler that you want to attach to the control in the appropriate event text box, as shown in Figure 4.24.

FIGURE 4.24

The Events pane in the Properties tab of Expression Blend

To switch back to the Properties view from the Events pane, click the Properties button next to the Events button.

> **TIP** If you press Tab inside the text box of one of the events in the Events pane, Expression Blend automatically generates the code to attach the event handler to the control and launches Visual Studio if it is installed. If Visual Studio is not installed, another editor is launched.

Applying brushes to controls

One of the biggest advantages to Silverlight is the ability to apply brushes to controls that modify the color and gradient. Using brushes gives you unlimited possibilities when designing the look and feel of your Silverlight applications.

The Brushes pane, shown in Figure 4.25, is made up of two main sections. The top section is a list of the available properties of the control that can accept some kind of brush setting. For example, Figure 4.25 shows the Brushes pane for a TextBox control. The TextBox control can accept a brush setting for the Background, BorderBrush, Foreground, SelectionBackground, SelectionForeground, and OpacityMask properties.

The bottom portion of the Brushes pane is a tabbed pane that includes the No brush, Solid color brush, Gradient brush, and Brush resources tabs that provide an interface to apply brushes to properties of the Silverlight control. To apply a brush to a property, first select the property and then click one of the brush tabs.

The No brush tab does not have an interface. If you click this tab, as shown in Figure 4.25, no brush is applied to the property selected in the top of the Brushes pane.

FIGURE 4.25

The Brushes pane in the Properties tab with the No brush tab selected

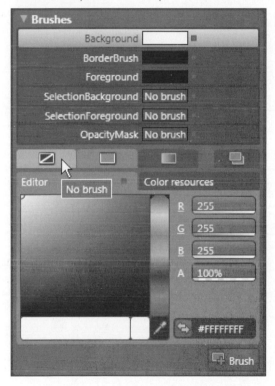

Solid color brushes

The Solid color brush tab, shown in Figure 4.26, allows you to specify a single color to use as the brush. This tab provides several methods of defining the color. You can use the color selector in the left portion of the tab.

You can specify the RGB color settings and set the Alpha channel of the color using the controls on the right-hand section of the tab. You can also type in the specific eight-digit color number if you have a specific color number that you want to use.

Figure 4.26 shows the `Background` property of a `TextBox` being set to a blue color with the Alpha channel set to 50%.

FIGURE 4.26

Setting a Solid Color brush in the Brush pane of the Properties tab in Expression Blend

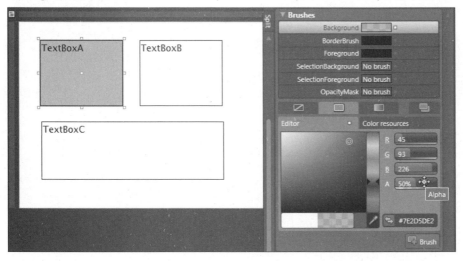

Gradient brushes

The Gradient Brush tab, shown in Figure 4.27, is similar to the Solid Color Brush tab except that it allows you to specify the same color options based on a gradient scale. You can specify a radial or linear gradient using the buttons on the lower left-hand corner of the tab.

You can use the color selector to set each color. You can specify the RGB color settings and set the Alpha channel of each color using the controls on the right-hand section of the tab. You can also type in the specific eight-digit color number if you have a specific color number that you want to use.

The gradient is based on the gradient scale at the bottom of the window. Initially, the gradient will have two gradient stops selected one at each end of the gradient scale. You can modify the gradient scale by adding additional gradient stops, changing existing gradient stops, and repositioning the gradient stops on the scale. New gradient stops are added to the scale by clicking on the scale. Gradient stops are changed by clicking on the gradient stop indicator on the scale and then modifying the color settings.

For example, Figure 4.27 shows a `TextBox` with the `Background` property being set to a gradient brush with three gradient stop settings.

FIGURE 4.27

Setting a gradient brush in the Brush pane of the Properties tab in Expression Blend

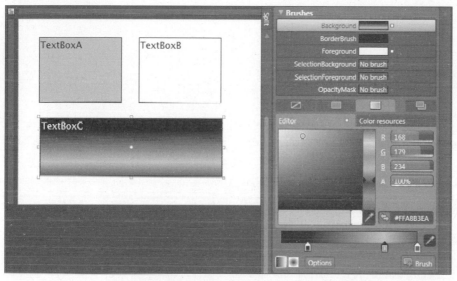

You may want to save any complex gradient images as brush resource brushes. This makes them available in the Brush Resources pane and allows you the ability to easily apply the exact gradient brush to other controls.

To save the gradient brush as a brush resource, click the Convert brush to resource button in the bottom right hand corner of the Gradient tab shown in Figure 4.27 to display the Create Brush Resource window, as shown in Figure 4.28. Name the brush resource and specify whether you want the resource available only in this file or in the entire project. A brush resource is created, and you can access it from the Brush Resources tab.

FIGURE 4.28

Creating a brush resource in the Create Brush Resource window in Expression Blend

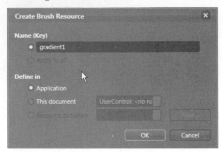

Image brush resources

A really cool feature of Silverlight is the ability to implement brushes that are based on `Image` controls. These brushes are called resource brushes. The Brush Resources tab, shown in Figure 4.29, allows you to specify a brush that has been created from an image or media resource in the project.

FIGURE 4.29

Selecting an image brush from brush resources in the Brush pane of the Properties tab in Expression Blend

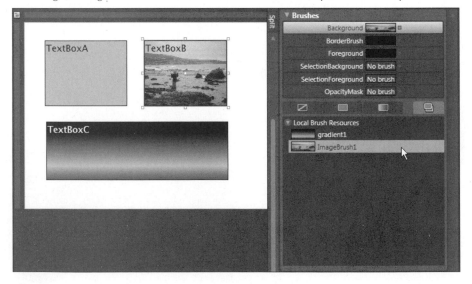

The first step in implementing a resource brush is to add the image to the project by selecting Project ➪ Add Existing Item from the main menu and then navigating to the image file and clicking OK. The file appears in the Media tab of the Asset Library (discussed earlier in this chapter) as an `Image` control.

Select the `Image` control from the Asset Library and add it to the Design view. Then select the newly added control and choose Tools ➪ MakeBrushResource ➪ MakeImageBrushResource. The image brush resource is now displayed in the Brush Resources tab.

To apply a resource brush to a property, simply select it from the Brush Resources tab. For example, Figure 4.29 shows a `TextBox Background` property being set to an image brush selected from the Brush Resources tab.

Setting appearance properties of controls

The Appearance pane, shown in Figure 4.30, allows you to set some of the appearance properties of controls. Most controls allow you to set their `Opacity` and `Visibility` properties in this pane. To make a control more transparent, use the mouse to drag the Opacity slider down to less than 100 percent. To change the visibility, use the Visibility drop down menu to select Visible or Collapsed.

Some controls have additional appearance properties that you can set. For example, the Border control allows you to set the `BorderThickness` and `CornerRadius` properties here, as shown in Figure 4.30.

FIGURE 4.30

Setting the Opacity and Visibility properties of a control in the Appearance pane of the Properties tab in Expression Blend

Setting the layout of controls in the Silverlight application

The most common settings that you work with in Expression Blend are the layout settings available on the Layout pane, as shown in Figure 4.31. These properties determine the layout size, positioning, and behavior of the controls. The following sections discuss the different settings available in the Layout pane.

FIGURE 4.31

Setting the Layout properties of a control in the Layout pane of the Properties tab in Expression Blend

Height and width

The first settings in the Layout pane are the Width and Height textboxes. The values in these text boxes determine the `Height` and `Width` properties of the control.

Positioning

The next settings are the positioning settings. These settings vary depending on whether the parent control is a `Canvas` or `Grid` control. For `Canvas`-based controls, these settings are Left and Top, allowing you to set the `Canvas.Left` and `Canvas.Top` properties of the control. For example:

```
<TextBox Canvas.Left="20" Canvas.Top="20" ...
```

For `Grid`-based controls, these settings are Row, Column, RowSpan, and ColumnSpan allowing you to set the `Grid.Row`, `Grid.Column`, `Grid.RowSpan`, and `Grid.ColumnSpan` properties of the control. For example:

```
<TextBox Grid.Row="2" Grid.Column="2"
         Grid.RowSpan="2" Grid.ColumnSpan="2"
    . . .
```

Alignment

The next settings in the Layout pane are the HorizontalAlignment and VerticalAlignment settings. These settings allow you to set the `HorizontalAlignment` and `VerticalAlignment` properties of the control.

You can set the value of the `HorizontalAlignment` property of the control by clicking one of the following alignment buttons shown in Figure 4.31. From left to right, they are: Left, Center, Right, Stretch.

Likewise, you can set the value of the `VerticalAlignment` property of the control by clicking one of the alignment buttons shown in Figure 4.31. From left to right, they are: Top, Center, Bottom, Stretch.

Margin

The next setting in the Layout pane is the Margin setting. The Margin setting allows you to set the top, left, right, and bottom margin for the control. These settings determine the margins around the control.

To set the margin settings, simply type the margin, in pixels, into the appropriate text box, as shown in Figure 4.31. The result is that the `Margin` property of the control is set to those values. For example:

```
<TextBlock Margin="5,5,20,20" . . .
```

Other settings

If you click the down arrow below the Margin settings, as shown in Figure 4.31, the Layout pane expands to reveal several other settings that can be set. The expanded pane includes settings such as the `MinWidth`, `MaxWidth`, `MinHeight`, and `MaxHeight` properties to control resizing the control. They also include the ability to set the `Padding` property of the control.

Applying transforms to controls

Another common task that you can perform on controls in Expression Blend is transforms. Transforms are typically used with animations to apply some kind of positioning, size, or behavior aspect to the control during the animation. Silverlight allows you to set Translate, Rotate, Scale, Skew, Center Point, and Flip Transform settings using different tabs in the Transform pane. The following sections discuss those settings.

Translate

The Translate tab of the Transform pane, shown in Figure 4.32, allows you to set the X and Y properties of the `TranslateTransform` setting for the control. These settings control the horizontal and vertical positioning in pixels of the control during animation. The result of setting these options is the following XAML statement inside the `<TransformGroup>` block of the control:

```
<TranslateTransform X="10" Y="10"/>
```

You can also set the `RenderTransformOrigin` property of the control by clicking one of the controls in the box in the left of the Transform pane. Each of these boxes changes the `RenderTransformOrigin` property based on the location of the box; for example, the center box sets the value to the following:

```
<TextBox RenderTransformOrigin="0.5,0.5" . . .
```

FIGURE 4.32

Setting the Translate Transform settings of a control in the Transform pane of the Properties tab in Expression Blend for the resulting effect

Rotate

The Rotate tab of the Transform pane, shown in Figure 4.33, allows you to set the `Angle` property of the `RotateTransform` setting for the control. This setting controls the clockwise rotation of the control during animation. The result of setting this option is the following XAML statement inside the `<TransformGroup>` block of the control:

```
<RotateTransform Angle="90"/>
```

FIGURE 4.33

Setting the Rotate Transform settings of a control in the Transform pane of the Properties tab in Expression Blend for the resulting effect

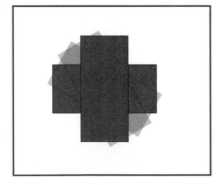

Scale

The Scale tab of the Transform pane, shown in Figure 4.34, allows you to set the `ScaleX` and `ScaleY` properties of the `ScaleTransform` setting for the control. These settings control the horizontal and vertical sizing, on a one-based scale, of the control during animation. The result of setting these options is the following XAML statement inside the `<TransformGroup>` block of the control:

```
<ScaleTransform ScaleX="2.5" ScaleY="2.5"/>
```

FIGURE 4.34

Setting the Scale Transform settings of a control in the Transform pane of the Properties tab in Expression Blend for the resulting effect

Skew

The Skew tab of the Transform pane, shown in Figure 4.35, allows you to set the `AngleX` and `AngleY` properties of the `SkewTransform` setting for the control. These settings control the horizontal and vertical skew, in pixels, of the control during animation. The result of setting these options is the following XAML statement inside the `<TransformGroup>` block of the control.

```
<SkewTransform AngleX="30" AngleY="30"/>
```

Setting the Skew Transform settings of a control in the Transform pane of the Properties tab in Expression Blend for the resulting effect

Center point

The Center Point tab of the Transform pane, shown in Figure 4.36, allows you to set very specific values for the `RenderTransformOrigin` property of the control. To set the value of the `RenderTransformOrigin`, you can either drag the X or Y slider or type a value into the slider box. Changing the values of X and Y sets the value of the `RenderTransformOrigin` property of the control as shown in the following code:

```
<TextBox RenderTransformOrigin="0.55,0.45" . . .
```

FIGURE 4.36

Setting the `RenderTransformOrigin` property of a control in the Transform pane of the Properties tab in Expression Blend

Flip

The Flip tab of the Transform pane, shown in Figure 4.37, allows you to quickly set the properties of the `ScaleTransform`, `SkewTransform`, and `RotateTransform` settings in the `<TransformGroup>` block for the control. Changing these settings flips the control either vertically or horizontally depending on what the settings are.

For example, consider the following `<TransformGroup>` block for a control:

```
<TransformGroup>
    <ScaleTransform/>
    <SkewTransform AngleX="10" AngleY="2"/>
    <RotateTransform Angle="2"/>
    <TranslateTransform X="10" Y="10"/>
</TransformGroup>
```

If you click the Flip X axis button in the Flip pane, the settings are changed to the following and the control is flipped on its X axis:

```
<TransformGroup>
    <ScaleTransform ScaleX="-1"/>
    <SkewTransform AngleX="-10" AngleY="-2"/>
    <RotateTransform Angle="-2"/>
    <TranslateTransform X="10" Y="10"/>
</TransformGroup>
```

If you click the Flip Y axis button in the Flip pane, then the settings are changed to the following and the control is flipped on its Y axis:

```
<TransformGroup>
    <ScaleTransform ScaleY="-1"/>
    <SkewTransform AngleX="-10" AngleY="-2"/>
    <RotateTransform Angle="-2"/>
    <TranslateTransform X="10" Y="10"/>
</TransformGroup>
```

FIGURE 4.37

Setting the Flip Transform settings of a control in the Transform pane of the Properties tab in Expression Blend for the resulting effect

Modifying other control properties

Silverlight provides so many different properties with the various controls that they are not easily coalesced into specific panes. Expression Blend provides several different panes in the Properties tab to facilitate setting these properties.

The following sections discuss briefly some of those panes including the Common, Miscellaneous, Text, and Media panes.

Common

The Common pane, shown in Figure 4.38, is a catchall pane that tries to incorporate some of the more common properties. The following are some of the properties available on the Common pane:

- **Cursor:** Sets the `Cursor` property of the control to display a specific cursor for the mouse when the mouse is over the control.
- **Text:** Sets the `Text` property of controls that have text properties, such as the `TextBox`.
- **Source:** Sets the `Source` property that specifies the URI for the `Image` control

FIGURE 4.38

Setting properties of a control in the Common pane of the Properties tab in Expression Blend

Miscellaneous

The Miscellaneous pane, shown in Figure 4.39, is another catchall pane that provides any properties that are not found elsewhere. The following are only a few of the properties available on the Miscellaneous pane:

- **AutoPlay:** Sets the `AutoPlay` property of a `MediaElement` control
- **Markers:** Sets the `Markers` property of a `MediaElement` control to a collection of marker elements
- **ClickMode:** Sets the `ClickMode` property of a `Button` control
- **Content:** Sets the `Content` property of a `Button` control
- **IsChecked:** Sets the `IsChecked` property of button controls such as a `RadioButton` control
- **Maximum:** Sets the `Maximum` property of a `Slider` or `ScrollBar` control

- **ToolTip:** Sets the `ToolTip` property of controls that can have tool tips, such as the `Button`
- **Source:** Sets the `Source` property that specifies the URI for the `Image` control

FIGURE 4.39

Setting properties of a control in the Miscellaneous pane of the Properties tab in Expression Blend

TIP   The Miscellaneous pane is where you find many of the properties that you cannot find elsewhere. If you cannot find a property on any of the Properties panes, you can still type the XAML code for the property using the XAML pane.

Text

The Text pane, shown in Figure 4.40, is a pane that is available only for `TextBlock` and `TextBox` controls. Using the Text pane, you can set the `FontSize`, `FontFamily`, `FontWeight`, `FontStyle`, `FontStretch`, and `MaxLength` properties of the `TextBlock` and `TextBox` controls using a familiar interface. You can also set the `TextAlignment` property by clicking the Paragraph tab, as shown in Figure 4.40.

FIGURE 4.40

Setting properties of a `TextBox` or `TextBlock` control in the Text pane of the Properties tab in Expression Blend

Media

The Media pane, shown in Figure 4.41, is a pane that is available only for `MediaElement` controls. Using the Media pane, you can set the following properties of the `MediaElement` controls:

- **Balance:** Sets the left/right sound `Balance` property of the `MediaElement` control
- **IsMuted:** Toggles the `IsMuted` property setting to `True` and `False` of the `MediaElement` control
- **Position:** Sets the `Position` property of the `MediaElement` control to a specific time
- **Source:** Sets the `Source` property of the `MediaElement` control to a URI that is either typed in or selected using the file dialog button shown in Figure 4.41
- **Volume:** Sets the playback sound `Volume` property of the `MediaElement`
- **Stretch:** Sets the `Stretch` property of the `MediaElement`

FIGURE 4.41

Setting properties of a `MediaElement` control in the Media pane of the Properties tab in Expression Blend

Creating Storyboards and Animations in Expression Blend

One of the most useful features of Expression Blend is the ability to generate `Storyboard` animation that implements smooth animation of Silverlight controls. Using Expression Blend to animate controls is very fast and simple. The following sections discuss how to implement a `Storyboard` animation using Expression Blend.

CROSS-REF For more information about implementing animations in Silverlight code-behind pages, see the chapters in Part III, specifically Chapter 8.

Creating a Storyboard

The first step in creating a Storyboard animation in Expression Blend is to create the Silverlight controls that you want to animate and then position them in the place where you want the animation to start. For example, Figure 4.42 shows a simple Silverlight application with three `Image` controls laid out across the top.

FIGURE 4.42

Creating a Storyboard animation in the Objects and Timeline pane in Expression Blend

TIP You should use the `x:Name` property to name the Silverlight controls that are involved in the animation before creating the animation. If you do not name them, then Expression Blend assigns a generic name to them to set the `Target` property for the animation.

With the Silverlight controls in place, click on the animation drop-down menu shown in Figure 4.42 and click New to display the Create Storyboard Resource window, as shown in Figure 4.43. Type a name for the animation in the Name text box and click OK to create the `Storyboard` resource. The name you specify here is assigned as the `x:Name` property of the `Storyboard` resource. A Timeline pane for the animation is displayed in the Objects and Timeline pane.

FIGURE 4.43

Creating a Storyboard resource in the Create Storyboard Resource window

Animating Silverlight controls in a Storyboard timeline

After you create a Storyboard, you can animate Silverlight controls in the timeline of the animation by setting the playhead of the timeline to a specific time and then modifying one or more controls.

To animate a control, first select it in the Design view. Then position the playhead in the timeline to a specific point in time where you want that specific animation to end, as shown in Figure 4.44.

FIGURE 4.44

Setting the time for an animation in the timeline

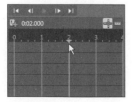

With the playhead in place, change the properties of the Silverlight control(s) to the final values for that animation. You can drag or resize a control using the mouse. You can use the Transform pane in the Properties tab to set transformations on the Silverlight controls. You can also set some other properties such as the Opacity on the Appearance pane.

For example, Figure 4.45 shows the location and size of an Image control that has been scaled up to three times its original size using the Scale tab of the Transform pane. Notice that a key frame has been created in the timeline, signified by the white oval, because the Silverlight controls were modified at that time. Also notice that a `DoubleAnimationUsingKeyFrames` and a `SplineDoubleKeyFrame` resource have been generated in the XAML file to handle the transforms made to the control at that time.

FIGURE 4.45

Setting properties of an `Image` control that is animated

You can create several key frames using this method. You can also involve multiple Silverlight objects in each key frame to get the end result that you want. The animation keys off these key frames and generates a smooth transition.

Playing animations in Expression Blend

You can test your animations in Expression Blend by clicking the Play button on the top of the timeline, as shown in Figure 4.46. When you click the Play button, the animation is rendered in the Design view.

For example, Figure 4.46 shows a sequence of animating the change of size and position of an `Image` control.

FIGURE 4.46

Testing an animation using the Play button in the timeline

You can also use the Go to next frame, Go to last frame, Go to previous frame, and Go to first frame buttons next to the Play button to navigate through the animation in the Design view. This can be useful as you develop the animation.

Recording and modifying key frames

A useful feature on the timeline is the ability to record a key frame in the middle of the animation. Recording a key frame means creating a key frame based on the settings that the Silverlight controls being animated would be set to at that point.

For example, consider an animation that sets the Scale.X property of a control from 1 to 2 between 0 and 2 seconds. If you record a key frame at 1 second in the timeline, the value of the Scale.X property of the control would be 1.5. A new DoubleAnimationUsingKeyFrames and a SplineDoubleKeyFrame resource are created to handle that key frame.

To record a key frame, position the Playhead slider at the time you want to record and click the Record Keyframe button, as shown in Figure 4.47. A new key frame appears in the timeline.

FIGURE 4.47

Recording a key frame using the timeline

Key frames can be modified by changing the XAML code in the XAML pane. You can modify the time of the key frame by sliding it along the timeline using the mouse. You can cut, copy, or delete a key frame by right-clicking on a key frame in the timeline to display the Edit menu.

You can also set the easing properties of the key frame by clicking on it in the timeline to display the Easing pane in the Properties tab, as shown in Figure 4.48. From this pane you can modify the X and Y plane behavior of the animation for that key frame.

FIGURE 4.48

Setting the Easing properties of a key frame in the Easing pane of the Properties tab in Expression Blend

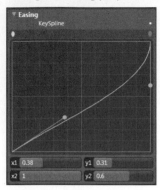

Importing Vector Images Using Expression Design and Expression Blend

Because XAML is based on vector images, it is possible to turn virtually any vector image into XAML that can be consumed in a Silverlight application. Expression Blend does not have the ability to import vector images; however, Expression Design does.

Using the design tools in Expression Design, you can create vector images that can be exported as XAML and added to your Silverlight applications. You can also import vector art that has been saved in Adobe Illustrator format (AI file) and exported as XAML.

This section discusses the process of exporting XAML from Expression Design and adding it to a Silverlight application in Expression Blend. The specifics of using Expression Design to create vector images are not discussed because that is beyond the scope of this book.

Exporting XAML from Expression Design

The first step in adding vector art to Silverlight applications is to add the artwork to Expression Design. This can be done by creating the artwork in Expression Design. You can also create the artwork in another application that can export the vector image as an Adobe Illustrator AI file and then import the artwork into Expression Design by choosing File ➪ Import from the main menu.

After the artwork is added to Expression Design, you can export it as XAML code. You can either export the entire document or you can select specific vector graphics in the document to export. This feature can be useful if you want to create separate XAML elements for different items in the document.

CAUTION   It is difficult to change the appearance of the XAML elements generated from vector images in Expression Blend. Make sure the elements are what you want before exporting them to XAML.

To export the vector art to XAML, choose File ⇨ Export from the main menu to display the Export window shown in Figure 4.49. Select either Whole document or Selected objects from the Items to Export section. Next select XAML Silverlight Canvas from the Format drop-down menu in the Export Properties section.

If you select the Always name objects option, then the exported XAML elements include generic `x:Name` properties. If you select the Place grouped objects in a XAML layout container option, then the vector components that are grouped together are encased in their own layout `Canvas` control.

Next, specify whether the text in the document should be exported as a `TextBlock` control or a `Path` element. Use a `TextBlock` control if you want the text to be editable in the Silverlight application. However, if you are using a special font that may not be easy to distribute with the application, it may be better to use a `Path` for the text.

Finally, set the filename and location and click Export All, as shown in Figure 4.49, to export the vector art to an XAML file. An XAML file is created with a `Canvas` control that contains the XAML equivalent of the vector art.

FIGURE 4.49

Exporting vector art as XAML using Expression Design

Adding exported XAML to a Silverlight application

After the vector art is exported from Expression Design as XAML, it can be easily added to Silverlight applications. The exported XAML file contains all of the XAML code necessary to render the vector art in a Silverlight application.

To add the Exported XAML to a Silverlight application in Expression Blend, open the file in any text editor. Cut and past the `Canvas` control code in the newly exported XAML file into the XAML pane of the `Page.xaml` file, as shown in Figure 4.50. You can remove the `xmlns` and `xmlns:x` properties from the `Canvas` object because they are already added in the root layout control of the `Page.xaml` file.

The vector images appear in the Design pane and can be repositioned by positioning the `Canvas` object. To change the size of the vector images, use the Scale tab in the Transform pane.

FIGURE 4.50

Importing vector art as XAML into Expression Blend

> **TIP**   You do not need Expression Blend to add exported XAML to Silverlight applications. You can simply cut and past the XAML code into the `Page.xaml` file in Visual Studio or any text editor. You can also add the exported XAML to custom Silverlight controls.

Summary

Expression Blend is by far the best utility to use when designing the UI elements and layout of Silverlight applications. Using Expression Blend provides a familiar graphical interface that allows you to use the mouse to create and modify the position of Silverlight controls. Expression Blend also provides the ability to quickly view and set almost all of the properties of each control in the Properties tab.

In this chapter, you learned how to:

- Use the Split view to see the XAML and rendered graphics at the same time
- Arrange Silverlight controls using the Design view
- Attach event handlers to Silverlight controls in Expression Blend
- Use images as brushes for foreground and background fills
- Create key frame animations of Silverlight objects
- Export vector art as XAML code using Expression Design

Chapter 5

Encoding Audio, Video, and Images for Silverlight Applications

P roviding audio and video elements is a great way to add a robust customer experience to your Web site. We already discussed the MediaElement in Chapter 2 that gives you the ability to implement audio and video in Silverlight applications.

Microsoft created Expression Encoder to help you create rich media files with metadata that enables you to implement a media-rich Silverlight application. Expression Encoder also provides you with the ability to determine the output size, quality, and other encoding settings that enable you to deliver the best media file for your needs.

Using Expression Encoder, you can import a wide variety of video and audio files that can then be encoded into a format that Silverlight can consume with the proper settings and metadata for the Silverlight application.

Image files are another important part of media-rich Internet applications. One of the biggest advancements in Internet media is the concept of multiscale images. The Microsoft Deep Zoom Composer product provides an easy-to-use interface to encode image files into multiscale images.

The following sections take you through the process of using Expression Encoder and Deep Zoom Composer to deliver encoded media files that can be consumed by Silverlight applications.

Configuring Video in a Job

The first step in building an encoded video project in Expression Encoder is to configure the video as it should appear in the Silverlight application. We are not going to spend much time in this section. Expression Encoder is very limited in its video edition capabilities. If your video needs a lot of modifications and editing, we strongly recommend editing it first in another application before importing it into Expression Encoder.

The following sections give you a brief overview of the process of importing video into Expression Encoder and then using the timeline tools to remove unwanted segments.

Importing audio and video into Expression Encoder

A big strength of Expression Encoder is its ability to import a wide variety of audio and video files that can be encoded. Importing audio and video into Expression Encoder is accomplished by clicking Import, or by choosing File ➪ Import from the main menu to display an open file dialog box.

You can use the open file dialog box to navigate the file system to locate and import the following types of files into Expression Encoder:

- **Audio Files:** WMA, MP3, WAV, AIFF, BWF, AC3, M4A, and M4B
- **Media Files:** AVI. MPG, MPEG, WVM, ASF, MOV, MP4, VOB, DV, MP2, M2V, M4V, M2T, DRV-MS, TS, 3PG, and 3G2

Each file that you import into Expression Encoder appears in the Media Content pane, as shown in Figure 5.1.

NOTE   Each media file that you import into Expression Encoder is its own track. You cannot combine two separate media files to be on the same track. You can sort of get around this by right-clicking on the timeline and selecting Add Leader to add one media file at the beginning, or Add Trailer to add one media file at the end. However, the leader and trailer files cannot be edited.

FIGURE 5.1

Microsoft Expression Encoder with media files imported

Using the timeline controls to cut audio or video

The timeline controls, as shown in Figure 5.2, allow you to remove segments of the video that you do not want to be encoded into the final project.

To remove a section of audio or video, position the playhead shown in Figure 5.2 at the beginning of the segment that you wish to remove and click the Add Edit button. Next, position the playhead at the end of the segment that you want to remove and click the Add Edit button again. This creates a spliced segment. To remove the spliced segment, position the playhead over it and click the Remove Segment button, as shown in Figure 5.2.

FIGURE 5.2

Using timeline controls to remove a segment of media

Configuring Audio and Video Encode Settings

Another great feature of Expression Encoder is the ability to quickly configure profile settings for audio and video that match the needs of your Web site users. The profile settings are accessed by clicking the Encode tab, as shown in Figure 5.3.

The following sections discuss configuring the media profile to specify the quality and output size of encoded media, the size of the rendered media file, and preprocessing audio levels.

Configuring an encoded media file profile

The first thing that you want to specify when configuring the encoded media file is the output file quality and encoded size. The quality of the video and audio is important to give the Silverlight application a richer experience; however, media files are very large. The size of the encoded media file may limit users due to their available bandwidth to access the application.

The quality and size is specified by setting the Video and Audio settings in the Profile pane, as shown in Figure 5.4.

FIGURE 5.3

The Encode tab in Expression Encoder

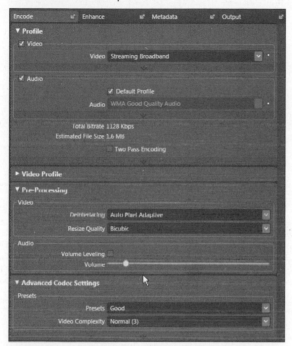

FIGURE 5.4

The Profile pane in the Encode tab in Expression Encoder

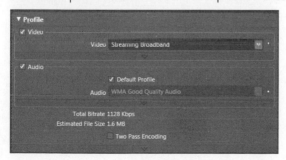

The Profile pane allows you to select a preconfigured video profile from a drop-down list. Each of these profiles contains settings used to encode the video, such as the frame rate, width, height, and bit rate. These settings determine the quality of the video as well as the encoded media file size. The standard rule is that the better the quality the larger the size.

To specify the profile to use for the video, click the down arrow next to the Video drop-down list shown in Figure 5.5 and then select a profile from the list. You can edit the settings implemented by the profile by clicking the down arrow below the Video drop-down list to display the settings, as shown in Figure 5.5.

FIGURE 5.5

The Video settings in the Encode tab in Expression Encoder

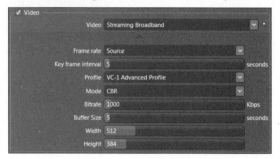

The Profile pane also allows you to select a preconfigured audio profile from a drop-down list. Each of these profiles contains settings used to encode the audio, such as the codec, sample rate, and bit rate. These settings determine the quality of the audio as well as the encoded media file size. Once again, the standard rule is that the better the quality the larger the size.

If the audio is part of a video file, the Default Profile option (see Figure 5.6) is selected and the Audio Profile settings are not available. You can still specify an audio profile by deselecting the Default Profile check box.

To specify the profile to use for the audio, click the down arrow next to the Audio drop-down list shown in Figure 5.6 and select a profile from the list. You can edit the settings implemented by the profile by clicking the down arrow below the Audio drop-down list to display the settings, as shown in Figure 5.6.

FIGURE 5.6

The Audio Profile settings in the Encode tab in Expression Encoder

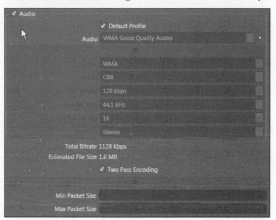

Configuring a video profile for display in Silverlight

After you configure the Audio and Video Profile settings in the Profile pane, you can configure the size of the video in the Video Profile pane, as shown in Figure 5.7. The Video Profile pane allows you to specify the size and shape of the rendered media output frame as well as crop the video to fit the appropriate size. This enables designers and developers to configure the video output to fit exactly in their Web pages.

The first step is to determine what mode you are going to use to size the video output frame. You can set the following options by clicking the Mode drop-down list, as shown in Figure 5.7:

- **Profile Adaptive:** The size will be determined based on settings made on the Profile pane without letterboxing.

- **Profile:** The size will be determined based on settings made on the Profile pane. Letterboxing will be used if necessary.

- **Source:** The size will be determined by the size of the original source file.

- **Custom:** Allows you to specify any size that you want.

You can also use the Resize Mode drop-down list to specify whether to stretch the image or use a letterbox method if the video aspect ratio does not match that of the size. Clicking the down arrow below the Resize Mode drop-down list expands the Video Profile pane allowing you to configure the Video Aspect ratio of the Video Profile pane, as shown in Figure 5.7.

FIGURE 5.7

The Video Profile settings in the Encode tab in Expression Encoder

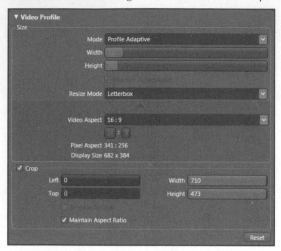

Setting audio and video preprocessing options

A very useful feature in the Encode pane of Expression Encoder is the ability to specify preprocessing options on the media files. Specifically, these options allow you to set deinterlace and resize options for the video and modify the volume of the audio. These options improve the quality of the encoded media.

The Deinterlacing option is set to Auto Pixel Adaptive by default. That is typically adequate for most video. However, if you need to modify this setting, you can simply click the down arrow next to the Deinterlacing drop-down list, as shown in Figure 5.8, and select one of the other options.

You can also specify the method for resizing the video. Depending on the video content and the adjustment in size, different methods may provide better results than others. If your video seems a bit pixelated or grainy, try selecting a different method from the Resize Quality drop-down list.

You can also modify the volume at which the media is encoded. This allows you to specify a good medium volume using the Volume slider.

Another helpful feature is the Volume Leveling check box. If this box is checked, the volume is evened out, meaning that very low volumes are raised to a more normal level and very high volume levels are lowered. You will likely want to use this feature if the media is poor quality or has abnormally high or low volume.

FIGURE 5.8

The Preprocessing settings in the Encode tab in Expression Encoder

Encoding Metadata in the Media File

The biggest benefit to developers using Expression Encoder to encode audio and video is the ability to encode metadata into the output file. Using Silverlight, that metadata can be extracted later and used to implement rich features in the video playback; for example, displaying chapter titles and embedding script commands that trigger application events at specific points in the media playback.

Metadata can be added to media files in Expression Encoder by clicking the Metadata tab, as shown in Figure 5.9. The following sections discuss using Expression Encoder to add metadata, markers, and script commands to audio and video files.

The Metadata tab in Expression Encoder

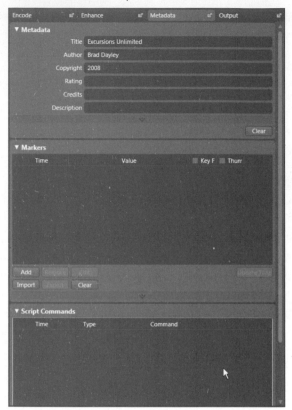

Adding metadata

Metadata such as the title, artist, and copyright information can be added to encoded media using the Metadata pane in the Metadata tab shown in Figure 5.10. This allows you to encode specific information about the audio or video with the media that is being encoded. You can expand the Metatdata pane to include more options by clicking the down arrow below the Description text box.

FIGURE 5.10

The Metadata pane in the Metadata tab in Expression Encoder

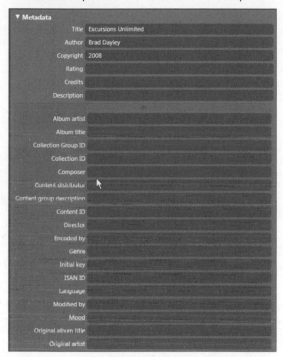

Adding timeline markers to video

A timeline marker is metadata that is associated with a specific point of time in the video or audio playback. Adding timeline markers allows you the ability to implement and name separate segments of the media file allowing users to skip to different scenes in the video.

Adding timeline markers in Expression Encoder

Timeline markers are added to media files using the Markers pane in the Metadata tab, as shown in Figure 5.11. First, position the playhead at the point in the video where you want to add a marker then click Add to add a timeline marker. On the marker line in the Markers pane, a new entry appears at the time selected in the video.

FIGURE 5.11

Adding timeline markers in the Markers pane in the Metadata tab in Expression Encoder

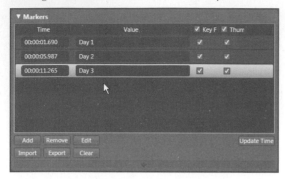

The first text box on the marker line shows the time. You can edit the time to be at the exact second that you want the marker to be added.

On the marker line, you can also specify a name that can be used to identify the segment of video. You can also select the Key Frame option if you want a key frame to be added to the video. This is necessary if you want users to be able to skip to that segment of the video using the media player controls.

You can also specify that a thumbnail should be created for that timeline marker. Thumbnails are displayed by most of the media player skins available for Silverlight. To create thumbnails, select the Thumbnail option.

Accessing timeline markers in Silverlight applications

In this section, we discuss using managed code to access timeline markers. Don't worry if you don't understand exactly what is going on. Coding Silverlight applications is discussed in the next several chapters.

When the video playback for the media file reaches the timeline marker, a `MarkerReached` event is triggered. Using the `MarkerReached` event, you can implement event handlers to provide functionality to your Silverlight applications that correspond to specific segments of the video playback.

The first step in accessing the markers in a Silverlight application is to add a `MediaElement` control to the application. For example, the following XAML adds a `MediaElement` named `myMovie` to a Silverlight application:

```
<MediaElement x:Name="myMovie"
              Source="Video.wmv"
              Height="300" Width="400" />
```

The next step is to add a `MarkerReached` event handler to the `MediaElement`. This is done in the managed code. For example, the following line of C# code adds the `MarkerReached` event handler to the `myMovie` `MediaElement`:

```
movie.MarkerReached +=
        new TimelineMarkerRoutedEventHandler(m_MarkerReached);
```

The `MarkerReached` event handler routine is passed a `TimelineMarkerRoutedEventHandler` argument object. You can use that argument to access information about the timeline marker. For example, the following event handler accesses the `Marker.Time`, `Marker.Text`, and `Marker.Type` attributes of the `TimelineMarkerRoutedEventHandler` argument object:

```
void m_MarkerReached(object sender, TimelineMarkerRoutedEventArgs
    e)
{
    string mType = e.Marker.Type.ToString();
    if (mType == "NAME")
    {
        mTime.Text = e.Marker.Time.ToString();
        mValue.Text = e.Marker.Text;
    }
}
```

The `Marker.Time` property is the time that you selected when adding the marker in Expression Encoder, as shown in Figure 5.11. The `Marker.Type` property is always the string `"NAME"` for timeline markers. The `Marker.Text` property is the value that you typed into the Value text box.

Adding script commands to a video file

Script commands are very similar to timeline markers. A script command is also metadata that is associated with a specific point of time in the video or audio playback. There are two big differences.

The first difference is that you cannot create key frames and thumbnails to coincide with a script command. The second difference is that you can specify different types of script commands where timeline markers are always of type "NAME".

Adding script commands allows you the ability to implement multiple types of functionality to specific points in the video.

Adding script commands in Expression Encoder

Script commands are added to media files using the Script Commands pane in the Metadata tab, as shown in Figure 5.12. First, position the playhead at the point in the video where you want to add a script command, then click Add to add a script command. On the script command line in the Script Commands pane, a new entry appears at the time selected in the video.

FIGURE 5.12

Adding script commands in the Script Commands pane in the Metadata tab in Expression Encoder

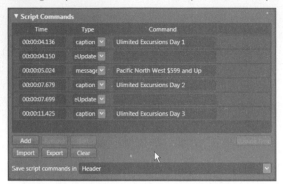

The first text box on the script command line shows the Time. You can edit the time to be at the exact second that you want the script command to be added.

On the script command line, you can also specify a Type value that can be used in your Silverlight applications to identify what actions to perform on the `MarkerReached` event. The Type value can be any user-defined string. Specifying different script commands allows you to apply different functionality on different script commands.

> **NOTE**   The default type is `caption` and has a special meaning for Silverlight media players. This is used to indicate a closed-caption media event. If the media player supports closed captioning and it is enabled, then the value specified in the Command text box is displayed as a closed caption.

You can also specify command text in the Command text box. The command text can be anything that is necessary to implement functionality in the media control. For example, if you are using the script command to display a message, then the message text would be the value of the command.

Accessing script commands in Silverlight applications

In this section, we discuss using managed code to access script commands encoded in video files.

When the video playback for the media file reaches the script command, a `MarkerReached` event is triggered just as with timeline markers. Using the `MarkerReached` event enables you to implement event handlers to provide functionality to your Silverlight applications that correspond to the specific type of script command.

The first step in accessing the script commands in a Silverlight application is to add a `MediaElement` control to the application. For example, the following XAML adds a `MediaElement` named `myMovie` to a Silverlight application:

```
<MediaElement x:Name="myMovie"
              Source="Video.wmv"
              Height="300" Width="400" />
```

The next step is to add a `MarkerReached` event handler to the `MediaElement`. This is done in the managed code. For example, the following line of C# code adds the `MarkerReached` event handler to the `myMovie` `MediaElement`:

```
movie.MarkerReached +=
        new TimelineMarkerRoutedEventHandler(m_MarkerReached);
```

The `MarkerReached` event handler routine is passed a `TimelineMarkerRoutedEventHandler` argument object. You can use that argument to access the type of script command and the command text. For example, the following event handler accesses the `Marker.Time`, `Marker.Text`, and `Marker.Type` attributes of the `TimelineMarkerRoutedEventHandler` argument object to implement different functionality for different command script types:

```
void m_MarkerReached(object sender, TimelineMarkerRoutedEventArgs
   e)
{
    string mType = e.Marker.Type.ToString();
    if (mType == "message")
    {
        myMessage.Text = e.Marker.Text();
    }
    if (mType == "caption")
    {
        videoCaption.Text = e.Marker.Text();
    }
    if (mType == "timeUpdate")
    {
        videoTimeIndex.Text = e.Marker.Time.ToString();
    }
}
```

The `Marker.Time` property is the time that you selected when adding the script command in Expression Encoder, as shown in Figure 5.12. The `Marker.Type` property is a string that is the value of the Type setting of the script command. The `Marker.Text` property is the value that you typed into the Command text box.

> **TIP** The value of the Command setting for script commands is a string. You can add several commands, arguments, or settings as part of that string and then parse the string in the event handler to determine how to implement the command. For example, the command string "640,480" could specify the height and width for a script command used to resize the video. In your code, you could split that command string and then change the values to integers and set the `Height` and `Width` properties of the `MediaElement`.

Configuring Silverlight Output

After you configure the encoding and metadata for the media in Expression Encoder, you are ready to output the encoded media. There are several output options that allow you to control exactly what is output. The very minimum that is output when the video or audio is encoded is an encoded WMV file for video jobs and an encoded WMA file for audio jobs, and a Settings.dat XML file containing the Expression Encoder job settings in XML format.

You can also have Expression Encoder automatically output thumbnail images and the XAML, HTML, and JavaScript code necessary to implement the encoded media in a Silverlight application. The following sections discuss the options available to output Expression Encoder jobs using the Output tab, as shown in Figure 5.13.

FIGURE 5.13

The Output tab in Expression Encoder

Generating a thumbnail

The Thumbnail pane, shown in Figure 5.14, allows you to specify the settings used when building a thumbnail from the video file when encoding the project. The Type setting allows you to set whether you want to use the Best Frame in the video, the 1st Frame, or a specific Custom time index to generate the thumbnail.

The Encoding section lets you set whether you want the thumbnail to be a JPEG, PNG, GIF, or BMP file type. The Size section of the Thumbnail pane allows you to set the height and width of the thumbnail image. You can select the Maintain Aspect Ratio option if you want the aspect ratio of the thumbnail image to remain consistent.

When the media file is rendered, a thumbnail image based on these settings is generated in the output directory.

FIGURE 5.14

The Thumbnail pane of the Output tab in Expression Encoder

Specifying a template

One of the coolest features of Silverlight is the ability to easily build and implement skins for almost any Silverlight control. That is especially true with the MediaElement control. The Silverlight SDK and Expression Encoder both ship with several MediaElement skins that can easily be applied to the media element to provide a professional look to the video.

A skin for the media player can be added to the job by selecting one of the options from the Template drop-down list in the Job Output pane, as shown in Figure 5.15. When you select a template from the list, the template is rendered in a preview directly below the list.

When you select a template, the supporting code for the template is generated in the output directory.

Modifying the template in Expression Blend

The media player skin that you select may not always be exactly what you are looking for. A really nice feature in Expression Encoder is the ability to link with Expression Blend to modify a copy of the template.

FIGURE 5.15

Adding a Media Player Skin template in the Job Output pane of the Output tab in Expression Encoder

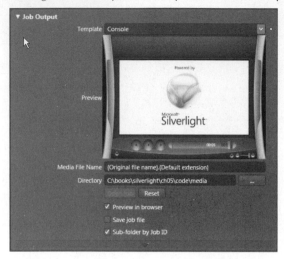

To access a copy of the template in Expression Blend, click the small white square next to the Template drop-down list and select Edit copy in Expression Blend from the pop-up menu. Name the copy and click OK to display the template as a project in Expression Blend, as shown in Figure 5.16. The copy of the project is used to output the media player skin, so any changes that you make in Expression Blend are part of the output media player.

In Expression Blend, you should see a root Canvas or Grid control. When you expand that control, a number of other controls and elements appear that are used to make up the media player. You can modify the existing controls or add new controls to modify the media player skin.

For example, if you select an element that has a Brush property, it specifies a gradient brush. You can modify the colors in the gradient by selecting the Brushes pane in the Properties tab and changing the colors in the gradient.

You can also access the XAML directly in Expression Encoder to make changes to the media player skin. When you finish modifying your settings, save the project and return to Expression Encoder.

Specifying output options

With the template selected, you are ready to encode the job. However, first you need to tell Expression Encoder where to put the encoded output. The encoded output is specified on the Job Output pane of the Output tab that was shown in Figure 5.15.

First, specify the filename and extension that you want the encoded media to be output to. The default filename is the first filename that was imported into the project. The default extension is .wmv for video files and .wma for audio files.

FIGURE 5.16

Modifying a Media Player Skin template in Expression Blend

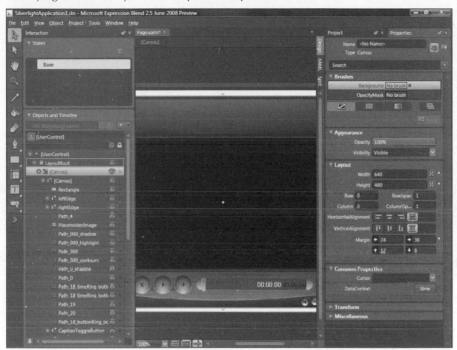

Then specify the directory by either typing the path into the text box or clicking the ... button to display a file dialog box. The Open Job button opens a Windows Explorer window at the location of the job output. The Reset button resets all output settings.

If you specify a template, you can select the Preview in browser option. When this is selected, then Expression Encoder launches a browser with the encoded project upon encoding completion.

If you select the Save job file option, the job file is saved in the output directory. This makes it easier to store the job for later changes.

If you select the Sub-folder by Job ID option, the output is placed in a subfolder of the one specified by the Directory setting. The name of the folder is based on the computer that encoded the job and a time and date stamp. For example: "Brad 8-1-2008 8.09.41 AM".

After you configure all output settings, click Encode or choose File ➪ Encode from the main menu to encode the media to the output location.

Implementing Encoded Media in Silverlight Applications

When Expression Encoder generates the encoded media to the output directory you have several options that you can use to implement that output as part of a Silverlight application. For example, you can simply use the encoded media file itself, or you can use the media player skin code generated as well as the thumbnail images.

The following sections discuss how to implement encoded media in Silverlight applications.

Understanding encoded output

The best place to start is to understand exactly what has been output by Expression Encoder. Figure 5.17 shows the contents of the typical Expression Encoder output folder for a media project that included thumbnails and a Media Player Skin template.

FIGURE 5.17

Adding Expression Encoder output to an ASP.NET Web page in Visual Studio

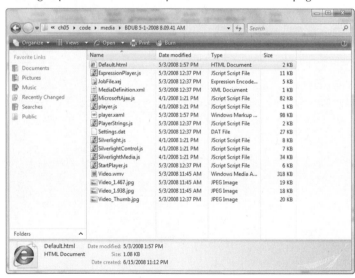

The project contains the following files:

- **Video.wmv:** This is the output media file that includes the encoded metadata.
- **Video*.jpg:** These are the thumbnail images generated by Expression Encoder.

- **Default.html:** This is a basic HTML page that implements the media file as a JavaScript Silverlight application.
- **player.xaml:** This is the XAML code used to generate all the UI for the media player skin.
- ***.js files:** These are the JavaScript files that are used to implement the functionality of the media player: for example, player control event handlers.
- **MediaDefinition.xml:** This is an XML file that contains the media file and chapter definitions.
- **Settings.dat:** This is the XML file that contains the Expression Encoder job settings.
- **JobFile.xej:** This is the saved Expression Encoder job file.

Using the encoded output in a Silverlight application

There are several different ways to use the output encoded by Expression Encoder when creating Silverlight applications. The output can be used as a stand-alone JavaScript Silverlight application. The output can also be consumed by other Silverlight applications.

The following sections describe some different methods for consuming Expression Encoder's output.

Using Expression Encoder output as a JavaScript Silverlight application

The easiest method of using Expression Encoder output in a Silverlight application is to simply add the output to your Web site and then modify or create a Web page to render the Silverlight application.

To understand this better, look at the contents of the Default.html file generated by Expression Encoder in Listing 5.1. The code loads the Silverlight.js and other JavaScript files using `script` tags and then implements the following `div` tag to add the media as a Silverlight application in the Web page:

```
<div id="divPlayer_0">
    <script  type='text/javascript'>
        var player = new StartPlayer_0();
    </script>
</div>
```

To add the Expression Encoder output as a Silverlight application to an existing Web page, all you need to do is add the `script` statements and the `div` statement from Listing 5.1 to the Web page.

CROSS-REF Implementing JavaScript Silverlight applications is discussed in much more detail in Chapter 9 and Chapter 11.

LISTING 5.1

Contents of the Default.html File Generated by Expression Encoder

```html
<!DOCTYPE HTML PUBLIC "-//W3C//DTD HTML 4.01 Transitional//EN"
"http://www.w3c.org/TR/1999/REC-html401-19991224/loose.dtd">
<html xmlns="http://www.w3.org/1999/xhtml">

<head>
<script type='text/javascript' src="MicrosoftAjax.js"></script>
<script type='text/javascript' src="Silverlight.js"></script>
<script type='text/javascript' src="SilverlightControl.js"></script>
<script type='text/javascript' src="SilverlightMedia.js"></script>
<script type='text/javascript' src="ExpressionPlayer.js"></script>
<script type='text/javascript' src="PlayerStrings.js"></script>
<script type='text/javascript' src="player.js"></script>
<script type='text/javascript' src="StartPlayer.js"></script>
<title></title>
<style type="text/css">
    html, body { margin: 0; padding: 0; height:100% }
    #divPlayer_0 { min-height: 100%; height:100%;  }
</style>
</head>

<body style="background-color:black;margin:0,0,0,0;overflow:auto;">
    <div id="divPlayer_0">
        <script  type='text/javascript'>
            var player = new StartPlayer_0();
        </script>
    </div>
</body>
</html>
```

> **TIP** You can modify the behavior of the media player by modifying the StartPlayer.js file. The object creation and the media event handlers are all in that file. You can also modify the player.xaml file if you want to change the appearance of the UI.

Using Expression Encoder output in .NET code

There are times that you may not want the visual effects of a media player as part of your Silverlight application. You may simply want to implement the media file output from Expression Encoder into an existing .NET Silverlight application.

This can be accomplished by importing the encoded video file into the project and then specifying that file as the source of a MediaElement control that is added to the project. You are then able to add your own playback control and functionality that fits in with your project. For example:

```
<MediaElement x:Name="movie" Source="Video1.wmv"
              Height="300" Width="400"
              HorizontalAlignment="Left"/>
```

CROSS-REF Implementing .NET Silverlight applications is discussed in much more detail in Chapters 6 and 8.

You can still add the media player skin as another element of your Silverlight application; however, this can be fairly difficult. The media player skin is simply a `Canvas` or `Grid` Silverlight control that contains several other controls and elements that make up the media player UI.

To add the media player skin to your .NET application, you can cut and paste the contents of the player.xaml file into an XAML file in your existing application. There are some changes that you need to make, however.

First the `xmlns` and `xmlns:x` properties need to be removed from the Canvas object because they are already present in your application, as shown in the following code:

```
<Canvas
    xmlns="http://schemas.microsoft.com/winfx/2006/xaml/
    presentation"
    xmlns:x="http://schemas.microsoft.com/winfx/2006/xaml"
    Width="640" Height="480">
```

Changes to:

```
<Canvas
    Width="640" Height="480">
```

You also need to add the encoded video and thumbnail images files to the Silverlight application project. After you add the video file to the project, you need to modify the `MediaElement` tag in the XAML you cut and pasted earlier to include that file in the `Source` attribute, as shown in the following code:

```
MediaElement x:Name="VideoWindow"
             Source="Video1.wmv"
             Width="510" Height="296"
             Canvas.Left="6
```

Finally, you need to look through the XAML and determine what functionality you want to implement in your .NET code. This is the difficult part. Most of the media controls will likely be a `Canvas` object with `x:Name` properties that include "Button" on the name, for example:

```
<Canvas x:Name="NextButton" . . .
```

In your .NET code, you need to implement `MouseLeftButtonUp` or `MouseLeftButtonDown` event handlers for these controls that implement the playback, volume control, and other functionality that you need.

Using Expression Encoder output in an asp:MediaPlayer control in an ASP. NET Web application

Implementing the Expression Encoder output in an ASP.NET Web page is actually very simple. Silverlight provides an ASP.NET control named `asp:MediaPlayer` that allows you to embed a Silverlight media player directly into an ASP.NET page.

Using the following steps, you can quickly add Expression Encoder output to an ASP.NET Web page in Visual Studio:

1. Add the encoded media file and the player.xaml file to the ASP.NET Web page project.

2. Add a ScriptManager control to the Web page.

3. Add an asp:MediaPlayer control to the Web page.

4. Select the Design view of the Web page.

5. Click the arrow button at the top right of the asp:MediaPlayer object to display the Media Player tasks menu, as shown in Figure 5.18.

6. Click the ... button next to the Player Skin text box.

7. Select the player.xaml file from the project folder and click OK.

8. Click the ... button next to the Media Source text box.

9. Select the encoded media file from the project folder and click OK.

When you build the application, the media player is included and the playback and other controls should work normally. This is because the `asp:MediaPlayer` tag is based off the standard media player skin framework that Expression Encoder uses to build the skin.

CROSS-REF Implementing media elements in an ASP.NET control is discussed in much more detail in Chapter 10. See that chapter for more details on the steps to add Expression Encoder output to an ASP.NET Web page as well as other options.

FIGURE 5.18

Adding Expression Encoder output to an ASP.NET Web page in Visual Studio.

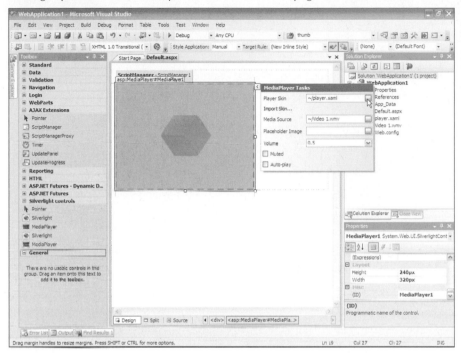

Encoding Multiscale Images Using Deep Zoom Composer

One of the coolest advancements for images in Web applications is the concept of a multiscale image. Multiscale images are designed to provide a means to implement high resolution images in Web pages without causing severe bandwidth issues.

A multiscale image is actually a series of images that represent different zoom states of a single original. Using the different zoom levels of a multiscaled image provides the ability to display an image and then zoom in on it without losing resolution.

The idea is to take a very large image and carve it up into a series of much smaller images that can be displayed at different stages of a zoom cycle. The higher the zoom, the higher pixel ration is taken from the original. For example, the original may be 10,000 pixels by 10,000 pixels. At 100 percent zoom, only one image may be generated at a 10:1 ratio meaning that the image is only

1,000 pixels by 1,000 pixels. However at 1,000 percent zoom, the image is carved up into 100 equal pieces at a ratio of 1:1 meaning that each image is still 1,000 pixels by 1,000 pixels even though they represent just one-hundredth of the original image.

Silverlight provides the `MultiScaleImage` control that allows you to implement multiscale images in your Silverlight applications. Deep Zoom Composer provides a simple-to-use interface that provides the ability to quickly create multiscale images that can be used by the `MultiScale Image` control. The following sections discuss the process of importing one or more images into Deep Zoom Composer, organizing them, and then exporting them as a multiscale image and Silverlight project.

Importing Images into Deep Zoom Composer

The first step in encoding images for a `MultiScaleImage` control is to import them into Deep Zoom Composer. Select File ⇨ New Project from the main menu. Then specify the name and location to create the new project in the New Project dialog box and click OK to create a new project.

Then click the Add Image button shown in Figure 5.19 to bring up a file dialog box. Select the image files you would like to add and click the Open button. The files will be displayed in the image list on the right.

FIGURE 5.19

Importing images into Deep Zoom Composer

Arranging Images in Deep Zoom Composer

After you have imported the images that you want to include, click the Compose button to bring up the Compose view. The images can be added to the Compose view by dragging them from the image list on the right. Then the images can be positioned and resized as necessary to create the high-resolution image that will make up the multiscale image as shown in Figure 5.20.

Compose view in Deep Zoom Composer

Notice at the bottom of the Compose view that there are several tools that help in aligning and resizing the images.

Exporting Multiscale Images from Deep Zoom Composer

Once you have the images arranged, you are ready to encode them into a multiscale image that can be used by the Silverlight `MultiScaleImage` control. Click on the Export tab to display the Export view shown in Figure 5.21.

FIGURE 5.21

Export view in Deep Zoom Composer

In the Export view, specify the name and export location of the Deep Zoom project. Then set the Image file format to JPEG or PNG. You have the option to export the images only or to export the images as part of a Silverlight project. Click the Export button to export the images into a multi-scale image.

If you specify the Export Images option, then a folder with the name specified by the Name option will be created in the Export location, and the images and XML files that make up the multiscale image will be exported to that location.

If you select the Export Images and Silverlight Project, then a folder with the name specified by the Name option will be created in the Export location, and the images and XML files that make up the multiscale image as well as a Visual Studio Silverlight application project will be exported to that location. A dialog box similar to the one in Figure 5.22 will be displayed.

Click on the Preview in Browser option to launch a Web page containing the Silverlight application exported by Deep Zoom Composer. You can view and play with the multiscale image as shown in Figure 5.23. Use the mouse to drag and position the image and the mouse wheel to zoom in and out of the image.

FIGURE 5.22

Export dialog box in Deep Zoom Composer

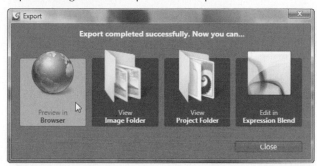

FIGURE 5.23

Multiscale image preview in a Web browser

Understanding the Exported Multiscale Image Project

When you export a multiscale image from Deep Zoom Composer, a series of folders is generated containing the image files that make up the multiscale image. There are also several XML files that are generated. These XML files are used by the `MultiScaleImage` control in Silverlight to render specific portions of the multiscale image.

Deep Zoom Composer creates a folder named GeneratedImages in the project output directory. When deploying Silverlight applications that use the multiscale image, this folder and contents must be accessible to that project. The following three files are created in the root GeneratedImages folder:

- **dzc_output.xml:** This file contains information that points to the image file. If the output was a collection, then there will be an entry in this file for each image file. This is the file that you will use as a source for the `MultiScaleImage` control.

- **SparseImageSceneGraph.xml:** This file contains the information for images in the multiscale image such as z-index.

- **Metadata.xml:** Contains similar information to that of `SparseImageSceneGraph.xml` in a slightly different format; however, it also includes a `Tag` property for each image.

The following two directories are generated in the GeneratedImages folder:

- **dzc_output_images:** Contains a composition tile set for each image in the collection.

- **dzc_output_file:** Contains a set of thumbnail tiles for the collection.

If you specified the Export Images and Silverlight Project setting, then a Visual Studio project for the multiscale image is also created. It is a good idea to have Deep Zoom Composer create a Silverlight project for you until you are familiar with how multiscale images work in Silverlight.

Summary

You can use Expression Encoder to quickly encode almost any type of media file with metadata that can be used in Silverlight applications. Expression Encoder allows designers and developers the ability to set size, quality, and other encoding options. It also allows developers the ability to encode timeline markers and script commands that can be consumed in Silverlight applications to provide time-based functionality. Using the Expression Encoder output, you can quickly add encoded video to existing or new Silverlight applications.

In this chapter, you learned how to:

- Set the size and quality for video output
- Customize encoding settings
- Access timeline markers in Silverlight applications
- Add script commands in Expression Encoder and use them to provide functionality in Silverlight applications
- Encode media player skins with video and modify them using Expression Blend
- Implement Expression Encoder output in .NET Silverlight applications
- Add Expression Encoder output to ASP.NET Web pages

Part III

Programming Silverlight Applications

Chapter 6

Using Visual Studio to Program Silverlight Applications

T**he** best place to start when developing .NET Silverlight applications is with Microsoft Visual Studio. Starting with Silverlight 2, Microsoft provides templates for creating Silverlight applications and libraries in C# and Visual Basic. This chapter is designed to briefly introduce you to some important concepts of using Visual Studio to build a Silverlight application.

CROSS-REF **This chapter is designed to quickly get you started developing Silverlight applications. We will discuss the structure of Silverlight applications in more detail in Chapter 7.**

If you are familiar with Visual Studio, you know that it provides a rich set of features such as IntelliSense that can speed up your application development. The following sections take you through the process of building a .NET Silverlight application in Visual Studio.

Developing a .NET Silverlight Application in Visual Studio

This section jumps right into programming Silverlight applications by stepping through a basic example. If you look at the basic makeup of most Silverlight applications, they are all the same. XAML code is used to render the UI from Silverlight controls, managed code-behind pages are used to handle functionality, and event handlers link the two together.

The following sections take you through the process of building a basic Silverlight application in Visual Studio that creates a TextBlock and a Button control and implements a mouse click event handler to modify the TextBlock when the mouse is clicked.

Creating a Silverlight project

The first step in creating a Silverlight application using Visual Studio is to create a C# or Visual Basic Silverlight application project.

Use the following steps to create a C# Silverlight application project:

1. Choose File ⇨ New ⇨ Project from the main menu in Visual Studio.

2. Select Visual C# from the Project types list, as shown in Figure 6.1.

3. Select the Silverlight Application template from the Visual Studio installed templates list.

4. Type the name of the project in the Name field, and set the location to create the new project.

5. Click OK to begin creating the project.

FIGURE 6.1

New Project creation window in Visual Studio with the Visual C# Silverlight Application template selected

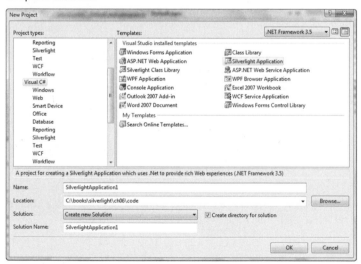

> **NOTE** In the top right of Figure 6.1, you can modify the .NET Framework from 3.5 to 3.0 or 2.0. This is useful if you need to create an application that is backwards compatible.

6. Specify that you want to add the hosting Web page to the project, as shown in Figure 6.2. If you select the option to allow Visual Studio to generate the HTML test page, Visual Studio automatically generates a page for you when you run the project in Visual Studio. You need to create your own Web page when deploying the application.

7. Set the Project Type to Web Site.

8. Click OK to create the project.

FIGURE 6.2

New project application window in Visual Studio with the Web Site project type selected

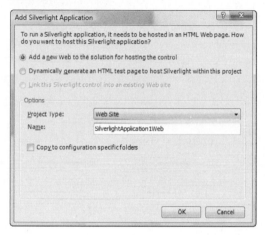

Visual Studio creates a Silverlight application project and a Web site project in the solution. The Silverlight Web site project contains the appropriate library assemblies to deploy a Silverlight application and the following four files shown in the Solution Explorer in Figure 6.3:

- `Default.aspx:` A blank ASPX file that can be used to deploy the Silverlight application
- `Default.aspx.cs:` The code-behind file that allows you to write .NET code to support the Default.aspx file
- `SilverlightApp1TestPage.aspx:` An ASPX page, named after the project, that is generated to host the Silverlight application when testing
- `SilverlightApp1TestPage.html:` An HTML page, named after the project, that is generated to host the Silverlight application when testing

The Silverlight application project contains the appropriate references to build a Silverlight application and the following six files shown in the Solution Explorer in Figure 6.3:

- `AppManifest.xml:` Manifest file used to build and deploy the Silverlight application.
- `AssemblyInfo.cs:` Source code used to build the Silverlight application assembly.
- `App.xaml:` XAML file that contains the Application object definition.

- `App.xaml.cs`: C# code-behind file that contains a partial Application class definition. This file is linked to the `App.xaml` file to create the complete Application class.

- `Page.xaml`: XAML file that contains the `UserControl` object definition.

- `Page.xaml.cs`: C# code-behind file that contains a partial `UserControl` class definition. This file is linked to the `Page.xaml` file to create the complete `UserControl` class.

FIGURE 6.3

Solution Explorer window in Visual Studio with the Web Site project type selected

Adding Silverlight controls

After you create a Silverlight application, you can begin building the user interface by adding Silverlight controls to the `Page.xaml` file. The easiest way to add Silverlight controls to an application is to use the Toolbox. Choose View ⇨ Toolbox from the main menu to enable the Toolbox shown in Figure 6.4.

Many of the Silverlight controls come from the `System.Windows.Controls.Extended` library. You should add a reference to this library to your project. This is done by right-clicking on the References folder in the Silverlight Application project located in the Solution Explorer and selecting Add Reference from the pop-up menu. The `System.Windows.Controls.Extended` library is listed in the .NET tab.

Use the following steps to add a `TextBlock` and a `Button` control to the `Page.xaml` file:

1. Double-click on the `Page.xaml` file in the Solution Explorer to display the `Page.xaml` in the editor, as shown in Figure 6.4.

FIGURE 6.4

`Page.xaml` open in the editor in Visual Studio

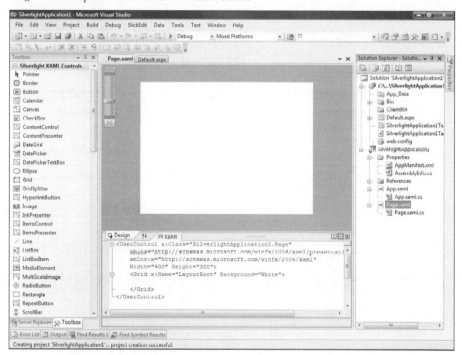

2. Drag a `TextBlock` control from the Toolbox to the XAML code for `Page.xaml`. The `TextBlock` needs to be dropped inside the `Grid` control that is already defined there.

NOTE At this time, the controls cannot be dragged onto the Designer view.

3. Drag a `Button` control from the Toolbox to the XAML code for `Page.xaml`. Notice in Figure 6.5 that the button takes up the entire application area.

FIGURE 6.5

Button control in the Page.xaml file in the editor in Visual Studio

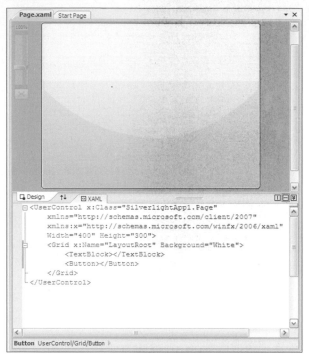

4. Set the Content attribute of the Button control to ClickMe, the Height to 40 and the Width to 200, as shown in Figure 6.6.

5. Set the Text attribute of the TextBlock to Waiting.

6. Set the VerticalAlignment attribute of the TextBlock to Top and the HorizontalAlignment to Center to center the TextBlock on the page.

7. Set the Margin attribute of the TextBlock to "0,40,0,0" to move the TextBlock lower on the page.

8. Save the file by pressing Ctrl+S.

The Result is a Button and a TextBlock control that are visible in the Designer view, as shown in Figure 6.6.

FIGURE 6.6

Button and TextBlock controls in the Designer view for Page.xaml file in Visual Studio

Naming Silverlight controls

In the previous section, you added a TextBlock and a Button control to the project; however, the two elements really don't do anything. To add functionality, you need to provide access to those controls to the .NET code-behind file Page.xaml.cs. This is accomplished by adding a scoped name to the Silverlight control that is accessible from the UserControl class defined in the code-behind file.

Use the following steps to add a scoped name to the Button and TextBlock controls:

1. Add the following line of code to the Button definition in Page.xaml to assign the namescope name myButton to the Button object:

   ```
   x:Name="myButton"
   ```

2. Add the following line of code to the TextBlock definition in Page.xaml to assign the namescope name myText to the TextBlock object as shown in Figure 6.7:

   ```
   x:Name="myText"
   ```

3. Save the file.

Adding the names to the namescope using the x:Name attribute does not change how the objects look; however, it makes them visible in the C# code-behind page.

Button and TextBlock controls with x:Name attributes set in the Designer view for Page.xaml file in Visual Studio

Adding event handlers to Silverlight controls

The first step in adding functionality to a Silverlight control is to attach an event handler to the control. Now that the Button and TextBlock objects have names in the namescope, you can access them in the C# code-behind page to attach the event handler.

Use the following steps to attach an event handler to the Button control:

1. Double-click on the Page.xaml file in the Solution Explorer to display the Page.xaml in the editor, as shown in Figure 6.8.

2. Attach a Click event handler to the Button object by adding the following line of code to the Page() constructor:

```
myButton.Click += new RoutedEventHandler(myButton_Click);
```

3. Define the myButton_Click() event handler function to the Page class using the following line of code:

```
void myButton_Click(object sender, RoutedEventArgs e)
```

4. Add the following line of code to the myButton_Click() event handler to set the Text attribute of the TextBlock named myText to "You Clicked".

```
myText.Text = "You Clicked";
```

5. Save the file.

You have now successfully attached a mouse event handler to the Button control.

CROSS-REF Event handlers are discussed in much more detail in Chapter 8.

FIGURE 6.8

Mouse click event handler attached to the Button control in the Page.xaml.cs C# code-behind file in Visual Studio

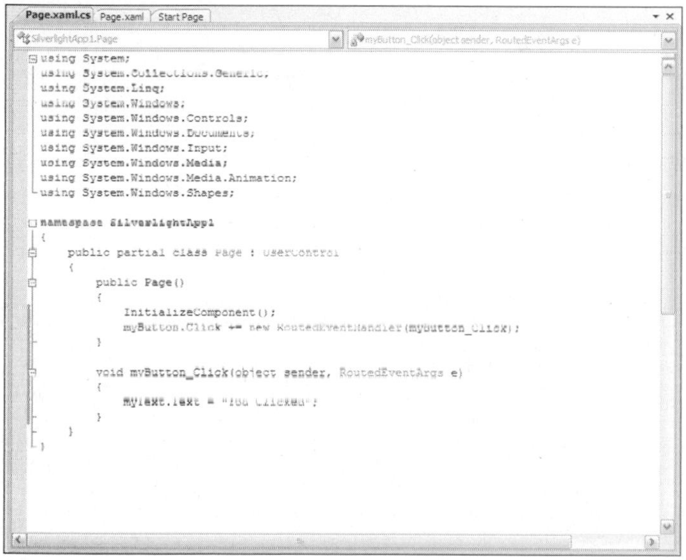

Testing Silverlight applications in Visual Studio

The last step in building Silverlight applications in Visual Studio is to use the built-in Web engine to test the application. After you complete your applications, you can press F5 to build and launch the Silverlight application in a Web browser.

NOTE When you run the application file for the first time, a new folder is created in the Web site project for the Silverlight solution. The folder is named ClientBin and contains an XAP application package that contains the compiled project. You learn more about this in Chapter 7.

When your example application runs and you click the button in the Web browser, the text should change, as shown in Figure 6.9.

Clicking on the button changes the content of the `Button` control and the `TextBlock`.

Using IntelliSense

One of the most useful features of Visual Studio is IntelliSense. IntelliSense is Microsoft's implementation to auto-complete code that you are typing into the editor. IntelliSense is intelligent enough to determine object types, so it is able to provide you with a drop-down list of available options. As you type more of the code, IntelliSense narrows the possibilities down for you. The Silverlight plug-in for Visual Studio enables IntelliSense on Silverlight projects. You can access IntelliSense from both XAML as well as the .NET languages.

For example, consider a Button control in an XAML file. When you press the Spacebar inside of the Button block, the IntelliSense list shown in Figure 6.10 appears.

IntelliSense providing a list of available attributes for a `Button` control in an XAML file

Another example of using IntelliSense is to add an event handler inside a code-behind page. Figure 6.11 shows an example of a partially typed statement to add the event handler and the rest that can be added from IntelliSense by pressing Tab.

FIGURE 6.11

IntelliSense filling in the rest of an event handler statement in a C# file

```
public partial class Page : UserControl
{
    public Page()
    {
        InitializeComponent();
        myButton.Click += new RoutedEventHandler(myButton_Click);

        myButton.MouseEnter +=
                        new MouseEventHandler(myButton_MouseEnter);    (Press TAB to insert)
    }
}
```

Using the Solution Explorer

Now that you know how to create and test a Silverlight application, you may want to know about some additional features in the Solution Explorer that can help when creating Silverlight applications. The following sections lightly touch on some of the features that are more useful when developing Silverlight applications. They are not meant to be inclusive, but only to give you an idea of where to go to find things.

Switching to Expression Blend

Because the designer in Visual Studio is very limited, a very helpful shortcut is to use the Solution Explorer to switch to Expression Blend to edit XAML files. That way you can use the robust graphical features of Blend to design your Silverlight elements and then switch back to Visual Studio to modify the code-behind functionality.

To switch to Expression Blend, right-click on the XAML file and select Open in Expression Blend, as shown in Figure 6.12. When you select Expression Blend, the project opens in Expression Blend for editing, as shown in Figure 6.13.

FIGURE 6.12

`Page.xaml` file open in Visual Studio after selecting Open in Expression Blend

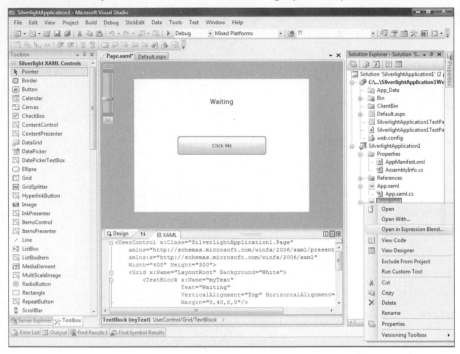

Adding resources

Most Silverlight applications comprise three types of files: the XAML file containing the UI elements, the .NET code-behind files containing the program logic, and resource files that contain non-code elements that are included in the application. An important part of building most Silverlight applications in Visual Studio is the ability to include those resource files in the project. There are several different types of resources that can be included in a Silverlight project; for example, images, movies, audio, and configuration.

Resource files are added to Silverlight projects in Visual Studio through the Solution Explorer. To illustrate an example of this, consider the XAML code in Listing 6.1 that defines an Image control that points to a file named `image.jpg`.

FIGURE 6.13

`Page.xaml` file opened in Expression Blend from Visual Studio

LISTING 6.1

XAML Code That Defines an Image Control That Points to a File Named image.jpg

```
<UserControl x:Class="SilverlightApp2.Page"
    xmlns="http://schemas.microsoft.com/client/2007"
    xmlns:x="http://schemas.microsoft.com/winfx/2006/xaml"
    Width="400" Height="300">
    <Grid x:Name="LayoutRoot" Background="White">
        <Image Source="/image.jpg"
               Height="200" Width="200"></Image>
    </Grid>
</UserControl>
```

If that image file used in Listing 6.1 is not available to the application when it is accessed, then an exception occurs. Use the following steps to add the image to the application:

1. Right-click on the Silverlight application project in the Solution Explorer, as shown in Figure 6.14.

2. Choose Add ⇨ Existing Item from the menu.

FIGURE 6.14

Adding an existing item to a Silverlight project in the Solution Explorer of Visual Studio

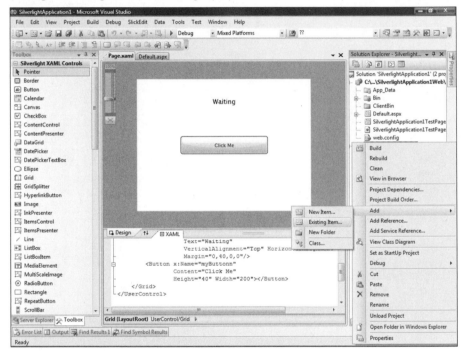

3. Use the file manager to navigate to the image file.

4. Click Add to add the image to the project.

5. Right-click on the newly added image file and select Properties from the menu to display the Properties pane shown in Figure 6.15.

FIGURE 6.15

Properties pane for an image file located in a Silverlight project in Visual Studio

6. Set the Build Action setting to Content.

7. Set the Copy to Output Directory setting to Copy Always.

These steps add the image file to the project. When the project is compiled, the image file is added to the XAP application page and deployed with the application.

You can also define the image file Build Action as None and copy the file to the output directory manually or you can set the image file Build Action as Embedded Resource and the image is compiled into the application assembly.

Build settings

This section is designed to give you a quick look at where to go in Visual Studio to configure the build settings for Silverlight applications.

Many of the build settings for Silverlight applications can be accessed from the Properties pane of the Silverlight project, as shown in Figure 6.16. The application-specific settings are located on the Application tab; for example, the assembly and XAP filenames and the startup object.

The build-specific settings are located on the Build tab; for example, the Output path and compilation symbols settings.

File-specific settings are located on the Properties pane for the code or resource file; for example, the BuildAction and Copy to Output Directory settings.

CROSS-REF For more information about the build settings and building Silverlight applications, refer to Chapter 7.

FIGURE 6.16

Properties window for a Silverlight project in Visual Studio

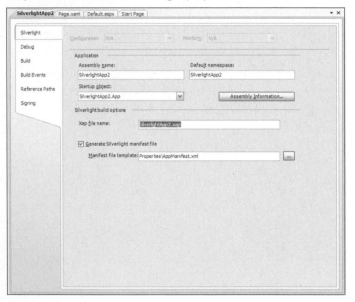

Summary

This chapter has given you a brief overview of using Visual Studio to create and implement Silverlight applications. We discussed the files created automatically by the Silverlight application template and how to add code to them to create a Silverlight application. You learned some features available in the Solution Explorer that help with adding resource files to projects. Finally we discussed where to find build-specific information for Silverlight applications so that you understand how to use Visual Studio to set up Silverlight application builds.

In this chapter, you learned:

- How to create a .NET Silverlight application project
- How to test Silverlight applications in Visual Studio
- How to use IntelliSense in Silverlight applications
- How to deploy image files as resources with a Silverlight application
- Where to configure Build settings for Silverlight applications

Chapter 7

Creating .NET Silverlight Applications

T his chapter is organized to help you understand the pieces that must be implemented to create a .NET Silverlight application, how they relate to each other, and how they are deployed. In their most basic sense, Silverlight applications are basically packages that are embedded in Web pages. The purpose of this chapter is to help you understand what pieces make up a Silverlight Web application and how they relate to each other.

If you are using Visual Studio to create and build your Silverlight applications, then most of the work in this chapter is done automatically for you. However, you need to understand these concepts to customize and deploy .NET applications.

The following sections discuss the anatomy of .NET Silverlight applications and how to deploy them in Web pages.

Understanding the Anatomy of a .NET Silverlight Application

Silverlight applications are composed of at least one application assembly that contains an entry point to begin execution. They can also include any number of optional libraries and resource files that provide additional functionality for the application. The following sections discuss each of these components and how they relate to the Silverlight application.

Application assembly package

The application assembly package is essentially a zipped-up package that contains a compiled Silverlight `Application` class with entry point metadata that allows the Silverlight browser plug-in to launch the application. The following sections discuss each component of the application assembly.

Implementing an application class with code-behind pages

The application class is the base class for the Silverlight application. It derives from `Application` and must implement the ability to start the Silverlight application. When creating .NET Silverlight applications, the application class actually spreads across two source files: an XAML file and a C# or Visual Basic code-behind file.

The first step in implementing a .NET Silverlight application is to link a C# or Visual Basic code-behind page to a Silverlight XAML application. Code-behind pages are managed code files that are a partial subset of a class defined in XAML code that is used to implement a Silverlight application or user control.

NOTE When you create a new Silverlight project in Visual Studio 2008, the code-behind pages are created automatically for you. There are two XAML documents with code-behind pages attached. The `App.xaml` file contains the `Application` definition. The `Page.xaml` file contains a `UserControl` definition for an in-project library that you actually use to implement controls in your application. Libraries are discussed later in this section.

Code-behind pages can be implemented in either C# or Visual Basic. They allow the developer to programmatically control the behavior of the Silverlight application. Code-behind pages are not unique to Silverlight, so we discuss only the fundamentals of how they are implemented in this book.

ON the WEB If you want more information about code-behind pages, you can go to `http://msdn2.microsoft.com/en-us/library/aa970568.aspx`.

NOTE Code-behind pages can be implemented in Python, managed JavaScript, and Ruby — not just in C# or Visual Basic — and are handled a little bit differently, as discussed in Chapter 9.

In Silverlight applications, code-behind pages are implemented using three fundamental components. Those components are the `x:Class` attribute, the `partial` keyword, and the `InitializeComponent()` method. To understand their relationship, consider the following code Listings 7.1, 7.2, and 7.3:

LISTING 7.1

XAML UserControl Definition Containing the x:Class Attribute

```
<Application xmlns="http://schemas.microsoft.com/client/2007"
             xmlns:x="http://schemas.microsoft.com/winfx/2006/xaml"
             x:Class="SilverlightApplication.App"
             >
    <Application.Resources>

    </Application.Resources>
</Application>
```

LISTING 7.2

C# Listing Implementing a Partial Class of the Application Element

```
using System;
using System.Windows;

namespace SilverlightApplication
{
    public partial class App : Application
    {
        public App()
        {
            InitializeComponent();
        }
    }
}
```

LISTING 7.3

Visual Basic Listing Implementing a Partial Class of the Application Element

```
Partial Public Class App
    Inherits Application

    Public Sub New()
        InitializeComponent()
    End Sub

End Class
```

In Listing 7.1, the XAML code declares a Silverlight application using the Application element and defines the class name as SilverlightApplication.App using the x:Class attribute. This definition ties the XAML code to the code-behind pages defined in Listings 7.2 and 7.3. The SilverlightApplication.App class is defined in Listings 7.2 and 7.3 as a partial class, using the partial keyword. The InitializeComponent() method starts the initial render of the Silverlight content area when the class is instantiated.

Application assembly

For .NET Silverlight applications, you need to compile the application class into an application assembly before adding it to the application assembly package. If you use Visual Studio, the ability to create the binary is automatically built into your Silverlight projects.

If you are not using a Visual Studio Silverlight project, then you need to use MSBuild to compile your application class. You need to provide MSBuild with an XML project configuration file similar to the one in Listing 7.4 that we borrowed from Microsoft's MSDN Web site:

LISTING 7.4

Sample MSBuild Configuration File for a Silverlight Application from Microsoft MSDN Web Site

```
<!-- SilverlightApplication.proj -->
<Project
  ToolsVersion="3.5"
  DefaultTargets="Build"
  xmlns="http://schemas.microsoft.com/developer/msbuild/2003">

  <!-- Application Configuration -->
  <PropertyGroup>

    <TargetFrameworkVersion>v3.5</TargetFrameworkVersion>
    <SchemaVersion>2.0</SchemaVersion>
    <NoStdLib>true</NoStdLib>
    <NoStdCfg>true</NoStdCfg>

    <!--
        Build a library assembly, SilverlightApplication.dll, with
        SilverlightApplication as the root namespace. Place the assembly
        in the ClientBin folder.
    -->
    <RootNamespace>SilverlightApplication</RootNamespace>
    <AssemblyName>SilverlightApplication</AssemblyName>
    <OutputType>Library</OutputType>
    <OutputPath>ClientBin</OutputPath>

  </PropertyGroup>

  <!-- Silverlight assembly references required by code -->
```

```
<ItemGroup>
  <Reference Include="mscorlib" />
  <Reference Include="system" />
  <Reference Include="System.Windows" />
</ItemGroup>

<!-- Files to build application class -->
<ItemGroup>
  <Compile Include="App.xaml.cs">
    <DependentUpon>App.xaml</DependentUpon>
  </Compile>
  <SilverlightPage Include="App.xaml">
    <Generator>MSBuild:CompileXaml</Generator>
  </SilverlightPage>
</ItemGroup>

<!--
The file that is used by MSBuild to Build C# Silverlight Applications,
and which specifies the C# compiler. Note that (MSBuildExtensionsPath)
is the path to the Program Files\MSBuild folder.
-->
<Import Project="$(MSBuildExtensionsPath)\
    Microsoft\Silverlight\v2.0\Microsoft.Silverlight.CSharp.targets" />
</Project>
```

The following is a list of the important configuration settings in the MSBuild project file:

- **OutputType:** Set to Library so that a managed library assembly is generated
- **OutputPath:** Defines the location to place the application assembly; is typically set to the CientBin folder
- **Mscorlib Reference:** Includes the required `mscorlib.dll` assembly
- **System Reference:** Includes the required `system.dll` assembly
- **System.Windows Reference:** Includes the required `System.Windows.dll` assembly
- **Compile Include:** Defines the .NET source file containing the `Application` class definition
- **DependentUpon:** Defines the XAML source file containing the `Application` class definition
- **SilverlightPage Include:** Defines the XAML file to be included in the SilverlightPage
- **Import Project:** Points to the MSBuild file used to build Silverlight applications and points to the compiler

When you build the Silverlight project, the following files are generated:

- **Silverlight Application DLL:** The application assembly file that is named after the Silverlight project. In the case of Listing 7.1, the assembly is named SilverlightApplication.dll.

- **Silverlight Application PDB:** The debug file for the application assembly that is also named after the Silverlight project.

 **For more information about the MSBuild, refer to the following MSDN Web page:**
http://msdn2.microsoft.com/en-us/library/0k6kkbsd.aspx

Entry point metadata

One additional piece is necessary for the Silverlight plug-in to be able to run your application. The plug-in needs an entry point to begin executing the Silverlight application. The Silverlight plug-in starts the CLR and then it creates an execution environment for the Silverlight application.

After the execution environment is set up for the Silverlight application, the plug-in needs to know where to begin executing code. If you are using Visual Studio to build your Silverlight project, this is handled automatically for you. If you are using MSBuild, you need to include the configuration shown in Listing 7.5 in your MSBuild project configuration file to create the entry point metadata necessary for the plug-in.

LISTING 7.5

MSBuild Configuration Code for Entry Point Metadata from the Microsoft MSDN Web Site

```
<!-- SilverlightApplication.csproj -->
<Project ... >

  <!-- Application Configuration -->
  <PropertyGroup>
    ...
    <OutputPath>ClientBin</OutputPath>
    ...
    <!--
        Generate the application package (.xap) that includes the
        application assembly and application class.
    -->
    <XapOutputs>true</XapOutputs>
    <XapFilename>SilverlightApplication.xap</XapFilename>

  </PropertyGroup>
  ...
</Project>
```

The following is a list of the important entry point metadata configuration settings in the MSBuild project file:

- **Silverlight Application:** Denotes whether the assembly that is being built by MSBuild is the application or library assembly. Should be set to `true` for Silverlight applications.

- **SilverlightAppEntry:** Specifies which class is the Silverlight `Application` class.

- **SilverlightManifestTemplate:** Specifies the location of the manifest template XML file to use when building the Silverlight application manifest.

- **GenerateSilverlightManifest:** Specifies whether a Silverlight application manifest should be built.

Listing 7.6 shows an example of a Silverlight application manifest that is generated when building the application assembly. The `EntryPointAssembly` attribute points to the application assembly, the `EntryPointType` points to the `Application` class, and the `Deployment.Parts` point to the assembly files.

LISTING 7.6

Example Silverlight Application Manifest File

```
<Deployment xmlns="http://schemas.microsoft.com/client/2007/deployment"
  xmlns:x="http://schemas.microsoft.com/winfx/2006/xaml"
  EntryPointAssembly="SilverlightApplication"
  EntryPointType="SilverlightApplication.App"
  RuntimeVersion="2.0.30226.2">
  <Deployment.Parts>
    <AssemblyPart x:Name="SilverlightApplication"
      Source="SilverlightApplication.dll" />
    <AssemblyPart x:Name="System.Windows.Controls"
      Source="System.Windows.Controls.dll" />
    <AssemblyPart x:Name="System.Windows.Controls.Extended"
      Source="System.Windows.Controls.Extended.dll" />
  </Deployment.Parts>
</Deployment>
```

XAP application package

The Silverlight application package is basically a ZIP file with a `.xap` extension. Packaging the Silverlight application into a package provides a number of benefits. Packages are much easier to distribute, they are easier to manage, large programs can be broken down into a series of smaller packages, and it is very easy to share packages between Silverlight applications.

You need to package the application assembly output into an application package so that your .NET Silverlight application can be deployed. Visual Studio automatically creates the package for you when you build a .NET Silverlight application. If you are using MSBuild, you need to include additional information in the MSBuild configuration file, as shown in Listing 7.7.

LISTING 7.7

MSBuild Configuration Code for Building Application Package File from the Microsoft MSDN Web Site

```
<!-- SilverlightApplication.csproj -->
<Project ... >

  <!-- Application Configuration -->
  <PropertyGroup>
    ...
    <OutputPath>ClientBin</OutputPath>
    ...
    <!--
        Generate the application package (.xap) that includes the
        application assembly and application class.
    -->
    <XapOutputs>true</XapOutputs>
    <XapFilename>SilverlightApplication.xap</XapFilename>

  </PropertyGroup>
  ...
</Project>
```

The following is a list of the important application package configuration settings in the MSBuild project file:

- **OutputPath:** Specifies the path where the assembly output is placed. The .xap file is placed in the same location as the assembly output.

- **XapOutputs:** If true, a .xap file is created that contains the application assembly and entry point information.

- **XapFilename:** Specifies the filename that is used when creating the .xap application package. This is the filename that is used when deploying a Silverlight application in a Web browser.

 If you want to look at the contents of a .xap file, you can change the extension to .zip and access it and extract files just as with any ZIP file.

Implementing library assemblies

Another useful Silverlight feature is the ability to develop Silverlight library assemblies. These libraries make it possible to break applications down and create reusable controls that can be consumed by multiple applications.

Library assemblies can be referenced by application assemblies as well as other library assemblies. This enables you to provide additional functionality to an application as part of the application package or on demand, allowing developers to create applications that initially are much smaller to download within the browser.

Silverlight library assemblies are similar to application assemblies except that they do not need to derive from the `Application` class. Library assemblies can be packaged with application assemblies or deployed separately.

The following sections discuss how to implement library classes, generate library assemblies, and package libraries for in-package or on-demand deployment.

Implementing a Silverlight library class with code-behind pages

As with application assemblies, .NET Silverlight library classes are actually spread across two source files: an XAML file and a C# or Visual Basic code-behind file.

The first step in implementing a .NET Silverlight library is to link a C# or Visual Basic code-behind page to a Silverlight XAML application. Code-behind pages are managed code files that are a partial subset of a class defined in XAML code that is used to implement a Silverlight application or user control.

In Silverlight libraries, code-behind pages are implemented using three fundamental components. Those components are the `x:Class` attribute, the `partial` keyword, and the `InitializeComponent()` method. To understand their relationship, consider the following code Listings 7.8, 7.9, and 7.10:

LISTING 7.8

XAML UserControl Definition Containing an x:Class Attribute That Matches the Class Defined in a Code-Behind Page

```
<UserControl x:Class="SilverlightApplication.Page"
    xmlns="http://schemas.microsoft.com/client/2007"
    xmlns:x="http://schemas.microsoft.com/winfx/2006/xaml"
    Width="400" Height="300">
    <Grid x:Name="LayoutRoot" Background="White">
        ...
    </Grid>
</UserControl>
```

LISTING 7.9

C# Listing Implementing a Partial Class of UserControl

```csharp
using System;
using System.Windows;

namespace SilverlightApplication
{
    public partial class Page : UserControl
    {
        public Page()
        {
            InitializeComponent();
        }
    }
}
```

LISTING 7.10

Visual Basic Listing Implementing a Partial Class of UserControl

```vb
Partial Public Class Page
    Inherits UserControl

    Public Sub New()
        InitializeComponent()
    End Sub

End Class
```

In Listing 7.8, the XAML code declares a Silverlight application using the UserControl element and defines the class name as SilverlightApplication.Page using the x:Class attribute. This definition ties the XAML code to the code-behind pages defined in Listings 7.9 and 7.10. The SilverlightApplication.Page class is defined in Listings 7.9 and 7.10 as a partial class, using the partial keyword. The InitializeComponent() method starts the initial render of the Silverlight content area when the class is instantiated.

Creating a library assembly

For .NET Silverlight applications, you need to compile the library class into an application assembly. If you use Visual Studio, the ability to build the assembly is automatically built into your Silverlight projects.

If you are not using a Visual Studio Silverlight project, use MSBuild to compile your library class. You need to provide MSBuild with an XML project configuration file similar to the one in Listing 7.11 that is borrowed from Microsoft's MSDN Web site:

LISTING 7.11

Sample MSBuild Configuration File for a Silverlight Library from Microsoft MSDN Web Site

```
<Project
  ToolsVersion="3.5"
  DefaultTargets="Build"
  xmlns="http://schemas.microsoft.com/developer/msbuild/2003">

  <!-- Library Configuration -->
  <PropertyGroup>

    <ProductVersion>9.0.21022</ProductVersion>
    <SchemaVersion>2.0</SchemaVersion>
    <NoStdLib>true</NoStdLib>
    <NoStdCfg>true</NoStdCfg>

    <!--
        Build a library assembly, SilverlightLibrary.dll, with
        SilverlightLibrary as the root namespace. The generated
        assembly is placed in the ClientBin folder.
    -->
    <RootNamespace>SilverlightLibrary</RootNamespace>
    <AssemblyName>SilverlightLibrary</AssemblyName>
    <TargetFrameworkVersion>v3.5</TargetFrameworkVersion>

    <!--
      Specify that this assembly is not a Silverlight application (eg
      does not contain an entry point). The decision on whether
      to deploy this assembly in-package or on-demand will be made by
      the developer later.
    -->
    <OutputType>Library</OutputType>
    <OutputPath>ClientBin</OutputPath>
    <SilverlightApplication>false</SilverlightApplication>

  </PropertyGroup>

  <!-- Silverlight assembly references required by code -->
  <ItemGroup>
    <Reference Include="System.Windows" />
    <Reference Include="mscorlib" />
    <Reference Include="system" />
  </ItemGroup>
```

continued

LISTING 7.11 *(continued)*

```
<!-- Code files to build library assembly -->
<ItemGroup>
  <SilverlightPage Include="Page.xaml">
    <Generator>MSBuild:CompileXaml</Generator>
  </SilverlightPage>
  <Compile Include="Page.xaml.cs">
    <DependentUpon>Page.xaml</DependentUpon>
  </Compile>
</ItemGroup>

<!--
  The File that is used by MSBuild to Build C# Silverlight Libraries,
  and which specifies the C# compiler. Note that SBuildExtensionsPath)
  is the path to the Program Files\MSBuild folder.
-->
<Import Project="$(MSBuildExtensionsPath)
    \Microsoft\Silverlight\v2.0\Microsoft.Silverlight.CSharp.targets" />
</Project>
```

The following is a list of the important configuration settings in the MSBuild project file for the library assembly:

- **OutputType:** OutputType is set to Library so that a managed library assembly is generated.

- **OutputPath:** OutputPath defines the location to place the library assembly.

- **SilverlightApplication:** Designates if this is an application or a library. Set this to false for a library.

- **Mscorlib Reference:** Includes the required mscorlib.dll assembly. (Required)

- **System Reference:** Includes the required system.dll assembly. (Required)

- **System.Windows Reference:** Includes the required System.Windows.dll assembly. (Required)

- **Compile Include:** Defines the .NET source file containing the UserControl class definition.

- **DependentUpon:** Defines the XAML source file containing the UserControl class definition.

- **SilverlightPage Include:** Defines the XAML file to be included in the SilverlightPage.
- **Import Project:** Points to MSBuild file used to build Silverlight applications and points to the compiler.

 There is no **XapOutputs** or **XapFilename** properties in the configuration file because an application package should not be generated for library assemblies.

When you build the Silverlight project, the following files are generated:

- **Silverlight Library DLL:** The library assembly file that is named after the Silverlight project
- **Silverlight Application PDB:** The debug file for the library assembly that is also named after the Silverlight project

Implementing in-package library assemblies

It is very simple to deploy library assemblies as part of your application assembly packages. Packaging libraries with an application allows you to reference the functionality of the library from your application code without having to download it first.

To configure a library for in-package deployment, first create a library assembly as described in the previous section. To add a library assembly to your application package using MSBuild, add a reference to the library assembly using the `ProjectReference` property in the MSBuild project configuration file for the Silverlight application, as shown in Listing 7.12.

CROSS-REF For more information about adding libraries to Visual Studio projects, see Chapter 6.

LISTING 7.12

MSBuild Configuration File Adding a Silverlight Library Reference

```
<Project ... >
  <!-- Application Configuration -->
  <PropertyGroup>
    ...
  </PropertyGroup>
  ...
  <!-- Reference a library assembly for in-package deployment -->
  <ItemGroup>
    <ProjectReference Include="myLibrary\myLibrary.proj" />
  </ItemGroup>
  ...
</Project>
```

Using Listing 7.12, the myLibrary assembly is packaged within the application and downloaded with the application package when the Silverlight application is accessed. You can reference the package from within your application source. For example, Listing 7.13 and Listing 7.14 show how an application project references the Page class in a library project to set the RootVisual property for the application's UI.

LISTING 7.13

Silverlight Application XAML Markup

```
<Application xmlns="http://schemas.microsoft.com/client/2007"
             xmlns:x="http://schemas.microsoft.com/winfx/2006/xaml"
             x:Class="SilverlightApplication.App"
             Startup="App_Startup">
</Application>
```

LISTING 7.14

Silverlight Application Code Referencing a Class Created in Library

```csharp
using System;
using System.Windows;
using myLibrary; // Silverlight library

namespace SilverlightApplication
{
    public partial class App : Application
    {
        public App()
        {
            InitializeComponent();
        }

        private void App_Startup(object sender, StartupEventArgs e)
        {
            // Load the main control from library
            this.RootVisual = new Page();
        }
    }
}
```

Implementing on-demand library assemblies

Silverlight libraries can also be downloaded when they are needed instead of packaging them with the application. This has a major advantage in that if certain functionality is not used, the assemblies for that functionality are not downloaded by the browser, thus reducing download time.

Implementing on-demand library assemblies is similar to in-package assemblies with two distinct differences. The reference in the MSBuild configuration file is slightly different, and you must add code to your application to download the library assembly file before it can be accessed.

To configure a library for on-demand deployment, first create a library assembly as described in the previous section. To add a library assembly to your application package using MSBuild, add a reference to the library assembly using the `ProjectReference` property in the MSBuild project configuration file for the Silverlight application. However, different from an in-package library, set the `Private` property to `false`, as shown in Listing 7.15.

LISTING 7.15

MSBuild Configuration File Adding an On-Demand Silverlight Library Reference

```
<Project ... >
  <!-- Application Configuration -->
  <PropertyGroup>
    ...
  </PropertyGroup>
  ...
  <!-- Reference a library assembly for in-package deployment -->
  <ItemGroup>
    <ProjectReference Include="myDownloadLibrary\myDownloadLibrary.proj">
      <Private>False</Private>
    </ProjectReference>
  </ItemGroup>
  ...
</Project>
```

Using Listing 7.15 with the `Private` property set to false, Silverlight only downloads the library upon request from the application itself. Therefore, you need to add code to your application to download the library assembly before you try to use it.

Listings 7.16 and 7.17 show examples of a Silverlight application that downloads a Library assembly prior to using it.

LISTING 7.16

Silverlight Application XAML File That Defines a Grid and TextBlock Control

```
<UserControl
    xmlns="http://schemas.microsoft.com/client/2007"
    xmlns:x="http://schemas.microsoft.com/winfx/2006/xaml"
    x:Class="SilverlightApplication.myPage">

    <Grid x:Name="ApplicationGrid">
        <TextBlock MouseLeftButtonUp="Clicked">
            Load Content From Library
        </TextBlock>
    </Grid>

</UserControl>
```

LISTING 7.17

Silverlight Application C# Code That Handles a Mouse Click Event and Downloads a File from the Server

```
namespace SilverlightApplication
{
    public partial class myPage : UserControl
    {
        public myPage()
        {
            InitializeComponent();
        }

        private void Clicked(
            object sender, MouseButtonEventArgs e)
        {
            // Download library assembly
            WebClient cli = new WebClient();
            cli.OpenReadCompleted +=
                new OpenReadCompletedEventHandler(cliReadCompleted);
            cli.OpenReadAsync(
                new Uri("myLibrary.dll", UriKind.Relative));
        }

        private void cliReadCompleted(
            object sender, OpenReadCompletedEventArgs e)
        {
            if ((e.Error == null) && (e.Cancelled == false))
```

```
        {
            // Convert downloaded stream into assembly
            AssemblyPart aPart = new AssemblyPart();
            aPart.Load(e.Result);

            AddPageFromLibrary();
        }
    }

    private void AddPageFromLibrary() {
        // Instantiate type from assembly
        Page page = new Page();

        // Add to grid
        this.ApplicationGrid.Children.Add(page);
    }
  }
}
```

In Listing 7.17, a Web client is created that downloads the library assembly as a stream, converts it to assembly, and then loads it in the application. Don't worry if you don't understand all of the code in Listing 7.17; those concepts are covered in subsequent chapters.

 If you try to access the library before trying to download it, your application throws a ManagedRuntimeError- System.IO.FileNotFoundException.

Using resource files

Another crucial part of most Silverlight applications are nonexecutable content files such as images, movies, audio, documents — basically any type of file that you need to render the Silverlight application. These types of files can be added to your application at three levels: the resource level, content level, or site level. The following sections discuss these levels and when to use each.

Resource file

Resource files are nonexecutable files that are actually embedded into either an application assembly or a library assembly. These resources are deployed when the application or library is deployed — for example, when an on-demand library resource file is only deployed to the browser when the library is loaded by the application.

The upside of resource files is that they are easily accessible and available to the application or library. The downsides are that they are always downloaded with the assembly and they are only available within that assembly.

In Visual Studio, Resources are added to a project by adding a `Resources` file. If you are not using Visual Studio, then a resource file can be added to an application or library assembly by using the `Resource` tag, as shown in Listing 7.18.

LISTING 7.18

MSBuild Configuration File Adding an Embedded Resource File

```
<Project ... >
    <!-- Application Configuration -->
    <PropertyGroup>
      ...
    </PropertyGroup>
    ...
    <!-- An image resource file that is embedded into the assembly -->
    <ItemGroup>
      <Resource Include="Image1.png" />
    </ItemGroup>
    ...
  </Project>
```

The `Resource Include` property shown in Listing 7.18 embeds the `Image1.png` file into the application assembly of the project. The image can them be accessed as a relative URI.

The following code illustrates how to access the image resource file from C#:

```
Image embeddedIMG = new Image();
embeddedIMG.Source = new BitmapImage(
                        new Uri("Image1.png", UriKind.Relative));
```

The following code illustrates how to access the image resource file from XAML:

```
<Image Source="Image1.png" />
```

If the image is embedded in a different library assembly, you need to specify the library in the URI.

For example, the following code illustrates how to access an image resource in another library assembly file from XAML:

```
<Image Source="/myLibrary;component/Image1.png" />
```

The leading slash indicates to reference a library relative to the assembly that the code is currently running in, and `myLibrary;component/` specifies the referenced assembly.

Content file

Content files are nonexecutable files that are packaged in the application package. These resource files are deployed when the application package is deployed.

The upside of content files is that the same file can be easily accessed by the application as well as by any libraries. If you have content that needs to be accessed by multiple assemblies, then it needs to be a content file or a site-of-origin file.

The downside of content files is that they are always downloaded with the application, which means that the application download is larger.

Visual Studio, Resources added to a project are automatically added to the application by setting their properties. If you are not using Visual Studio, a content file can be added to an application or library assembly by using the Content tag, as shown in Listing 7.19.

LISTING 7.19

MSBuild Configuration File Adding a Content File

```
<Project ... >
    <!-- Application Configuration -->
    <PropertyGroup>
        ...
    </PropertyGroup>
    ...
    <!-- An image resource file deployed in the package -->
    <ItemGroup>
      <Content Include="Image1.png" />
    </ItemGroup>

    </Project>
```

The Content Include property shown in Listing 7.19 packages the Image1.png file into the application package. The image can them be accessed as a relative URI.

The following code illustrates how to access the image content file from C#:

```
Image contentIMG = new Image();
contentIMG.Source = new BitmapImage(
                        new Uri("/Image1.png", UriKind.Relative));
```

The following code illustrates how to access the image content file from XAML:

```
<Image Source="/Image1.png" />
```

Because the image file is located at the same level as the assembly files, you need to use the leading slash to reference it.

Site-of-origin file

Site-of-origin files are nonexecutable files that are deployed to the site with — but are not a part of — the application package. In effect, because they are not part of the package, site-of-origin files are always deployed on demand when they are used.

The upside of site-of-origin files is that they are only downloaded when they are used, which reduces the size of the application download.

> **TIP** **If you have content files that are not always needed, they should be site-of-origin files whenever possible.**

The downside of site-of-origin files is that they are not part of the package, so you need to make certain that they are actually available on the Web site.

If you are not using Visual Studio, a site-of-origin file can be added to an application or library assembly by using the None tag, as shown in Listing 7.20.

LISTING 7.20

MSBuild Configuration File Adding a Site of Origin File

```
<Project ... >
    <!-- Application Configuration -->
    <PropertyGroup>
      ...
    </PropertyGroup>
    ...
    <!-- An image resource file deployed outside the package -->
    <ItemGroup>
      <None Include="Image1.png">
        <CopyToOutputDirectory>Always</CopyToOutputDirectory>
      </None>
    </ItemGroup>
    ...
  </Project>
```

The `None Include` property shown in Listing 7.20 includes the image file in the build; however, it is not placed in the package or embedded in an assembly. Instead, you must copy the file to the site of origin. The `CopyToOutputDirectory` property is set to `Always` for site-of-origin files. This instructs MSBuild to copy the file to the output directory of the project. The image can then be accessed as a relative URI.

The following code illustrates how to access the image site-of-origin file from C#:

```
Image siteIMG = new Image();
siteIMG.Source = new BitmapImage(
                    new Uri("/Image1.png", UriKind.Relative));
```

The following code illustrates how to access the image site-of-origin file from XAML:

```
<Image Source="/Image1.png" />
```

The image file is not relative to the code because it is not embedded in an assembly or in the package; therefore, you need to use the leading slash to reference it.

Implementing the Application Class

All Silverlight applications are based on an implementation of an `Application` class. The application class is responsible for handling any parameters that are passed to the Silverlight application, constructing the Silverlight `application` object, starting the application, displaying the UI, and exiting the application when finished.

The following sections discuss the class methods used during the lifetime of the `application` class, how to display the UI from the `application` class, and how to handle initialization parameters.

Application class methods

The Silverlight application class derives from `Application` and should implement a constructor, application startup, application exit, and an unhandled exception method. These methods are used to implement the creation, start, and end of the application.

Application constructor

Each Silverlight application should implement a constructor that calls the `InitializeComponent()` method for the application. The `InitializeComponent()` function merges the application XAML with the application class, as discussed earlier in this chapter. The constructor can also be used to implement any properties or events that need to be initialized upon object creation.

The following code in Listings 7.21 and 7.22 shows the implementation of a basic application constructor.

LISTING 7.21

XAML Code for a Basic Silverlight Application

```
<Application
    xmlns="http://schemas.microsoft.com/client/2007"
    xmlns:x="http://schemas.microsoft.com/winfx/2006/xaml"
    x:Class="SilverlightApplication.App">
</Application>
```

LISTING 7.22

C# Code Containing a Basic Silverlight Application Constructor

```
using System.Windows;

namespace SilverlightApplication
{
    public partial class App : Application
    {
        public App()
        {
            // Merge application class and XAML markup
            InitializeComponent();
        }
    }
}
```

The application constructor always has the same name as the application class and is automatically called when a Silverlight application is loaded.

Application startup

After the Silverlight application has been created using the constructor, the application startup method is called prior to allowing the user access. This allows Silverlight applications to perform any initialization activities, such as processing initialization parameters, initializing resources or properties, loading data, and displaying the application UI.

The following code in Listings 7.23 and 7.24 shows the implementation of a basic application startup method.

LISTING 7.23

XAML Code for a Basic Silverlight Application Including a Startup Property

```
<Application
    xmlns="http://schemas.microsoft.com/client/2007"
    xmlns:x="http://schemas.microsoft.com/winfx/2006/xaml"
    x:Class="SilverlightApplication.App"
    Startup="AppStart">
</Application>
```

LISTING 7.24

C# Code Containing a Basic Silverlight Application Startup Method

```
using System.Windows;

namespace SilverlightApplication
{
    public partial class App : Application
    {
        public App()
        {
            // Merge application class and XAML markup
            InitializeComponent();
        }

        private void AppStart(object sender, StartupEventArgs e)
        {
            this.RootVisual = new Page();
        }
    }
}
```

In Listing 7.23, the Startup property points to the AppStart() function in the App class. The AppStart() function is used to set the application UI. Two parameters are passed to the application startup method. The first parameter points to the entry point object that raised the startup event. The second parameter contains a dictionary containing any initialization parameters that were passed to the application.

Application exit

The application exit method is called when the Silverlight application ends. This allows Silverlight applications to perform any cleanup activities such as processing and storing data, logging, and so on. The application exit method is called when any one of the following events occur:

- The user navigates to another Web page.
- The user refreshes the Web page hosting the Silverlight application.
- The browser window or current browser tab is closed.
- The operating system is shut down.
- The Silverlight control is removed using the HTML DOM from a Web script.

The following code in Listings 7.25 and 7.26 shows the implementation of a basic application exit method.

LISTING 7.25

XAML Code for a Basic Silverlight Application Including an Exit Property

```
<Application
    xmlns="http://schemas.microsoft.com/client/2007"
    xmlns:x="http://schemas.microsoft.com/winfx/2006/xaml"
    x:Class="SilverlightApplication.App"
    Startup="AppStart"
    Exit="AppExit">
</Application>
```

LISTING 7.26

C# Code Containing a Basic Silverlight Application Exit Method

```
using System.Windows;

namespace SilverlightApplication
{
    public partial class App : Application
    {
        public App()
        {
            // Merge application class and XAML markup
            InitializeComponent();
        }
```

```
        private void AppStart(object sender, StartupEventArgs e)
        {
            this.RootVisual = new Page();
        }

        private void AppExit(object sender, EventArgs e)
        {
            do_log("Exiting");
        }
    }
}
```

In Listing 7.25, the `Exit` property points to the `AppExit()` method in the App class. The `AppMethod()` function simply adds an entry to a log file. Two parameters are passed to the application exit method. The first parameter points to the entry point object that raised the exit event. The second parameter contains a dictionary containing any arguments passed to the exit handler.

CAUTION Be careful not to implement any code that would create an exit routine that would result in a re-entrant or looping situation; for example, setting the `Source` property of the Silverlight plug-in.

Unhandled exception

The unhandled exception method is called when an exception is thrown in the Silverlight application but never handled. This allows developers the ability to protect users from unsightly exceptions in their Silverlight applications.

 The unhandled exception method is not required; however, it is always a very good idea to implement it.

The following code in Listings 7.27 and 7.28 shows the implementation of a basic unhandled exception method.

LISTING 7.27

XAML Code for a Basic Silverlight Application Including an Unhandled Exception Property

```
<Application
    xmlns="http://schemas.microsoft.com/client/2007"
    xmlns:x="http://schemas.microsoft.com/winfx/2006/xaml"
    x:Class="SilverlightApplication.App"
    UnhandledException="AppException">
</Application>
```

LISTING 7.28

C# Code Containing a Basic Silverlight Unhandled Exception Method

```csharp
using System.Windows;

namespace SilverlightApplication
{
    public partial class App : Application
    {
        public App()
        {
            // Merge application class and XAML markup
            InitializeComponent();
        }

        private void AppException(object sender,
                    ApplicationUnhandledExceptionEventArgs e)
        {
            do_log("Exception" + e.ToString());
        }
    }
}
```

In Listing 7.28, the UnhandledException property points to the AppException() method in the App class. The AppException() function simply adds an exception entry to a log file. Two parameters are passed to the unhandled exception method. The first parameter points to the entry point object that raised the event. The second parameter contains a dictionary containing any arguments passed to the exception handler.

Displaying the application UI

The application UI is specified by setting the RootVisual property of the Application class to a Silverlight class that derives from UIElement. The most common example is the UserControl class.

The best way to illustrate this is to look at a basic Silverlight application project created by Visual Studio. There are four main source files involved, two that create a UserControl class and two that create an Application class.

Listings 7.29 and 7.30 contain the contents of the Page.xaml and Page.xaml.cs files that create the Page UserControl class.

LISTING 7.29

XAML Code for a Basic Silverlight UserControl Class

```xaml
<UserControl x:Class="SilverlightApplication.Page"
    xmlns="http://schemas.microsoft.com/client/2007"
    xmlns:x="http://schemas.microsoft.com/winfx/2006/xaml"
    Width="400" Height="300">
    <Grid x:Name="LayoutRoot" Background="White">

    </Grid>
</UserControl>
```

LISTING 7.30

C# Code Containing a Basic Silverlight UserControl Class

```csharp
using System;
using System.Windows;
using System.Windows.Controls;

namespace SilverlightApplication
{
    public partial class Page : UserControl
    {
        public Page()
        {
            InitializeComponent();
        }
    }
}
```

Listings 7.31 and 7.32 contain the contents of the App.xaml and App.xaml.cs files that create the App Application class.

LISTING 7.31

XAML Code for a Basic Silverlight Application Class

```
<Application xmlns="http://schemas.microsoft.com/client/2007"
             xmlns:x="http://schemas.microsoft.com/winfx/2006/xaml"
             x:Class="SilverlightApplication.App"
             >
    <Application.Resources>

    </Application.Resources>
</Application>
```

LISTING 7.32

C# Code Containing a Basic Silverlight Application Class

```
using System;
using System.Windows;
using System.Windows.Controls;

namespace SilverlightApplication
{
    public partial class App : Application
    {
        public App()
        {
            this.Startup += this.Application_Startup;
            this.Exit += this.Application_Exit;
            this.UnhandledException += this.Application_UnhandledException;

            InitializeComponent();
        }

        private void Application_Startup(object sender, StartupEventArgs e)
        {
            // Load the main control
            this.RootVisual = new Page();
        }

        private void Application_Exit(object sender, EventArgs e)
        {

        }
    }
}
```

The UserControl class Page, which is created in Listings 7.27 and 7.28, contains the actual UI for the Silverlight application. That UI is displayed using the following line of code from the App Application class created in Listings 7.29 and 7.30:

```
this.RootVisual = new Page();
```

 The RootVisual property can only be set once. Make certain that you know exactly which UI element this should be before setting this property.

Using initialization parameters

You can pass in and handle initialization parameters in Silverlight applications using the initParams property of the StartupEventArgs parameter passed into the application startup method. The initParams needs to be set in the HTML element that implements the Silverlight application.

Listing 7.33 illustrates an example of setting an initial parameter named PageName when creating a Silverlight application in an HTML object element.

LISTING 7.33

HTML Code That Implements Initialization Parameters for a Silverlight Application

```
<object
  data="data:application/x-silverlight,"
  type="application/x-silverlight"
  width="100%" height="100%">
  <param name="source" value="SilverlightApplication.xap"/>
  <param name="initParams" value="/PageName=MyCoolApp" />
</object>
```

If there are multiple parameters specified by the initParams property, they should be separated by commas; for example:

```
<param name="initParams" value="/PageName=MyCoolApp,/
    PageNumber=1" />
```

 The initialization parameter support in Silverlight is designed to handle alpha-numeric characters only.

Listing 7.34 shows an implementation of accessing the initialization parameter PageName in the startup method of a Silverlight application.

LISTING 7.34

Startup Method That Accesses Initialization Parameters

```
using System;
using System.Windows;

namespace SilverlightApplication
{
    public partial class App : Application
    {
        public App()
        {
            InitializeComponent();
        }

        private void AppStart(object sender, StartupEventArgs e) {

            string pageName = "/PageName";
            if( !e.InitParams.ContainsKey(pageName) )
            {
                appTitle = "Generic Application";
            }
            else
            {
                appTitle = e.InitParams[pageName];
            }
        }
    }
}
```

The AppStart() function in Listing 7.34 uses the ContainsKey method of the InitParams dictionary of the StartupEventArgs argument to determine if the PageName parameter exists. If the PageName parameter exists then it is able to access it by name; otherwise a Generic name is used for the title.

Deploying .NET Silverlight Applications in Web Pages

Deploying .NET Silverlight applications involves creating an instance of the Silverlight plug-in control by embedding it in an <OBJECT> tag in an HTML or ASPX file. When the Web page is rendered, the Silverlight plug-in is instantiated and the entry point into the Silverlight application is called. Embedding the Silverlight plug-in in a Web page allows you to access the Silverlight application from HTML code as well as access the HTML code from the Silverlight application.

The following sections discuss how to embed a Silverlight plug-in control in a Web page and configure the attributes, parameters, and events to create and manage an instance of a Silverlight application as well as using the asp:Silverlight tag to add Silverlight applications to Web pages. If you use Visual Studio to create a Silverlight project, a Web page is automatically created for you with the Silverlight object embedded. However, you can use the following sections to modify the configuration of the Silverlight plug-in.

CROSS-REF You can use the JavaScript helper file `Silverlight.js` to initialize an instance of a Silverlight application, which is covered in Chapter 11.

Embedding a Silverlight plug-in in an HTML Web page

The first step in deploying a Silverlight application is to create a host tag with an `id` attribute in the Web page. Typically, this is a `<DIV>` tag, as shown in the following line of code:

```
<div id=mySilverlightControlHost>  </div>
```

The next step is to add an `<OBJECT>` tag inside the host tag as shown in the following:

```
<div id=mySilverlightControlHost>
  <object id="mySilverlightControlID">
  </object>
</div>
```

The `<OBJECT>` tag provides an element in the DOM in which to load and configure the Silverlight application. The host tag and object tag allow you to place the Silverlight application as an element in your Web pages.

Setting Silverlight plug-in attributes

After you add an `<OBJECT>` tag to the Web page, add the `id`, `data`, `type`, `height`, and `width` attributes, as described in Table 7.1, to configure the Silverlight plug-in as shown in the following code:

```
<div id=mySilverlightControlHost>
  <object
    id="mySilverlightControlID"
    data="data:application/x-silverlight,"
    type="application/x-silverlight-2-b1"
    height="100%"
    width="100%">
  </object>
</div>
```

Table 7.1 describes the attributes that you should add to an embedded Silverlight plug-in `<OBJECT>` tag.

TABLE 7.1	

Attributes of the Silverlight Plug-in <OBJECT> Tag

Attribute	Description
id	Required. Sets the name for the plug-in instance within the HTML DOM. This allows you to access the plug-in using the DOM.
data	Required. Streamlines the instantiation process. Should be set to the Silverlight application MIME type — data:application/x-silverlight.
type	Required. Specifies the MIME type that determines which version of the Silverlight plug-in control should be loaded.
height	Required. Sets the height of the Silverlight content area. This value can be an integer that specifies the height in pixels or a percentage of the height of the parent object. For example: height="100%".
width	Required. Sets the width of the Silverlight content area. This value can be an integer that specifies the height in pixels or a percentage of the height of the parent object. For example: width="100%".

Setting Silverlight plug-in parameters

After you configure the attributes of the <OBJECT> tag, add the source parameter to point to the Silverlight application. The source parameter specifies the Silverlight application package to download and launch to render the content for the Web page as shown in the following code:

```
<div id=mySilverlightControlHost>
  <object
    id="mySilverlightControlID"
    data="data:application/x-silverlight,"
    type="application/x-silverlight-2-b1"
    height="100%"
    width="100%">
    <param name="source"
           value="ClientBin/SilverlightApplication.xap"/>
  </object>
  <iframe style='visibility:hidden;height:0;width:0;border:0px'>
  </iframe>
</div>
```

Table 7.2 describes parameters that can be added to an embedded Silverlight plug-in <OBJECT> tag.

TABLE 7.2

Parameters of the Silverlight Plug-in <OBJECT> Tag

Parameter	Description
source	Required. Specifies a URI containing the location of the source file. This should point to the Silverlight application package (XAP) file.
background	The color used to render the background of the Silverlight plug-in. The default is white. Background uses the same syntaxes available to the managed Color in code or XAML. For example: background="Black" or background="#FFFFFFFF"
enableHtmlAccess	Boolean. Specifies whether the Silverlight plug-in allows hosted content or its runtime to access the HTML DOM. When true, the Silverlight application has access to the browser DOM. Note: enableHtmlAccess cannot be changed after plug-in initialization.
initParams	String. Contains a comma-separated list of parameters that can be used to pass specific initialization information to a Silverlight application. Initialization parameters are discussed earlier in this chapter.
maxFramerate	Integer. Specifies the desired frame rate for the rendering engine. Defaults to 60. The actual frame rate depends on system load and processing power; it may be slower on some systems.
splashScreenSource	Specifies an XAML splash screen that is displayed while the Silverlight application package is downloading.
windowless	Boolean. Specifies whether the plug-in renders windowed or windowless. Defaults to false. This parameter cannot be changed during runtime.

Adding Silverlight plug-in events

You also need to add the onError and onResize parameters to point to error and resize event handlers as well as an <IFRAME>. The event handler parameters specify the name of event handler functions, either in JavaScript or in managed code, to call when an error occurs. Listing 7.35 shows a fully deployed Silverlight application including JavaScript onError and onResize event handler functions.

LISTING 7.35

Silverlight Application Embedded in a Web Page

```
<!DOCTYPE html PUBLIC "-//W3C//DTD XHTML 1.0 Transitional//EN" "http://
    www.w3.org/TR/xhtml1/DTD/xhtml1-transitional.dtd">
<html xmlns="http://www.w3.org/1999/xhtml" >
<head>
    <title>Silverlight Project Test Page </title>

    <script type="text/javascript">
        function onError(sender, args) {
            if (args.errorType == "InitializeError")  {
                var errorDiv = document.getElementById("errorLocation");
                if (errorDiv != null)
                    errorDiv.innerHTML = args.errorType + "- " +
                    args.errorMessage;
            }
        }
        function onResize(sender, args) {
            <!-- Resize Code Here -->
        }
    </script>

</head>

<body>
  <div id="silverlightControlHost">
    <object
      data="data:application/x-silverlight,"
      type="application/x-silverlight-2-b1"
      width="100%"
      height="100%">
      <param name="source" value="ClientBin/SilverlightApplication.xap"/>
      <param name="onError" value="onError" />
      <param name="onResize" value="onResize" />
    </object>
    <iframe style='visibility:hidden;height:0;width:0;border:0px'>
    </iframe>
  </div>
</body>
</html>
```

Table 7.3 describes events that can be added to an embedded Silverlight plug-in <OBJECT> tag.

TABLE 7.3	

Events of the Silverlight Plug-in <OBJECT> Tag

Event	Description
onError	Specifies the handler function to call when an error is generated and not handled in the Silverlight application.
onResize	Specifies the handler function to call when the ActualHeight or ActualWidth property of the Silverlight plug-in control changes.
onLoad	Specifies the handler function to call when the Silverlight application is successfully instantiated and all content is loaded. This allows the application to perform any last minute operations before the Silverlight application content is presented to the user.
onSourceDownloadComplete	Specifies the handler function to call when the Silverlight application package specified by the source parameter has been downloaded.
onSourceDownloadProgressChanged	Specifies the handler function to call while the Silverlight application package specified by the source parameter is downloading.

Embedding a Silverlight application using the asp:Silverlight tag

When you create asp.net Silverlight applications, you should use the asp.net tag to embed the application in the Web page. The first step in deploying an asp.net Silverlight application is to create a host tag with an id attribute in the Web page. Just as with HTML, this is typically a <DIV> tag, as shown in the following code:

```
<div id=mySilverlightControlHost>  </div>
```

The next step is to add an <asp:Silverlight> tag inside the host tag, as shown in the following code:

```
<div  style="height:100%;">
   <asp:Silverlight
      ID="mySilverlightApp"
      runat="server"
      Source="~/ClientBin/SilverlightApplication.xap"
      Version="2.0"
      Width="100%"
      Height="100%" />
</div>
```

211

The `<asp:Silverlight>` tag allows you to define the Silverlight application as an ASP element. You need to still provide the `ID`, `Source`, `Version`, `Width`, and `Height` attributes to configure the Silverlight plug-in. Specifying the `runat="server"` attribute tells the server to render the content at the server before delivering it to the browser. This is discussed in more detail in Chapter 9.

Summary

This chapter has focused on helping you understand the basics of Silverlight application development. We discussed the anatomy of a Silverlight application to help you understand how the Silverlight class, assembly, and package relate to each other. I also discussed how to use library assemblies and resource files to help you develop more robust applications. You also learned how to deploy an application package as an embedded object in a Web page.

In this chapter, you learned how to:

- Create a Silverlight class with code-behind pages
- Build a Silverlight application package
- Deploy Silverlight applications in Web pages

Chapter 8

Programming .NET Silverlight Applications

This chapter covers how to take advantage of the relationship between XAML and code-behind pages to build .NET Silverlight programs. Using .NET languages such as C# and Visual Basic enables you to do almost everything you need to generate impressive interfaces using Silverlight.

This chapter focuses on three main areas to illustrate how to use .NET languages to provide a rich interface for users. The first section covers manipulating the XAML elements programmatically to show you how to use code-behind pages to generate user interface functionality. The next section discusses event handling to handle user and program events to implement a very dynamic user interface. The final section discusses using code-behind pages to create robust functionality in your animations.

Manipulating XAML Elements Programmatically

A very useful feature of code-behind pages when programming .NET Silverlight applications is the ability to access and manipulate the controls defined by XAML elements. XAML is very limited when it comes to providing functionality to a Web site. That is where the code-behind pages come in. With the code-behind pages, you can programmatically access XAML elements to modify the user interface dynamically to provide a much better experience for the user.

The following sections take you through the basics of accessing XAML elements, creating new XAML elements, and deleting existing XAML elements.

Accessing namescoped XAML elements

The first step in accessing XAML element is to give them a name using the x:Name attribute. The x:Name exposes the XAML element as an object in the code-behind page by adding it to the XAML namescope when the XAML is parsed. Objects in the namescope are accessible in the code-behind pages using C# or Visual Basic.

For example, the following XAML TextBlock element uses x:Name="myText" to expose the XAML element:

```
<TextBlock x:Name="myText"
           Text="Some Plain Text"
           HorizontalAlignment="Center"
           VerticalAlignment="Top" />
```

From the code-behind page, you can access the TextBlock element and get the value of the Text attribute by using the following C# code:

```
String textValue = myText.Text;
```

Using this method, you can access almost all attributes, methods, and events of the Silverlight XAML elements.

Modifying existing Silverlight XAML elements

You can also modify the Silverlight XAML elements from code-behind pages by accessing the exposed object. You can change values, add event handlers, and use any of the object's methods. Most of the programming that you do with Silverlight involves using the code-behind pages to manipulate the XAML elements that are rendered to the browser.

Consider the following code in Listing 8.1 of a basic Silverlight XAML file that adds a TextBlock and a Button control to a Grid.

LISTING 8.1

Simple XAML File That Implements the x:Name Attribute to a TextBlock and Button Element

```
<UserControl x:Class="proj0801.Page"
    xmlns="http://schemas.microsoft.com/client/2007"
    xmlns:x="http://schemas.microsoft.com/winfx/2006/xaml"
    Width="400" Height="200">
    <Grid x:Name="LayoutRoot"
          Background="White">
        <TextBlock x:Name="myText"
                   Text="Some Plain Text"
                   HorizontalAlignment="Center"
                   VerticalAlignment="Top" />
```

```
        <Button x:Name="myButton"
                Content="Change Text"
                Height="30"
                Width="80"/>
    </Grid>
</UserControl>
```

The `TextBlock` element is added to the XAML namescope as `myText` and the `Button` is added as `myButton`. Using the C# code-behind file in Listing 8.2, the `TextBlock` control can be modified.

LISTING 8.2

C# Code-Behind File That Accesses the TextBlock XAML Element and Modifies It Dynamically

```csharp
using System;
using System.Windows;
using System.Windows.Controls;
using System.Windows.Input;
using System.Windows.Media;
using System.Windows.Media.Animation;

namespace proj0801
{
    public partial class Page : UserControl
    {
        public Page()
        {
            InitializeComponent();
            myButton.Click += new RoutedEventHandler(myButton_Click);
        }

        void myButton_Click(object sender, RoutedEventArgs e)
        {
            myText.FontFamily = new FontFamily("Comic Sans MS");
            myText.FontSize = 30;
            myText.Text = "Some Cool Text";
            myButton.Content = "Clicked";
        }
    }
}
```

The code in Listing 8.2 is able to implement an event handler for the `Button` element using the following line of code because the `Button` element was added to the `namescope` as `myButton`:

```
myButton.Click += new RoutedEventHandler(myButton_Click);
```

Figure 8.1 shows the results of clicking the button in the Web browser. Inside the event handler for the button, the code in Listing 8.2 is able to modify the `FontFamily`, `FontSize`, and `Text` attributes of the `TextBlock` element and modify the `Content` attribute of the `Button` element using the `myText` and `myButton` names in the namespace.

FIGURE 8.1

Simple Silverlight application that adds a `Button` and `TextBlock` element to the namescope and then modifies them programmatically when the button is clicked

Dynamically adding/removing XAML elements

In addition to modifying existing XAML elements, Silverlight provides the ability to dynamically add and remove elements. This gives you the flexibility to change the complete look and feel of your application during runtime. For example, you could create a Silverlight form element that implements a series of `TextBlock` and `TextBox` elements to collect data and then when the data is entered, remove all of the `TextBlock` and `TextBox` elements and replace them with a rich media view with images and movies.

The following sections describe the process and give an example of creating and removing elements from a Silverlight application.

Dynamically creating XAML elements

The simplest way to create XAML elements is to generate them dynamically in managed code and then add them to an existing XAML element as a child. XAML elements that can contain child elements such as a `Grid` or `Canvas` have a `Children` object as an attribute when they are exposed in the namescope. You can use the `Add` method of the `Children` object to add objects to an existing object.

For example consider the following code that exposes a Canvas object using the name blank-Canvas:

```
<Canvas x:name="blankCanvas" />
```

You could use the following C# code to add a button to the Canvas:

```
Button btn = new Button();
blankCanvas.Children.Add(btn);
```

 The Children.Add() method accepts any object that derives from the UIElement class.

You are responsible for setting any needed attributes of the new object being added to XAML prior to adding it as a child. To illustrate this, consider the code in Listing 8.3.

LISTING 8.3

XAML Code That Defines a Child Grid to the Root Element That Is Used to Create New XAML Objects

```
<UserControl x:Class="proj0802.Page"
    xmlns="http://schemas.microsoft.com/client/2007"
    xmlns:x="http://schemas.microsoft.com/winfx/2006/xaml"
    Width="400"
    Height="300">
    <Grid x:Name="LayoutRoot"
          Background="LightGray">
        <Grid x:Name="playArea"
              VerticalAlignment="Top"
              Height="200"
              Width="400"
              Background="Gray"/>
    </Grid>
</UserControl>
```

The code in Listing 8.3 defines two Grid elements. The first Grid is the root element and is added to the namescope as LayoutRoot. The second Grid element is a child of the first and is added to the namescope as playArea. The C# code-behind page in Listing 8.4 adds an event handler for the playArea Grid that dynamically adds a Rectangle object to the LayoutRoot Grid.

LISTING 8.4

C# Code-Behind File That Adds an Event Handler to a Grid Element and Dynamically Adds Rectangle Objects to Another XAML Grid

```csharp
using System;
using System.Windows;
using System.Windows.Controls;
using System.Windows.Input;
using System.Windows.Media;
using System.Windows.Media.Animation;
using System.Windows.Shapes;

namespace proj0802
{
    public partial class Page : UserControl
    {
        public Page()
        {
            InitializeComponent();

            playArea.MouseLeftButtonUp +=
                new MouseButtonEventHandler(playArea_Add);
        }

        void playArea_Add(object sender, MouseButtonEventArgs e)
        {
            Point location = e.GetPosition(null);
            Rectangle aBlock = new Rectangle();
            aBlock.Height = 40;
            aBlock.Width = 40;
            aBlock.StrokeThickness = 3;
            aBlock.Stroke = new SolidColorBrush(Colors.Blue);
            aBlock.Fill = new SolidColorBrush(Colors.Red);
            aBlock.HorizontalAlignment = HorizontalAlignment.Left;
            aBlock.VerticalAlignment = VerticalAlignment.Top;
            aBlock.Margin = new Thickness(location.X, location.Y, 0, 0);

            LayoutRoot.Children.Add(aBlock);
        }
    }
}
```

The event handler in Listing 8.4 first gets the coordinates of the mouse click from the `MouseEventArgs` parameter to use later when determining the location to place the block. Then it creates a `Rectangle` object. At this point the `Rectangle` object has no color, stroke, or size.

The next few lines of code set the `Height`, `Width`, and `StrokeThickness`. So far, setting the attributes is similar to the XAML definition.

Notice that when it comes to setting the Stroke and Fill for the rectangle, they cannot simply be set as text; instead, a SolidColorBrush object is created with the appropriate color. This is a little different than creating the XAML. The same approach must be taken with the Margin using a Thickness object.

> **CAUTION** When setting attributes in code-behind pages, you need to understand what type is expected. In XAML, everything is a string; in code-behind pages, some values are strings, some are numbers, and some are specific objects.

The HorizontalAlignment and VerticalAlignment attributes are set using HorizontalAlignment and VerticalAlignment objects. These cannot simply be set to "Left" or "Top" strings.

Once the appropriate attributes are set for the Rectangle object, it is added as a child attribute of the Grid element LayoutRoot.

In essence, what has been done is similar to the following XAML code:

```
<Rectangle Height="40"
           Width="40"
           StrokeThickness="3"
           Stroke="Blue"
           Fill="Red"
           VerticalAlignment="Top"
           HorizontalAlignment="Left"
           Margin="20,20,0,0" />
```

Figure 8.2 shows the results of clicking on the playArea Grid object in the Web browser. Inside the event handler for the Grid in Listing 8.4, a new Rectangle object is generated and placed at the coordinates where the mouse is clicked.

FIGURE 8.2

Silverlight application that dynamically adds new rectangle objects to the rendered XAML each time the mouse is clicked

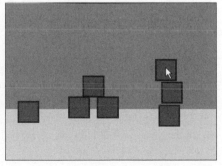

Dynamically deleting XAML elements

Using code-behind pages, you can also dynamically remove XAML elements from an object. This is done by accessing the `Children` attribute of an XAML element that contains child elements. You can use the `Remove` method of the `Children` object to remove child objects from an existing object.

For example, consider the following code that exposes a `Canvas` object using the name `myCanvas`, the canvas contains a child `TextBlock` object name `txtBlock`:

```
<Canvas x:Name="myCanvas">
    <TextBlock x:Name="txtBlock"
               Text="MssEd UP Txt!" />
</Canvas>
```

You could use the following C# code to remove the `TextBlock` element from the `Canvas`:

```
myCanvas.Children.Remove(txtBlock);
```

Using the `Children.Remove()` method, you can remove any object that is a `UIElement` and a child of the current object. To illustrate this further, consider the code in Listing 8.5.

LISTING 8.5

C# Code-Behind File That Adds an Event Handler to a Grid Element and Dynamically Adds Rectangle Objects with Event Handlers That Handle the Removal of the Object

```csharp
using System;
using System.Windows;
using System.Windows.Controls;
using System.Windows.Input;
using System.Windows.Media;
using System.Windows.Media.Animation;
using System.Windows.Shapes;

namespace proj0802
{
    public partial class Page : UserControl
    {
        public Page()
        {
            InitializeComponent();
```

```
        playArea.MouseLeftButtonUp +=
                new MouseButtonEventHandler(playArea_Add);
    }

    void playArea_Add(object sender, MouseButtonEventArgs e)
    {
        Point location = e.GetPosition(null);
        Rectangle aBlock = new Rectangle();
        aBlock.Height = 40;
        aBlock.Width = 40;
        aBlock.StrokeThickness = 3;
        aBlock.Stroke = new SolidColorBrush(Colors.Blue);
        aBlock.Fill = new SolidColorBrush(Colors.Red);
        aBlock.HorizontalAlignment = HorizontalAlignment.Left;
        aBlock.VerticalAlignment = VerticalAlignment.Top;
        aBlock.Margin = new Thickness(location.X, location.Y, 0, 0);
        aBlock.MouseLeftButtonUp +=
                new MouseButtonEventHandler(blockDelete);

        LayoutRoot.Children.Add(aBlock);
    }

    void blockDelete(object sender, MouseButtonEventArgs e)
    {
        Rectangle block = sender as Rectangle;
        LayoutRoot.Children.Remove(block);
    }
  }
}
```

Listing 8.5 adds some additional functionality to that of Listing 8.4. Now when a Rectangle is created, a MouseLeftButtonUp event handler is added before adding it to the root canvas. Inside that event handler, we retrieve the sender as a Rectangle object and then implement the Children.Remove() method to remove the Rectangle that was clicked from the root canvas.

Figure 8.3 shows the results of clicking on Rectangle objects in the Web browser. Inside the event handler for the Rectangle objects in Listing 8.5, the Rectangle is removed from the rendered XAML when you click it with the mouse.

FIGURE 8.3

Silverlight application that removes the added rectangle objects from the rendered XAML each time they are clicked by the mouse

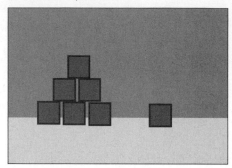 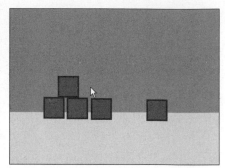

Implementing Event Handling

One of the strengths of Silverlight is how easy it is to implement event handling in applications. Event handling is accomplished by attaching a specific event handler to an object. In Silverlight, this can be done either in the XAML code or in the managed code-behind file.

In XAML, an event handler can be attached to an object by setting the event attribute to the name of the handler function in the code-behind page. For example, the following code attached the `MouseEnterHandler()` function to the `MouseEnter` attribute of a `TextBlock` element:

```
<TextBlock MouseEnter="MouseEnterHandler"/>
```

To attach an event handler in the code-behind page, you need to create a new event handler object and add it to the event handler attribute of the Silverlight control. For example, the following code attached the `myText_MouseLeave()` function to the `MouseLeave` attribute of a `TextBlock` control named `myText`:

```
myText.MouseLeave += new MouseEventHandler(myText_MouseLeave);
```

Listings 8.6 and 8.7 show the full implementation of the `MouseEnter` and `MouseLeave` events in the XAML and C# code-behind files.

LISTING 8.6

XAML File That Attaches a MouseEnter Event Handler to a TextBlock Silverlight Control

```
<UserControl x:Class="proj0803.Page"
    xmlns="http://schemas.microsoft.com/client/2007"
```

```
    xmlns:x="http://schemas.microsoft.com/winfx/2006/xaml"
    Width="400" Height="300" >
    <Grid x:Name="LayoutRoot" Background="White">
        <TextBlock x:Name="myText"
                   Text="Mouse is Gone"
                   MouseEnter="MouseEnterHandler"/>
    </Grid>
</UserControl>
```

LISTING 8.7

C# Code-Behind File That Implements MouseEnter and MouseLeave Event Handlers

```
using System;
using System.Windows;
using System.Windows.Controls;
using System.Windows.Input;

namespace proj0803
{
    public partial class Page : UserControl
    {
        public Page()
        {
            InitializeComponent();
            myText.MouseLeave += new MouseEventHandler(myText_MouseLeave);
        }

        private void MouseEnterHandler(object sender, MouseEventArgs e)
        {
            var txtBlock = sender as TextBlock;
            txtBlock.Text = "Mouse at " +
                            e.GetPosition(LayoutRoot).ToString();
            txtBlock.FontSize = 20;
        }

        void myText_MouseLeave(object sender, MouseEventArgs e)
        {
            myText.Text = "Mouse is Gone";
            myText.FontSize = 10;
        }
    }
}
```

In Listing 8.6, the MouseEnter handler is attached to the MouseEnterHandler function defined in Listing 8.7. The MouseLeave handler is attached in Listing 8.7 using the myText name that was assigned to the TextBlock in Listing 8.6. To attach a mouse leave handler, a new MouseEventHandler object must be created and added to the MouseLeave attribute of the myText TextBlock, as shown in the following line of code from Listing 8.7:

```
myText.MouseLeave += new MouseEventHandler(myText_MouseLeave);
```

Event handler functions can accept two parameters: a sender and an event arguments parameter. The sender parameter should be defined as object type. The event handler passes the object that triggered the event as the sender parameter.

> **TIP** If your handler function does not reference the sender or event arguments parameter, then you do not need to define them as part of the function declaration.

Because the sender parameter is always an object class, you need to cast the sender attribute to the appropriate type prior to using it in the handler. In Listing 8.7, the sender argument must be cast to a TextBlock using the following line of code before setting the Text attribute:

```
var txtBlock = sender as TextBlock;
```

The event argument's parameter type depends on the event for which you are creating the handler. In the Listing 8.7, the event argument's parameter type is MouseEventArgs because the handler is handling a MouseEvent.

The code in Listing 8.7 accesses the MouseEventArgs parameter using the following code to get the coordinates of the mouse when it entered the TextBlock element and include that as part of the string that the TextBlock is set to:

```
e.GetPosition(LayoutRoot).ToString();
```

Figure 8.4 illustrates what happens when the application defined in Listings 8.6 and 8.7 is loaded. When the mouse enters the TextBlock, the Text attribute is set to the position of the mouse, and when the mouse leaves, the Text attribute is modified to reflect that.

FIGURE 8.4

Silverlight application that captures the coordinates of the mouse when it enters a TextBlock and then modifies the text to display those coordinates

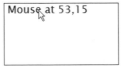

Mouse is Gone

Mouse at 53,15

Mouse is Gone

There are basically two types of events that you deal with in Silverlight applications: events that are triggered by user input and events that are triggered by program events.

Events that are triggered by user input include things such as mouse and keyboard events. Events that are triggered by program events include things such as the page loaded or an animation completed event. Different objects have different events available. The following sections discuss the different types of events and how they work.

Application events

Application events can only be attached to an `Application` class object. There are three application events that apply to three distinct parts of the application lifecycle, the `Startup`, `Stop`, and `UnhandledException` events.

Application events can be defined either in the definition for the `Application` object in the XAML file as shown in the following code:

```
<Application xmlns="http://schemas.microsoft.com/client/2007"
             xmlns:x="http://schemas.microsoft.com/winfx/2006/xaml"
             x:Class="proj0804.App"
             Startup="Application_Startup"
             Exit="Application_Exit"
             UnhandledException="Application_UnhandledException"
             >
    . . .
</Application>
```

Application events can also be defined in the constructor of the `Application` class in the code-behind page, as shown in the following C# example:

```
public App()
{
    this.Startup += this.Application_Startup;
    this.Exit += this.Application_Exit;
    this.UnhandledException += this.Application_UnhandledException;

    InitializeComponent();
}
```

Table 8.1 describes the different types of application events that can be applied to a Silverlight application.

TABLE 8.1

Application Events

Event	Event Arguments	Event Description
Startup	StartupEventArgs	Triggered when the application is first started, before the UI is presented to the user.
Exit	EventArgs	Triggered when the application shuts down due to the browser closing, user navigating to a new page, or a system shutdown. Allows the application to perform any cleanup.
Unhandled-Exception	ApplicationUnhandled ExceptionEventArgs	Triggered when an exception occurs somewhere in the Silverlight application and is not handled. Allows you to provide protection so that the user does not see exception errors in the browser.

CAUTION   Never include long, time-consuming or reentrant code in the `Exit` event handler. This can cause problems for the user when he or she tries to navigate to other pages, reloads the current page, or closes the browser.

Silverlight control events

Silverlight control events include a set of events that can be attached to most of the Silverlight control objects. Silverlight control events are used to handle generic events that occur in every Silverlight control; for example, the `GotFocus` event is used when an element gains focus in the application.

Many of the Silverlight control events are inherited from the `UIElement` class, such as the keyboard, mouse, and focus events. Others are inherited from the `FrameworkElement` class, such as the `Loaded`, `LayoutUpdated`, and `SizeChanged` events.

Table 8.2 describes the different types of control events that can be applied to a Silverlight control.

TABLE 8.2

Silverlight Control Events

Event	Event Handler	Event Description
Loaded	Routed-EventHandler	Triggered when the element has been rendered and is accessible to the user. Child elements with no children are triggered first. This event does not bubble up to parent elements.
GotFocus	Routed-EventHandler	Triggered when the element receives focus. This event can bubble up when multiple handlers are registers for a sequence of elements.

Event	Event Handler	Event Description
LostFocus	Routed-EventHandler	Triggered when the element loses focus. This event can bubble up when multiple handlers are registers for a sequence of elements.
LayoutUpdated	EventHandler	Triggered when the layout of various child elements in the Silverlight application change; for example, a property change, window resize, or user request.
Size-Changed	SizeChanged-EventHandler	Triggered when the ActualHeight or ActualWidth properties of an element changes. This event does not bubble up to parent elements.

A common use of control events is to modify or add things to a Silverlight control after it has been loaded. To show an example of this, Listings 8.8 and 8.9 illustrate an example Silverlight application that dynamically adds 100 buttons to a Grid element after it has been loaded. This is a lot simpler than trying to manually place those buttons in the XAML file.

LISTING 8.8

XAML File That Implements a Simple Grid Control

```
<UserControl x:Class="proj0804.Page"
    xmlns="http://schemas.microsoft.com/client/2007"
    xmlns:x="http://schemas.microsoft.com/winfx/2006/xaml"
    Width="400" Height="300">
    <Grid x:Name="LayoutRoot" Background="White">
        <Crid x:Name="gameBoard"
            Height="200"
            Width="200"
            Background="Gray">
        </Grid>
    </Crid>
</UserControl>
```

LISTING 8.9

C# Code-Behind File That Implements Code to Dynamically Add Button Objects in the Loaded Event for a Grid Object

```
using System;
using System.Windows;
using System.Windows.Controls;
```

continued

LISTING 8.9   *(continued)*

```csharp
using System.Windows.Input;


namespace proj0804
{
    public partial class Page : UserControl
    {
        public Page()
        {
            InitializeComponent();
            //Initialize Control Loaded Event
            gameBoard.Loaded += new RoutedEventHandler(gameBoard_Loaded);
        }

        void gameBoard_Loaded(object sender, RoutedEventArgs e)
        {
            //Add Rows
            for (int y=0; y<10; y++)
            {
                //Add Columns
                for (int x=0; x<10; x++)
                {
                    //Add button
                    Button b = new Button();
                    b.Height = 20;
                    b.Width = 20;
                    b.Margin = new Thickness(x*20, y*20, 0, 0);
                    b.VerticalAlignment = VerticalAlignment.Top;
                    b.HorizontalAlignment = HorizontalAlignment.Left;
                    gameBoard.Children.Add(b);
                }
            }
        }
    }
}
```

The first thing the code in Listing 8.9 does is to implement a loaded event handler, gameBoard_ Loaded, for the Grid control named gameBoard that was defined in Listing 8.8 using the following line of code:

```csharp
gameBoard.Loaded += new RoutedEventHandler(gameBoard_Loaded);
```

In the gameBoard_Loaded() event handler, two for loops are used to construct ten rows of ten button objects and add them to the gameBoard object using the following line of code:

```csharp
gameBoard.Children.Add(b);
```

When the Silverlight application defined in Listings 8.8 and 8.9 is loaded, the event handler for the gameBoard object is called and 100 buttons are dynamically generated, as shown in Figure 8.5.

FIGURE 8.5

Silverlight application that dynamically adds 100 buttons to a Grid object after it has been loaded

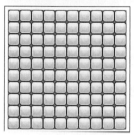

Mouse events

Mouse events include a set of events that can be attached to most of the Silverlight control objects. The mouse events are inherited from the UIElement class. Mouse events are used to handle basic events that occur in the Silverlight control; for example, the MouseEnter event is used to determine when the mouse enters a control as was illustrated earlier in this chapter. You can use mouse events to provide users with a very dynamic and fun interface.

Table 8.3 describes the different types of mouse events that can be applied to a Silverlight control.

TABLE 8.3

Mouse Events

Event	Event Handler	Event Description
MouseEnter	MouseEventHandler	Triggered when mouse enters the bounding area of an element. If both a parent and a child define this event, the parent's handler is called first.
MouseLeave	MouseEventHandler	Triggered when mouse leaves the bounding area of an element. If both a parent and a child define this event, the parent's handler is called first.
MouseLeft-ButtonDown	MouseButton-EventHandler	Triggered when the left button of the mouse is clicked when over the bounding area of the element. This event can bubble up when multiple handlers are registers for a sequence of elements.

continued

TABLE 8.3	(continued)	

Event	Event Handler	Event Description
MouseLeft- ButtonUp	MouseButton- EventHandler	Triggered when the left button of the mouse is released when over the bounding area of the element or while the mouse is captured. This event can bubble up when multiple handlers are registers for a sequence of elements.
MouseMove	MouseEventHandler	Triggered when the coordinate position of the mouse changes. This event can bubble up when multiple handlers are registers for a sequence of elements.

TIP Typically when both the MouseEnter and MouseMove events are used, the MouseMove event is triggered first. However, in the case where the object moves to the location of the mouse or the object is capturing mouse movements during drag-and-drop operations, the MouseEnter event can be triggered without a MouseMove event.

CAUTION The MouseLeave event does not provide information about the location of the mouse in the event arguments parameter because the mouse is out of bounds.

CAUTION The MouseMove event is triggered frequently as the user moves the mouse around the screen. Avoid adding complex or time-consuming code to the MouseMove event handler.

One of the most common uses of mouse events is to add drag-and-drop functionality to applications. The code in Listings 8.10 and 8.11 illustrate an example of adding drag-and-drop functionality to a Silverlight application allowing the user to position three images using the mouse.

LISTING 8.10

XAML File That Implements a Simple Canvas Control and Three Image Controls

```
<UserControl x:Class="proj0805.Page"
    xmlns="http://schemas.microsoft.com/client/2007"
    xmlns:x="http://schemas.microsoft.com/winfx/2006/xaml"
    Width="600" Height="400">
    <Grid x:Name="LayoutRoot" Background="White">
        <Canvas x:Name="myCanvas"
                Background="LightBlue">
            <Image x:Name="Image1"
                Source="/image1.jpg"
                Height="100"
                MouseLeftButtonDown="dragMouseLeftButtonDown"
                MouseLeftButtonUp="dragMouseLeftButtonUp"
                MouseMove="dragMouseMove"/>
```

```
        <Image x:Name="Image2"
                Source="/image2.jpg"
                Height="100"
                MouseLeftButtonDown="dragMouseLeftButtonDown"
                MouseLeftButtonUp="dragMouseLeftButtonUp"
                MouseMove="dragMouseMove"/>
        <Image x:Name="Image3"
                Source="/image3.jpg"
                Height="100"
                MouseLeftButtonDown="dragMouseLeftButtonDown"
                MouseLeftButtonUp="dragMouseLeftButtonUp"
                MouseMove="dragMouseMove"/>
    </Canvas>
  </Grid>
</UserControl>
```

LISTING 8.11

C# Code-Behind File That Implements Drag-and-Drop Handlers for Image Objects

```
using System;
using System.Collections.Generic;
using System.Linq;
using System.Windows;
using System.Windows.Controls;
using System.Windows.Documents;
using System.Windows.Input;
using System.Windows.Media;
using System.Windows.Media.Animation;
using System.Windows.Shapes;

namespace proj0805
{
    public partial class Page : UserControl
    {
        Point lastPosition;
        Boolean isCaptured = false;

        public Page()
        {
            InitializeComponent();
        }

        void dragMouseMove(object sender, MouseEventArgs e)
        {
            var img = sender as Image;
```

continued

LISTING 8.11 *continued*

```
            //Check to see if image is captured
            if (isCaptured)
            {
                //Re-position the Image based on the mouse movement
                double moveX = e.GetPosition(this).X - lastPosition.X;
                double moveY = e.GetPosition(this).Y - lastPosition.Y;
                Canvas.SetTop(img, moveY);
                Canvas.SetLeft(img, moveX);
            }
        }

        void dragMouseLeftButtonUp(object sender, MouseButtonEventArgs e)
        {
            var img = sender as Image;
            //Release capture
            img.ReleaseMouseCapture();
            isCaptured = false;
        }

        void dragMouseLeftButtonDown(object sender, MouseButtonEventArgs e)
        {
            var img = sender as Image;
            //Begin Capture
            lastPosition = e.GetPosition(img);
            isCaptured = true;
            img.CaptureMouse();
        }
    }
}
```

The code in Listing 8.10 defines a Canvas control named myCanvas that is used as the container for an Image object. It also defines three Image controls that each attach to MouseLeftButtonDown, MouseLeftButtonUp, and MouseMove event handlers using the following code:

```
  MouseLeftButtonDown="dragMouseLeftButtonDown"
  MouseLeftButtonUp="dragMouseLeftButtonUp"
  MouseMove="dragMouseMove"/>
```

NOTE By defining the event handlers in the XAML code, you do not need to implement them in the code-behind page. Each `Image` attaches to the same handlers, so the handlers need to be able to handle the `Image` objects generically.

The first thing the code in Listing 8.11 does is to define a `lastPosition` `Point` object to keep track of the last position of the mouse when dragging began. An `isCaptured` `Boolean` is also defined to keep track of whether a dragging operation is currently under way.

The code in Listing 8.11 implements dragging and dropping `Images` objects through a series of three event handlers. Dragging is started in the `MouseLeftButtonDown` handler named `drag-MouseLeftButtonDown()`. Inside this handler, we first get the object that initiated the event and cast it to an `Image` object using the following line of code:

```
var img = sender as Image;
```

To begin dragging, the `lastPosition` is set to the current position of the mouse and `isCaptured` is set to `true`. You should also capture the mouse to the specific `Image` object using the following line of code:

```
img.CaptureMouse();
```

CAUTION If you do not use the `CaptureMouse()` function to capture the mouse to a specific object, you run the risk of losing dragging if the mouse moves faster than the update does.

Once the drag is started, the movement of the object is handled in the `MouseMove` handler named `dragMouseMove()`. The `dragMouseMove()` first checks to see if `isMouseCaptured` is set to `true`, meaning that a drag operation is underway. If a drag is currently underway, then the `Image` object is repositioned in the `Canvas` using the following code:

```
Canvas.SetTop(img, moveY);
Canvas.SetLeft(img, moveX);
```

To stop the drag and drop of the image in the new location, the application uses the `MouseLeftButtonUp` handler named `dragMouseLeftButtonUp()`. Dragging is stopped by setting the `isMouseCaptured` to `false` and executing the `ReleaseMouseCapture()` function of the `Image` object.

When the Silverlight application defined in Listings 8.10 and 8.11 is loaded, three `Image` objects are displayed on top of each other in the top-left corner of the `Canvas`. The images can be repositioned by dragging and dropping them using the mouse, as shown in Figure 8.6.

FIGURE 8.6

Silverlight application that implements drag and drop to position three image files

Keyboard events

Keyboard events include a set of events that can be attached to most of the Silverlight control objects. The keyboard events are inherited from the UIElement class. Keyboard events capture interrupts from the keyboard that occur while the Silverlight control is in focus. For example, the KeyPressed event is used to detect that the user pressed a key. Implementing keyboard events can be critical in adding functionality to your Silverlight applications such as hot keys.

Table 8.4 describes the different types of keyboard events that can be applied to a Silverlight control.

TABLE 8.4

Keyboard Events

Event	Event Handler	Event Description
KeyDown	KeyEvent-EventHandler	Triggered when a keyboard key is pressed while the element is in focus. This event can bubble up when multiple handlers are registers for a sequence of elements.
KeyUp	KeyEvent-EventHandler	Triggered when a keyboard key is released while the element is in focus. This event can bubble up when multiple handlers are registers for a sequence of elements.

 **Keyboard event handling may be different in different browsers. You should test applications that implement keyboard events in all browsers that you plan to support.**

To illustrate an example of using keyboard events in a Silverlight application, Listings 8.12 and 8.13 create an application that implement a KeyDown and KeyUp event to display key text dynamically when a keyboard key is pressed by the user.

LISTING 8.12

XAML File That Implements a TextBlock to Display Key Data Captured from a TextBox Control

```
<UserControl x:Class="proj0806.Page"
    xmlns="http://schemas.microsoft.com/client/2007"
    xmlns:x="http://schemas.microsoft.com/winfx/2006/xaml"
    Width="400" Height="300">
    <Grid x:Name="LayoutRoot" Background="Black">
            <TextBlock x:Name="txt"
                    Foreground="Blue"
                    VerticalAlignment="Center"
                    HorizontalAlignment="Center"/>
            <TextBox x:Name="txtBox"
                    Height="30"
                    Width="30"
                    VerticalAlignment="Bottom"
                    HorizontalAlignment="Center">
            </TextBox>
    </Grid>
</UserControl>
```

LISTING 8.13

C# Code-Behind File That Implements Code Capture Keyboard Input to a TextBox Control and Displays the Key in a TextBlock

```
using System;
using System.Windows;
using System.Windows.Controls;
using System.Windows.Input;

namespace proj0806
{
    public partial class Page : UserControl
    {
        int txtSize = 10;

        public Page()
        {
            InitializeComponent();

            //Implement Key Event Handlers
            txtBox.KeyDown += new KeyEventHandler(myCanvas_KeyDown);
            txtBox.KeyUp += new KeyEventHandler(txtBox_KeyUp);
```

continued

LISTING 8.13   *(continued)*

```
        }

        void myCanvas_KeyDown(object sender, KeyEventArgs e)
        {
            //Capture keyboard input from the KeyDown event
            txt.FontSize = txtSize;
            txt.Text = e.Key.ToString();
            txtBox.Text = "";
            txtSize += 5;
        }

        void txtBox_KeyUp(object sender, KeyEventArgs e)
        {
            //Reset TextBlock
            txt.Text = "";
            txtSize = 10;
        }
    }
}
```

The code in Listing 8.13 first attaches a KeyDown event handler named txtBox_KeyDown()
and a KeyUp event handler named txtBox_KeyUp()to the txtBox TextBox control defined
in Listing 8.12 using the following code:

```
    txtBox.KeyDown += new KeyEventHandler(txtBox_KeyDown);
    txtBox.KeyUp += new KeyEventHandler(txtBox_KeyUp);
```

In the txtBox_KeyDown() event handler, the Text attribute of the txt TextBlock object
defined in Listing 8.12 is set to the string value of the key that is pressed using the following code:

```
    txt.Text = e.Key.ToString();
```

The KeyDown event continues to be triggered over and over again as long as the key is still
pressed. The example shows this by incrementing the size of the text displayed. The longer you
hold down the key, the bigger the text becomes.

The Silverlight application defined in Listings 8.12 and 8.13 captures the key pressed by the user
in the text box and displays the key in the Grid, as shown in Figure 8.7.

FIGURE 8.7

Using keyboard events in a Silverlight application to display characters

Media events

Media events include a set of events that can be attached specifically to Silverlight `MediaElement` control objects. Media events provide extra functionality specific to handling video and audio. Media events provide you with the ability to detect the current state of the `MediaElement` control. For example, the `BufferingProcessChanged` event is used to determine that additional data is received when loading the media file.

Table 8.5 describes the different types of events that can be applied to a Silverlight `MediaElement` control.

TABLE 8.5

Media Events

Event	Event Handler	Event Description
`BufferingProgress-Changed`	`RoutedEvent-Handler`	Triggered when the `BufferingProgress` property of the `MediaElement` changes .05 or more compared to the last time it was raised. It is also triggered when the `BufferingProgress` reaches 1.0, meaning the file is fully buffered.
`CurrentStateChanged`	`RoutedEvent-Handler`	Triggered when the `CurrentState` property of the `MediaElement` changes compared to the last time it was raised; for example, from Playing to Buffering.
`DownloadProgress-Changed`	`RoutedEvent-Handler`	Triggered when the `DownloadProgress` property of the `MediaElement` changes .05 or more compared to the last time it was raised. It is also triggered when the `DownloadProgress` reaches 1.0, meaning the file is fully downloaded.
`MarkerReached`	`TimelineMarker-RoutedEvent-Handler`	Triggered when an embedded timeline marker is reached in the `MediaElement` during playback.

continued

TABLE 8.5	*(continued)*	
Event	**Event Handler**	**Event Description**
`MediaEnded`	`RoutedEvent-Handler`	Triggered when the media playback has ended. If multiple streams are used, the event is only triggered when the last stream has ended.
`MediaFailed`	`EventHandler`	Triggered when an error occurs in relation to the `Source` property of the `MediaElement`; for example, a file is not found or is invalid.
`MediaOpened`	`RoutedEvent-Handler`	Triggered when the media has been validated and opened.

> **TIP** Many properties of the `MediaElement` are not valid until after the `MediaOpened` Event is raised; for example, `BufferingProgress`, `Markers`, and `AudioStreamIndex`.

To illustrate an example of using media events in a Silverlight application, Listings 8.14 and 8.15 implement a `MediaElement` with event handlers attached to play, pause, and stop buttons. They also illustrate the use of using a timer event handler to implement a progress indicator.

LISTING 8.14

XAML File That Defines a MediaElement Control with Playback Button and a Progress Slider Control

```
<UserControl x:Class="proj0807.Page"
    xmlns="http://schemas.microsoft.com/client/2007"
    xmlns:x="http://schemas.microsoft.com/winfx/2006/xaml"
    Width="500" Height="400">
    <Grid x:Name="LayoutRoot" Background="White">
        <Canvas Height="300" Width="300"
                HorizontalAlignment="Center"
                VerticalAlignment="Center">
            <Border Height="300" Width="300"
                    BorderBrush="DarkGray" BorderThickness="6"/>
            <MediaElement x:Name="myMovie"
                    Source="/movie1.wmv"
                    Height="180" Width="240"
                    Canvas.Top="20" Canvas.Left="30"/>
            <TextBlock x:Name="txtPosition"
                    Height="30" Width="60"
                    Canvas.Top="200" Canvas.Left="80"
                    Foreground="White"/>
            <Slider x:Name="timeSlide" Maximum="1"
                    Height="25" Width="210"
                    Canvas.Top="220" Canvas.Left="45" />
            <Button x:Name="playButton" Content="Play"
```

```
                        Height="25"  Width="50"
                        Canvas.Top="260" Canvas.Left="70"/>
            <Button x:Name="pauseButton" Content="Pause"
                        Height="25" Width="50"
                        Canvas.Top="260" Canvas.Left="125"/>
            <Button x:Name="stopButton" Content="Stop"
                        Height="25" Width="50"
                        Canvas.Top="260" Canvas.Left="180"/>
        </Canvas>
    </Grid>
</UserControl>
```

LISTING 8.15

C# Code-Behind File That Uses MediaElement Event Handlers to Implement Playback Controls and a Progress Indicator

```csharp
using System;
using System.Windows;
using System.Windows.Controls;
using System.Windows.Input;
using System.Windows.Media;
using System.Windows.Media.Animation;
using System.Windows.Threading;

namespace proj0807
{
    public partial class Page : UserControl
    {
        DispatcherTimer timer;

        public Page()
        {
            InitializeComponent();
            //Initialize Player Control Event Handlers
            playButton.Click += new RoutedEventHandler(playMovie);
            pauseButton.Click += new RoutedEventHandler(pauseMovie);
            stopButton.Click += new RoutedEventHandler(stopMovie);
            //Initialize Playter Event Handlers
            myMovie.MediaEnded +=
                    new RoutedEventHandler(myMovie_MediaEnded);
            //Initialize Timer
            timer = new DispatcherTimer();
            timer.Interval = new TimeSpan(0, 0, 0, 0, 500);
            timer.Tick += new EventHandler(time_Tick);
            timer.Start();
        }
```

continued

LISTING 8.15   *(continued)*

```
    void time_Tick(object sender, EventArgs e)
    {
        txtPosition.Text = myMovie.Position.ToString();
        timeSlide.Value = myMovie.Position.TotalMilliseconds /
                myMovie.NaturalDuration.TimeSpan.TotalMilliseconds;
    }

    void myMovie_MediaEnded(object sender, RoutedEventArgs e)
    {
        myMovie.Stop();
    }

    void playMovie(object sender, RoutedEventArgs e)
    {
        myMovie.Play();
    }
    void pauseMovie(object sender, RoutedEventArgs e)
    {
        myMovie.Pause();
    }
    void stopMovie(object sender, RoutedEventArgs e)
    {
        myMovie.Stop();
    }
  }
}
```

To define a media player, the code in Listing 8.14 defines a `MediaElement` control to display a movie, three `Button` controls to control playback, and a `Slider` and `TextBlock` control to display progress.

To implement the functionality of the media player, the code in Listing 8.15 first attaches the `playMovie()`, `pauseMovie()`, and `stopMovie()` event handlers to the playback control buttons defined in Listing 8.14. Inside the handlers, the `Play()`, `Pause()`, and `Stop()` functions of the `myMovie MediaElement` object are used to provide the playback functionality.

To reset the playback to the beginning, the code in Listing 8.15 attaches the `MediaEnded` event handler `myMovie_MediaEnded()` event handler to the `myMovie` object using the following code:

```
    myMovie.MediaEnded += new RoutedEventHandler(myMovie_MediaEnded);
```

Inside the `myMovie_MediaEnded()` event handler, the `Stop()` function of the myMovie `MediaElement` object is used to reset the media player to the beginning.

Updating the progress text and slider is accomplished by adding a `DispatcherTimer` named `timer` to the application and attaching a `Tick` event handler named `time_Tick()` using the following code:

```
timer = new DispatcherTimer();
timer.Interval = new TimeSpan(0, 0, 0, 0, 500);
timer.Tick += new EventHandler(time_Tick);
timer.Start()
```

Inside the `time_Tick()` event handler, the `txtPosition` TextBlock and the `timeSlide` Slider controls, as defined in Listing 8.14, are updated each time the timer `Tick` event is triggered using the following lines of code:

```
txtPosition.Text = myMovie.Position.ToString();
timeSlide.Value = myMovie.Position.TotalMilliseconds /
        myMovie.NaturalDuration.TimeSpan.TotalMilliseconds;
```

The Silverlight media player application defined in Listings 8.14 and 8.15 allows a user to play, pause, and stop a movie as well as keep track of playback progress, as shown in Figure 8.8.

FIGURE 8.8

Simple Silverlight media player application that implements playback and progression controls

Other control events

There are several events that are limited to specific Silverlight controls. These events provide functionality specific to the type of control that is being implemented; for example, the `DateSelected` event is used to determine when a date is selected in the Silverlight `Calendar` control.

Table 8.6 describes the different types of special events that can be applied to a specific Silverlight control.

TABLE 8.6

Specific Silverlight Control Events

Event	Silverlight Control	Event Description
CalendarOpened	DatePicker	Triggered when the drop-down calendar is opened in a DatePicker
CalendarClosed	DatePicker	Triggered when the drop-down calendar is closed in a DatePicker
Checked	CheckBox, RadioButton, ToggleButton	Triggered when a CheckBox, RadioButton, or ToggleButton is checked
Click	Button, CheckBox, HyperlinkButton, RadioButton, ToggleButton	Triggered when the mouse is clicked on a Button, CheckBox, HyperlinkButton, RadioButton, or ToggleButton control
Closed	ToolTip	Triggered when the ToolTip is closed
Completed	Animation, Storyboards	Triggered when an Animation or Storyboard object has finished rendering
DisplayDate-Changed	Calendar	Triggered when the DisplayDate property is changed in a Calendar control
DisplayMode-Changed	Calendar	Triggered when the DisplayMode property is changed in a Calendar control
ImageFailed	Image	Triggered when an Image, ImageBrush, or MultiScaleImage fails to load
Indeterminate	CheckBox, RadioButton, ToggleButton	Triggered when the state of a CheckBox, RadioButton, or ToggleButton is neither on nor off
Open	ToolTip	Triggered when the ToolTip is opened
SelectedDates-Changed	Calendar	Triggered when date is selected in a Calendar control
SelectionChanged	ListBox, TextBox	Triggered when a selection of text is changed in a TextBox. Is also triggered when the selection is changed in a ListBox.

Event	Silverlight Control	Event Description
TextChanged	TextBox	Triggered when the Text property is changed in a TextBox
UnChecked	CheckBox, RadioButton, ToggleButton	Triggered when a CheckBox, RadioButton, or ToggleButton is unchecked
ValueChanged	Slider, ScrollBar	Triggered when the Value property of a Slider or ScrollBar control is changed

To illustrate an example of using specific control events in a Silverlight application, Listings 8.16 and 8.17 implement a simple Web form that uses a Calendar, ListBox, and RadioButton controls to input data.

LISTING 8.16

XAML File That Defines a Web Form with TextBox, Calendar, ListBox, and RadioButton Controls

```
<UserControl x:Class="proj0808.Page"
    xmlns="http://schemas.microsoft.com/client/2007"
    xmlns:x="http://schemas.microsoft.com/winfx/2006/xaml"
    Width="500" Height="400">
<Grid x:Name="LayoutRoot" Background="White">
    <Border BorderBrush="DarkBlue" BorderThickness="5"/>

    <TextBlock Text="First:"
                Height="30" Margin="20,30,0,0"
                VerticalAlignment="Top"/>
    <TextBlock Text="Last:"
                Height="30" Margin="20,80,0,0"
                VerticalAlignment="Top"/>
    <TextBlock Text="Date:"
                Height="30" Margin="20,125,0,0"
                VerticalAlignment="Top"/>
    <TextBlock Text="State:"
                Height="30" Margin="20,175,0,0"
                VerticalAlignment="Top"/>

    <TextBox Height="30" Margin="75,25,220,0"
            VerticalAlignment="Top"/>
    <TextBox Height="30" Margin="75,75,220,0"
            VerticalAlignment="Top"/>
    <TextBlock x:Name="txtDate"
```

continued

LISTING 8.16 *(continued)*

```
                    Height="30" Margin="75,125,220,0"
                    VerticalAlignment="Top"/>
        <TextBlock x:Name="txtState"
                    Height="30" Margin="75,175,220,0"
                    VerticalAlignment="Top"/>

        <TextBlock Text="Place:"
                    Height="30" Margin="20,0,0,120"
                    VerticalAlignment="Bottom"/>
        <TextBlock x:Name="txtPlace"
                    Height="30" Margin="75,0,0,120"
                    VerticalAlignment="Bottom"/>

        <Grid Margin="30,0,0,20"
            VerticalAlignment="Bottom" HorizontalAlignment="Left">
            <Border BorderBrush="DarkGray" BorderThickness="3" />
            <StackPanel Height="100" Width="150">
                <RadioButton Click="placeClick"
                            Height="30" Width="100" Content="First"/>
                <RadioButton Click="placeClick"
                            Height="30" Width="100" Content="Second"/>
                <RadioButton Click="placeClick"
                            Height="30" Width="100" Content="Third"/>
            </StackPanel>
        </Grid>

        <Calendar x:Name="myCalendar"
                    Margin="0,10,10,180" Width="200"
                    HorizontalAlignment="Right" />
        <ListBox x:Name="myStateList"
                    Height="120" Width="200" Margin="0,0,10,20"
                    HorizontalAlignment="Right"
                    VerticalAlignment="Bottom">
            <TextBlock Text="California"/>
            <TextBlock Text="Florida"/>
            <TextBlock Text="Texas"/>
            <TextBlock Text="New York"/>
            <TextBlock Text="Utah"/>
            <TextBlock Text="Washington"/>
        </ListBox>
    </Grid>
</UserControl>
```

LISTING 8.17

C# Code-Behind File That Implements Event Handlers to Handle User Input

```csharp
using System;
using System.Windows;
using System.Windows.Controls;
using System.Windows.Input;

namespace proj0808
{
    public partial class Page : UserControl
    {
        public Page()
        {
            InitializeComponent();
            //Initialize Date and State Selection Handlers
            myCalendar.SelectedDatesChanged +=
                new EventHandler< SelectionChangedEventArgs>(dateSelected);
            myStateList.SelectionChanged +=
                new SelectionChangedEventHandler(stateSelected);
        }

        void stateSelected(object sender, SelectionChangedEventArgs e)
        {
            var state = c.AddedItems[0] as TextBlock;
            txtState.Text = state.Text;
        }

        void dateSelected(object sender, SelectionChangedEventArgs e)
        {
            txtDate.Text = string.Format("{0:D}", myCalendar.SelectedDate);
        }

        private void placeClick(object sender, RoutedEventArgs e)
        {
            var btnPlace = sender as RadioButton;
            txtPlace.Text = btnPlace.Content.ToString();
            btnPlace.IsChecked = false;
        }
    }
}
```

The XAML code in Listing 8.16 defines a Web form by implementing a series of `TextBox` and `TextBlock` elements. The data to fill in the `TextBlock` controls are set using a set of `Calendar`, `ListBox`, and `RadioButton` controls also defined in Listing 8.16.

The C# code in Listing 8.17 gathers data from the `Calendar` control named `myCalendar` and the `ListBox` control name `myStateList` by attaching the `dateSelected()` and `stateSelected()` event handlers using the following code:

```
myCalendar.SelectedDatesChanged+=
        new EventHandler<SelectionChangedEventArgs>(dateSelected);
myStateList.SelectionChanged +=
        new SelectionChangedEventHandler(stateSelected);
```

Inside the `SelectedDateChanged` event handler `dateSelected()`, the handler sets the `Text` property of the `txtDate` object using the date from the `SelectedDate` property of the `myCalendar` `Calendar` control.

```
txtDate.Text = String.Format("{0:D}", myCalendar.SelectedDate);
```

The `stateSelected()` event handler in Listing 8.17 casts the first element in the `AddedItems` property of the event argument e to a `TextBlock` object named `state`. The `Text` attribute of `txtState` can then be set as shown in the following code:

```
var state = e.AddedItems[0] as TextBlock;
txtState.Text = state.Text;
```

The event handlers for the radio buttons are handled a bit differently. The `placeClick()` event handler is added to the `RadioButton` controls in the XAML file in Listing 8.16. Then inside the event handler, the event argument e is cast as a `RadioButton` and the `Text` attribute of the `txtPlace` object is set to the value of the `Content` attribute of the `RadioButton` that triggered the event.

```
var btnPlace = sender as RadioButton;
txtPlace.Text = btnPlace.Content.ToString();
```

The Silverlight form application defined in Listings 8.16 and 8.17 allows a user to use `TextBox`, `Calendar`, `ListBox`, and `RadioButton` controls to add data to the form, as shown in Figure 8.9.

FIGURE 8.9

Simple Silverlight form application that implements `TextBox`, `Calendar`, `ListBox`, and `RadioButton` controls

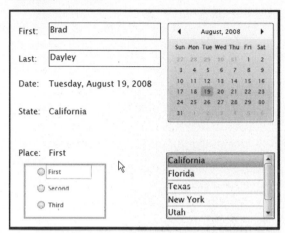

Controlling Animations Programmatically

One of the most dramatic features that Silverlight provides to create rich Internet content is the ability to create and control animations. As you learned in Chapter 3, you can use `Storyboard` and `DoubleAnimation` elements in XAML to animate Silverlight controls. The following sections discuss how to start and stop animations and how to dynamically create animations of objects in code-behind pages.

Starting and stopping the animation

When an animation is started, Silverlight begins rendering the animation as a sequence of frames to the browser based on the duration set in the animation. What is animated is defined by any `DoubleAnimation` or `DoubleAnimationWithKeyFrame` children that belong to the `Storyboard`. Starting and stopping animations is handled through the `Begin()` and `Stop()` functions of a `Storyboard` object. For example, if you define a `Storyboard` with the name `myAnimation`, then the following lines of C# code start the animation:

```
myAnimation.Begin();
```

To stop a `Storyboard` named `myAnimation` that is already rendering, you can use the following line of code:

```
myAnimation.Stop;
```

One of the most common uses of animations is to provide added style to buttons or links when the mouse is over them. The code in Listing 8.18 and 8.19 illustrates two examples of using XAML code to define animations and then using mouse event handlers in the code-behind page to start and stop the animation.

LISTING 8.18

XAML File That Defines a Two-Button Control with Storyboard Animations That Animate the Resize and Opacity Change of a Silverlight Control

```
<UserControl x:Class="proj0809.Page"
    xmlns="http://schemas.microsoft.com/client/2007"
    xmlns:x="http://schemas.microsoft.com/winfx/2006/xaml"
    Width="400" Height="300">
<UserControl.Resources>
    <Storyboard x:Name="FadeIt">
        <DoubleAnimation Storyboard.TargetName="btnFade"
                Storyboard.TargetProperty="(UIElement.Opacity)"
                From=".25" To="1" Duration="00:00:01"/>
    </Storyboard>
    <Storyboard x:Name="SizeIt">
        <DoubleAnimation Storyboard.TargetName="btnSize"
                Storyboard.TargetProperty="(UIElement.RenderTransform).
                (TransformGroup.Children)[0].(ScaleTransform.ScaleX)"
                From="1" To="2" Duration="00:00:01"/>
        <DoubleAnimation Storyboard.TargetName="btnSize"
                Storyboard.TargetProperty="(UIElement.RenderTransform).
                (TransformGroup.Children)[0].(ScaleTransform.ScaleY)"
                From="1" To="2" Duration="00:00:01"/>
    </Storyboard>
</UserControl.Resources>
<Grid x:Name="LayoutRoot" Background="Black">
    <Button x:Name="btnSize" Content="Resize"
            Height="50" Width="150" Margin="100,41,0,0"
            HorizontalAlignment="Left" VerticalAlignment="Top"
            RenderTransformOrigin="0.5,0.5">
        <Button.RenderTransform>
            <TransformGroup>
                <ScaleTransform/>
```

```
                <SkewTransform/>
                <RotateTransform/>
                <TranslateTransform/>
            </TransformGroup>
        </Button.RenderTransform>
    </Button>
    <Button x:Name="btnFade" Content="Fade In"
            Height="50" Width="150" Margin="100,120,0,0"
            HorizontalAlignment="Left"  VerticalAlignment="Top"
            Opacity="0.25"/>
    </Grid>
</UserControl>
```

LISTING 8.19

C# Code-Behind File That Uses Mouse Event Handlers to Start and Stop Button Animation

```
using System;
using System.Windows;
using System.Windows.Controls;
using System.Windows.Input;
using System.Windows.Media;
using System.Windows.Media.Animation;


namespace proj0809
{
    public partial class Page : UserControl
    {
        public Page()
        {
            InitializeComponent();

            //Initialize mouse enter events to begin animation
            btnFade.MouseEnter += new MouseEventHandler(btnFade_MouseEnter);
            btnSize.MouseEnter += new MouseEventHandler(btnSize_MouseEnter);

            //Initialize mouse leave events to stop animation
            btnFade.MouseLeave += new MouseEventHandler(btnFade_MouseLeave);
            btnSize.MouseLeave += new MouseEventHandler(btnSize_MouseLeave);
        }
        void btnSize_MouseEnter(object sender, MouseEventArgs e)
```

continued

LISTING 8.19   *(continued)*

```
    {
        SizeIt.Begin();
    }
    void btnFade_MouseEnter(object sender, MouseEventArgs e)
    {
        FadeIt.Begin();
    }
    void btnSize_MouseLeave(object sender, MouseEventArgs e)
    {
        SizeIt.Stop();
    }
    void btnFade_MouseLeave(object sender, MouseEventArgs e)
    {
        FadeIt.Stop();
    }
  }
}
```

The code in Listing 8.18 defines two Button controls and two Storyboard elements, one for each button. For the Button named btnSize, a Storyboard named SizeIt is defined that implements two DoubleAnimation children to perform scale transforms along the X and Y axis. For the Button named btnFade, a Storyboard named FadeIt is defined that implements a single DoubleAnimation that animates the Opacity attribute of the Button object from .25 to 1.

The animations defined in Listing 8.18 are implemented in Listing 8.19 by adding a MouseEnter and MouseExit event handler to each button. To animate the button when the user moves the mouse over it, the code in Listing 8.19 starts the animation in the MouseEnter event handlers using the following lines of code:

```
SizeIt.Begin();
. . .
FadeIt.Begin();
```

To stop the animation and return the object to a preanimated state when the mouse leaves the button, the code stops the animation in the MouseExit event handlers using the following lines of code:

```
SizeIt.Stop();
. . .
FadeIt.Stop();
```

The Silverlight application defined in Listings 8.18 and 8.19 displays two buttons; when the mouse is navigated over the top button the button resizes, when the mouse is moved over the bottom button the button fades in, as shown in Figure 8.10.

FIGURE 8.10

Simple Silverlight form application that implements two animated buttons

  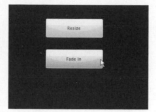

Handling the animation completed event

The Storyboard object provides the Completed event, similar to the Completed event that is provided by the MediaElement control. When the Storyboard is completely rendered, the Completed event is triggered.

The Completed event is very useful when you need to do cleanup work after an event or if you want to run multiple animations in a sequence. For example, consider two Storyboard objects named animateFirst and animateSecond. If you want to run the animations in a sequence one after another, use the following code to add a Completed event handler to the first Storyboard:

```
animateFirst.Completed += new EventHandler(firstCompleted);
```

Inside the firstCompleted event handler, you would then start the second animation using the following code:

```
void firstCompleted(object sender, EventArgs e)
{
    animateSecond.Start();
}
```

Dynamically creating animations in code

Defining animations in XAML works well for most button animations; however, there are times that you want to dynamically create animations in your .NET code. This allows you to reuse the same animation for multiple objects easily and gives you much more flexibility in defining the behavior of the animation. Creating an animation programmatically uses much of the same logic as creating one in XAML. You create a Storyboard object and then add to it DoubleAnimation or DoubleAnimationWithKeyFrame objects that render the animation.

 When adding animations programmatically, write a function that creates a TransformGroup that can be added to the object being animated.

The code in Listings 8.20 and 8.21 shows an example of creating animations in .NET code dynamically and adding them to Image objects that are defined in XAML.

LISTING 8.20

XAML File That Defines Six Image Controls That Are Animated in the Code-Behind File

```xaml
<UserControl x:Class="Proj0810.Page"
    xmlns="http://schemas.microsoft.com/client/2007"
    xmlns:x="http://schemas.microsoft.com/winfx/2006/xaml"
    Width="400" Height="300">
    <Grid x:Name="LayoutRoot" Background="Black">
        <Image x:Name="image1" Source="/test.jpg"
                MouseEnter="imageMouseEnter"
                Height="100" Width="100"
                VerticalAlignment="Top" HorizontalAlignment="Left"
                Margin="40,40,0,0"/>
        <Image x:Name="image2" Source="/test.jpg"
                MouseEnter="imageMouseEnter"
                Height="100" Width="100"
                VerticalAlignment="Top" HorizontalAlignment="Left"
                Margin="140,40,0,0"/>
        <Image x:Name="image3" Source="/test.jpg"
                MouseEnter="imageMouseEnter"
                Height="100" Width="100"
                VerticalAlignment="Top" HorizontalAlignment="Left"
                Margin="240,40,0,0"/>
        <Image x:Name="image4" Source="/test.jpg"
                MouseEnter="imageMouseEnter"
                Height="100" Width="100"
                VerticalAlignment="Top" HorizontalAlignment="Left"
                Margin="40,120,0,0"/>
        <Image x:Name="image5" Source="/test.jpg"
                MouseEnter="imageMouseEnter"
                Height="100" Width="100"
                VerticalAlignment="Top" HorizontalAlignment="Left"
                Margin="140,120,0,0"/>
        <Image x:Name="image6" Source="/test.jpg"
                MouseEnter="imageMouseEnter"
                Height="100" Width="100"
                VerticalAlignment="Top" HorizontalAlignment="Left"
                Margin="240,120,0,0"/>
    </Grid>
</UserControl>
```

LISTING 8.21

C# Code-Behind File That Dynamically Creates Animations and Applies Them to Image Objects

```csharp
using System;
using System.Windows;
using System.Windows.Controls;
using System.Windows.Input;
using System.Windows.Media;
using System.Windows.Media.Animation;

namespace Proj0810
{
    public partial class Page : UserControl
    {
        public Page()
        {
            InitializeComponent();
        }

        TransformGroup makeTG(int x, int y, double angle, double scale)
        {
            TransformGroup tg = new TransformGroup();
            TranslateTransform transT = new TranslateTransform();
            transT.X = x;
            transT.Y = y;
            tg.Children.Add(transT);

            ScaleTransform scaleT = new ScaleTransform();
            scaleT.ScaleX = scale;
            scaleT.ScaleY = scale;
            tg.Children.Add(scaleT);

            RotateTransform rotateT = new RotateTransform();
            rotateT.CenterX = transT.X;
            rotateT.CenterY = transT.Y;
            rotateT.Angle = angle;
            tg.Children.Add(rotateT);
            return tg;
        }

        void initAnimation(Image img)
        {
            //Set animation duration
            Duration duration = new Duration(TimeSpan.FromSeconds(1));
```

continued

LISTING 8.21 *(continued)*

```
//Add transform group
img.RenderTransform = makeTG(0, 0, 0, 1);
img.RenderTransformOrigin = new Point(0.5, 0.5);

//Create Storyboard
Storyboard story = new Storyboard();
story.AutoReverse = true;
string storyName = "story_" + img.Name;
if (LayoutRoot.Resources[storyName] == null) //First time
{
    LayoutRoot.Resources.Add(storyName, story);
    story.Completed += new EventHandler(story_Completed);
}
else //story already exists
{
    story = LayoutRoot.Resources[storyName] as Storyboard;
    story.Stop();
    story.Children.Clear();
}

//Scale X to flip image
DoubleAnimation scaleX = new DoubleAnimation();
story.Children.Add(scaleX);
scaleX.To = -1;
scaleX.Duration = duration;
Storyboard.SetTarget(scaleX, img);
PropertyPath pPath = new PropertyPath(
    "(UIElement.RenderTransform)." +
    "(TransformGroup.Children)[1]." +
    "(ScaleTransform.ScaleX)");
Storyboard.SetTargetProperty(scaleX, pPath
);

//Rotate
DoubleAnimation rotate = new DoubleAnimation();
story.Children.Add(rotate);
rotate.To = 360;
rotate.Duration = duration;
Storyboard.SetTarget(rotate, img);
pPath = new PropertyPath(
    "(UIElement.RenderTransform)." +
    "(TransformGroup.Children)[2]." +
    "(RotateTransform.Angle)");
Storyboard.SetTargetProperty(rotate, pPath
);

story.Begin();
}
```

```
void story_Completed(object sender, EventArgs e)
{
    var story = sender as Storyboard;
    story.Stop();
}

void imageMouseEnter(object sender, MouseEventArgs e)
{
    var img = sender as Image;
    initAnimation(img);
}
}
}
```

The code in Listing 8.20 simply implements six Button controls that attach to a MouseEnter event handler named imageMouseEnter() that implemented in Listing 8.21.

In Listing 8.21, the imageMouseEnter() handler function calls the initAnimation() function that creates and starts an animation on the Image control that triggered the event.

To create the animation, the function first creates a Duration object that can be applied to all animations in the Storyboard. Then a TransformGroup is created and attached to the Image control using the following line of code that calls the makeTG() function defined earlier in the code:

```
img.RenderTransform = makeTG(0, 0, 0, 1);
```

Next, the origin of the transform is set to the center of the Image object using the following line of code:

```
img.RenderTransformOrigin = new Point(0.5, 0.5);
```

The next lines of code create a Storyboard object that is named after the Image object name, and if it hasn't already been added to the RootLayout object the Storyboard is added as a Resource using the following line of code:

```
LayoutRoot.Resources.Add(storyName, story);
```

If, however, the Storyboard has already been added to the RootLayout object, then it is stopped and any children are removed using the following lines of code:

```
story = LayoutRoot.Resources[storyName] as Storyboard;
story.Stop();
story.Children.Clear();
```

The next lines of code create a `DoubleAnimation` named `scaleX` that is added to the `Storyboard` as a child. The `To` attribute of the `DoubleAnimation` object is set to -1, meaning flip the object on the X scale, and the `Duration` attribute is set to `duration`. The `SetTarget()` function is used to set the `Image` object as the target for the animation, and the `SetTargetProperty()` function is used to set property that is animated to `ScaleTransform.ScaleX` using the following lines of code:

```
Storyboard.SetTarget(scaleX, img);
PropertyPath pPath = new PropertyPath(
             "(UIElement.RenderTransform)." +
             "(TransformGroup.Children)[1]." +
             "(ScaleTransform.ScaleX)");
Storyboard.SetTargetProperty(scaleX, pPath);
```

The next lines of code create a `DoubleAnimation` named `rotate` that is added to the `Storyboard` as a child. The `To` attribute of the `DoubleAnimation` object is set to 360 degrees, meaning completely rotate the object, and the `Duration` attribute is set to `duration`. The `SetTarget()` function is used to set the `Image` object as the target for the animation, and the `SetTargetProperty()` function is used to set property that is animated to `RotateTransform.Angle` using the following lines of code:

```
Storyboard.SetTarget(rotate, img);
pPath = new PropertyPath(
             "(UIElement.RenderTransform)." +
             "(TransformGroup.Children)[2]." +
             "(RotateTransform.Angle)");
Storyboard.SetTargetProperty(rotate, pPath);
```

The Storyboard is then started using the following command:

```
story.Begin();
```

The `story_Completed()` event handler is implemented to stop the animation when the Storyboard is first added to the `RootLayout` object using the following line of code:

```
story.Completed += new EventHandler(story_Completed);
```

The Silverlight application defined in Listings 8.20 and 8.21 displays six images. When the mouse is navigated over an image, an animation is created and rendered that rotates and flips the image, as shown in Figure 8.11.

FIGURE 8.11

Silverlight application that implements animations on images when the mouse is moved over them

Implementing Multiscale Images in Silverlight Applications

In Chapter 5, we discussed how to use Deep Zoom Composer to encode and generate a multiscale image. This section discusses how to actually implement a multiscale image in a Silverlight application. Silverlight provides the `MultiScaleImage` control to implement multiscale images in Silverlight applications.

The `MultiScaleImage` control allows you to use the XML and image output from Deep Zoom Composer to implement high-resolution images in your Silverlight applications that users can zoom in and out on.

Multiscale images are implemented in XAML by designing a `MultiScaleImage` control, for example:

```
<MultiScaleImage x:Name="msi"
                 UseSprings = "False"
                 Source="GeneratedImages/dzc_output.xml"
                 height="480" Width="640"/>
```

The `Source` attribute of the `MultiScaleImage` control points to the location of the XML file that describes the image files that make up the multiscale image. This file is automatically generated by Deep Zoom Composer when you create the multiscale image. The `UseSprings` property tells Silverlight whether to use animations when rendering changes to size or position of the image.

The `MultiScaleImage` control is similar to an `Image` control with a few important additions. The `MultiScaleImage` provides the `ViewportHeight` and `ViewportWidth` properties that set the height and width of the rendered multiscale image. The `ViewPortOrigin` property specifies `Point` object that determines the center coordinates used when rendering the multiscale image. For example, the following code sets the center of the `ViewPortOrigin` property to the center of the multiscale image:

```
msImage.ViewportOrigin = new Point(0, 0);
```

The `MultiScaleImage` also provides the function `ZoomAboutLogicalPoint()` that adjusts the zoom factor and `ViewPortOrigin` and re-renders the `MultiScaleImage`. The function accepts a zoom factor, where 1 is actual size, as the first argument, a `double` specifying the x offset from center as the second, and a `double` specifying the y offset from center as the third. For example, the following code sets the zoom factor to 50 percent and renders the multiscale image with a `ViewPortOrigin` 100 pixels to the right and 50 pixels down from the center of the multiscale image:

```
Point p = new Point(0, 0);
msImage.ZoomAboutLogicalPoint(.5, 100, -50);
```

The code in Listings 8.22, 8.23, and 8.24 shows an example of implementing a `MultiScaleImage` control in a Silverlight application. Most of the code in Listings 8.22 and 8.23, as well as all of the code in Listing 8.24, was generated using the Export Images and Silverlight Project option in Deep Zoom Composer. The GeneratedImages folder and contents need to be placed in the ClientBin directory of the Visual Studio project for the image to render when you are testing and will also need to be deployed with the project.

The code in Listing 8.22 implements a `MultiScaleImage` control named `msi`, a `TextBlock` control named `loadText`, and three `Button` controls named `inBtn`, `outBtn`, and `allBtn`.

LISTING 8.22

XAML Code Defining a MultiScaleImage Control

```xaml
<UserControl x:Class="multiScale.Page"
    xmlns="http://schemas.microsoft.com/winfx/2006/xaml/presentation"
    xmlns:x="http://schemas.microsoft.com/winfx/2006/xaml"
    Width="660" Height="580">
    <Grid x:Name="LayoutRoot" Background="#FFFFFFFF">
        <Border BorderThickness="1,1,1,1"
                Margin="10,10,10,100"
                BorderBrush="#FF9F9F9F">
            <MultiScaleImage x:Name="msi" UseSprings="False"
                             MinHeight="480"
                             MinWidth="640"
                             Height="480"
                             Width="640"/>
        </Border>
        <TextBlock x:Name="loadText" Text="Loading . . ."
                   HorizontalAlignment="Center"
                   VerticalAlignment="Bottom"
                   Margin="0, 0, 0, 60"/>
        <Button x:Name="inBtn" Content="Zoom In"
                HorizontalAlignment="Center"
                VerticalAlignment="Bottom"
                Margin="0, 0, 200, 10"
                Height="30" Width="100"/>
        <Button x:Name="allBtn" Content="Show All"
                HorizontalAlignment="Center"
                VerticalAlignment="Bottom"
                Margin="0, 0, 0, 10"
                Height="30" Width="100"/>
        <Button x:Name="outBtn" Content="Zoom Out"
                HorizontalAlignment="Center"
                VerticalAlignment="Bottom"
                Margin="0, 0, -200, 10"
                Height="30" Width="100"/>
    </Grid>
</UserControl>
```

The code in Listing 8.23 provides the functionality to zoom in an out on the multiscale image. In the Page() constructor, the code sets the Source attribute of the msi object to the GeneratedImages/dzc_output.xml file that was created by Deep Zoom Composer. Next, the code attaches the msi_Loaded and msi_ImageOpenSucceeded event handlers to the Loaded and ImageOpenSucceeded events of the msi object using the following code:

```
this.msi.Loaded += new RoutedEventHandler(msi_Loaded);
this.msi.ImageOpenSucceeded +=
                    new RoutedEventHandler(msi_ImageOpenSucceeded);
```

Then the code attaches the zoomInClick, zoomOutClick, and ShowAllClick event handlers to the inBtn, outBtn, and allBtn Click events.

The rest of the Page() constructor attaches delegate functions for mouse events that allow multi-scaled images to be dragged and resized using the mouse and mouse wheel. This code is generated by Deep Zoom Composer; however, you can easily modify any of it to adjust behavior for your application.

The msi_ImageOpenSucceeded() event handler uses the SubImages property of the MultiScaleImage to iterate through the subimages in the collection. If you specified the Export as Collection option, then the subimages of the multiscale image can be accessed in using the SubImages property. The code simply sets the Text attribute of the loadText control when the multiscale image has been opened successfully.

The msi_Loaded() event handler simply sets the zoom factor to .5 for the image and the ViewPointOrigin to the center when the image is loaded using the Zoom() function. The Zoom() function accepts a double that specifies the zoom factor and a Point that specifies the coordinate in the MultiScaleImage object to use for the ViewPointOrigin. The actual coordinate needs to be translated to a logical coordinate inside the multiscale image. This is done using the ElementToLogicalPoint() function as shown below:

```
Point logicalPoint = this.msi.ElementToLogicalPoint(pointToZoom);
```

The code renders the desired zoom on the multiscale image using the ZoomAboutLogicalPoint() function of the MultiScaleImage object as shown below:

```
this.msi.ZoomAboutLogicalPoint(zoom, logicalPoint.X, logicalPoint.Y);
```

The code in the ShowAllClick() handler sets the ViewPointOrigin to the center of the multiscale image. The ViewPortWidth is set to 1 to reset the view port to the full size of the MultiScaleImage control. Then the ZoomFactor is set to 1, which resets the image view to the full multiscale image.

The zoomInClick() handler uses the Zoom() function to set the zoom factor to 1.2 of the current size and the x and y offsets to half the width and height of the current size. The zoomOutClick() handler uses the Zoom() function to set the zoom factor to .8 of the current size and the x and y offsets to half the width and height of the current size.

LISTING 8.23

C# Code That Implements MultiScaleImage Zooming Functionality

```csharp
using System;
using System.Collections.Generic;
using System.Linq;
using System.Net;
using System.Windows;
using System.Windows.Controls;
using System.Windows.Documents;
using System.Windows.Input;
using System.Windows.Media;
using System.Windows.Media.Animation;
using System.Windows.Shapes;

namespace multiScale
{
    public partial class Page : UserControl
    {
        //
        // Based on prior work done by
        // Lutz Gerhard, Peter Blois, and Scott Hanselman
        //
        Point lastMousePos = new Point();

        double _zoom = 1;
        bool mouseButtonPressed = false;
        bool mouseIsDragging = false;
        Point dragOffset;
        Point currentPosition;

        public double ZoomFactor
        {
            get { return _zoom; }
            set { _zoom = value; }
        }

        public Page()
        {
            InitializeComponent();

            //Sets the MultiScale Image Source
            this.msi.Source =
                new DeepZoomImageTileSource(
                    new Uri("GeneratedImages/dzc_output.xml",
                        UriKind.Relative));

            this.msi.Loaded += new RoutedEventHandler(msi_Loaded);
```

continued

LISTING 8.23 *(continued)*

```
this.msi.ImageOpenSucceeded +=
    new RoutedEventHandler(msi_ImageOpenSucceeded);

inBtn.Click += new RoutedEventHandler(zoomInClick);
allBtn.Click += new RoutedEventHandler(ShowAllClick);
outBtn.Click += new RoutedEventHandler(zoomOutClick);

//Events implemented by DeepZoomComposer
this.MouseMove += delegate(object sender, MouseEventArgs e)
{
    if (mouseButtonPressed)
    {
        mouseIsDragging = true;
    }
    this.lastMousePos = e.GetPosition(this.msi);
};

this.MouseLeftButtonDown +=
    delegate(object sender, MouseButtonEventArgs e)
{
    mouseButtonPressed = true;
    mouseIsDragging = false;
    dragOffset = e.GetPosition(this);
    currentPosition = msi.ViewportOrigin;
};

this.msi.MouseLeave +=
    delegate(object sender, MouseEventArgs e)
{
    mouseIsDragging = false;
};

this.MouseLeftButtonUp +=
    delegate(object sender, MouseButtonEventArgs e)
{
    mouseButtonPressed = false;
    if (mouseIsDragging == false)
    {
        bool shiftDown =
            (Keyboard.Modifiers & ModifierKeys.Shift) ==
            ModifierKeys.Shift;

        ZoomFactor = 2.0;
        if (shiftDown) ZoomFactor = 0.5;
        Zoom(ZoomFactor, this.lastMousePos);
    }
    mouseIsDragging = false;
};
```

```
        this.MouseMove += delegate(object sender, MouseEventArgs e)
        {
            if (mouseIsDragging)
            {
                Point newOrigin = new Point();
                newOrigin.X = currentPosition.X -
                    (((e.GetPosition(msi).X - dragOffset.X) /
                    msi.ActualWidth) * msi.ViewportWidth);
                newOrigin.Y = currentPosition.Y -
                    (((e.GetPosition(msi).Y - dragOffset.Y) /
                    msi.ActualHeight) * msi.ViewportWidth);
                msi.ViewportOrigin = newOrigin;
            }
        };

        new MouseWheelHelper(this).Moved +=
            delegate(object sender, MouseWheelEventArgs e)
        {
            e.Handled = true;
            if (e.Delta > 0)
                ZoomFactor = 1.2;
            else
                ZoomFactor = .80;

            Zoom(ZoomFactor, this.lastMousePos);
        };
}

void msi_ImageOpenSucceeded(object sender, RoutedEventArgs e)
{
    //If collection, SubImages list of all MultiScaleSubImages
    int x=0;
    foreach (MultiScaleSubImage subImage in msi.SubImages)
    {
        x++;
    }
    loadText.Text = "Loaded " + x + " sub-images.";
}

void msi_Loaded(object sender, RoutedEventArgs e)
{
    Zoom(.5, new Point(0 , 0));
}

public void Zoom(double zoom, Point pointToZoom)
{
    Point logicalPoint =
        this.msi.ElementToLogicalPoint(pointToZoom);
    this.msi.ZoomAboutLogicalPoint(zoom, logicalPoint.X,
```

continued

263

LISTING 8.23   *(continued)*

```
                                              logicalPoint.Y);
        }

        private void ShowAllClick(object sender, RoutedEventArgs e)
        {
            this.msi.ViewportOrigin = new Point(0, 0);
            this.msi.ViewportWidth = 1;
            ZoomFactor = 1;
        }

        private void zoomInClick(object sender, RoutedEventArgs e)
        {
            Zoom(1.2, new Point(this.ActualWidth / 2,
                this.ActualHeight / 2));
        }

        private void zoomOutClick(object sender, RoutedEventArgs e)
        {
            Zoom(.8, new Point(this.ActualWidth / 2,
                this.ActualHeight / 2));
        }
    }
}
```

The code in Listing 8.24 is a C# helper file that is generated by Deep Zoom Composer to provide mouse wheel event support that is used in Listing 8.23.

LISTING 8.24

C# File That Implements Mouse Wheel Event Handling Functionality

```
using System;
using System.Net;
using System.Windows;
using System.Windows.Controls;
using System.Windows.Documents;
using System.Windows.Ink;
using System.Windows.Input;
using System.Windows.Media;
using System.Windows.Media.Animation;
using System.Windows.Shapes;
using System.Windows.Browser;
```

```
namespace multiScale
{
    // Courtesy of Pete Blois
    public class MouseWheelEventArgs : EventArgs
    {
        private double delta;
        private bool handled = false;

        public MouseWheelEventArgs(double delta)
        {
            this.delta = delta;
        }

        public double Delta
        {
            get { return this.delta; }
        }

        // Use handled to prevent the default browser behavior!
        public bool Handled
        {
            get { return this.handled; }
            set { this.handled = value; }
        }
    }

    public class MouseWheelHelper
    {

        public event EventHandler<MouseWheelEventArgs> Moved;
        private static Worker worker;
        private bool isMouseOver = false;

        public MouseWheelHelper(FrameworkElement element)
        {

            if (MouseWheelHelper.worker == null)
                MouseWheelHelper.worker = new Worker();

            MouseWheelHelper.worker.Moved += this.HandleMouseWheel;

            element.MouseEnter += this.HandleMouseEnter;
            element.MouseLeave += this.HandleMouseLeave;
            element.MouseMove += this.HandleMouseMove;
        }
```

continued

LISTING 8.24   *(continued)*

```
private void HandleMouseWheel(object sender,
                             MouseWheelEventArgs args)
{
    if (this.isMouseOver)
        this.Moved(this, args);
}

private void HandleMouseEnter(object sender, EventArgs e)
{
    this.isMouseOver = true;
}

private void HandleMouseLeave(object sender, EventArgs e)
{
    this.isMouseOver = false;
}

private void HandleMouseMove(object sender, EventArgs e)
{
    this.isMouseOver = true;
}

private class Worker
{

    public event EventHandler<MouseWheelEventArgs> Moved;

    public Worker()
    {

        if (HtmlPage.IsEnabled)
        {
            HtmlPage.Window.AttachEvent("DOMMouseScroll",
                                    this.HandleMouseWheel);
            HtmlPage.Window.AttachEvent("onmousewheel",
                                    this.HandleMouseWheel);
            HtmlPage.Document.AttachEvent("onmousewheel",
                                    this.HandleMouseWheel);
        }

    }

    private void HandleMouseWheel(object sender, HtmlEventArgs args)
```

```
        {
            double delta = 0;

            ScriptObject eventObj = args.EventObject;

            if (eventObj.GetProperty("wheelDelta") != null)
            {
                delta =
            ((double)eventObj.GetProperty("wheelDelta"))/120;


                if (HtmlPage.Window.GetProperty("opera") != null)
                    delta = -delta;
            }
            else if (eventObj.GetProperty("detail") != null)
            {
                delta = -((double)eventObj.GetProperty("detail")) / 3;

                if (HtmlPage.BrowserInformation.UserAgent.IndexOf(
                                            "Macintosh") != -1)
                    delta = delta * 3;
            }

            if (delta != 0 && this.Moved != null)
            {
                MouseWheelEventArgs wheelArgs =
                    new MouseWheelEventArgs(delta);
                this.Moved(this, wheelArgs);

                if (wheelArgs.Handled)
                    args.PreventDefault();
            }
        }
    }
  }
}
```

The results of the application defined in Listings 8.22, 8.23, and 8.24 are shown in Figure 8.12. When the application starts, the multiscale image is loaded, the text of the loadText control is loaded, and the image can be resized using the button controls and the mouse.

FIGURE 8.12

Silverlight application that implements a `MultiScaleImage` control to dynamically resize a high resolution image

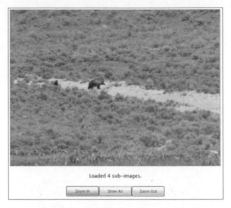

Summary

In this chapter, we first discussed how to access the XAML elements in your .NET code using their namescope names. Then we covered adding and removing XAML objects using code-behind pages. Next, we covered the various types of event handlers and how to use them to implement mouse and keyboard events as well as handling program events such as the `MediaElement` `Completed` event. Finally, we discussed how to use .NET code to control and create animations for objects.

In this chapter, you learned how to:

- Access an XAML object in the namescope
- Add and remove XAML objects using .NET code
- Implement application events
- Implement control events
- Implement mouse and keyboard events
- Implement drag-and-drop functionality
- Create animations dynamically
- Implement Deep Zoom images to Silverlight applications

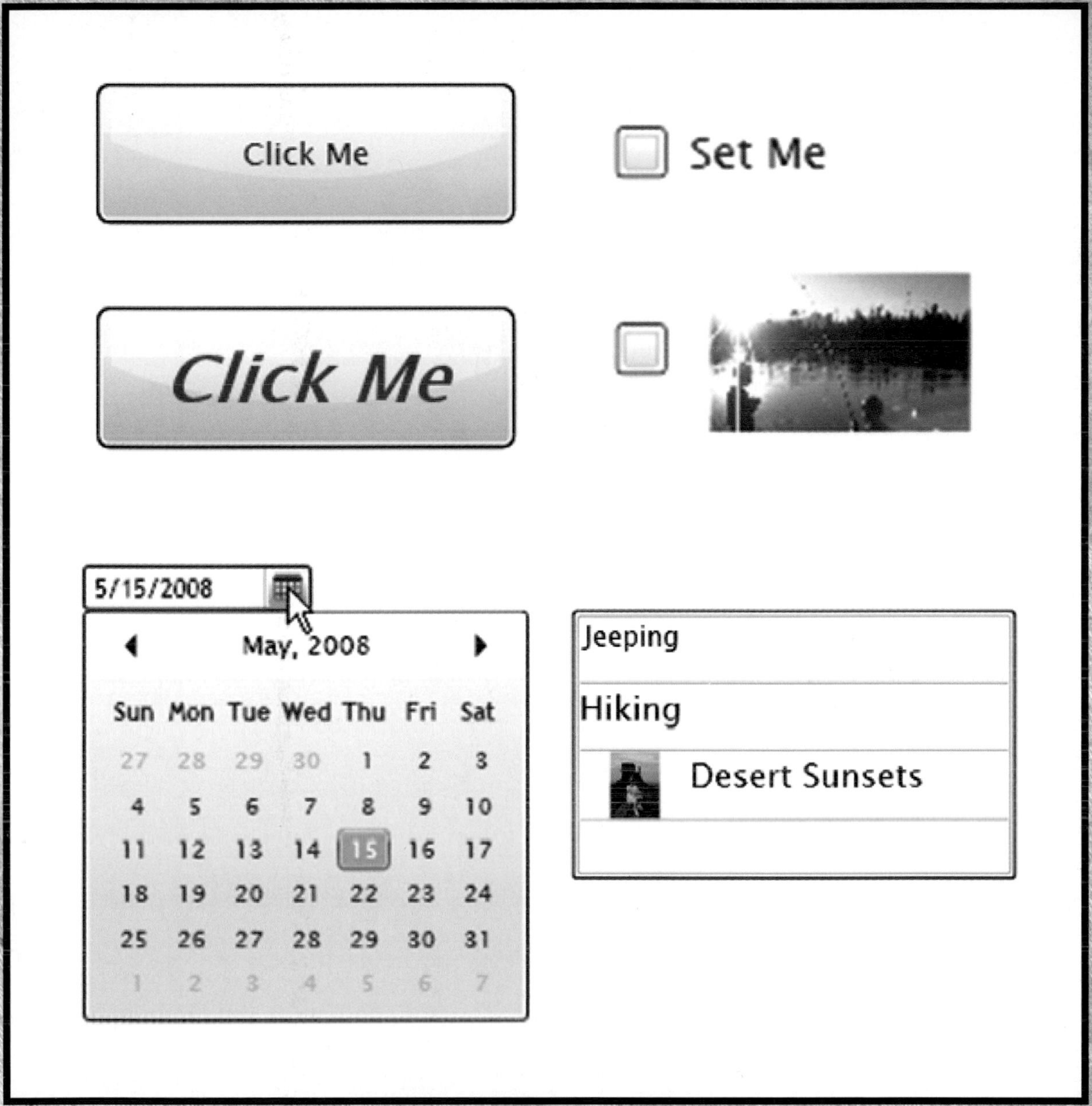

Click Me

Set Me

Click Me

5/15/2008

◀		May, 2008				▶
Sun	Mon	Tue	Wed	Thu	Fri	Sat
27	28	29	30	1	2	3
4	5	6	7	8	9	10
11	12	13	14	15	16	17
18	19	20	21	22	23	24
25	26	27	28	29	30	31
1	2	3	4	5	6	7

Jeeping

Hiking

Desert Sunsets

Silverlight enables developers to quickly add a wide variety of controls to their Web applications. Silverlight uses a subset of the Windows Presentation Foundation to provide elements such as buttons, calendars, list boxes, data grids, and other controls. Chapter 3 discusses adding these controls in Silverlight applications.

One of the best features of Silverlight is that it enables the designer to apply custom transformations on UI elements during the design phase and at runtime. The appearance of UI elements can be adjusted by applying transformations such as rotation, skew, size, and opacity.

Silverlight provides additional controls that can be used to help designers and developers lay out applications. These controls offer developers the option to use grid, panel, and tab methods to organize UI elements in their applications. Chapter 3 discusses using these layout controls to align and organize the UI controls in applications.

Describe the Image

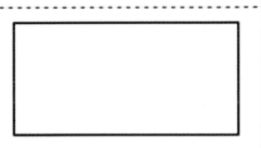

With the powerful design capability of Silverlight, it is easy to create special effects that will give Web applications a rich look and feel. Using the concepts discussed in Chapter 3, developers will be able to implement special effects such as adding reflections to images.

Adding custom brushes to UI elements enables designers to change the look and feel of UI controls. Solid, gradient, and custom brushes can be used to adjust aspects of UI elements such as borders, backgrounds, and foregrounds. For example, adding a gradient brush to a simple ellipse can give it a completely different look.

Expression Blend is a powerful tool that will speed up the design and layout of Silverlight applications. UI elements can quickly be added to Silverlight applications and their appearance and position adjusted using the mouse. Chapter 4 discusses using Expression Blend to create and lay out Silverlight applications.

Expression Blend also provides a graphical interface to create and design animations. UI elements can be adjusted on a series of key frames to create an animation by using the animation timeline in Expression Blend. Chapter 4 discusses how to implement animation of UI elements using Expression Blend.

A great feature of Silverlight is that XAML is based on vector graphics. Therefore, vector art of almost any format can be imported into Expression Design and then exported as XAML code. The XAML code can then be added to Silverlight applications. This enables designers and developers to make use of already existing vector art in their Web applications. Chapter 4 discusses the process of importing vector art into Silverlight applications using Expression Design and Expression Blend.

A big challenge when developing Web applications that use media files is getting the files into the appropriate size and format. Also, Silverlight is fairly limited in the media file types that it can implement. Expression Encoder solves these two problems. Almost any type of media file can be imported into Expression Encoder. The size, quality, metadata, and other properties of the media can then be adjusted and encoded into a format that can be consumed by Silverlight applications. Chapter 5 discusses how to encode media using Expression Encoder.

A powerful feature of Silverlight is the ability to apply templates to controls. One of the most useful templates is the video player template. Chapter 5 discusses how to add video player templates to Silverlight projects.

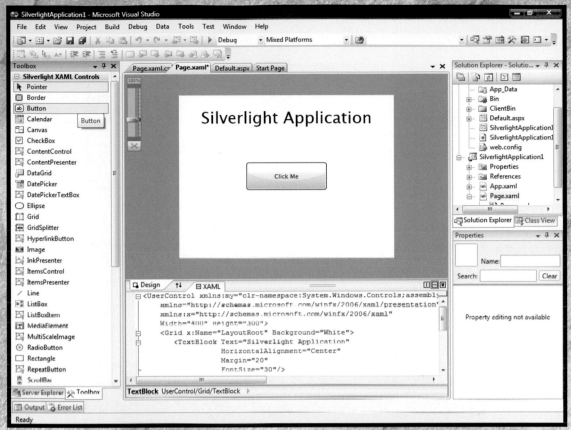

Microsoft has added a lot of capability to Visual Studio to support developing Silverlight applications and libraries. Chapter 6 discusses how to get started with Visual Studio to create Silverlight applications.

Silverlight controls provide a rich set of events that can be used to provide robust functionality to Web applications. These events provide a means of handling user input, monitoring progress of downloads, and much more. Chapter 8 discusses using events to handle keyboard and mouse input into Web applications.

One of the most important capabilities of Silverlight is that it enables developers to easily create XAML and manipulate elements during runtime from managed code. This allows Web applications to be highly interactive with users. Chapter 8 discusses how to add, modify, and remove UI elements in Silverlight applications.

Using the Silverlight mouse events, developers can implement rich animations to UI elements that provide a professional, next-generation look and feel to Web applications. Chapter 8 discusses how to use mouse and animation events to animate images and other controls.

Silverlight provides a JavaScript library that enables developers to quickly implement functionality to Silverlight applications using unmanaged JavaScript. Chapter 9 discusses how to use JavaScript to add XAML elements to Silverlight applications dynamically.

Using unmanaged JavaScript, developers can also load content into Silverlight applications on demand. Chapter 9 also discusses the process of loading images and other content into Silverlight applications using unmanaged JavaScript.

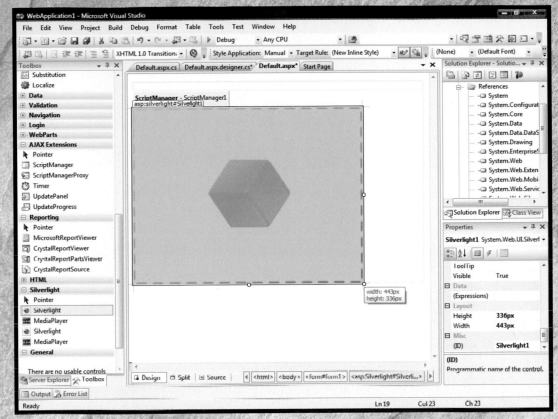

Visual Studio provides the ability to quickly add a Silverlight application to an existing ASP.NET Web application. This enables developers to implement rich Silverlight UI features to existing ASP.NET applications. Chapter 10 discusses using Visual Studio to implement Silverlight in ASP.NET AJAX applications.

The ability to integrate with ASP.NET applications opens a big window to access a variety of Web services. Chapter 10 discusses implementing a Silverlight application using ASP.NET AJAX to access a remote WSDL service.

Using the ASP.NET AJAX extensions for Silverlight also enables developers to quickly add rich, fully functional media players to their Web pages. Chapter 10 discusses the process of using the ASP.NET Silverlight media control to add a movie player to an ASP.NET Web page.

Silverlight DLR Application

Welcome to IronPython Sudoku

7	8		3			9		
			9			3	1	
				6	1			2
	6			1	8		3	
1		2				8		4
	7		5	9			6	
2			7	8				
	4	7			3			
		5			6		8	7

Started

Silverlight provides a Dynamic Language Runtime (DLR) library that allows developers to use Python, Ruby, and managed JavaScript to provide the backend functionality to Silverlight applications. This enables developers to work in a language that they are more familiar with and use code that has already been written. Chapter 11 discusses how to implement Silverlight applications using IronPython, IronRuby, and JavaScript.

A powerful feature of Silverlight is that it enables developers to create custom controls that can be reused in the same application or as a library for other applications. Using custom controls, developers can implement a library that can be consumed by the entire Web site. This gives all pages of the Web site the same look and feel. Chapter 12 discusses the process of creating custom controls and libraries.

Silverlight applications are hosted in the HTML DOM; therefore, interaction between HTML and Silverlight can be very useful. Silverlight applications have access to the DOM enabling developers to modify and interact with HTML elements. Chapter 13 discusses interaction between Silverlight applications and the HTML DOM.

Because Silverlight applications are hosted in the HTML DOM, HTML elements can interact with Silverlight application controls using JavaScript. Chapter 13 discusses interaction between the HTML DOM and Silverlight applications.

Silverlight applications can implement timer threads that will wake up and perform tasks on a scheduled interval. Timer threads enable developers to quickly implement timed control to their Silverlight applications. Chapter 13 discusses implementing a timer thread in Silverlight applications.

Using the Common Language Runtime (CLR) libraries, Silverlight provides a robust development platform. Using the CLR library, Silverlight applications can access the client file system, implement background threads, and do a wide variety of other tasks. Chapter 13 discusses implementing background threads to update UI in Silverlight applications.

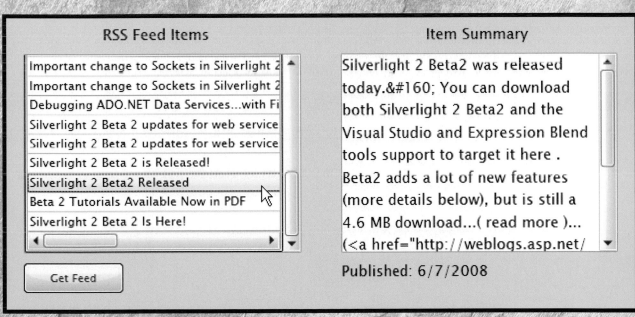

The Silverlight communication framework provides libraries that enable developers to quickly add interaction between Silverlight applications and RSS or Atom feeds. Chapter 14 discusses using the Silverlight communication framework to retrieve data from an RSS feed and view it in a Silverlight application.

The Silverlight communication framework also provides libraries that allow Silverlight applications to implement HTML Web requests and responses. This allows Silverlight applications the ability to easily interact with existing Web services. Chapter 14 discusses implementing HTML Web requests and responses in Silverlight applications.

The Silverlight data framework provides libraries that simplify the process of reading and writing XML data. This feature is often critical when interfacing with Web services that transmit data via XML. Chapter 15 discusses different ways to read and write XML data in Silverlight applications.

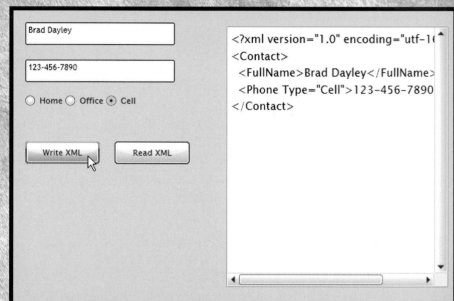

The Silverlight data framework also provides a library to implement LINQ access to SQL and XML sources. Chapter 15 discusses accessing an SQL database from a Silverlight application and using LINQ to access SQL data.

Chapter 9

Programming Silverlight Applications with JavaScript

When Silverlight 1.0 was released, unmanaged JavaScript was the only method of adding event handling and other functionality to applications. Using unmanaged JavaScript creates some limitations and the .NET model discussed in Chapter 8 and the DLR discussed in Chapter 11 are typically better models to use. However, you can still create very robust Silverlight applications using unmanaged JavaScript.

In fact unmanaged Javascript may be a much better choice in some situations. For example, if you would like to add a splash screen to your Web page using Silverlight, then unmanaged JavaScript is the best programming model.

This chapter helps you understand how to use unmanaged JavaScript to programmatically control the design and flow of your Silverlight applications. The following sections introduce the JavaScript relationship to Silverlight and discuss how to use JavaScript to dynamically access and manipulate the content in a Silverlight application.

Understanding the Silverlight–JavaScript Relationship

Unmanaged JavaScript Silverlight applications contain at least three types of code: HTML, XAML, and JavaScript. JavaScript can play two main roles in Silverlight applications. The first role is to create the Silverlight object in the Web page. The second role is to provide a means of programmatically working with the Silverlight plug-in to provide a rich interactive environment.

Managed JavaScript versus unmanaged JavaScript

Using the DLR, you can implement JavaScript that is managed similarly to how .NET applications use managed C# and Visual Basic. The big difference between the unmanaged and managed programming model is that in the managed programming model, the code-behind pages are tied as part of the same class to the XAML code. In the unmanaged JavaScript model, the JavaScript code is not part of the same class as the XAML code. Instead, it accesses the XAML using functionality that is exposed through a JavaScript library named Silverlight.js.

The advantage to using unmanaged JavaScript is that it is easier to implement already existing JavaScript that is embedded in HTML pages to interact with Silverlight applications. The disadvantage is that the unmanaged JavaScript model does not support the newer Silverlight 2 controls that provide much more robust functionality, and it does not directly tie in with other .NET projects such as Web services.

NOTE   The JavaScript programming model is determined by the x:Class attribute. If the x:Class attribute is absent from the root XAML object, then the programming model that applies for the page defaults to the unmanaged JavaScript programming model. If the x:Class attribute is present, the programming model for the page is the managed JavaScript programming model. The programming models cannot be mixed on a single XAML page because the declaration of the programming model affects the resolution of event handlers.

Using the Silverlight.js library

Every JavaScript Silverlight application includes a reference to Microsoft's Silverlight.js JavaScript library. The Silverlight.js library is a set of JavaScript functions that provide interaction between unmanaged JavaScript, the Silverlight plug-in, and Silverlight applications.

The Silverlight.js library exposes functions that help you implement Silverlight applications in Web pages using JavaScript. This library allows you to use JavaScript to create a Silverlight object in the DOM, load Silverlight applications into the object, and then handle load events.

The Silverlight.js library must be loaded in the Web page using a <script> tag, as shown in the following HTML example:

```
<!DOCTYPE html PUBLIC "-//W3C//DTD XHTML 1.0 Transitional//EN"
"http://www.w3.org/TR/xhtml1/DTD/xhtml1-transitional.dtd">
<html xmlns="http://www.w3.org/1999/xhtml" >
<head>
    <title>Silverlight Project Page </title>
    <script type="text/javascript" src="Silverlight.js"></script>
</head>
```

NOTE   The Silverlight.js JavaScript library is included in the Silverlight 2 SDK. If you want to use the unmanaged JavaScript model, pull the Silverlight.js file out of the SDK and include it with your code.

Creating and Embedding the Silverlight Application

When the `Silverlight.js` library is added to the HTML document, you can add a Silverlight application to the Web page. Adding a Silverlight application to a Web page is a two-step process. The first step is to add JavaScript code to create a Silverlight object. The second step is to add code to the `<body>` of the HTML document to actually embed the Silverlight object.

The `Silverlight.js` library exposes two functions to create Silverlight application objects: `createObject()` and `createObjectEx()`. The `Silverlight.js` library determines the type of browser being used and embeds the Silverlight application in the rendered HTML document with the appropriate tags. For example, some browsers expect the `<object ... />` tag and others expect the `<embed ... />` tag.

This section focuses on how to implement JavaScript that uses the `CreateObjectEx()` function to create a Silverlight application object.

The JavaScript code in Listing 9.1 defines a JavaScript function named `createSilverlight()` that creates the Silverlight object and then embeds that object in the HTML document.

LISTING 9.1

A Basic Web Page Containing an Embedded Silverlight Application

```
<!DOCTYPE html PUBLIC "-//W3C//DTD XHTML 1.0 Transitional//EN"
"http://www.w3.org/TR/xhtml1/DTD/xhtml1-transitional.dtd">
<html xmlns="http://www.w3.org/1999/xhtml" >
<head>
    <title>Silverlight Project Test Page </title>
    <script type="text/javascript" src="Silverlight.js"></script>
    <script type="text/javascript">
    function createSilverlight()
    {
        Silverlight.createObjectEx({
            source: "Page.xaml",
            parentElement:
            document.getElementById("SilverlightControlHost"),
            id: "SilverlightControl",
            properties: {
                width: "400",
                height: "400",
                version: "1.1",
                background: "#1111FF"
            },
            events: {},
                initParams: null,
```

continued

LISTING 9.1   *(continued)*

```
                context: null
        });
    }
    </script>
</head>

<body>
    <div id="SilverlightControlHost">
        <script type="text/javascript">
            createSilverlight();
        </script>
    </div>
</body>
</html>
```

The createSilverlight() function in Listing 9.1 handles the creation of the Silverlight object. The Silverlight object is created by calling the createObjectEx() function that was exposed by loading the Silverlight.js library. Then the code in Listing 9.1 embeds the Silverlight application in the <body> of the HTML document by using the following <div> tag:

```
    <div id="SilverlightControlHost">
```

The <div> tag acts as the parent element that hosts the Silverlight object. Notice that the id value of SilverlightControlHost matches the value that is used to obtain the parent element in the createObjectEx() function. Those values must match to embed the Silverlight object. Inside the <div> tag, the Silverlight object is embedded by simply calling the createSilverlight() JavaScript function defined in the header.

Configuring parameters of the createObject and createObjectEx functions

The createObject() and createObjectEx() functions perform the same basic task, the only difference is how parameters are passed to them. The createObject() function accepts the parameters using basic comma-separated syntax as follows:

```
    createObject(Source, Parent, ID, Properties,
            Events, initParams, Context)
```

The createObjectEx() function accepts the parameters using a single JavaScript Object Notation (JSON) dictionary that contains the parameters as a single package, as shown in the following createObjectEx() function call:

```
Silverlight.createObjectEx({
  source: "Page.xaml",
  parentElement: document.getElementById("SilverlightControlHost"),
  id:"SilverlightControl",
  properties: {
    width:"400",
    height:"200",
    version: "2.0",
    enableHtmlAccess: "true",
    background:"#1FFFFF"
  },
  events:{},
  initparams:null,
  context:null
});
```

Table 9.1 lists the parameters that can be passed to the createObject() and createObjectEx() functions.

TABLE 9.1

Parameters for createObject() and createObjectEx()

Parameter	Description
Source	Specifies the URL of the Silverlight XAP assembly or the XAML file that should initially be loaded by the plug-in. A reference to an embedded object can also be specified if the XAML is embedded in the HTML document.
parent-Element	Specifies the ID of the Silverlight object's parent HTML element. The Silverlight object can be accessed from this object in the DOM.
Id	Specifies a unique ID in the DOM for the Silverlight object.
Properties	Specifies an array of properties for the Silverlight object.
Events	Specifies an array of events that is set when the Silverlight object is initialized.
initParams	Specifies an array of user-defined parameters available when the Silverlight object is initialized.
Context	Specifies a unique identifier that can be passed into the onLoad event handler. This allows the event handler to determine which Silverlight application was loaded without having to check the HTML DOM.

Specifying the source parameter

The `source` parameter of the `createObjectEx()` function specifies the location of the Silverlight XAP assembly or the XAML file that should be used to initially render the Silverlight object. Typically, the value of `source` is a URL that points to an XAP assembly file, as shown in the following line of code:

```
source: "SilverlightApplication.xap"
```

The value of `source` can also be a reference to XAML that is embedded in the HTML document. The following code snippet shows an example accessing embedded XAML in an HTML document:

```
source: "#xamlembedded",
. . .
<script type="text/xaml" id="xamlembedded"><?xml version="1.0"?>
    <Canvas x:Name="parentCanvas"
            xmlns="http://schemas.microsoft.com/client/2007"
            xmlns:x="http://schemas.microsoft.com/winfx/2006/xaml">
        . . .
    </Canvas>
</script>
```

Notice in the code snippet that the `source` parameter uses the `#id` syntax to access the DOM ID of the embedded XAML script.

Configuring the parent ID

The `parent` parameter specifies the DOM ID of an object in the HTML document that acts as the parent object for the Silverlight object. Typically a Silverlight application is embedded in a `<div>` or a `<span>` tag. The tag must be given the same ID as is specified in the parent parameter as shown by the following code example:

```
id: "SilverlightControl",
. . .
<div id="SilverlightControlHost">
```

Setting the Silverlight object ID

The `id` parameter specifies a unique element ID that can be used to identify the Silverlight object in the DOM. The `id` parameter must follow standard DOM element ID rules. The `getElementById()` function, discussed later in this chapter, uses this ID to find the Silverlight object.

Configuring the Silverlight application properties

The `properties` parameter specifies an array of properties that are used to render the initial Silverlight application. These properties control the look and the behavior of the rendered Silverlight application. Table 9.2 lists the properties that can be configured for a Silverlight application using the `properties` parameter.

TABLE 9.2	

Properties of a Silverlight Application

Property	Description
version	Specifies the exact version or a range of versions of the Silverlight plug-in that is required to initialize the Silverlight application. If the version requirement is not available, then the plug-in download link provided by the Silverlight.js library is displayed.
background	Defines what background color should be used for the Silverlight application. If no value is set, then it defaults to white.
height	Specifies the height in either pixels or percentage for the Silverlight application. Default is 0.
width	Specifies the width in either pixels or percentage for the Silverlight application. Default is 0.
isWindowless	Default false. If set to true, then the Silverlight application is displayed as a windowless control in the browser, and the background color becomes the alpha value for the control.
inplace-InstallPrompt	Default false. If this is set to false, then the normal plug-in download link is displayed. If set to true, then a different plug-in download is displayed that links directly to the plug-in download and also includes links to the Silverlight license agreement and privacy pages.
ignore-BrowserVer	Default false. If set to true, then Silverlight does not try to verify that the requesting browser type and version supports Silverlight control. If set to false, then only supported browsers load the Silverlight application.
enable-Html-Access	Default true. If set to true, then the Silverlight application can access data in the browser's DOM.
framerate	Specifies the maximum frames per second that the Silverlight application renders. The default is 24. The maximum is 64.

Using the IsInstalled method to determine which Silverlight plug-in is installed

The Silverlight.js library includes the IsInstalled() function that accepts a version string and returns true if the version of the currently installed Silverlight plug-in is compatible with that version. This allows you to determine if the correct Silverlight plug-in is installed before trying to create the Silverlight application object.

For example, the following code verifies that the Silverlight 2 plug-in is installed before calling createObjectEx(); if Silverlight 2 is not installed, a notification alert is sent to the user:

```
var version = "2.0";
var isInstalled = Silverlight.isInstalled(version);
if (isInstalled)
{
  Silverlight.createObjectEx({
    . . .
  });
}
else
{
    alert("Silverlight plug-in version " + version +
          " not installed.");
}
```

CAUTION   If your Silverlight application requires a specific version of the Silverlight plug-in, then it is a good idea to use `IsInstalled()` method to ensure that the appropriate version of Silverlight is installed.

Adding load and error events to Silverlight at initialization time

The `events` parameter allows you to specify functions that are executed on certain events during the Silverlight application initialization. Currently, Silverlight allows you to register handlers for onLoad and onError events. The following code snippet creates a Silverlight object that implements onLoad and onError event handling:

```
<script type="text/javascript">
function createSilverlight()
{
    Silverlight.createObjectEx({
        source: "Page.xaml",
        parentElement: document.getElementById("SLHost"),
        id: "SilverlightControl",
        properties: {
            width: "400",
            height: "400",
            version: "1.1",
            background: "#1111FF"
    },
        events: {
            onLoad:silverlightLoad,
            onError:silverlightError
        }
    });
}
function silverlightLoad(control, userContext, sender)
{
    alert("Silverlight successfully rendered.");
}
function silverlightError(control, userContext, sender)
```

```
    {
        alert("The browser encountered an error rendering Silverlight.");
    }
    </script>
```

Notice that the event parameter defines the event handler by using the `event:handlerfunction` syntax. If the `onError` event is raised, then the `silverlightError` handler function is called and simply displays an alert message that indicates an error was encountered. If the `onLoad` event is raised, meaning that the page loaded successfully, then the `silverlightLoad` handler function is called and simply displays an alert message that indicates the page loaded successfully. Using event handlers at initialization time enables you to be more dynamic with your Silverlight applications.

Configuring user-defined parameters in the Silverlight application

The `initParams` parameter allows you to add custom defined parameters that get passed to the Silverlight application when it is initialized. These parameters can be accessed using the `initParams` attribute of the Silverlight control object.

The following example code adds a list of comma-delineated strings as the `initParms` setting for the Silverlight object and then uses the Silverlight control object in an `onLoad` event handler to access the list of strings:

```
function createSilverlight()
{
    Silverlight.createObjectEx({
        source: "Page.xaml",
        parentElement: document.getElementById("SLHost"),
        id: "SilverlightControl",
        properties: {
            width: "100%",
            height: "100%",
            version: "1.1",
            },
        events: {
                onLoad:onLoad
        },
        initParams:"one,two,three,four"
    });
}
function onLoad(control, userContext, sender)
{
    var paramList = control.initParams.split(",");
    var txt = "User Defined Parameters\r\n";
    for (var i=0; i<paramList.length; i++)
    {
        txt += "Parameter: " + paramList[i] + "\r\n";
    }
    alert(txt);
}
```

The onLoad event handler accesses the initParams that were defined in the createObjectEx() function directly from the Silverlight control object that was passed as the first argument of the event handler. It then parses the string and generates an alert displaying the list of user-defined parameters.

Creating the Silverlight object in a separate JavaScript file

Embedding the JavaScript necessary to create the Silverlight object in the HTML file itself works well for some Silverlight applications. However, for most applications you should create a separate JavaScript file that contains the object creation as well as other JavaScript functions.

Keeping the JavaScript code in a separate file helps you organize your code better and reuse code in multiple applications. Another major advantage of keeping your JavaScript code separately is that you may take advantage of browser caching because the HTML file takes up a much smaller footprint.

Breaking the JavaScript code out into a separate file is simple. First, copy the contents inside the JavaScript <script> tags to a separate document and save it. Then load the new JavaScript file in the HTML document, as shown in the following code snippet:

```
<!DOCTYPE html PUBLIC "-//W3C//DTD XHTML 1.0 Transitional//EN"
"http://www.w3.org/TR/xhtml1/DTD/xhtml1-transitional.dtd">
<html xmlns="http://www.w3.org/1999/xhtml" >
<head>
    <title>Silverlight Project</title>
    <script type="text/javascript" src="Silverlight.js"></script>
    <script type="text/javascript" src="myJavaScript.js"></script>
</head>
```

 The JavaScript file containing your JavaScript code must be loaded after the Silverlight.js library so that the library helper function is available.

Accessing XAML Using Unmanaged JavaScript

One of the most powerful features of Silverlight is the ability to access and programmatically change a Silverlight application after it is loaded. Accessing the Silverlight application can be broken down into three main areas: accessing the Silverlight object, accessing the Silverlight application settings, and accessing the XAML content.

You should already be familiar with the Silverlight object from earlier in this chapter. The Silverlight application settings define the look and behavior of the Silverlight application. The content of the Silverlight object is generated from the XAML file that is defined by the source property. The following sections discuss how to access the object, settings, and content of a Silverlight application and dynamically modify them to provide a rich experience in the browser.

Accessing the Silverlight object

You can access the Silverlight object from a JavaScript file in three ways. The first way is through the HTML DOM using the document.getElementById() function. The getElementById() function accepts an object ID as its only parameter and searches the HTML DOM and tries to find the object with the specified ID.

To illustrate an example of using the HTML DOM to access the Silverlight object, look at the following code example that creates a Silverlight object:

```
createObjectEx({
    source: "Page.xaml",
    parentElement: document.getElementById("SilverlightControlHost"),
    id: "SilverlightControl",
    properties: {
        width: "100%",
        height: "100%",
        version: "1.1",
        background: "#1FFFFFF",
        enableHtmlAccess: "true"
    },
    events: {},
  initParams: null,
  context: null,
});
```

Using the previous code, the following line of code accesses the HTML DOM and assigns the Silverlight object created previously to the variable control:

```
var control = document.getElementById('SilverlightControl');
```

> **CAUTION**   A common mistake is to specify the ID of the HTML element that is hosting the Silverlight object instead of the ID of the Silverlight object itself.

The second way to access the Silverlight object is to use the getHost() function of an XAML object; for example, inside an event handler. Each XAML object has a getHost() function that returns the Silverlight object that is hosting it. The following code example accesses the Silverlight object from an event handler function and assigns it to the variable control:

```
function myEvent(sender, eventArgs)
```

```
    {
        var control = sender.getHost();
    }
```

Both methods of accessing the Silverlight object host are acceptable and work well. Typically, if an XAML object is available, it is much easier to use the getHost() method because you do not need to know the ID of the Silverlight object.

Accessing the Silverlight application settings

Now that you know how to access the Silverlight object, you can access the settings for the Silverlight application. You can access the settings used by the createObject() and createObjectEx() functions. This can be useful for a lot of reasons. For example, accessing the settings allows you to determine what source file was used to render the Silverlight application.

Many of the Silverlight settings can be accessed directly from the Silverlight object. The settings defined by the properties argument are accessed using the settings attribute of the Silverlight object. The code example in Listing 9.2 illustrates accessing the Silverlight object in an event handler onLoad that is attached to the root canvas object of the XAML file. The onLoad handler collects information about the Silverlight object and displays it in an alert window, as shown in Figure 9.1.

LISTING 9.2

JavaScript Code Enabling an onLoad Event Handler

```
function createSilverlight()
{
    Silverlight.createObjectEx({
        source: "Page.xaml",
        parentElement: document.getElementById("silverlightHost"),
        id: "SilverlightControl",
        properties: {
            width: "100%",
            height: "100%",
            version: "1.1",
            background: "#1FFFFF",
            enableHtmlAccess: "true"
        },
        events: {onLoad:onLoad},
        initParams: null,
        context: null
    });
}
```

```
function onLoad(control, context, sender)
{
  var plugin = sender.getHost();
  var msg = "Silverlight Control Properties\r\n";
  msg += "\r\nControl : " + sender.toString();
  msg += "\r\nParent : " + plugin.parentElement.id;
  msg += "\r\nSource : " + plugin.source;
  msg += "\r\nID : " + plugin.id;
  msg += "\r\nBackground : " + plugin.settings.background;
  msg += "\r\nMaxFrameRate : " + plugin.settings.maxFrameRate;
  alert(msg);
}
```

FIGURE 9.1

The alert window displaying the settings assigned to the Silverlight application

The example in Listing 9.2 accesses the Silverlight object from the XAML object that initiated the onLoad event. Notice that the source, id, and parentElement values are accessed directly from the object itself; however, the background and maxFrameRate values are accessed from the settings attribute.

Using the Silverlight object, you are also able to modify the Silverlight application settings from JavaScript. Changes that are made to the Silverlight object modify how the object is rendered. This can be useful to dynamically change the look and feel of the Silverlight application based on environment or user settings.

To illustrate changing the Silverlight object dynamically, look at the code examples in Listings 9.3, 9.4, and 9.5 that dynamically set the height, width, and background attributes of the Silverlight object using random values when the page is loaded.

LISTING 9.3

XAML File Named Page.xaml That Renders a Simple Canvas That Contains a TextBlock

```
<Canvas x:Name="parentCanvas"
        xmlns="http://schemas.microsoft.com/client/2007"
        xmlns:x="http://schemas.microsoft.com/winfx/2006/xaml"
        >
    <TextBlock x:Name="myText" Text="Silverlight"/>
 </Canvas>
```

LISTING 9.4

HTML File That Embeds as Silverlight Application

```
<!DOCTYPE html PUBLIC "-//W3C//DTD XHTML 1.0 Transitional//EN"
"http://www.w3.org/TR/xhtml1/DTD/xhtml1-transitional.dtd">
<html xmlns="http://www.w3.org/1999/xhtml" >
<head>
    <title>Silverlight JavaScript Project Test Page </title>

    <script type="text/javascript" src="Silverlight.js"></script>
    <script type="text/javascript" src="TestPage.html.js"></script>
</head>

<body>
    <div id="silverlightHost">
        <script type="text/javascript">
            createSilverlight();
        </script>
    </div>
</body>
</html>
```

LISTING 9.5

JavaScript Code That Creates a Silverlight Application Object and Dynamically Sets the Height, Width, and Background Color

```
function createSilverlight()
{
    Silverlight.createObjectEx({
        source: "Page.xaml",
        parentElement: document.getElementById("silverlightHost"),
```

```
        id: "SilverlightControl",
        properties: {
            width:"400",
            height:"200",
            version: "2.0",
            enableHtmlAccess: "true",
            background:"#1FFFFF"
        },
        events:{
            onLoad: onLoad
            },
        initparams: null,
        context: null
    });
}

function onLoad(control, context, sender)
{
  var plugin = sender.getHost();
  var sizes = [100, 200, 300];
  var colors = ["Blue", "LightGray", "Gray"];
  var randNum = Math.round(Math.random() * 2);
  plugin.width = sizes[randNum];
  plugin.height = sizes[randNum];
  plugin.settings.background = colors[randNum];
}
```

In this example, the onLoad function randomly gets a color and size setting from an array and then sets the source attribute of the Silverlight object. The result is that the size and background color of the Silverlight application are changed dynamically each time the Web page is loaded, as shown in Figure 9.2.

FIGURE 9.2

Dynamically rendering random size and background color settings in a Silverlight application

Accessing XAML content

The Silverlight object also gives you direct access to the XAML content from JavaScript. Accessing the XAML content gives you the ability to dynamically change the XAML content programmatically from JavaScript. The following sections discuss how to access the XAML content to set content properties, find specific XAML elements, and then manipulate the content.

Using the content attribute

The Silverlight object implements an attribute named content that provides access to the content of the Silverlight object. Using the content attribute, you can access information about the status of the current content as well as the current content itself. For example, the following code snippet uses the content attribute to determine if the application is in fullScreen mode:

```
control = document.getElementById("SilverlightControl");
if (control.content.fullScreen){
  control.content.fullScreen = false;
}
```

Table 9.3 lists the properties of the content attribute.

TABLE 9.3

Properties of the Silverlight Object's Content Attribute

Property	Description
Accessibility	Read-only. Specifies accessibility information about the content.
actualHeight	Read-only. Specifies the actual height of the content.
actualWidth	Read-only. Specifies the actual width of the content.
createFromXaml()	Function that creates a Silverlight object from XAML. Syntax: createFromXaml(xamlContent, nameScope)
createFromXaml-Downloader()	This is a function that creates a Silverlight object from a file in a downloader object. Syntax: createFromXamlDownloader(downloader, part)
findName()	Function that searches the content and returns a reference to a given object.
fullScreen	Specifies whether the Silverlight application is in full-screen mode.
onFullScreenChange	Specifies the event handler that is triggered when the status of the fullScreen property changes.
onResize	Specifies the event handler that is triggered when the content is resized.

Finding and modifying XAML elements in JavaScript

You can use the findName() function of the content attribute of a Silverlight XAML control to search through the content and find a specific XAML element that has been given a unique name using the x:Name attribute. For example, consider the following XAML element:

```
<TextBlock x:Name="appText" Canvas.Top="20" Canvas.Left="27"
           FontSize="12" Text="Silverlight Application"/>
```

You can use the following lines of code in JavaScript to access the appText TextBlock:

```
var control = document.getElementById("SilverlightControl");
var txtBlock = control.content.findName("appText");
```

After you use the findName() function to retrieve an XAML element, you have access to the attributes of the XAML element. For example, the following line of code sets the Text attribute of the txtBlock used earlier in this section:

```
txtBlock.Text = "New Text";
```

Silverlight also provides the getValue() and setValue() methods to get and set properties of the object. For example, the following line of code sets the Canvas.Left property for the txtBlock object:

```
txtBlock.setValue("Canvas.Left",  20);
```

To illustrate accessing and modifying XAML elements better, consider the XAML code in Listing 9.6. The code is simple and only defines a basic TextBlock control with the name appText and a Rectangle control named appBox.

LISTING 9.6

Simple XAML Code That Defines a TextBlock and Rectangle Element

```
<Canvas x:Name="parentCanvas"
        xmlns="http://schemas.microsoft.com/client/2007"
        xmlns:x="http://schemas.microsoft.com/winfx/2006/xaml">
    <Rectangle x:Name="appBox"/>
    <TextBlock x:Name="appText"/>
</Canvas>
```

The code in Listing 9.7 defines an onLoad function named updateXAML() that does all the work to configure and lay out the TextBlock and Rectangle controls as they appear in Figure 9.3.

LISTING 9.7

JavaScript Code That Accesses the TextBlock and Rectangle Objects to Set the Properties

```javascript
function createSilverlight()
{
    Silverlight.createObjectEx({
        source: "Page.xaml",
        parentElement: document.getElementById("silverlightHost"),
        id: "SilverlightControl",
        properties: {
            width: "400",
            height: "200",
            version: "2.0",
            background: "LightGray",
            enableHtmlAccess: "true"
        },
        events: {onLoad:updateXAML},
        initParams: null,
        context: null
    });
}

function updateXAML(control, context, sender)
{
    var plugin = sender.getHost();
    var txtBlock = plugin.content.findName("appText");
    var rect = plugin.content.findName("appBox");

    txtBlock.Text="New Silverlight Application";
    txtBlock.Foreground="White";
    txtBlock.FontSize="20";
    txtBlock.setValue("Canvas.Top", 70);
    txtBlock.setValue("Canvas.Left", 50);

    rect.Fill="Blue";
    rect.Height=50;
    rect.Width=300;
    rect.setValue("Canvas.Top", 60);
    rect.setValue("Canvas.Left", 40);
}
```

Inside the updateXAML() function in Listing 9.7, the code uses the findName() function to get the TextBlock and Rectangle objects and then sets the Text, Height, Width, Fill, FontSize, and Foreground attributes to define the look of the elements. The code uses the setValue() function to set the Canvas.Top and Canvas.Left properties to set the layout of the elements, as shown in Figure 9.3.

A Silverlight application with a TextBlock and Rectangle that were configured in JavaScript

Accessing child elements of XAML objects in JavaScript

Another very valuable attribute that Silverlight adds to XAML objects is the `children` attribute. The `children` attribute provides access to a collection of child elements that are attached to the XAML element. Silverlight also provides several properties and functions attached to the `children` attribute that help in working with the child attributes. Table 9.4 lists the attributes and functions attached to the `children` attribute.

TABLE 9.4

Attributes and Functions of the children Attribute of an XAML Object in JavaScript

Attribute	Description
`add()`	Accepts an object as an argument and adds it as a child to the end of the list.
`clear()`	Removes all objects from the list.
`Count`	Integer that specifies the number of children in the list.
`getItem()`	Accepts an integer and returns the child element at that index.
`getValue()`	Accepts a string and returns the value of the property specified by the string.
`insert()`	Accepts an integer index as the first argument and an object as the second object and inserts the object as a child at the index specified.
`name`	Returns the name of the child object if available.
`remove()`	Accepts an object and removes it from the list
`removeAt()`	Accepts an integer and removes the child at that index from the list.
`setValue()`	Accepts a string as the first argument that specifies the property and the value that the property should be set to as the second argument.

The code in Listings 9.8 and 9.9 shows an example of using the `children` attribute of a root `Canvas` object to add a checkers game board to a Silverlight application. The code in Listing 9.8 is simple and only defines a basic `Canvas` object with the name `parentCanvas`.

LISTING 9.8

Simple XAML Code That Defines a Root Canvas Element

```
<Canvas x:Name="parentCanvas"
        xmlns="http://schemas.microsoft.com/client/2007"
        xmlns:x="http://schemas.microsoft.com/winfx/2006/xaml">
</Canvas>
```

The code in Listing 9.9 defines an onLoad function named createGame() that creates a series of Rectangle objects and uses the children attribute the parentCanvas control to add them as checker board squares, as shown in Figure 9.3.

LISTING 9.9

JavaScript Code That Creates a Checkerboard and Adds It as a Child Element to the Root Canvas Object

```
function createSilverlight()
{
    Silverlight.createObjectEx({
        source: "Page.xaml",
        parentElement: document.getElementById("silverlightHost"),
        id: "SilverlightControl",
        properties: {
            width: "400",
            height: "450",
            version: "2.0",
            background: "LightGray",
            enableHtmlAccess: "true"
        },
        events: {onLoad:createGame},
        initParams: null,
        context: null
    });
}

function createGame(control, context, sender)
{
    var plugin = sender.getHost();
    var game = plugin.content.findName("parentCanvas");
    var doBlack = true;

    var blackBlock =
      "<Rectangle Fill=\"Black\" Height=\"50\" Width=\"50\"/>";
    var redBlock =
```

```javascript
  "<Rectangle Fill=\"Red\" Height=\"50\" Width=\"50\"/>";
var boardCanvas =
  "<Canvas Height=\"400\" Width=\"400\" Canvas.Top=\"50\"/>";
var titleBlock =
  "<TextBlock Text=\"Checkers\" Canvas.Top=\"15\" Canvas.Left=\"150\"/>";

var board = plugin.content.createFromXaml(boardCanvas);

board.children.clear();
for (var x=0; x<8; x++)
{
    for (var y=0; y<8; y++)
    {
        if(doBlack)
        {
            var square = plugin.content.createFromXaml(blackBlock);
            square.setValue("Canvas.Left", y*50);
            square.setValue("Canvas.Top", x*50);
            board.children.add(square);
            doBlack = false;
        }
        else
        {
            var square = plugin.content.createFromXaml(redBlock);
            square.setValue("Canvas.Left", y*50);
            square.setValue("Canvas.Top", x*50);
            board.children.add(square);
            doBlack = true;
        }
    }
    if(doBlack)
        doBlack = false;
    else
        doBlack = true;
}

var title = plugin.content.createFromXaml(titleBlock);
game.children.add(title);
game.children.add(board);
}
```

Inside the createGame() function in Listing 9.9, the code first gets the root Canvas object using the findName() function. Then the code defines the XAML code used to create a Canvas game board, Rectangles for the red and black blocks, and a TextBlock for the title. Next, the code uses the clear() function of the children attribute of the root Canvas to clear any elements that might already exist. The createFromXaml() function is used to create the XAML object from text.

The code uses two `for` loops to create rows of alternating red and black squares. Inside the `for` loops the values of the index are used in the `setValue()` function to set the `Canvas.Top` and `Canvas.Left` properties of each block to place it at the correct coordinates of the `Canvas`.

The `add()` function is used to add the squares to the game board `Canvas` and then to add the game board and title objects to the root `Canvas` object. The result is the checkerboard shown in Figure 9.4.

FIGURE 9.4

A Silverlight application that generates a checkers game board

Implementing Event Handling in Unmanaged JavaScript

There are two major types of events when dealing with unmanaged JavaScript. The first type is the plug-in events `onLoad` and `onError` that have already been discussed in this chapter. The second type of event is events that are triggered by Silverlight controls, such as a mouse enter event for a `TextBlock` control. You can attach unmanaged JavaScript event handler functions to Silverlight controls allowing you to add functionality to your Silverlight applications using JavaScript functions to manage events such as mouse or keyboard interaction.

CROSS-REF This section only introduces you to how to implement event handlers in unmanaged JavaScript. Refer to Chapter 8 for more detailed information about events.

Implementing event handling for Silverlight controls using unmanaged JavaScript is similar to implementing event handlers in .NET code-behind pages. Event handler functions can be declared as part of the XAML declaration for the control. For example, the following code defines a TextBlock element and attaches a MouseLeftButtonDown event handler named onClick() to the control:

```
<TextBlock x:Name="myText"
           Text="Some Text"
           MouseLeftButtonDown="onClick"/>
```

Event handlers can also be attached to Silverlight controls in your unmanaged JavaScript code. Typically this is done in the onLoad event handler for the Silverlight plug-in. For example, the following onLoad event handler function attaches a MouseEnter event handler named mouseOver() to a Rectangle control named myBox:

```
function onLoad(control, context, sender)
{
    var box = sender.findName('myBox');
    box.addEventListener('MouseEnter',mouseOver);
}
```

The code in Listings 9.10 and 9.11 provides an example of how to attach event handlers by declaring them as part of the XAML as well as using the addEventListener() function in JavaScript.

LISTING 9.10

Simple XAML Code That Defines a TextBlock Element That Attaches a MouseLeftButtonDown Event Handler

```
<Canvas x:Name="parentCanvas"
        xmlns="http://schemas.microsoft.com/client/2007"
        xmlns:x="http://schemas.microsoft.com/winfx/2006/xaml">
    <Image x:Name="myImage"
           Source="image.jpg"
           Canvas.Top="10" Canvas.Left="110"
           Width="640" Height="480"/>
    <TextBlock x:Name="Larger"
               Text="640x480"
               Canvas.Top="20" Canvas.Left="10"/>
    <TextBlock x:Name="Smaller"
               Text="320x240"
               Canvas.Top="50" Canvas.Left="10"
               MouseLeftButtonDown="smallSize"/>
</Canvas>
```

The code in Listing 9.10 defines an Image element named myImage, a TextBlock control named Larger, and another TextBlock element named Smaller. The code attaches a MouseLeftButtonDown event handler named smallSize to the Smaller TextBlock.

LISTING 9.11

JavaScript Code That Attaches MouseLeftButtonUp Event Handler to a TextBlock and Uses the Event to Resize an Image Element

```
function createSilverlight()
{
    Silverlight.createObjectEx({
        source: "Page.xaml",
        parentElement: document.getElementById("silverlightHost"),
        id: "SilverlightControl",
        properties: {
            width: "760",
            height: "500",
            version: "2.0",
            background: "LightGray",
            enableHtmlAccess: "true"
        },
        events: {onLoad:onLoad},
        initParams: null,
        context: null
    });
}

function onLoad(control, context, sender)
{
    var textblock = sender.findName('Larger');
    textblock.addEventListener('MouseLeftButtonUp',largeSize);
}

function largeSize(sender, args)
{
    plugin = sender.getHost();
    var shrinkText = plugin.content.findName('Smaller');
    var image = plugin.content.findName('myImage');
    sender.FontSize="20";
    shrinkText.FontSize="15";
    image.Width="640";
    image.Height="480";
}
function smallSize(sender, args)
{
    plugin = sender.getHost();
    var shrinkText = plugin.content.findName('Larger');
```

```
    var image = plugin.content.findName('myImage');
    sender.FontSize="20";
    shrinkText.FontSize="15";
    image.Width="320";
    image.Height="240";
}
```

To show how event handlers can also be added in the JavaScript code, the code in Listing 9.11 attaches an event handler to the Larger TextBlock element using the following lines of code:

```
    var textblock = sender.findName('Larger');
    textblock.addEventListener('MouseLeftButtonUp',largeSize);
```

The code in Listing 9.11 also implements two event handlers to handle resizing the Image element and adjusting the size of the TextBlock to designate which size is selected. The result is that the image is resized when your user clicks on the TextBlock elements, as shown in Figure 9.5.

FIGURE 9.5

A Silverlight application that uses JavaScript events to resize an Image element

Dynamically Loading Content in Unmanaged JavaScript

One of the more useful features provided by Silverlight for unmanaged JavaScript code is the ability to dynamically download and render content. This is done by the Downloader object. The Downloader object is a specialized Silverlight object that provides functionality to download and access content on demand from JavaScript. Content can be downloaded after the Silverlight application is instantiated and then rendered without having to refresh the entire Web page.

The content that can be downloaded can be XAML, text, or media and can be downloaded as a single file or as a package that is zipped together as a ZIP file. The following sections discuss using the `Downloader` object to download and render content dynamically.

Understanding the Downloader object

The `Downloader` object provides functionality to initiate data transfer, monitor the progress of the download, and retrieve the downloaded contents. `Downloader` objects can be created by using the `createObject()` function of the Silverlight application and passing the string `downloader`, as shown in the following code:

```
function makeDownloader(sender, eventArgs) {
    var plugin = sender.getHost();
    var dLoader = plugin.createObject('downloader');
}
```

The `Downloader` object exposes several additional methods, properties, and events that provide a means to initiate the download, monitor the progress, and access the content that is downloaded. Table 9.5 lists the `Downloader`-specific properties that are exposed by a `Downloader` object.

TABLE 9.5

Downloader-Specific Properties That Are Exposed through a Downloader Object

Property	Description
DownloadProgress	Double between 0 and 1. Represents the amount of the total content that has been downloaded. You can determine the percentage of the total content that has been downloaded by multiplying this value by 100.
Name	String. Specifies the name of the XAML object. This value is read-only in JavaScript and write-only in XAML.
ResponseText	String. Represents a string version of the downloaded content. This property is only valid inside the `Completed` event handler. This value is only used if you are downloading a single file; if you are downloading a ZIP package, then use the `GetResponseText()` method.
Status	Integer. Specifies the current state of the Downloader request. This value defaults to 0. A value of 200 designates "OK" meaning the request was successful. A value of 204 designates "no content" meaning that the server could not find the content specified in the request.
StatusText	String. A string representation of the value of the `Status` property.
Uri	String. Specifies a string corresponding to the URI of the `Downloader` object request.

Table 9.6 lists the `Downloader`-specific methods that are exposed by a `Downloader` object.

TABLE 9.6

Downloader-Specific Methods That Are Exposed through a Downloader Object

Attribute	Description
`Abort()`	Cancels the current `Downloader` request and resets the `DownloadProgress`, `Status`, and `StatusText` properties to their initial state.
`AddEventListener (event, handler)`	Accepts two arguments. The first argument specifies a string representation of the downloader event. The second argument specifies an event handler function that handles the event. This method attaches the event handler to the `Downloader` object.
`Equals(object)`	Accepts an object as the only argument and compares it to the `Downloader` object. `True` is returned if the objects match; otherwise, `false` is returned.
`FindName(name)`	Accepts a string specifying an object name as the only argument and returns the object if it can be found referencing the object's `x:Name` attribute. If the object is not found, `null` is returned.
`GetHost()`	Returns a reference to the Silverlight plug-in instance that contains the `Downloader` object.
`GetResponse-Text(part)`	Accepts a string specifying a package part name as the only argument and returns a string representation of the part if it is found. For example, if you are downloading a ZIP package containing a text file named `config.txt`, the following call to `GetResponseText()` would retrieve the content: `myDownloader.GetResponseText("config.txt");`
`GetValue (property)`	Accepts a string representing a Silverlight property name as the only argument and returns the value of the Silverlight property. Most properties can be accessed using standard dot syntax; however, this can be useful if you need to access properties such as `Canvas.Top`.
`Open(verb, uri)`	Accepts two arguments. The first argument is a string representing the verb used in the `Downloader` (currently only `GET` is supported). The second argument specifies the URI of the content file or package to download. The `Open()` function initializes the `Downloader` object; however, the request is not sent until the `Send()` method is called. Note: Backslashes are not permitted in the URI; use forward slashes. Also, cross domain addresses are not permitted.
`Send()`	Executes the `Downloader` request specified in the `Open()` function asynchronously.
`SetValue (property, value)`	Accepts a string representing a Silverlight property name as the first argument and a value as the second argument. `SetValue()` sets the value of the Silverlight property to the value argument. Most properties can be accessed using standard dot syntax; however, this can be useful if you need to access properties such as `Canvas.Top`.

Table 9.7 lists the `Downloader`-specific events that are exposed by a `Downloader` object.

TABLE 9.7

Downloader-Specific Events That Are Exposed Through a Downloader Object

Event	Description
Completed	The `Completed` event is triggered when the content is fully downloaded. The `Status` and `StatusText` properties of the `Downloader` object are valid in the `Completed` event handler.
Download-Failed	The `DownloadFailed` event is triggered when the request is completed with an error. The `Status` and `StatusText` properties of the `Downloader` object are valid in the `Completed` event handler.
DownloadProgress-Changed	The `DownloadProgressChanged` event is triggered when the total content downloaded has changed by 0.05 or more as a factor of 1 signifying a 5 percent change in the content.

 **NOTE** `AddEventListener()` returns a token as an integer value that can be passed to the `RemoveEventListener()` function to detach an event handler from a `Downloader`.

Creating a Downloader object

The first step in implementing dynamically downloaded content is to create a `Downloader` object using the `createObject()` function, as shown in the following lines of code:

```
function loadXAML(sender, eventArgs) {
    var plugin = sender.getHost();
    var dLoader = plugin.createObject('downloader');
    . . .
```

After you create the `Downloader` object, you need to attach a completion handler to it so that you know when the download is finished and you can begin using the downloaded content. The following line of code implements that `AddEventListener()` function to attach a `Completed` event handler:

```
dLoader.addEventListener('completed', addXAML);
```

Next, you need to define the request that is used to download the content using the `open()` function of the `Downloader` object. The method of download is GET and you need to specify either a single content file or a ZIP content package, as shown in the following code:

```
dLoader.open('GET', 'content.xaml');
```

After you define the request, the `Downloader` is instantiated and you can use the `Send()` function to execute the download request, as shown in the following code:

```
dLoader.send();
```

Creating a Completed event handler

After you create the `Downloader` object, as described in the previous section, you need to create the event handler function that was attached to the `Downloader` object. The `Completed` event handler needs to retrieve the contents from the download request and then implement them as part of the Silverlight application.

If you are downloading a single file, the dynamically downloaded content can be accessed using the `ResponseText` property of the `Downloader`, as shown in the following code:

```
function handleDownload(sender, eventArgs) {
    var text = sender.ResponseText;
```

If you are downloading a file that is part of a ZIP package, the dynamically downloaded content can be accessed using the `GetResponseText()` method of the `Downloader`, as shown in the following code:

```
function handleDownload(sender, eventArgs) {
    var text = sender.GetResponseText("file.txt");
```

If you are downloading a single XAML file, the dynamically downloaded content can be accessed using the `createFromXamlDownloader()` method of the Silverlight plug-in, as shown in the following code:

```
function handleDownload(sender, eventArgs) {
    var plugin = sender.getHost();
    var xamlFragment =
            plugin.content.createFromXamlDownloader(sender, "");
```

If you are downloading an XAML file as part of a package, the dynamically downloaded content can be accessed using the `createFromXamlDownloader()` method of the Silverlight plug-in and specifying the XAML content file, as shown in the following code:

```
function handleDownload(sender, eventArgs) {
    var plugin = sender.getHost();
    var xamlFragment =
            plugin.content.createFromXamlDownloader(sender, "new.xaml");
```

If you are downloading an image or media file as a single file, the dynamically downloaded content can be assigned to the `MediaElement` or `Image` object using the `setSource()` method of the object, as shown in the following code:

```
function handleDownload(sender, eventArgs) {
    var img = sender.FindName("myImage");
    img.setSource(sender, "");
```

If you are downloading an image or media file as part of a package, the dynamically downloaded content can be assigned to the MediaElement or Image object using the setSource() method of the object and specifying the content filename, as shown in the following code:

```
function handleDownload(sender, eventArgs) {
    var img = sender.FindName("myImage");
    img.setSource(sender, "image.txt");
```

Dynamically loading XAML

A common use of the Downloader object is to dynamically download and render XAML as part of the Silverlight application. Using the Downloader to download XAML gives you the flexibility to implement several different XAML files in your application; but only download those that are necessary during runtime.

The code in Listings 9.12, 9.13, and 9.14 provides an example of how to dynamically add XAML to a Silverlight application after it has already been instantiated. The code in Listing 9.12 simply defines a basic Silverlight application with a single TextBlock element.

LISTING 9.12

Simple XAML Code That Defines a TextBlock Element

```
<Canvas x:Name="parentCanvas"
        xmlns="http://schemas.microsoft.com/client/2007"
        xmlns:x="http://schemas.microsoft.com/winfx/2006/xaml">
    <TextBlock x:Name="txtLoad" Text="Load XAML Dynamically"/>
</Canvas>
```

The code in Listing 9.13 defines a series of Rectangle elements that are transformed to shape three sides of a box, each with its own color. When the initial Silverlight application is rendered, the content in Listing 9.13 is not loaded.

LISTING 9.13

Simple XAML Code That Defines a Cube That Is Not Rendered When the Application Is Loaded

```
<Canvas>
    <TextBlock Text="Dynamically Loaded XAML"
               Width="205" Height="27"
```

```
                                Canvas.Left="50" Canvas.Top="25"/>
        <Rectangle Width="50" Height="50"
                   Fill="Red" Stroke="#FF000000"
                   Canvas.Left="91" Canvas.Top="93"
                   RenderTransformOrigin="0.5,0.5">
            <Rectangle.RenderTransform>
                <TransformGroup>
                    <ScaleTransform ScaleX="1" ScaleY="1"/>
                    <SkewTransform AngleX="0" AngleY="20"/>
                    <RotateTransform Angle="0"/>
                    <TranslateTransform X="0" Y="0"/>
                </TransformGroup>
            </Rectangle.RenderTransform>
        </Rectangle>
        <Rectangle Width="50" Height="50"
                   RenderTransformOrigin="0.5,0.5"
                   Fill="Blue" Stroke="#FF000000"
                   Canvas.Left="138" Canvas.Top="93">
            <Rectangle.RenderTransform>
                <TransformGroup>
                    <ScaleTransform ScaleX="1" ScaleY="1"/>
                    <SkewTransform AngleX="0" AngleY="-20"/>
                    <RotateTransform Angle="0"/>
                    <TranslateTransform X="0" Y="0"/>
                </TransformGroup>
            </Rectangle.RenderTransform>
        </Rectangle>
        <Rectangle Width="48" Height="48"
                   RenderTransformOrigin="0.5,0.5"
                   Fill="Green" Stroke="#FF000000"
                   Canvas.Left="115" Canvas.Top="61">
            <Rectangle.RenderTransform>
                <TransformGroup>
                    <ScaleTransform ScaleX="1" ScaleY="1"/>
                    <SkewTransform AngleX="25" AngleY="25"/>
                    <RotateTransform Angle="-45"/>
                    <TranslateTransform X="0" Y="0"/>
                </TransformGroup>
            </Rectangle.RenderTransform>
        </Rectangle>
    </Canvas>
```

The code in Listing 9.14 does all of the work of downloading the XAML from Listing 9.13 and adding it as a child to the XAML from Listing 9.12 where it appears in the Web browser.

LISTING 9.14

JavaScript Code That Dynamically Downloads XAML Content and Adds It to an Existing Silverlight Application

```javascript
function createSilverlight()
{
    Silverlight.createObjectEx({
        source: "Page.xaml",
        parentElement: document.getElementById("silverlightHost"),
        id: "SilverlightControl",
        properties: {
            width: "300",
            height: "200",
            version: "2.0",
            background: "LightGray",
            enableHtmlAccess: "true"
        },
        events: {onLoad:onLoad},
        initParams: null,
        context: null
    });
}

function onLoad(control, context, sender)
{
    var textblock = sender.findName('txtLoad');
    textblock.addEventListener('MouseLeftButtonUp',loadXAML);
}

function loadXAML(sender, eventArgs) {
    var plugin = sender.getHost();
    var dLoader = plugin.createObject('downloader');
    dLoader.addEventListener('completed', addXAML);
    dLoader.open('GET', 'content.xaml');
    dLoader.send();
}

function addXAML(sender, eventArgs) {
    var plugin = sender.getHost();
    var xamlFragment = plugin.content.createFromXamlDownloader(sender, "");

    var root = sender.findName("parentCanvas");
    root.children.clear();
    root.children.add(xamlFragment);
}
```

The first thing the code in Listing 9.14 does is attach a `MouseLeftButtonUp` event handler named `loadXAML()` to the `TextBlock` already defined in Listing 9.12. The `loadXAML()` event handler creates a `Downloader` object named `dLoader`, attaches a `Completed` event handler named `addXAML()` to it, and then builds and sends a request to download the `content.xaml` file shown in Listing 9.13.

Inside the `addXAML()` event handler, the code uses the `createFromXamlDownloader()` function to render the contents of `content.xaml` to an XAML fragment named `xamlFrag-ment`. The code then gets the `parentCanvas` object from Listing 9.12, clears the existing `TextBlock` element, and appends the `xamlFragment`. The result is that when you click the text shown on the left in Figure 9.6, the content of Listing 9.13 is rendered in the application, as shown on the right side in Figure 9.6.

FIGURE 9.6

A Silverlight application that dynamically downloads and renders XAML content

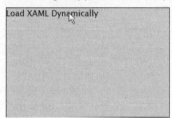
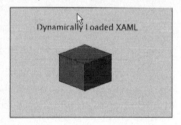

Dynamically loading text and media

Another common use of the `Downloader` object is to dynamically download a package that contains related content of different types and then implement that content to update or modify the Silverlight application. Using the `Downloader` to download zipped files gives you the flexibility to create packages that include text, XAML, media, and images that are related, and only download those that are necessary during runtime.

The code in Listings 9.15 and 9.16 provides an example of how to dynamically add content to a Silverlight application after it has already been instantiated. The code in Listing 9.15 simply defines a basic Silverlight application with a `TextBlock` element that is used to dynamically update another `TextBlock` and an `Image` element using content that is downloaded from a ZIP package.

LISTING 9.15

Simple XAML Code That Defines a TextBlock and Image Element That Is Dynamically Updated from Downloaded Content

```
<Canvas x:Name="parentCanvas"
        xmlns="http://schemas.microsoft.com/client/2007"
        xmlns:x="http://schemas.microsoft.com/winfx/2006/xaml">
    <TextBlock x:Name="appText"
               Text="Load Content"
               Canvas.Left="10"/>
    <TextBlock x:Name="imgDesc"
               FontSize="20"
               Canvas.Top="20" Canvas.Left="30" />
    <Image x:Name="appImage"
           Height="200" Width="200"
           Canvas.Top="40" Canvas.Left="20"/>
</Canvas>
```

The code in Listing 9.16 does all of the work of downloading a zipped file containing a text file and image file and using them to update a TextBlock and Image element from Listing 9.15.

LISTING 9.16

JavaScript Code That Dynamically Downloads Text and Image Content in a ZIP File and Adds Them to an Existing Silverlight Application

```
function createSilverlight()
{
    Silverlight.createObjectEx({
        source: "Page.xaml",
        parentElement: document.getElementById("silverlightHost"),
        id: "SilverlightControl",
        properties: {
            width: "250",
            height: "250",
            version: "2.0",
            background: "LightGray",
            enableHtmlAccess: "true"
        },
        events: {onLoad:onLoad},
        initParams: null,
        context: null
    });
}

function onLoad(control, context, sender)
```

```
{
    var textblock = sender.findName('appText');
    textblock.addEventListener('MouseLeftButtonUp',loadPackage);
}

function loadPackage(sender, eventArgs) {
    var plugin = sender.getHost();
    var dLoader = plugin.createObject('downloader');
    dLoader.addEventListener('completed', renderContent);
    dLoader.open('GET', 'content.zip');
    dLoader.send();
}

function renderContent(sender, eventArgs) {
    var textBlock = sender.findName('imgDesc');
    textBlock.Text = sender.GetResponseText('desc.txt');
    var image = sender.findName("appImage");
    image.setSource(sender, "image.jpg");
}
```

The first thing the code in Listing 9.16 does is attach a MouseLeftButtonUp event handler named loadPackage() to the TextBlock named appText defined in Listing 9.15. The loadPackage() event handler creates a Downloader object named dLoader, attaches a Completed event handler named renderContent() to it, and then builds and sends a request to download the content.zip file.

Inside the renderContent() event handler, the code uses the GetResponseText() function to set the Text attribute of the TextBlock named imgDesc. The code then uses the setSource() function to set the Source attribute of the Image named appImage from Listing 9.15. The result is that when you click the text shown in Figure 9.7, the content of content.zip file is downloaded and used to set the text and image displayed in the application shown in Figure 9.7.

FIGURE 9.7

A Silverlight application that dynamically loads an image and description text from a ZIP package

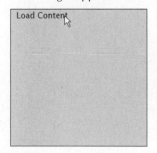

Summary

In this chapter, we discussed the difference between managed and unmanaged JavaScript. You learned how to use unmanaged JavaScript to create and embed Silverlight applications in Web pages. You also learned how to use the `Silverlight.js` library to manipulate XAML elements, implement event handling, and dynamically download and render content without refreshing the Web page.

In this chapter, you learned how to:

- Use the `Silverlight.js` library to embed a Silverlight application in a Web page.
- Manipulate XAML elements using unmanaged JavaScript.
- Implement application loading events in unmanaged JavaScript.
- Implement mouse and other events in Unmanaged JavaScript.
- Download and add XAML elements dynamically.
- Download and render media and text dynamically.

Chapter 10

Programming Silverlight Applications with ASP.NET Services and AJAX

S ilverlight provides two controls that allow you to quickly and easily implement the rich functionality of Silverlight in your ASP.NET Web pages. These controls provide the necessary framework for you to implement Silverlight in applications that are based on ASP.NET services.

Using these controls, you can quickly add video, imaging, and other rich graphical components to existing AJAX applications. The following sections discuss using the `asp:Silverlight` and `asp:MediaPlayer` controls to integrate Silverlight with ASP.NET services and AJAX.

This chapter is organized almost as a walk-through. The code examples go together to implement an ASP.NET service-based Silverlight application and a media player. Therefore, this chapter makes more sense if you read it from beginning to end.

Creating an ASP.NET Web Service to Use Silverlight

Silverlight 2 was designed to be able to directly interface with ASP.NET Web applications. The ASP.NET control `asp:Silverlight` was created to directly embed a Silverlight application in an ASP.NET Web page (typically the `.aspx` file). Using the `asp:Silverlight` control enables developers to implement Silverlight applications with a rich user interface to their existing Web service applications.

The following sections discuss how to create an ASP.NET Web application that is able to implement a Silverlight application to provide a nice user interface. We are not going to devote much time discussing ASP.NET Web development; however, for those who are not very familiar with ASP.NET Web applications and services, we provide the bare-bones help to get started using Visual Studio in this section.

Creating an ASP.NET Web application

The first step in implementing Silverlight in an ASP.NET application is to create a new ASP.NET Web application or use an already existing one. To create a new ASP.NET Web application in Visual Studio, choose File ➪ New ➪ Project and select ASP.NET Web Application from the Project window, as shown in Figure 10.1. Set the Name, Location, Solution, and Solution Name settings, and click OK.

FIGURE 10.1

New project window used to create a new ASP.NET Web application project

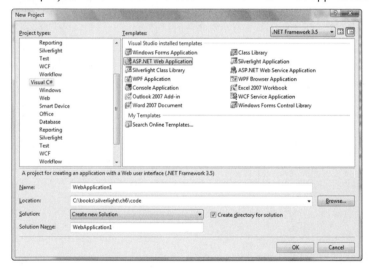

Registering the Silverlight assembly

The first step in implementing Silverlight in an ASP.NET Web service is to register the Silverlight assembly dynamically linked library (dll) in the ASP.NET Web page (typically the `Default.aspx` file) that hosts the Silverlight application. This is done by adding a `Register` tag with the Silverlight `Assembly` and `Namespace` attributes as well as the `asp TagPrefix`. For example:

```
<%@ Register Assembly="System.Web.Silverlight"
    Namespace="System.Web.UI.SilverlightControls"
    TagPrefix="asp" %>
```

Once the Silverlight assembly is registered, you can add Silverlight applications to the Web page using the `asp:Silverlight` control.

Adding a ScriptManager

To use AJAX scripting with your Silverlight application, you need to add an AJAX `ScriptManager` control to the ASP.NET Web page. The `ScriptManager` reacts to events in the ASP.NET page life cycle and coordinates event handling in all of the controls and code-behind pages.

To add a `ScriptManager` to the ASP.NET Web page, select the Design view for the ASP.NET Web page and drag and drop a `ScriptManager` control from the AJAX Extensions list in the Toolbox onto the page, as shown in Figure 10.2.

FIGURE 10.2

`ScriptManager` control being added to a Default.aspx ASP.NET Web page in the Design view of Visual Studio

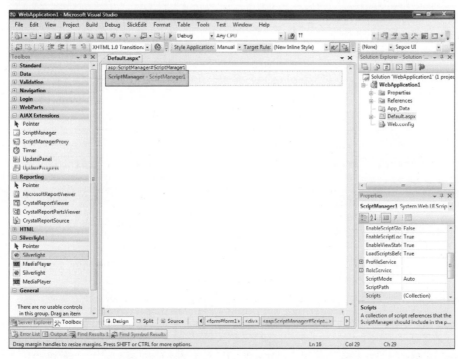

Adding the `ScriptManager` control adds the following code to the ASP.NET Web page:

```
<asp:ScriptManager ID="ScriptManager1" runat="server">
</asp:ScriptManager>
```

Embedding an asp:Silverlight tag in an ASP.NET Web page

Registering the Silverlight assembly in the ASP.NET Web page allows you to implement Silverlight functionality by embedding an `asp:Silverlight` or `asp:MediaPlayer` control in the Web page. The `asp:Silverlight` control hosts the Silverlight application.

The `asp:Silverlight` control exposes several properties that allow you to configure the look and initial behavior of the Silverlight application. Table 10.1 contains a list of some of the more important properties that you can configure for the `asp:Silverlight` control.

TABLE 10.1

Properties of the asp:Silverlight Control

Property	Description
Enabled	Boolean. Specifies whether the `asp:Silverlight` control is enabled or disabled. You can set this to `false` to temporality disable the control. Default is `true`.
EnableHtmlAccess	Boolean. Specifies whether the Silverlight plug-in can access the browser DOM. Default is `true`.
Height	Integer. Specifies the height in pixels in the Web page that the `asp:Silverlight` control consumes in the Web page.
ID	String. Specifies the object ID in the browser DOM assigned to the control.
InitParameters	Specifies optional user-defined initialization parameters that can be consumed by the `onLoad` event handler of the Silverlight application.
runat	String. Specifies if the control should be run at the server or the client. Default is set to "server". Typically this should be left at "server".
OnPluginError	String. Specifies the name of the JavaScript event handler function that is called if an error occurs in the Silverlight application at runtime.
OnPluginFullScreenChanged	String. Specifies the name of the JavaScript event handler function that is called when the full screen mode is modified.
OnPluginLoaded	String. Specifies the name of the JavaScript event handler function that is called when the Silverlight application is loaded.
OnPluginResized	String. Specifies the name of the JavaScript event handler function that is called if the Silverlight application is resized. This can be very useful if you allow users to modify the size of the Silverlight application.
Source	String. Specifies the URL of the XAML or XAP file that contains the Silverlight application.
Version	String. Represents the minimum version of Silverlight plug-in that is required for the Silverlight application.

Property	Description
`Width`	Integer. Specifies the width in pixels in the Web page that the `asp:Silverlight` control consumes in the Web page.
`Windowless`	Boolean. Specifies whether the Silverlight application is displayed in a windowless state. Default is `false`.

To add an `asp:Silverlight` control to the ASP.NET Web page, select the Design view for the ASP.NET Web page and drag and drop an `asp:Silverlight` control from the Silverlight controls list in the Toolbox onto the Design view as shown in Figure 10.3.

FIGURE 10.3

An `asp:Silverlight` control being added to a Default.aspx ASP.NET Web page in the Design view of Visual Studio

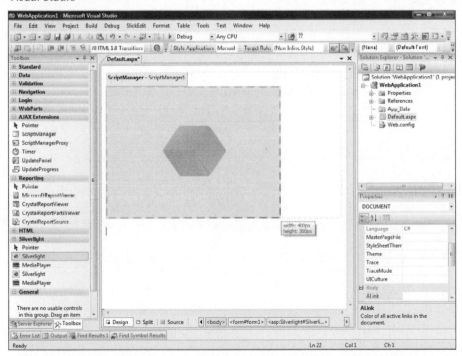

Adding the `asp:Silverlight` control adds the following code to the ASP.NET Web page:

```
<asp:Silverlight ID="Silverlight1" runat="server"
                 Height="100px" Width="100px"/>
```

After the `asp:Silverlight` control is added to the page, you can modify the properties of the control by changing the values in the Properties pane shown or by setting them directly in the source code. Listing 10.1 shows an example ASP.NET Web page that has been fully configured with an embedded `asp:Silverlight` control.

You can also resize and move the `asp:Silverlight` control in the Design view using the mouse. This allows designers an easier method of setting the placement and size in relation to other page elements.

LISTING 10.1

A Default.aspx ASP.NET Web Page Containing an Embedded asp:Silverlight Control

```
<%@ Page Language="C#" AutoEventWireup="true"
    CodeBehind="Default.aspx.cs"
    Inherits="proj1001._Default" %>

<%@ Register Assembly="System.Web.Silverlight"
    Namespace="System.Web.UI.SilverlightControls"
    TagPrefix="asp" %>

<!DOCTYPE html PUBLIC "-//W3C//DTD XHTML 1.0 Transitional//EN"
  "http://www.w3.org/TR/xhtml1/DTD/xhtml1-transitional.dtd">

<html xmlns="http://www.w3.org/1999/xhtml" >
<head runat="server">
    <title>Image Service for Silverlight</title>
</head>
<body>
    <h1>Image Service Using Silverlight</h1>
    <form id="form1" runat="server">
        <asp:ScriptManager ID="ScriptManager1"
                           runat="server">
        </asp:ScriptManager>
        <div>
            <asp:Silverlight ID="SilverlightImageView"
                Source="ClientBin/SilverlightImageShow.xap"
                runat="server"
                Version="2.0"
                Height="540px" Width="660px" />
        </div>
    </form>
</body>
</html>
```

Creating a Web service

After the `asp:Silverlight` control is added to the ASP.NET Web page, you can create and add a Web service to the ASP.NET Web application that provides server-based functionality for the Silverlight application.

To add a new Web service to the ASP.NET Web application in Visual Studio, right-click on the Web application in the Solution Explorer pane and choose Add ⇨ New Item . . . from the pop-up menu. Then select Web Service from the New Item window, as shown in Figure 10.4, and click Add.

New Item window used to add a new Web service to an ASP.NET Web application project

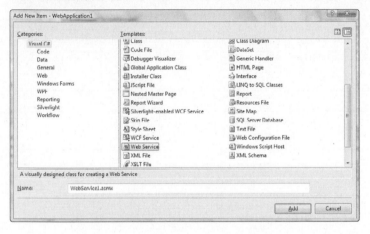

Visual Studio creates two new files in the project, a `.asmx` file and either a C# or Visual Basic code-behind file for the `.asmx` file. The code in the Web service code-behind file typically contains a simple `System.Web.Services.WebService` class.

You need to enable the `WebService` class for ASP.NET AJAX by adding a `ScriptService` attribute to the class definition, as shown in the following code:

```
[System.Web.Script.Services.ScriptService]
public class WebService1 : System.Web.Services.WebService
{
    ...
```

Adding the `ScriptService` attribute opens the `WebService` class to the AJAX script manager allowing methods and events to be accessed by AJAX scripts.

Adding Web methods to the ASP.NET Web service

After you enable the WebService for access by AJAX, you can begin adding methods to the service that are accessible by your Silverlight application. Web methods are simply methods of the WebService class that are preceded by the WebMethod attribute, as shown in the following example:

```
[WebMethod]
        public string getCount()
{
    . . .
```

The WebMethod attribute exposes the function as a Web Services Description Language (WSDL) service of the ASP.NET Web service, allowing you to access it via a service reference from the Silverlight application.

Listing 10.2 shows an example ASP.NET Web service that has been enabled for AJAX scripting access using the ScriptService attribute and has two WebMethod functions defined.

LISTING 10.2

A Web Service asmx.cs C# File That Implements Two WebMethod Functions

```
using System;
using System.Collections;
using System.ComponentModel;
using System.Data;
using System.Linq;
using System.Web;
using System.Web.Services;
using System.Web.Services.Protocols;
using System.Xml.Linq;

namespace proj1001
{
    [WebService(Namespace = "http://tempuri.org/")]
    [WebServiceBinding(ConformsTo = WsiProfiles.BasicProfile1_1)]
    [ToolboxItem(false)]
    [System.Web.Script.Services.ScriptService]
    public class imageService : System.Web.Services.WebService
    {
```

```csharp
        string[] images = new string[5];

        public imageService()
        {
            //init Images
            for (int x = 1; x <= 5; x++)
                images[x-1] = "image" + x.ToString() + ".jpg";
        }

        [WebMethod]
        public int getCount()
        {
            return images.Length;
        }

        [WebMethod]
        public string getImage(int index)
        {
            return images[index];
        }
    }
}
```

The code in Listing 10.2 simulates a service that might access a database to retrieve a list of image files and then exposes two functions as WebMethod services. For simplicity, the code simply creates an array of image filenames as if it had retrieved them from a database. The getCount() service simply returns the number of images available as an int. The getImage() service accepts an int argument index and uses that value to return a specific image filename from the images array as a string.

You can test the Web services to verify that they are working by selecting the .asmx file in the Solution Explorer pane and pressing F5 to run the Web service. The Web service is loaded in the default browser, as shown in Figure 10.5. You can click one of the Web methods to load that method in the browser. Specify values for any parameters and click Invoke to execute the WebMethod and see the results.

FIGURE 10.5

Testing the `getImage()` Web method in Visual Studio

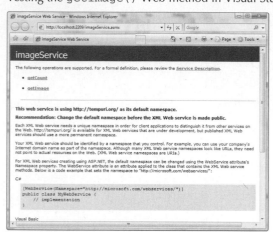

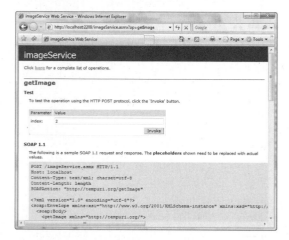

Creating a Silverlight Application for ASP.NET Web Services

In the previous section, you prepared an ASP.NET Web application to implement a Silverlight application that accesses an ASP.NET Web service. After the Web application is ready, you need to create a Silverlight application and link it to the ASP.NET Web application. Then a service reference to the `WebService` must be added to the Silverlight application project so that your Silverlight code is able to access the `WebMethod` services.

In the following sections, you learn how to link the Silverlight application to the ASP.NET Web application in Visual Studio. Then you learn how to add a service reference to the `WebService` that is defined in the ASP.NET Web application project and access the `WebMethod` services from Silverlight.

Linking a Silverlight application to an ASP.NET Web application

The first step in accessing an ASP.NET Web service from Silverlight is to provide the Silverlight assembly as part of the ASP.NET Web application project. This is necessary so that the ASP.NET Web page from Listing 10.1 can access the Silverlight application using the `Source` attribute. Creating a Silverlight link links the output of the Silverlight application to the output of the ASP.NET Web application so that the XAP file and any other output from the Silverlight application build are available to the ASP.NET Web application.

Linking a Silverlight application to an ASP.NET Web application project can be accomplished in one of two ways depending on whether you are creating a new Silverlight application project. The following sections describe each method.

Linking a new Silverlight application

If the Silverlight application does not already exist, right-click on ASP.NET Web Application in the Solution Explorer pane in Visual Studio and select Add ➪ New Item from the drop-down menu. Then select Silverlight Application from the available templates, specify the project name, and click Add to display the Add Silverlight Application dialog box, as shown in Figure 10.6. The Create a new Silverlight project and add it to the solution option will be set. Name the Silverlight project, specify the location to create it, and set the language option.

Specify the Destination folder to store the output of the Silverlight application. The Destination folder refers to the path, relative to the output path of the ASP.NET Web application project, where the Silverlight application build output is placed.

FIGURE 10.6

Adding a new Silverlight application in an ASP.NET Web application project

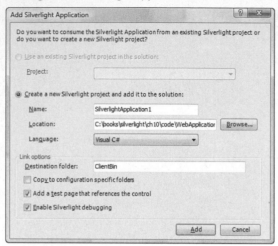

> **NOTE** When adding a Silverlight link, you do not need to select the Add a test page that references the control option because the Silverlight application is embedded in an ASP.NET Web page.

Click Add to create the Silverlight link. Visual Studio creates a new Silverlight application and adds it to the solution as well as links the output of the Silverlight application to the output of the ASP.NET Web application.

Linking an existing Silverlight application

If the Silverlight application already exists, then you must first add it to the ASP.NET Web application project. Right-click on the Solution in the Solution Explorer pane and choose Add ➪ Existing Project from the pop-up menu. Then navigate to the Silverlight application project and add it to the ASP.NET Web application project.

After the Silverlight application is added to the solution, right-click on ASP.NET Web Application in the Solution Explorer pane in Visual Studio and select Add ➪ New Item from the drop-down menu. Then select Silverlight Application from the available templates, specify the project name, and click Add to display the Add Silverlight Application dialog box, as shown in Figure 10.6. The Create a new Silverlight project and add it to the solution option will be set. Change this option to the Use an existing Silverlight project in the solution as shown in Figure 10.7. Select the project from the Project drop-down list.

Specify the Destination folder to store the output of the Silverlight application. Click Add to create the Silverlight link. Visual Studio links the output of the existing Silverlight application to the output of the ASP.NET Web application.

FIGURE 10.7

Adding a Silverlight link to an existing Silverlight application in an ASP.NET Web application project

Adding a service reference to the Silverlight application

The Silverlight application project needs to contain a Web reference to the `WebService` in order for the Silverlight code to be able to implement a `WebMethod` exposed by the service.

To add a Web reference to a Silverlight application, right-click on the Silverlight application project in the Solution Explorer pane of Visual Studio and select Add Service Reference from the pop-up menu to display the Add Service Reference, as window shown in Figure 10.8. Click Discover to discover Web services and then select the `WebService` from the Services list shown in Figure 10.8.

Specify a Namespace that is used to access the `WebService` from the Silverlight application. The namespace that you specify is used in the managed code of the Silverlight application to access the Web service. After you specify a namespace, click OK to add the service reference.

When you add a service reference to a Web service, Visual Studio wires up the WebService to the Silverlight application, and you can access the WebMethod as a SOAP client from your managed code.

FIGURE 10.8

Adding a service reference to a Silverlight application in Visual Studio

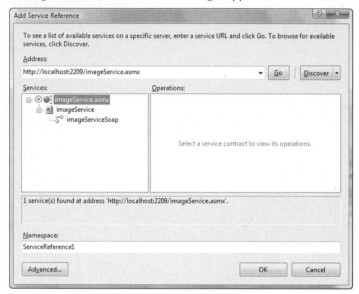

> **TIP**   If you make changes to your Web service, it is a good idea to update the service reference in the Silverlight application project in case any of the changes break code there. To update the service reference, right-click on the Web reference in the Solution Explorer and select Update Service Reference from the pop-up menu. Visual Studio updates the reference with any changes that have been made in **WebService**.

Accessing an ASP.NET Web service from Silverlight

Using the service reference created in the previous section, you are able to access the WebService from the managed code in your Silverlight application as a SOAP client. Using a SOAP client, managed code is able to access the WebMethod functionality exposed by the WebService.

Add code to implement service reference namespace

The first step in providing access to the WebService in your managed code is to include a reference to the namespace specified when creating the service reference. For example, consider a

Silverlight application implemented in C# using the namespace `SilverlightImageShow`. If the namespace of the Web reference is `imageServiceReference`, then you add the following `using` statement to the managed code to provide access to the `WebService`:

```
using SilverlightImageShow.imageServiceReference;
```

Creating a SOAP client to access the Web service

Using the Web service reference, you can create a SOAP client. The service reference exposes a class named after the `WebService` with `SoapClient` appended onto it. You use this class to create an image reference. For example, if the `WebService` is named `imageService`, then the following line of code creates a SOAP client that can connect to the `WebService`:

```
imageServiceSoapClient client = new imageServiceSoapClient();
```

 Currently, Silverlight only implements asynchronous communication between Silverlight applications and Web services.

Executing server-based Web methods

The SOAP client exposes the `WebMethod` services of the `WebService` as functions of the client object by appending Async on the end of the `WebMethod` name. For example, if the `WebMethod` name is `getCount()`, then you can execute the server-based function using the following line of code:

```
client.getCountAsync();
```

This line of code sends an asynchronous request to the server to execute the `WebMethod` function. When a response to the request is returned, a completed event is triggered for the client.

Adding a completed event handler to get a response

To handle the response of the request to a `WebMethod`, you need to attach a completed event handler to the client and get the value of the response in the handler when the request is received. There is a completed event property for each `WebMethod` that is exposed by the service.

The completed event property is named after the `WebMethod`. For example, if the Web method is named `getCount`, then the completed event is named `getCountCompleted`. The following code shows an example of attaching a completed event handler to a SOAP client:

```
client.getCountCompleted +=
    new EventHandler<getCountCompletedEventArgs>(getCountCompleted);
```

Notice that there is a `CompletedEventArgs` parameter named after the `WebMethod` specified for the event handler. When you define the event handler function, you need to define the `args` parameter of the event handler as this type. For example:

```
void getCountCompleted(object sender, getCountCompletedEventArgs e)
{
    . . .
```

Example Silverlight application

To fully illustrate implementing ASP.NET Web services in Silverlight applications, consider the code in Listing 10.3 and Listing 10.4. The code in Listing 10.3 is an XAML file that contains an `Image` control and two `Button` controls that are used to display images in the ASP.NET Web page defined in Listing 10.4.

LISTING 10.3

XAML Code That Implements an Image Control to Display Images Retrieved from a Web Service

```xml
<UserControl x:Class="SilverlightImageShow.Page"
    xmlns="http://schemas.microsoft.com/client/2007"
    xmlns:x="http://schemas.microsoft.com/winfx/2006/xaml"
    Width="660" Height="540">
    <Grid x:Name="LayoutRoot" Background="Black">
        <Image x:Name="appImage"
                VerticalAlignment="Top" HorizontalAlignment="Left"
                Height="480" Width="640"
                Margin="10,10,0,0"/>
        <Button x:Name="prevButton" Content="Previous"
                Height="20" Width="80"
                VerticalAlignment="Bottom" HorizontalAlignment="Left"
                Margin="220,0,0,10" />
        <Button x:Name="nextButton" Content="Next"
                Height="20" Width="80"
                VerticalAlignment="Bottom" HorizontalAlignment="Left"
                Margin="320,0,0,10" />
        <TextBlock x:Name="myText"
                Height="20" Width="200"
                Foreground="White"
                VerticalAlignment="Bottom" HorizontalAlignment="Left"
                Margin="10,0,0,10" />
    </Grid>
</UserControl>
```

The code in Listing 10.4 implements event handlers for the `nextButton` and `prevButton` controls that allow the user to toggle through images from an image list that is accessed using a SOAP client.

LISTING 10.4

A Web service asmx.cs C# File That Implements Two WebMethod Functions

```csharp
using System;
using System.Collections.Generic;
using System.Windows;
using System.Windows.Controls;
using System.Windows.Documents;
using System.Windows.Input;
using System.Windows.Media;

using SilverlightImageShow.imageServiceReference;

namespace SilverlightImageShow
{
  public partial class Page : UserControl
  {
    int index = 0;
    int count = 0;
    imageServiceSoapClient client;

    public Page()
    {
      InitializeComponent();

      //Initialize Button Event Handlers
      prevButton.Click += new RoutedEventHandler(prevButton_Click);
      nextButton.Click += new RoutedEventHandler(nextButton_Click);

      //Initialize Soap Client and Event Handlers
      client = new imageServiceSoapClient();
      client.getCountCompleted +=
       new EventHandler<getCountCompletedEventArgs>(getCountCompleted);
      client.getImageCompleted +=
       new EventHandler<getImageCompletedEventArgs>(updateImageCompleted);

      client.getCountAsync();
    }

    void getCountCompleted(object sender, getCountCompletedEventArgs e)
    {
      count = e.Result;
    }

    void nextButton_Click(object sender, RoutedEventArgs e)
    {
      if (index < count-1)
          index += 1;
```

continued

323

LISTING 10.4   *(continued)*

```
        else
            index = 0;
      client.getImageAsync(index);
   }

   void prevButton_Click(object sender, RoutedEventArgs e)
   {
      if (index > 0)
          index -= 1;
      else
          index = count-1;
      client.getImageAsync(index);
   }

   void updateImageCompleted(object sender, getImageCompletedEventArgs e)
   {
      appImage.SetValue(Image.SourceProperty, e.Result.ToString());
      myText.Text = String.Format("{0} ({1} of {2})",
                                  e.Result,
                                  index+1, count);

   }
 }
}
```

The code in Listing 10.4 defines an imageServiceSoapClient member named client that is used throughout the class. In the class constructor, the client is initialized using the following command:

```
    client = new imageServiceSoapClient();
```

Completed event handlers for the getCount() and getImage() WebMethod functions defined in Listing 10.2 are also added in the class constructor. The number of images available at the server is determined by executing the getImageAsync() function of the client object and then setting the value of count in the getCountCompleted() event handler function.

When the nextButton and prevButton buttons are clicked, their event handlers adjust the current index and send a request to the server to get the new image name using the getImageAsync() function. The Image object appImage and myText controls are updated with the results from that request in the getImageCompleted() event handler function.

The result is that when the user clicks Next and Previous in the ASP.NET Web page, as shown in Figure 10.9, the Silverlight application requests the name of the next or previous image in the list from an ASP.NET Web service and updates the image accordingly.

FIGURE 10.9

An ASP.NET Web application that implements an asp:Silverlight control to display images that are retrieved from an ASP.NET Web service

Image Service Using Silverlight

image1.jpg (1 of 5)   Previous   Next

Using asp:MediaPlayer AJAX Element to Directly Embed Video

Silverlight 2 provides the ASP.NET control asp:MediaPlayer to directly interface with ASP. NET Web services. The asp:MediaPlayer was created to directly embed a Silverlight media player element in an ASP.NET Web page (typically the .aspx file). Using the asp:MediaPlayer control allows developers to easily employ Silverlight's media capabilities to implement rich video content on their Web sites.

The advantage of implementing Silverlight media players in ASP.NET AJAX Web pages is that developers can use AJAX scripting to interact with media events. The following sections discuss how to implement a Silverlight media player in an ASP.NET Web page, add encoded video to the player, and implement AJAX scripting to interact with media events.

Registering the Silverlight assembly

The first step in implementing a Silverlight media player in an ASP.NET AJAX Web page is to register the Silverlight assembly dll file in the ASP.NET Web page (typically the `Default.aspx` file) that hosts the Silverlight application. This is done by adding a `Register` tag with the Silverlight `Assembly` and `Namespace` attributes as well as the `asp TagPrefix`. For example:

```
<%@ Register Assembly="System.Web.Silverlight"
    Namespace="System.Web.UI.SilverlightControls"
    TagPrefix="asp" %>
```

Once the Silverlight assembly is registered, you can add a Silverlight media player to the Web page using the `asp:MediaPlayer` control.

Adding a ScriptManager

To use AJAX scripting with your Silverlight media player, you need to add an AJAX `ScriptManager` control to the ASP.NET Web page also. The `ScriptManager` reacts to events in the ASP.NET page life cycle and coordinates event handling in all of the controls and code-behind pages.

To add a `ScriptManager` to the ASP.NET Web page, select the Design view for the ASP.NET Web page and drag and drop a `ScriptManager` control from the AJAX Extensions list in the Toolbox onto the page, as shown in Figure 10.10.

Adding the `ScriptManager` control adds the following code to the ASP.NET Web page:

```
<asp:ScriptManager ID="ScriptManager1" runat="server">
</asp:ScriptManager>
```

Embedding an asp:MediaPlayer tag in an ASP.NET Web page

Registering the Silverlight assembly in the ASP.NET Web page allows you to implement Silverlight media functionality by embedding an `asp:MediaPlayer` control in the Web page. The `asp:MediaPlayer` control hosts the Silverlight media player implemented in XAML.

The `asp:MediaPlayer` control exposes several properties that allow you to configure the look and behavior of the media player as well as hook into media events with JavaScript event handlers. Table 10.2 contains a list of some of the more important properties that you can configure for the `asp:MediaPlayer` control.

FIGURE 10.10

`ScriptManager` control being added to a Default.aspx ASP.NET Web page in the Design view of Visual Studio

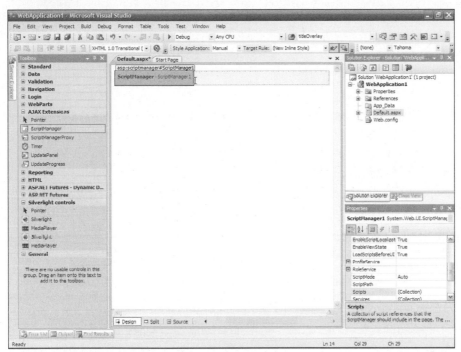

TABLE 10.2

Properties of the asp:MediaPlayer Control

Property	Description
AutoLoad	Boolean. Specifies whether to load the media file immediately or wait until the user clicks the Start button. Default is true.
AutoPlay	Boolean. Specifies whether to play the media file immediately or wait until the user clicks the Start button. Default is true.
Chapters	MediaChapterCollection. Contains a collection of asp:MediaChapter controls that apply to the MediaSource.
EnableCaptions	Boolean. Specifies whether to show captions with the video. Default is true.
Enabled	Boolean. Specifies whether the asp:MediaPlayer control is enabled or disabled. You can set this to false to temporarily disable the control. Default is true.

continued

TABLE 10.2 *(continued)*

Property	Description
EnableHtmlAccess	Boolean. Specifies whether the Silverlight plug-in can access the browser DOM. Default is `true`.
Height	Integer. Specifies the height in pixels in the Web page that the `asp:MediaPlayer` control consumes in the Web page.
ID	String. Specifies the object ID in the browser DOM assigned to the control.
MediaDefinition	String. Specifies the URL to the media definition XML file that contains data about the media source, such as chapters and thumbnails.
MediaSkinSource	String. Specifies the URL of the XAML file that is used as the skin for the media player. These skins are found in the SDK, created by Expression Encoder or created by the developer.
MediaSource	String. Specifies the URL of the media file that is played.
Muted	Boolean. Specifies if the volume of the player is muted. Default is `false`.
OnClientChapterSelected	String. Specifies the name of the JavaScript event handler function that is called when a chapter is selected in the player.
OnClientChapterStarted	String. Specifies the name of the JavaScript event handler function that is called when a chapter is started in the player.
OnClientCurrentStateChanged	String. Specifies the name of the JavaScript event handler function that is called when state of the media player is changed.
OnClientMarkerReached	String. Specifies the name of the JavaScript event handler function that is called when a marker is reached in the media.
OnClientMediaEnded	String. Specifies the name of the JavaScript event handler function that is called when the media has played completely to the end.
OnClientMediaFailed	String. Specifies the name of the JavaScript event handler function that is called if the media fails to load.
OnClientMediaOpened	String. Specifies the name of the JavaScript event handler function that is called when media has been downloaded and is opened by the player.
OnClientVolumeChanged	String. Specifies the name of the JavaScript event handler function that is called when volume is changed in the media player.
runat	String. Specifies if the control should be run at the server or the client. Default is set to "server." Typically this should be left at "server."
Volume	Double. Specifies the volume in a range between 0 and 1.
Width	Integer. Specifies the width in pixels in the Web page that the `asp:MediaPlayer` control consumes in the Web page.
Windowless	Boolean. Specifies whether the Silverlight application is displayed in a windowless state. Default is `false`.

To add an `asp:MediaPlayer` control to the ASP.NET Web page, select the Design view for the ASP.NET Web page and drag and drop an `asp:MediaPlayer` control from the Silverlight controls list in the Toolbox onto the Design view as shown in Figure 10.11.

FIGURE 10.11

An `asp:MediaPlayer` control being added to a Default.aspx ASP.NET Web page in the Design view of Visual Studio

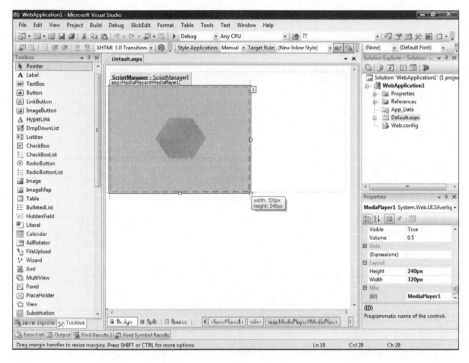

Adding the `asp:MediaPlayer` control adds the following code to the ASP.NET Web page:

```
<asp:MediaPlayer ID="MediaPlayer1" runat="server"
                 Height="480px" Width="640px">
</asp:MediaPlayer>
```

After the `asp:MediaPlayer` control is added to the page, you can quickly set the media file to be played and the XAML code to use as a skin for the media player by clicking the arrow button at the top right of the `asp:MediaPlayer` control in the Design view of Visual Studio. This displays the MediaPlayer Tasks tool, as shown in Figure 10.12.

Inside the MediaPlayer Tasks tool, you can specify the XAML source to use as the player skin; the media file to use as the source for the player; an image to use as a place holder until the media plays; and volume, muted, and auto-play options.

> **TIP**
>
> **The Silverlight SDK ships with several skins. You can import one of these skins or another skin that you have created by clicking Import Skin in the MediaPlayer Tasks tool. This displays a file dialog box, initially in the SDK directory containing the provided skins, which allows you to select an XAML file to import as the media player skin.**

FIGURE 10.12

The MediaPlayer Tasks tool for an `asp:MediaPlayer` control in the Design view of Visual Studio

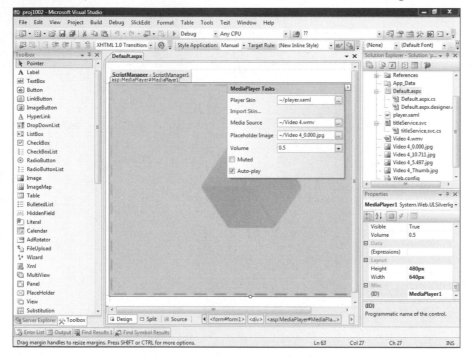

You can modify all of the properties of the control by changing the values in the Properties pane shown or by setting them directly in the source code. Listing 10.5 shows an example ASP.NET Web page that has been fully configured with an embedded `asp:MediaPlayer` control.

LISTING 10.5

A Default.aspx ASP.NET Web Page Containing an Embedded asp:Silverlight Control

```
<%@ Page Language="C#" AutoEventWireup="true"
    CodeBehind="Default.aspx.cs" Inherits="proj1002._Default" %>

<%@ Register assembly="System.Web.Silverlight"
    namespace="System.Web.UI.SilverlightControls" tagprefix="asp" %>

<!DOCTYPE html PUBLIC "-//W3C//DTD XHTML 1.0 Transitional//EN"
    "http://www.w3.org/TR/xhtml1/DTD/xhtml1-transitional.dtd">

<html xmlns="http://www.w3.org/1999/xhtml" >
<head runat="server">
    <title>ASP.NET AJAX Silverlight Media Player</title>
</head>
<body>
    <form id="form1" runat="server">
    <div>
        <asp:ScriptManager ID="ScriptManager1" runat="server">
        </asp:ScriptManager>
        <asp:MediaPlayer ID="MediaPlayer1" runat="server" AutoPlay="True"
                         MediaSkinSource="~/player.xaml"
                         MediaSource="~/Video4.wmv"
                         Height="480px" Width="640px">
        </asp:MediaPlayer>
    </div>
    </form>
</body>
</html>
```

Figure 10.13 shows the ASP.NET page in Listing 10.5 in a Web browser. The player.xaml and Video4.wmv files came from a video job that was encoded using Expression encoder with the Professional skin.

FIGURE 10.13

A Silverlight media player implemented in an ASP.NET Web page using the `asp:MediaPlayer` control

Adding MediaChapters controls

One of the cool things about most of the Silverlight media player skins is the ability to display chapters that allow the user to quickly navigate to a specific location in the video. Chapters can be added to an `asp:MediaPlayer` control using the `Chapters` property of the control and adding `asp:MediaChapter` controls.

The following code shows an example of adding three chapters to the `asp:MediaPlayer` control in Listing 10.5:

```
<asp:MediaPlayer ID="MediaPlayer1" runat="server" AutoPlay="True"
                 MediaSkinSource="~/player.xaml"
                 MediaSource="~/Video 4.wmv"
                 PlaceholderSource="~/Video 4_0.000.jpg"
                 Height="480px" Width="640px"
                 OnClientMarkerReached="onMarkerReached">
    <Chapters>
        <asp:MediaChapter Position="0.1"
                          ThumbnailSource="~/Video 4_0.000.jpg"
                          Title="Beginning" />
        <asp:MediaChapter Position="5.5"
                          ThumbnailSource="~/Video 4_5.497.jpg"
                          Title="Middle" />
        <asp:MediaChapter Position="10.7"
                          ThumbnailSource="~/Video 4_10.711.jpg"
                          Title="End" />
```

```
        </Chapters>
    </asp:MediaPlayer>
```

The `Position` attribute specifies the time in seconds in the video to apply the chapter. The `ThumbnailSource` property specifies the image file to use as a thumbnail. The `Title` property assigns a title to the chapter that can be consumed by the Silverlight application.

Figure 10.14 shows the ASP.NET page with the newly added chapter elements showing.

FIGURE 10.14

A Silverlight media player implemented in an ASP.NET Web page using the `asp:MediaPlayer` control with chapter controls displayed

The thumbnails used for the example in Figure 10.14 were created using Expression Encoder and then added as files to the ASP.NET Web application project.

Encoding video for AJAX scripting

One of the key features of implementing media using Silverlight is the ability to encode metadata in the media that can be consumed by Silverlight applications. Encoding metadata using Microsoft's Expression Encoder is discussed in detail in Chapter 5; however, in this section We touch lightly on it to explain the setup necessary to implement AJAX scripting event handlers.

If you want your AJAX scripts to be able to perform certain tasks at specific points in the video, you need to encode script commands at that point in the video. For example, consider the partial Silverlight media player XAML skin code in Listing 10.6. The code defines a `Storyboard` named `titleOverlay` that animates a `TextBlock` control named `myText` to fade in and then back out.

LISTING 10.6

Partial Code from a Silverlight Media Player XAML Skin

```
<Canvas xmlns="http://schemas.microsoft.com/winfx/2006/xaml/presentation"
        xmlns:x="http://schemas.microsoft.com/winfx/2006/xaml"
        Width="800" Height="600">
    <Canvas.Resources>
        <Storyboard x:Name="titleOverlay">
            <DoubleAnimationUsingKeyFrames BeginTime="00:00:00"
                    Storyboard.TargetName=" myText"
                    Storyboard.TargetProperty="(UIElement.Opacity)">
                <SplineDoubleKeyFrame KeyTime="00:00:00" Value="0"/>
                <SplineDoubleKeyFrame KeyTime="00:00:01" Value="1"/>
                <SplineDoubleKeyFrame KeyTime="00:00:02" Value="0"/>
            </DoubleAnimationUsingKeyFrames>
        </Storyboard>
    </Canvas.Resources>
    . . .
    <TextBlock x:Name="myText"
            FontSize="48" FontWeight="Bold" Foreground="DarkBlue"
            Width="595" Height="111"
            Canvas.Left="109" Canvas.Top="101"/>
</Canvas>
```

To be able to implement the `titleOverlay` animation in an AJAX script, you need to encode a script command in the media file to provide an event and information about the control.

This is done by adding a script command to the media file in Expression Encoder at the time that you want the title overlay to be displayed. Figure 10.15 shows a media job in Encoder that implements a script command for the `titleOverlay` animation. The type is specified as `overlay` and the value of the script command is `titleOverlay`.

The type will be used later in an AJAX script to determine that the marker is the defined `overlay` marker. Notice in Figure 10.15 that we also added some caption script commands to the video. It is necessary in the AJAX script to use the value of type to differentiate between the `caption` markers and the `overlay` marker.

FIGURE 10.15

A media job in Expression Encoder with a script command configured for a file

We also added markers to the video to create thumbnail images that we could add to the Web application project. Those images are used later to set up chapters in the asp:MediaPlayer control.

Adding an AJAX-enabled WCF service

The TextBlock implemented in Listing 10.6 does not have a value set for the Text element. To help you better understand the value of using AJAX with Silverlight media players, this section takes you through the process of adding an AJAX-enabled WCF service to the ASP.NET Web application and using that service to retrieve the text for the title overlay from the server.

First, right-click on the Web application project in the Solution Explorer of Visual Studio and choose Add ⇨ New Item to display the Add New Item window, as shown in Figure 10.16. Then select AJAX-enabled WCF Service, specify the name of the service, and click OK to add it to your project.

FIGURE 10.16

Adding a new AJAX-enabled WCF service to the ASP.NET Web application project in Visual Studio

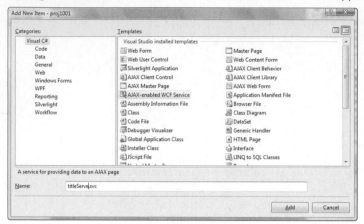

The WCF service is added to the project and a code-behind file is created. Inside the code-behind page you need to add a function with the [OperationContract] attribute that returns the title that is displayed as an overlay of the video. The code in Listing 10.7 shows the complete C# code-behind file for the WCF service titleService that provides an OperationContract service method named getTitle() that returns a title string.

LISTING 10.7

C# Code-Behind Page for an AJAX-Enabled WCF Web Service

```csharp
using System;
using System.Linq;
using System.Runtime.Serialization;
using System.ServiceModel;
using System.ServiceModel.Activation;
using System.ServiceModel.Web;

namespace proj1002
{
    [ServiceContract(Namespace = "")]
    [AspNetCompatibilityRequirements(RequirementsMode =
                AspNetCompatibilityRequirementsMode.Allowed)]
    public class titleService
    {
        [OperationContract]
```

```
    public string getTitle()
    {
        var title = "Sit Back and Enjoy the Ride";
        return title;
    }
  }
}
```

After you add the WCF service to the project, you need to modify the `asp:ScriptManager` control to provide access to the service in the ASP.NET Web page. The following code adds the `titleService` to the `asp:ScriptManager` control:

```
<asp:ScriptManager ID="ScriptManager1" runat="server">
    <Services>
        <asp:ServiceReference Path="~/titleService.svc" />
    </Services>
</asp:ScriptManager>
```

Implementing marker events in AJAX

After the media is encoded with script commands and the AJAX-enabled WCF service is config-ured in the project, you can implement AJAX scripts that consume the media player events and use the WCF service to update the XAML elements in the media player.

To implement an AJAX script handler for a script command, you need to add an event handler to the `asp:MediaPlayer` control that handles the marker event raised by the script command. This is done by setting the `onClientMarkerReached` property, as shown in the following code:

```
<asp:MediaPlayer ID="MediaPlayer1" runat="server" AutoPlay="True"
                 MediaSkinSource="~/player.xaml"
                 MediaSource="~/Video 4.wmv"
                 PlaceholderSource="~/Video 4_0.000.jpg"
                 Height="480px" Width="640px"
                 OnClientMarkerReached="onMarkerReached">
```

Next, you need to add a JavaScript function that handles the `onClientMarkerReached` event. The code in Listing 10.8 contains the full contents of the ASP.NET Web page that implements the `onClientMarkerReached` event in an `asp:MediaPlayer`.

LISTING 10.8

ASP.NET Web Page That Embeds a Silverlight MediaPlayer Control and Provides Functionality Using AJAX

```
<%@ Page Language="C#" AutoEventWireup="true"
    CodeBehind="Default.aspx.cs" Inherits="proj1002._Default" %>

<%@ Register assembly="System.Web.Silverlight"
    namespace="System.Web.UI.SilverlightControls" tagprefix="asp" %>

<!DOCTYPE html PUBLIC "-//W3C//DTD XHTML 1.0 Transitional//EN"
    "http://www.w3.org/TR/xhtml1/DTD/xhtml1-transitional.dtd">

<html xmlns="http://www.w3.org/1999/xhtml" >
<head runat="server">
    <title>ASP.NET AJAX Silverlight Media Player</title>
    <script type="text/javascript">
        function setTitle(title)
        {
            var player = $find('MediaPlayer1');
            var tb = player.get_element().content.root.findname('myTitle');
            tb.Text = title;
        }
        function doOverlay(story)
        {
            var player = $find('MediaPlayer1');
            var sb = player.get_element().content.root.findName(story);
            titleService.getTitle(setTitle);
            sb.begin();
        }
        function onMarkerReached(sender, args)
        {
            var marker = args.get_marker();
            if (marker.type === 'overlay')
            {
                var storyboard = marker.text;
                doOverlay(storyboard);
            }
        }
    </script>
</head>
<body>
    <form id="form1" runat="server">
    <div>
        <asp:ScriptManager ID="ScriptManager1" runat="server">
            <Services>
```

```
                    <asp:ServiceReference Path="~/titleService.svc" />
            </Services>
        </asp:ScriptManager>
        <asp:MediaPlayer ID="MediaPlayer1" runat="server" AutoPlay="True"
                         MediaSkinSource="~/player.xaml"
                         MediaSource="~/Video 4.wmv"
                         PlaceholderSource="~/Video 4_0.000.jpg"
                         Height="480px" Width="640px"
                         OnClientMarkerReached="onMarkerReached">
            <Chapters>
                <asp:MediaChapter Position="0.1"
                                  ThumbnailSource="~/Video 4_0.000.jpg"
                                  Title="Beginning" />
                <asp:MediaChapter Position="5.5"
                                  ThumbnailSource="~/Video 4_5.497.jpg"
                                  Title="Middle" />
                <asp:MediaChapter Position="10.7"
                                  ThumbnailSource="~/Video 4_10.711.jpg"
                                  Title="End" />
            </Chapters>
        </asp:MediaPlayer>
    </div>
    </form>
</body>
</html>
```

The asp:MediaPlayer control attaches the onClientMarkerReached event to the onMarkerReached() JavaScript event handler. Inside the onMarkerReached() event handler, the code uses the get_marker() function of the event to get the marker object and then accesses the marker.type attribute to determine if it is actually the overlay script command that was added using Expression Encoder using the following lines of code:

```
var marker = args.get_marker();
if (marker.type === 'overlay')
```

If this is the overlay script command, then the code calls the doOverlay() function and passes the marker.text attribute that contains the name of the Storyboard control that was defined in Expression Encoder as shown in Figure 10.15.

Inside the doOverlay() JavaScript function from Listing 10.8, the following lines of code get the MediaPlayer control and use it to find the Storyboard control:

```
var player = $find('MediaPlayer1');
var sb = player.get_element().content.root.findName(story);
```

Next, because this is AJAX and the `titleService` has been added to the `ScriptManager`, the function can call into the `getTitle()` operation of the WCF service described in Listing 10.7. The following line of code calls the `getTitle()` operation and uses the `setTitle()` JavaScript function to set the `Text` attribute of the `TextBlock` `myTitle` in the media player XAML:

```
titleService.getTitle(setTitle);
```

When the `Text` attribute of the `myTitle` `TextBlock` is set, the `Storyboard` animation to display the overlay starts, using the following line of code:

```
sb.begin();
```

The result is that when the overlay script command is triggered by the movie player, the Web page calls to the WCF service and gets a title and then uses the titleOverlay storyboard animation to fade the title into the video and back out, as shown in Figure 10.17.

FIGURE 10.17

A Silverlight media player implemented in a title overlay using AJAX scripts and a WCF service

Summary

This chapter has taken you through the process of configuring ASP.NET Web applications that implement Silverlight to provide a rich interface. Using the `asp:Silverlight` and `asp:MediaPlayer` controls, you can quickly embed Silverlight applications and media players in your ASP.NET applications. Silverlight can access ASP.NET Web services to request information from the server. We also covered using AJAX scripting to interact with the Silverlight controls to implement event handling and access to Web services.

In this chapter, you learned how to:

- Implement Silverlight applications in ASP.NET Web pages
- Link Silverlight projects to ASP.NET projects in Visual Studio
- Access ASP.NET services from Silverlight applications
- Embed a Silverlight video player in an ASP.NET Web page
- Access Silverlight controls from AJAX scripts
- Implement AJAX scripts to handle Silverlight events

Chapter 11

Programming Silverlight Applications Using the Dynamic Language Runtime

S ilverlight includes support for the Dynamic Language Runtime (DLR), including support for IronPython, IronRuby, and managed JavaScript. DLR support allows developers that are more familiar with these languages to implement Silverlight applications. This also allows developers to integrate new Silverlight applications with their existing Web applications and services.

The purpose of this chapter is to familiarize you with the process of implementing Silverlight applications in each of the IronPython, IronRuby, and managed JavaScript languages. The following sections introduce you to DLR programming concepts and then take you through some examples of creating DLR Silverlight applications.

Configuring a Silverlight DLR Application

When creating Silverlight DLR applications, you need to configure your project to include some basic elements that are required for all Silverlight DLR applications. Silverlight DLR applications require the following five basic parts:

- **Host Web Page:** An HTML or ASPX file that has been embedded with the Silverlight application

- **XAML Code:** Silverlight XAML file that defines the interface for the application

- **Dynamic Language Code:** An `app.py`, `app.rb`, or `app.jsx` file that contains the dynamic language code to implement the functionality of the application

- **Manifest:** An `AppManifest.xml` file that contains `AssemblyPart` elements for each assembly that is required by the application

- **Assemblies:** DLL libraries that are required by the application

You use these elements to build an XAP package that contains the compiled code assembly, manifest, and any necessary assemblies for the Silverlight DLR application.

> **NOTE**   The main dynamic language script must be named app: app.py for Python, app.rb for Ruby, or app.jsx for JavaScript. This is because Silverlight keys off the word app to locate the access point into the application. You can include several dynamic language scripts in the application, but only the initial one must be named app.

Embedding a Silverlight DLR application in a Web page

Silverlight applications must be embedded in Web pages. To embed the Silverlight DLR application, the host Web page needs to include HTML code that implements the Silverlight application. There are two methods of doing this. The most common method is to use an `object` or `embed` tag, as shown in code Listing 11.1. This method is discussed more in Chapter 7.

LISTING 11.1

Example HTML Code That Embeds a Silverlight Application Using an Object Tag

```
<!DOCTYPE html PUBLIC "-//W3C//DTD XHTML 1.0 Transitional//EN"
  "http://www.w3.org/TR/xhtml1/DTD/xhtml1-transitional.dtd">

<html xmlns="http://www.w3.org/1999/xhtml">
<head runat="server">
    <title>Dynamic Language Runtime and Silverlight</title>
</head>
<body>
    <h1>Silverlight DLR Application</h1>
    <form id="form1" runat="server">
        <div id="silverlightControlHost" width="500" height="500">
            <object data="data:application/x-silverlight,"
                type="application/x-silverlight-2-b1"
                width="500" height="500">
                <param name="source" value="app.xap"/>
                <param name="onerror" value="onSilverlightError" />
                <param name="onload" value="onSilverlightLoad" />
                <param name="background" value="LightGray" />
                <param name="initParams" value="" />
```

```
                    <param name="windowless" value="true" />
                </object>
            <iframe style='visibility:hidden;height:0;width:0;border:0px'>
            </iframe>
            </div>
        </form>
    </body>
    </html>
```

The second method is to use the `Silverlight.js` library and JavaScript to create the Silverlight object and embed it in the Web page. That method is discussed more in Chapter 9.

The `source` parameter should point to the XAP package that is created for the Silverlight DLR application. When the Web page is loaded, the XAP package is downloaded and the application is started in the Web page.

Building the AppManifest.xml file

When building Silverlight DLR applications, you need to use libraries for the appropriate language. These libraries must be included in the XAML manifest file so that the libraries are compiled and included in the XAP package.

Each language requires different libraries. The following is a list of the language-specific libraries required for each language:

- **IronPython:** IronPython.dll, IronPython.Modules.dll
- **IronRuby:** IronRuby.dll, IronRubyLibraries.dll
- **Managed Jscript:** Microsoft JScript Compiler.dll, Microsoft.JScript.Runtime.dll

In addition to the language-specific libraries, you need to include the following libraries for basic Silverlight applications:

- **Microsoft.Scripting.Silverlight.dll**
- **Microsoft.Scripting.dll**

If you are going to use the user controls introduced in Silverlight 2, you need to include the following user control libraries:

- **System.Windows.Controls.dll**
- **System.Windows.Controls.Extended.dll**

The code in Listing 11.2 shows an example `AppManifest.xml` file for an IronRuby Silverlight application. For more information about the `AppManifest.xml` file, see Chapter 7.

LISTING 11.2

Example AppManifest.xml File for a DLR Silverlight Application

```
<Deployment xmlns="http://schemas.microsoft.com/client/2007/deployment"
    xmlns:x="http://schemas.microsoft.com/winfx/2006/xaml"
    RuntimeVersion="2.0.30226.00"
    EntryPointAssembly="Microsoft.Scripting.Silverlight"
    EntryPointType="Microsoft.Scripting.Silverlight.DynamicApplication">
  <Deployment.Parts>
    <!-- Add any additional assemblies here -->
    <AssemblyPart Name="Microsoft.Scripting.Silverlight"
        Source="Microsoft.Scripting.Silverlight.dll" />
    <AssemblyPart Source="Microsoft.Scripting.dll" />
    <AssemblyPart Source="IronRuby.dll" />
    <AssemblyPart Source="IronRuby.Libraries.dll" />
    <AssemblyPart Name="System.Windows.Controls"
        Source="System.Windows.Controls.dll" />
    <AssemblyPart Name="System.Windows.Controls.Extended"
        Source="System.Windows.Controls.Extended.dll" />
  </Deployment.Parts>
</Deployment>
```

Using Chiron

The Silverlight SDK ships with an extremely useful tool called Chiron. Chiron can be used to test Silverlight DLR applications as well as create XAP packages. Chiron is a console application named `Chiron.exe`. In the same directory as Chiron is an XML configuration file named `Chiron.exe.config`. The Chiron configuration file contains the information Chiron needs to find the necessary libraries to build and test Silverlight DLR applications.

 You should add Chiron to your PATH environment variable. The Chiron path will be located in a path similar to the following depending on the location where the SDK is installed:

```
C:\Program File\Microsoft SDKs\Silverlight\v2.0\Tools\Chiron
```

Using Chiron as a Web server to test applications

One of the most common uses you have for Chiron is to test your Silverlight DLR applications as you develop them. Chiron has the ability to dynamically generate the XAP package needed by the browser on the fly.

This allows you to load the Silverlight application in the Web page, make changes to the code, and then simply refresh the Web page to implement the changes in the browser. Chiron acts as a Web server. When the page refreshes, a new version of the XAP package is dynamically generated and loaded in the browser.

To use Chiron as a Web server to test your applications, you need to put your source files and the `AppManifest.xml` file in a subfolder named `app`. The app subfolder should be a subfolder of the path where the application's host Web page is located. For example:

```
\DLRapp\TestPage.html
\DLRapp\app\app.py
\DLRapp\app\AppManifest.xml
\DLRapp\app\app.xaml
```

After you place your files in the correct paths, run Chiron using the following command from the command prompt:

```
chiron /b
```

You should see a Web page similar to the one in Figure 11.1 displayed. If you click on the host Web page, the application should load.

FIGURE 11.1
_____

A Web browser launched by Chiron to test a Silverlight DLR application

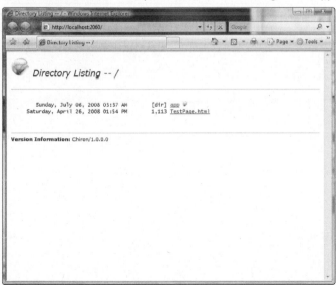

You can also use the `chiron /w` option instead of `chiron /b`. Chiron is loaded as a Web server that is serving the current directory as the root; however, no Web page is launched. Chiron serves on localhost port 2060.

 **To stop Chiron from running as a Web server, press Ctrl+C in the console window from where it was launched.**

Creating an XAP file

When you are ready to deploy your Silverlight DLR application, you need to use Chiron to create an XAP package that can be distributed. Use the following console command syntax:

```
Chiron /d:<dir name> /z:<xap filename>
```

The `/d:` option specifies the directory name of the location where the source files and `AppManifest.xml` file are stored. The `/z:` option specifies the filename of the XAP package that is created by Chiron.

CAUTION **Chiron works on a directory basis. Everything that is in the directory specified by the `/d:` option is included in the package.**

DLR Console on the Web

There is a great Web site that you can use to play around with DLR languages in Silverlight applications. The folks at dynamicsilverlight.net have created a Web-based console utility that allows you to add XAML and DLR code and have it dynamically applied to a Canvas element that is part of the same Web page. This allows you to test code snippets and play around with the language.

The address of the DLR console utility, shown in Figure 11.2 is:

```
http://dynamicsilverlight.net/see/dlrconsole/
```

FIGURE 11.2

A DLR console utility on the Web that allows developers to play around with DLR languages and Silverlight

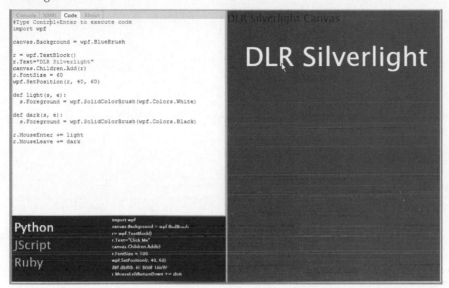

Creating an IronPython Silverlight Application

IronPython is an implementation of Python that is currently being developed by Microsoft. Using IronPython, developers are able to implement Python as the client side language for Silverlight applications. Using Python to code Silverlight applications allows developers to use current Python libraries and modules to provide rich functionality to the Silverlight application.

The first step in creating an IronPython Silverlight application is to create a folder for the application. Inside that folder you need to create a Web page similar to the one in Listing 11.1 to host the application.

Creating XAML for the IronPython Silverlight application

In your application folder, create a subfolder named app. In the app subfolder, create the XAML file containing the visual layout for the IronPython Silverlight application. We recommend using the UserControl as the root visual element for the XAML file.

Listing 11.3 shows an example XAML file that can be used to implement an IronPython Silverlight application. The code in Listing 11.3 implements a TextBlock control named titleBlock, a Button control named myButton, and a Canvas control named gamePage. Throughout this section, we refer to these controls as we describe how to implement an IronPython application to interact with them.

LISTING 11.3

Example app.xaml File for an IronPython Silverlight Application

```
<UserControl x:Class="System.Windows.Controls.UserControl"
    xmlns="http://schemas.microsoft.com/client/2007"
    xmlns:x="http://schemas.microsoft.com/winfx/2006/xaml"
    Width="500" Height="500">
    <Grid x:Name="LayoutRoot" Background="LightGray">
        <TextBlock x:Name="titleBlock"
                   HorizontalAlignment="Center"
                   FontSize="30"/>
        <Button x:Name="myButton" Content="StartGame"
                Height="20" Width="80"
                VerticalAlignment="Bottom"
                HorizontalAlignment="Center"
                Margin="15"/>
        <Canvas x:Name="gamePage" Background="Black"
                Height="410" Width="410">
        </Canvas>
    </Grid>
</UserControl>
```

Creating a manifest for the IronPython Silverlight application

With the XAML file in place, you should create an XML file named AppManifest.xml. Although this file is created automatically by Chiron, Chiron does not automatically add all of the assembly libraries you need.

Listing 11.4 shows an example of an AppManifest.xml file for an IronPython Silverlight application. This manifest file includes the standard Silverlight assemblies, the assemblies for IronPython, and the assemblies to implement the Silverlight 2 controls.

LISTING 11.4

Example AppManifest.xml File for an IronPython Silverlight Application

```xml
<Deployment xmlns="http://schemas.microsoft.com/client/2007/deployment"
    xmlns:x="http://schemas.microsoft.com/winfx/2006/xaml"
    RuntimeVersion="2.0.30226.00"
    EntryPointAssembly="Microsoft.Scripting.Silverlight"
    EntryPointType="Microsoft.Scripting.Silverlight.DynamicApplication">
  <Deployment.Parts>
    <!-- Add any additional assemblies here -->
    <AssemblyPart Name="Microsoft.Scripting.Silverlight"
        Source="Microsoft.Scripting.Silverlight.dll" />
    <AssemblyPart Source="Microsoft.Scripting.dll" />
    <AssemblyPart Source="IronPython.dll" />
    <AssemblyPart Source="IronPython.Modules.dll" />
    <AssemblyPart Name="System.Windows.Controls"
        Source="System.Windows.Controls.dll" />
    <AssemblyPart Name="System.Windows.Controls.Extended"
        Source="System.Windows.Controls.Extended.dll" />
  </Deployment.Parts>
</Deployment>
```

Providing access to CLR libraries and namespaces in Python

With the AppManifest.xml created, you can begin creating an IronPython application by creating a file named app.py in the same folder as the XAML file. The first step in Python programming is to add references to the libraries that are consumed by the application.

To provide access to the assemblies in your IronPython program, import the clr library and use the AddReference function to add a reference to the assembly. For example, to provide access to the Controls and Controls.Extended libraries, use the following code:

```
import clr
clr.AddReference('System.Windows.Controls,Version=1.0.0.0, \
Culture=neutral, PublicKeyToken=31bf3856ad364e35')
clr.AddReference('System.Windows.Controls.Extended,Version=1.0.0.0, \
Culture=neutral, PublicKeyToken=31bf3856ad364e35')
```

After the references are established, you can use the import statement to add specific namespaces or modules. For example, to add the System.Windows.Application and System.Windows.Controls.UserControl namespaces, use the following code:

```
from System.Windows import Application
from System.Windows.Controls import UserControl
```

Accessing XAML from IronPython

With the `Application` namespace imported, you can access the XAML code in the application using the Silverlight `Application` namespace. This is done by using the `Application.Content.RootVisual()` function.

The `RootVisual()` function accepts two arguments. The first is a `DependencyObject` of the same type as the root element in the XAML. The second argument is a `string` specifying the location of the XAML file relative to the currently executing code.

For example, the following line of code retrieves the root element of the XAML file named `app.xaml` with a `UserControl` as the root element:

```
xaml = Application.Current.LoadRootVisual(UserControl(), "app.xaml")
```

The code uses the `UserControl()` constructor to build the `DependencyObject`.

Using the root element of the XAML, you can access other objects in the XAML file. Consider the code in Listing 11.3 that specifies a `TextBlock` control named `titleBlock`. You can modify the `Text` attribute of `titleBlock` using the following line of Python code:

```
xaml.titleBlock.Text = 'Welcome to IronPython'
```

Implementing event handling in IronPython

The Silverlight DLR also gives you the ability to implement event handling for XAML objects inside your IronPython code. This provides you with the ability to implement fully functional event-driven IronPython applications that drive a rich Silverlight UI.

Using the root element of the XAML, you can access objects in the XAML and attach event handlers to them. Consider the code in Listing 11.3 that specifies a `Button` control named `myButton`. You can use the following IronPython code to attach a `MouseLeftButtonUp` event handler to the `myButton` control:

```
xaml.myButton.MouseLeftButtonUp += onClick
```

Then you can implement an IronPython event handler function similar to the following to handle the `MouseLeftButtonUp` event on the button:

```
def onClick (sender, args):
    sender.Content = "Clicked"
```

The IronPython event handler function gets the sender object, which in this case is a `Button` control, and sets the `Content` attribute to `Clicked`.

CROSS-REF Event handlers are discussed in much more detail in Chapter 8. Although that chapter focuses on C# and Visual Basic programming, the event types and arguments are very similar, and you can use that chapter as a reference for IronPython event handlers.

Adding dynamic XAML using IronPython

You can use IronPython code to dynamically add XAML objects that are rendered to the browser in the Silverlight application. This is one of the most powerful features of the DLR because it allows you to employ the strengths of the scripting language to create a content-rich interface for the user.

One of the biggest strengths of the DLR is that almost every Silverlight object has a constructor. You can use that constructor rather than having to use `CreateFromXaml()` or an `XamlReader` to build XAML objects.

To create an XAML object in IronPython, simply call the constructor function. For example, to create a `Canvas` and a `TextBlock` object, you use the following IronPython code:

```
c = Canvas()
t = TextBlock()
```

After creating the object, you can modify its properties using standard dot syntax. For example, to set the size of a `Canvas` object you use the following IronPython code:

```
c = Canvas()
c.Height = 50
c.Width = 200
```

As with .NET programming, you cannot use string values for properties such as the `Source` property of an `Image` control or the `Margin` property of a `StackPanel` control. To set those values, you need to use the appropriate object from the CLR library.

For example, the following IronPython code creates a `SolidColorBrush` object to set the `Foreground` color of a `TextBlock`:

```
xaml.titleBlock.Foreground = SolidColorBrush(Colors.Red)
```

To be able to create the `SolidColorBrush` object using `Colors` in this manner, you need to import them from the CLR using the following import statement:

```
from System.Windows.Media import SolidColorBrush, Colors
```

At times you may still want to use an XAML reader to generate an XAML DOM from a well-formed XAML string. To do this you can use the `Load` function of an `XamlReader` object to generate the XAML from a string. For example, the following IronPython code creates an XAML DOM with the root object being a `Canvas`:

```
myXaml = XamlReader.Load("""<Canvas
xmlns='http://schemas.microsoft.com/client/2007'
Width='200' Height='200' Background='Blue'
Canvas.Top='%d' Canvas.Left='%d'>
<TextBlock Text='%s' Canvas.Top='10' Canvas.Left='15'
Text="SomeText"/>
</Canvas>""")
```

You need to import the XamlReader using the following import statement:

```
from System.Windows.Markup import XamlReader
```

CAUTION   The XAML text needs to be well formed and *must* include an xmlns property, typically xmlns='http://schemas.microsoft.com/client/2007', for Silverlight to be able to generate the XAML DOM.

Example of an IronPython Silverlight application

The code in Listing 11.5 contains IronPython code that implements all of the techniques that have been discussed in this section. The full IronPython Silverlight application comprises the Web page in Listing 11.1, the XAML in Listing 11.3, the manifest in Listing 11.4, as well as the Python code in Listing 11.5.

LISTING 11.5

Example app.py File for an IronPython Silverlight Application

```
import clr
clr.AddReference('System.Windows.Controls, Version=1.0.0.0, \
Culture=neutral, PublicKeyToken=31bf3856ad364e35')
clr.AddReference('System.Windows.Controls.Extended, Version=1.0.0.0, \
Culture=neutral, PublicKeyToken=31bf3856ad364e35')

from System.Windows import Application
from System.Windows.Markup import XamlReader
from System.Windows.Media import SolidColorBrush, Colors
from System.Windows.Controls import UserControl, Canvas, TextBlock

gameData = ['7','8','','','','','','','',
'3','','','9','','','','6','1',
'9','','','3','1','','','','2',
'','6','','1','','2','','7','',
'','1','8','','','','5','9','',
'','3','','8','','4','','6','',
'2','','','','4','7','','','5',
'7','8','','','','3','','','6',
'','','','','','','','8','7']
```

```
def makeSquare(top, left, value):
    square = """<Canvas
xmlns='http://schemas.microsoft.com/client/2007'
Width='40' Height='40' Background='White'
Canvas.Top='%d' Canvas.Left='%d'>
<TextBlock Text='%s' Canvas.Top='10' Canvas.Left='15'/>
</Canvas>""" % (top, left, value)
    return square

def buildSet(setRow, setCol):
    c = Canvas()
    for x in range(3):
        for y in range(3):
            top = setRow*140 + x*45
            left = setCol*140 + y*45
            value = gameData[setRow*27 + setCol*9 + x*3 + y]
            c2 = XamlReader.Load(makeSquare(top,left, value))
            c.Children.Add(c2)
    return c

def buildGame():
    for x in range(3):
        for y in range(3):
            set = buildSet(x, y)
            xaml.gamePage.Children.Add(set)

def onClick (sender, args):
    buildGame()
    sender.Content = "Started"

xaml = Application.Current.LoadRootVisual(UserControl(), "app.xaml")
xaml.titleBlock.Text = 'Welcome to IronPython Suduko'
xaml.titleBlock.Foreground = SolidColorBrush(Colors.Red)
xaml.myButton.MouseLeftButtonUp += onClick
```

The XAML code in Listing 11.3 defines a Button control named myButton, a TextBlock control named titleBlock, and a Canvas control named gamePage. The code in Listing 11.5 accesses these elements and implements an event handler and dynamic XAML to create a Sudoku game sheet.

The code first imports the clr and uses it to add references to the Controls and Controls.Extended libraries. Then it imports the necessary modules and namespaces required by the application using from import statements.

To simplify the application, a simple list is implemented named gameData to generate the application. The gameData list is consumed by the makeSquare() function that simply generates a well-formed XAML statement to create a Canvas control to represent one square in the Sudoku game.

The buildSet() function uses a nested for loop to create a 3 × 3 set in the Sudoku game. The buildSet() function uses the XamlReader.load() function to dynamically generate the Canvas objects from the makeSquare() function and adds those to a Canvas object that is returned by the function using the following line of code:

```
c2 = XamlReader.Load(makeSquare(top,left, value))
c.Children.Add(c2)
```

The buildGame() function also uses a nested for loop to create a 3 × 3 grid of Canvas objects from buildSet() and adds them to the gamePage Canvas object in the XAML file using the following line of code:

```
xaml.gamePage.Children.Add(set)
```

To access the Silverlight XAML, the IronPython code uses the Application.Current. LoadRootVisual() function to get the UserControl control from the app.xaml file using the following line of code.

```
xaml = Application.Current.LoadRootVisual(UserControl(), "app.xaml")
```

Using the UserControl object xaml, the code is then able to set the Text and Foreground attributes using the following lines of code. Notice that the Foreground attribute is set to a SolidColorBrush object type:

```
xaml.titleBlock.Text = 'Welcome to IronPython Suduko'
xaml.titleBlock.Foreground = SolidColorBrush(Colors.Red)
```

The code in Listing 11.5 implements a MouseLeftButtonUp event handler to call the buildGame() function in the onClick() event handler function. Notice that in the onClick() event handler function, the Content property of the Button control that triggered the event is modified using the following code:

```
sender.Content = "Started"
```

The onClick() event handler is attached to the Button control mybutton using the following line of code:

```
xaml.myButton.MouseLeftButtonUp += onClick
```

The result is that the Silverlight application creates a Web page similar to the one in Figure 11.3. When the StartGame button is clicked, a Sudoku game page is dynamically rendered.

FIGURE 11.3

An IronPython Silverlight application that dynamically generates a Sudoku game sheet

Creating an IronRuby Silverlight Application

IronRuby is an implementation of the Ruby programming language that is currently being developed by Microsoft. Using IronRuby, developers can implement Ruby code as the client-side language for Silverlight applications. Using Ruby to code Silverlight applications allows developers to use already existing Ruby applications to provide rich functionality to the Silverlight application.

The first step in creating an IronRuby Silverlight application is to create a folder for the application. Inside that folder, you need to create a Web page similar to the one in Listing 11.1 to host the application.

Creating XAML for the IronRuby Silverlight application

In your application folder, you need to create a subfolder named app. In the app subfolder, create the XAML file containing the visual layout for the IronRuby Silverlight application. We recommend using the UserControl as the root visual element for the XAML file.

Listing 11.6 shows an example XAML file that can be used to implement an IronRuby Silverlight application. The code in Listing 11.6 implements a `TextBlock` control named `titleBlock`, a `Button` control named `myButton`, and a `Canvas` control named `rubyForm`. Throughout this section we refer to these controls as we describe how to implement an IronRuby application to interact with them.

LISTING 11.6

Example app.xaml File for an IronRuby Silverlight Application

```
<UserControl x:Class="System.Windows.Controls.UserControl"
    xmlns="http://schemas.microsoft.com/client/2007"
    xmlns:x="http://schemas.microsoft.com/winfx/2006/xaml"
    x:Name="Page">
    <Grid x:Name="LayoutRoot" Background="LightGray">
        <TextBlock x:Name="titleBlock"
                    HorizontalAlignment="Center"
                    FontSize="30"/>
        <Button x:Name="myButton" Content="Populate"
                Height="20" Width="80"
                VerticalAlignment="Bottom"
                HorizontalAlignment="Center"
                Margin="15"/>
        <Canvas x:Name="rubyForm" Background="White"
                Height="300" Width="400">
        </Canvas>
    </Grid>
</UserControl>
```

Creating a manifest for the IronRuby Silverlight application

With the XAML file in place, you should create an XML file named `AppManifest.xml`. Although this file is created automatically by Chiron, Chiron does not automatically add all of the assembly libraries you need.

Listing 11.7 shows an example of an `AppManifest.xml` file for an IronRuby Silverlight application. This manifest file includes the standard Silverlight assemblies, the assemblies for IronRuby, and the assemblies to implement the Silverlight 2 controls.

LISTING 11.7

Example AppManifest.xml File for an IronRuby Silverlight Application

```
<Deployment xmlns="http://schemas.microsoft.com/client/2007/deployment"
    xmlns:x="http://schemas.microsoft.com/winfx/2006/xaml"
    RuntimeVersion="2.0.30226.00"
    EntryPointAssembly="Microsoft.Scripting.Silverlight"
    EntryPointType="Microsoft.Scripting.Silverlight.DynamicApplication">
  <Deployment.Parts>
    <AssemblyPart Name="Microsoft.Scripting.Silverlight"
        Source="Microsoft.Scripting.Silverlight.dll" />
    <AssemblyPart Source="Microsoft.Scripting.dll" />
    <AssemblyPart Source="IronRuby.dll" />
    <AssemblyPart Source="IronRuby.Libraries.dll" />
    <AssemblyPart Name="System.Windows.Controls"
        Source="System.Windows.Controls.dll" />
    <AssemblyPart Name="System.Windows.Controls.Extended"
        Source="System.Windows.Controls.Extended.dll"/>
  </Deployment.Parts>
</Deployment>
```

Providing access to CLR libraries and namespaces in IronRuby

With the AppManifest.xml created, you can begin creating an IronRuby application by creating a file named app.py in the same folder as the XAML file. The first step in Ruby programming is to add references to the libraries that are consumed by the application.

To provide access to the assemblies in your IronRuby program, you need to use a require statement to add a reference to the assembly. For example, to provide access to the Controls and Controls.Extended libraries, use the following code:

```
require 'System.Windows.Controls, Version=1.0.0.0,
    Culture=neutral, PublicKeyToken=31bf3856ad364e35'
require 'System.Windows.Controls.Extended, Version=1.0.0.0,
    Culture=neutral, PublicKeyToken=31bf3856ad364e35'
```

After the references are established, you can use include statements to add namespaces. For example, to add the System.Windows.Application and System.Windows.Controls.UserControl namespaces, use the following code:

```
include System::Windows
include System::Windows::Controls
```

Accessing XAML from IronRuby

With the Windows namespace imported, you can access the XAML code in the application using the Silverlight `Application` namespace. This is done by using the `Application.current.load_root_visual()` function.

The `load_root_visual()` function accepts two arguments. The first is a `DependencyObject` of the same type as the root element in the XAML. The second argument is a `string` specifying the location of the XAML file relative to the currently executing code.

For example, the following line of code retrieves the root element of the XAML file named `app.xaml` with a `UserControl` as the root element:

```
@xaml = Application.current.load_root_visual(UserControl.
    new,"app.xaml")
```

The code uses the `UserControl.new` constructor to build the `DependencyObject`.

Using the root element of the XAML, you can access other objects in the XAML file. Consider the code in Listing 11.6 that specifies a `TextBlock` control named `titleBlock`. You can modify the `Text` attribute of `titleBlock` using the following line of Ruby code:

```
@xaml.titleBlock.Text = 'Welcome to IronRuby'
```

Implementing event handling in IronRuby

The Silverlight DLR also gives you the ability to implement event handling for XAML objects inside your IronRuby code. This provides you with the ability to implement fully functional event-driven IronRuby applications that drive a rich Silverlight UI.

Using the root element of the XAML, you can access objects in the XAML and attach event handlers to them. Consider the code in Listing 11.6 that specifies a `Button` control named `myButton`. You can use the following IronRuby code to attach a `Click` event handler to the `myButton` control:

```
@xaml.myButton.click{|sender, args| onClick(sender, args)}
```

Then you can implement an IronRuby event handler function similar to the following to handle the `Click` event on the button:

```
def onClick(sender, args)
    sender.content = 'Clicked'
end
```

The IronRuby event handler function gets the sender object, which in this case is a `Button` control, and sets the `Content` attribute to `Clicked`.

CROSS-REF Event handlers are discussed in much more detail in Chapter 8. Although that chapter focuses on C# and Visual Basic programming, the event types and arguments are very similar, and you can use that chapter as a reference for IronRuby event handlers.

Adding dynamic XAML using IronRuby

You can use IronRuby code to dynamically add XAML objects that will be rendered to the browser in the Silverlight application. This is one of the most powerful features of the DLR because it allows you to employ the strengths of the scripting language to create a content-rich interface for the user.

One of the biggest strengths of the DLR is that almost every Silverlight object has a constructor. You can use that constructor rather than having to use `CreateFromXaml()` or a `XamlReader` to build XAML objects.

To create an XAML object in IronRuby, simply call the constructor function. For example, to create a `StackPanel`, `TextBlock`, and `TextBox` object, you use the following IronRuby code:

```
panel = StackPanel.new
label = TextBlock.new
text = TextBox.new
```

Once the object has been created, you can modify its properties using standard dot syntax. For example, to set the size of a `Panel` object, use the following IronRuby code:

```
panel = StackPanel.new
panel.Height = 50
panel.Width = 200
```

As with .NET programming, you are not able to use string values for properties such as the `Source` property of an `Image` control or the `Margin` property of a `StackPanel` control. To set those values, you need to use the appropriate object from the CLR library.

For example, the following IronRuby code creates a `Thickness` object to set the `Margin` property of a `StackPanel`:

```
panel.margin = Thickness.new 50
```

Example of an IronRuby Silverlight application

The code in Listing 11.8 contains IronRuby code that implements all of the techniques that have been discussed in this section. The full IronRuby Silverlight application comprises the Web page in Listing 11.1, the XAML in Listing 11.6, the manifest in Listing 11.7, as well as the Ruby code in Listing 11.8.

LISTING 11.8

Example app.rb File for an IronRuby Silverlight Application

```ruby
require 'System.Windows.Controls, Version=1.0.0.0, Culture=neutral,
    PublicKeyToken=31bf3856ad364e35'
require 'System.Windows.Controls.Extended, Version=1.0.0.0, Culture=neutral,
    PublicKeyToken=31bf3856ad364e35'

include System::Windows
include System::Windows::Controls

@xaml = Application.current.load_root_visual(UserControl.new, "app.xaml")

def addItem(name)
    panel = StackPanel.new
    panel.margin = Thickness.new 5
    panel.Orientation = Orientation.horizontal
    label = TextBlock.new
    label.Width = 80
    label.TextAlignment = TextAlignment.right
    label.Text = name
    tBox = TextBox.new
    tBox.Width = 200
    panel.children.add(label)
    panel.children.add(tBox)
    return panel
end

def onClick(sender, args)
    panel = StackPanel.new
    panel.margin = Thickness.new 50
    panel.children.add(self.addItem("First"))
    panel.children.add(self.addItem("Last"))
    panel.children.add(self.addItem("Address"))
    panel.children.add(self.addItem("Phone"))
    panel.children.add(self.addItem("Email"))
    @xaml.rubyForm.children.add(panel)
    sender.content = 'Clicked'
end

class FrameworkElement
    def method_missing(method)
        find_name(method.to_s.to_clr_string)
    end
end

@xaml.titleBlock.Text = 'Dynamic IronRuby Form'
@xaml.find_name('myButton').click{|sender, args| onClick(sender, args)}
```

The XAML code in Listing 11.6 defines a Button control named myButton, a TextBlock control named titleBlock, and a Canvas control named rubyForm. The code in Listing 11.8 accesses these controls to implement an event handler and dynamic XAML to create a simple Silverlight Web form.

The code first adds references to the Controls and Controls.Extended libraries. Then it imports the necessary namespaces required by the application using required statements.

To access the Silverlight XAML, the IronRuby code uses the Application.current.load_root_visual() function to get the UserControl control from the app.xaml file using the following line of code.

```
@xaml =
Application.current.load_root_visual(UserControl.new,"app.xaml")
```

The addItem() function accepts a single argument name. It then creates a StackPanel, TextBlock, and TextBox object. It then sets the necessary attributes for the controls. The Text property of the TextBox control is set to the value of the name argument. Notice that the TextAlignment and Orientation properties are set using TextAlignment and Orientation objects using the following code:

```
panel.Orientation = Orientation.horizontal
. . .
label.TextAlignment = TextAlignment.right
```

The TextBlock and TextBox objects are added to the StackPanel using the following lines of code, and the StackPanel is returned by the function:

```
panel.children.add(label)
panel.children.add(tBox)
```

Using IronRuby, the namescope is not directly linked up. Therefore you cannot use dot syntax to access elements that have been named in the namescope. To solve this problem, the code in Listing 11.8 overrides the method_missing() method of the FrameworkElement class so that the method_missing() method implements a find_name() method to get the name as shown in the following code snippet:

```
class FrameworkElement
    def method_missing(method)
        find_name(method.to_s.to_clr_string)
    end
end
```

Without overridding the method_missing() method, you have to access items in the namescope using the following syntax:

```
@xaml.find_name(titleBlock).Text = 'Welcome to Dynamic IronRuby'
```

You can use dot syntax to access the namescope names if you do override the method_missing() method. The following code shows an example of using the UserControl object xaml to modify the Text attribute of a TextBlock that is defined in app.xaml:

```
@xaml =
Application.current.load_root_visual(UserControl.new,"app.xaml")
@xaml.titleBlock.Text = 'Welcome to Dynamic IronRuby'
```

The code in Listing 11.8 implements a Click event handler to dynamically build a Web form by calling the addItem() function in the onClick() event handler function. Notice that in the onClick() event handler function, the Content property of the Button control that triggered the event will be modified using the following code:

```
sender.content = 'Clicked'
```

The onClick() event handler is attached to the Button control myButton using the following line of code:

```
@xaml.find_name('myButton').click{|sender, args| onClick(sender,
args)}
```

The result is that the Silverlight application creates a Web page similar to the one in Figure 11.4. Clicking the Populate button dynamically generates a Silverlight Web form.

FIGURE 11.4

An IronRuby Silverlight application that dynamically generates a Silverlight Web form

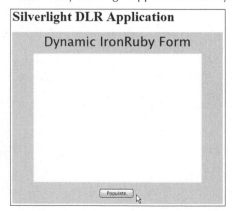

Creating a Managed JavaScript Silverlight Application

The DLR functionality of Silverlight allows developers the ability to implement the code for Silverlight applications using managed JavaScript. In Chapter 9, we discuss using unmanaged JavaScript to build Silverlight applications. This section focuses on using managed JavaScript that is compiled and delivered in the Silverlight XAP file.

The first step in creating a managed JavaScript Silverlight application is to create a folder for the application. Inside that folder you need to create a Web page similar to the one in Listing 11.1 to host the application.

Creating XAML for the managed JavaScript Silverlight application

In your application folder, you need to create a subfolder named app. In the app subfolder, create the XAML file containing the visual layout for the managed JavaScript Silverlight application. We recommend using the UserControl as the root visual element for the XAML file.

Listing 11.9 shows an example XAML file that can be used to implement a managed JavaScript Silverlight application. The code in Listing 11.9 implements a TextBlock control named titleBlock; three Button controls named zoomOut, zoomIn, and zoomInMore; as well as an Image control named myImage. The XAML code also defines a StoryBoard animation that scales the myImage control. Throughout this section we refer to these controls as we describe how to implement a managed JavaScript application to interact with them.

LISTING 11.9

Example app.xaml File for a Managed JavaScript Silverlight Application

```
<UserControl x:Class="System.Windows.Controls.UserControl"
    xmlns="http://schemas.microsoft.com/client/2007"
    xmlns:x="http://schemas.microsoft.com/winfx/2006/xaml"
    x:Name="Page">
    <UserControl.Resources>
        <Storyboard x:Name="zoomImage">
            <DoubleAnimationUsingKeyFrames
                Storyboard.TargetName="myImage"
                Storyboard.TargetProperty="(UIElement.RenderTransform).
(TransformGroup.Children)[0].(ScaleTransform.ScaleX)"
                BeginTime="00:00:00">
```

continued

LISTING 11.9 *(continued)*

```
                        <SplineDoubleKeyFrame x:Name="xFactor"
                                        KeyTime="00:00:03"
                                        Value="10"/>
                </DoubleAnimationUsingKeyFrames>
                <DoubleAnimationUsingKeyFrames
                        Storyboard.TargetName="myImage"
                        Storyboard.TargetProperty="(UIElement.RenderTransform).
(TransformGroup.Children)[0].(ScaleTransform.ScaleY)"
                        BeginTime="00:00:00">
                        <SplineDoubleKeyFrame x:Name="yFactor"
                                        KeyTime="00:00:03"
                                        Value="10"/>
                </DoubleAnimationUsingKeyFrames>
            </Storyboard>
        </UserControl.Resources>

        <Grid x:Name="LayoutRoot" Background="DarkGray">
            <TextBlock x:Name="titleBlock"
                    HorizontalAlignment="Center"
                    FontSize="30"/>
            <Grid x:Name="imagePad" Background="LightGray"
                    Height="300" Width="400">
                <Image x:Name="myImage" Source="image.jpg"
                        Height="30" Width="40"
                        RenderTransformOrigin="0.5,0.5" >
                    <Image.RenderTransform>
                        <TransformGroup>
                            <ScaleTransform/>
                            <SkewTransform/>
                            <RotateTransform/>
                            <TranslateTransform/>
                        </TransformGroup>
                    </Image.RenderTransform>
                </Image>
            </Grid>
            <Button x:Name="zoomOut" Content="Zoom Out"
                    Height="20" Width="80"
                    VerticalAlignment="Bottom"
                    HorizontalAlignment="Left"
                    Margin="100,0,0,15"/>
            <Button x:Name="zoomIn" Content="Zoom In"
                    Height="20" Width="80"
                    VerticalAlignment="Bottom"
                    HorizontalAlignment="Left"
                    Margin="200,0,0,15"/>
            <Button x:Name="zoomInMore" Content="Zoom More"
                    Height="20" Width="80"
```

```
                    VerticalAlignment="Bottom"
                    HorizontalAlignment="Left"
                    Margin="300,0,0,15"/>
        </Grid>
</UserControl>
```

> **CAUTION** The JavaScript programming model is determined by the `x:Class` attribute. If the `x:Class` attribute is absent from the root XAML object, then the programming model that applies for the page will default to the unmanaged JavaScript programming model. If the `x:Class` attribute is present, the programming model for the page is the managed JavaScript programming model. The programming models cannot be mixed on a single XAML page because the declaration of the programming model affects the resolution of event handlers.

Creating a manifest for the managed JavaScript Silverlight application

With the XAML file in place, you should create an XML file named `AppManifest.xml`. Although this file is created automatically by Chiron, Chiron does not automatically add all of the assembly libraries you need.

Listing 11.10 shows an example of an `AppManifest.xml` file for a managed JavaScript Silverlight application. This manifest file includes the standard Silverlight assemblies, the assemblies for managed JavaScript, and the assemblies to implement the Silverlight 2 controls.

LISTING 11.10

Example AppManifest.xml File for a Managed JavaScript Silverlight Application

```xml
<Deployment xmlns="http://schemas.microsoft.com/client/2007/deployment"
    xmlns:x="http://schemas.microsoft.com/winfx/2006/xaml"
    RuntimeVersion="2.0.30226.00"
    EntryPointAssembly="Microsoft.Scripting.Silverlight"
    EntryPointType="Microsoft.Scripting.Silverlight.DynamicApplication">
    <AssemblyPart Name="Microsoft.Scripting.Silverlight"
        Source="Microsoft.Scripting.Silverlight.dll" />
    <AssemblyPart Source="Microsoft.Scripting.dll" />
    <AssemblyPart Source="Microsoft.JScript.Compiler.dll" />
    <AssemblyPart Source="Microsoft.JScript.Runtime.dll" />
    <AssemblyPart Name="System.Windows.Controls"
        Source="System.Windows.Controls.dll" />
    <AssemblyPart Name="System.Windows.Controls.Extended"
        Source="System.Windows.Controls.Extended.dll" />
    </Deployment.Parts>
</Deployment>
```

Providing access to CLR libraries and namespaces in managed JavaScript

With the `AppManifest.xml` created, you can begin creating a managed JavaScript application by creating a file named app.jsx in the same folder as the XAML file. The first step in JavaScript programming is to add references to the libraries that will be consumed by the application.

To provide access to the assemblies in your managed JavaScript program, use the `Import` statements to add specific namespaces or modules. For example, to add the `System.Windows.Application` and `System.Windows.Controls.UserControl` namespaces, use the following code:

```
Import("System.Windows.Application");
Import("System.Windows.Controls.UserControl");
```

Accessing XAML from managed JavaScript

With the `Windows` namespace imported, you can access the XAML code in the application using the Silverlight `Application` namespace. This is done by using the `Application.Current.LoadRootVisual()` function.

The `LoadRootVisual()` function accepts two arguments. The first is a `DependencyObject` of the same type as the root element in the XAML. The second argument is a `string` specifying the location of the XAML file relative to the currently executing code.

For example, the following line of code will retrieve the root element of the XAML file named `app.xaml` with a `UserControl` as the root element:

```
xaml =
Application.Current.LoadRootVisual(new UserControl(), "app.xaml")
```

The code uses the `new UserControl()` constructor to build the `DependencyObject`.

Using the root element of the XAML, you can access other objects in the XAML file. Consider the code in Listing 11.9 that specifies a `TextBlock` control named `titleBlock`. You can modify the `Text` attribute of `titleBlock` using the following line of JavaScript code:

```
xaml.titleBlock.Text = 'Welcome to Managed JavaScript'
```

Implementing event handling in managed JavaScript

The Silverlight DLR also gives you the ability to implement event handling for XAML objects inside your managed JavaScript code. This provides you with the ability to implement fully functional event-driven managed JavaScript applications that drive a rich Silverlight UI.

Using the root element of the XAML, you can access objects in the XAML and attach event handlers to them. Consider the code in Listing 11.9 that specifies a `Button` control named `zoomOut`. You can use the following managed JavaScript code to attach a `Click` event handler to the `zoomOut` control:

```
xaml.zoomOut.Click += unZoom
```

Then you can implement a managed JavaScript event handler function similar to the following to handle the `Click` event on the button:

```
function unZoom (sender, args) {
    sender.Content = "Clicked"
```

The managed JavaScript event handler function gets the `sender` object, which in this case is a `Button` control, and sets the `Content` attribute to `Clicked`.

CROSS-REF Event handlers are discussed in much more detail in Chapter 8. Although that chapter focuses on C# and Visual Basic programming, the event types and arguments are very similar, and you can use that chapter as a reference for managed JavaScript event handlers.

Adding dynamic XAML using managed JavaScript

You can use managed JavaScript code to dynamically add XAML objects that are rendered to the browser in the Silverlight application. This is one of the most powerful features of the DLR because it allows you to employ the strengths of the scripting language to create a content-rich interface for the user.

One of the biggest strengths of the DLR is that almost every Silverlight object has a constructor. You can use that constructor rather than having to use `CreateFromXaml()` or a `XamlReader` to build XAML objects.

To create an XAML object in managed JavaScript, simply call the constructor function. For example, to create a `Canvas` and a `TextBlock` object, use the following managed JavaScript code:

```
c = new Canvas()
t = new TextBlock()
```

After you create the object, you can modify its properties using standard dot syntax. For example, to set the size of a `Canvas` object, use the following managed JavaScript code:

```
c = new Canvas()
c.Height = 50
c.Width = 200
```

As with .NET programming, you cannot use string values for properties such as the `Source` property of an `Image` control or the `Margin` property of a `StackPanel` control. To set those values, you need to use the appropriate object from the CLR library.

For example, the following managed JavaScript code creates a `SolidColorBrush` object to set the `Foreground` color of a `TextBlock`:

```
xaml.titleBlock.Foreground = new SolidColorBrush(Colors.Red)
```

At times you may still want to use an XAML reader to generate an XAML DOM from a well-formed XAML string. To do this you can use the `Load` function of an `XamlReader` object to generate the XAML from a string. For example, the following managed JavaScript code creates an XAML DOM with the root object being a `Canvas`:

```
myXaml = XamlReader.Load("""<Canvas
xmlns='http://schemas.microsoft.com/client/2007'
Width='200' Height='200' Background='Blue'
Canvas.Top='%d' Canvas.Left='%d'>
<TextBlock Text='%s' Canvas.Top='10' Canvas.Left='15'
Text="SomeText"/>
</Canvas>"""
```

> **CAUTION** The XAML text needs to be well formed and *must* include an `xmlns` property, typically `xmlns='http://schemas.microsoft.com/client/2007'`, for Silverlight to be able to generate the XAML DOM.

Example of a managed JavaScript Silverlight application

The code in Listing 11.11 contains managed JavaScript code that implements all of the techniques that have been discussed in this section. The full managed JavaScript Silverlight application comprises the Web page in Listing 11.1, the XAML in Listing 11.9, the manifest in Listing 11.10, as well as the JavaScript code in Listing 11.11.

LISTING 11.11

Example app.jsx File for a Managed JavaScript Silverlight Application

```
Import("System.Windows.Application");
Import("System.Windows.Controls.UserControl");

xaml = Application.Current.LoadRootVisual(new UserControl(), "app.xaml")
xaml.titleBlock.Text = "JavaScript Image Zoom"
xaml.zoomOut.Click += unZoom
xaml.zoomIn.Click += doZoom
xaml.zoomInMore.Click += bigZoom

function unZoom (sender, args) {
```

```
    xaml.xFactor.Value = 1
    xaml.yFactor.Value = 1
    xaml.zoomImage.Begin()
    sender.Content = "Clicked"
}

function doZoom (sender, args) {
    xaml.xFactor.Value = 5
    xaml.yFactor.Value = 5
    xaml.zoomImage.Begin()
    sender.Content = "Clicked"
}

function bigZoom (sender, args) {
    xaml.xFactor.Value = 10
    xaml.yFactor.Value = 10
    xaml.zoomImage.Begin()
    sender.Content = "Clicked"
}
```

The XAML code in Listing 11.9 defines Button controls named zoomOut, zoomIn, and zoomInMore. It also defines a TextBlock control named titleBlock and a StoryBoard control named zoomImage. The code in Listing 11.11 accesses these elements to implement event handlers that control zooming an image.

The code first imports the necessary namespaces required by the application using Import statements. To access the Silverlight XAML, the managed JavaScript code uses the Application. Current.LoadRootVisual() function to get the UserControl control from the app.xaml file using the following line of code:

```
    xaml =
    Application.Current.LoadRootVisual(new UserControl(), "app.xaml")
```

Using the UserControl object xaml, the code is then able to set the Text property of the titleBlock control using the following line of code:

```
    xaml.titleBlock.Text = "JavaScript Image Zoom"
```

The code in Listing 11.11 then implements a Click event handler for each button using the following code:

```
    xaml.zoomOut.Click += unZoom
    xaml.zoomIn.Click += doZoom
    xaml.zoomInMore.Click += bigZoom
```

Three JavaScript event handler functions named unZoom(), doZoom(), and bigZoom() are implemented to handle Click events from the Button controls. Inside Listing 11.9, we added the xFactor and yFactor names to the SplineDoubleKeyFrame element of the ScaleTransform.ScaleX and ScaleTransform.ScaleY animation properties. Inside the event handler functions, the xFactor and yFactor names are accessed to set the Value used by the zoomImage Storyboard. This allows JavaScript to control the size that the Image control is changed to by the animation using the following code:

```
xaml.xFactor.Value = 5
xaml.yFactor.Value = 5
```

Notice that in the event handler functions, the Content property of the Button control that triggered the event is modified using the following code:

```
sender.Content = "Clicked"
```

The zoomImage animation is started in the event handler functions using the begin() function as shown in the following code:

```
xaml.zoomImage.Begin()
```

The result is that the Silverlight application creates a Web page similar to the one in Figure 11.5. When the Zoom Out, Zoom In, and Zoom In More buttons are clicked, the image size is changed using a StoryBoard animation.

FIGURE 11.5

A managed JavaScript Silverlight application that dynamically zooms in and out on an image

Summary

In this chapter, we discussed how to create Silverlight applications using the DLR languages IronPython, IronRuby, and managed JavaScript. Using the Chiron tool that ships with the Silverlight SDK, you can test and deploy Silverlight applications that are written in IronPython, IronRuby, or managed JavaScript. Silverlight's DLR support provides developers with access to XAML code allowing them to provide functionality to the Silverlight UI from DLR code.

In this chapter, you learned:

- What components are necessary for a DLR application
- How to create a manifest file for a DLR application
- How to use Chiron to test DLR applications
- How to access XAML elements in DLR applications
- How to implement event handling in DLR applications
- How to dynamically create XAML in DLR applications
- How to create IronPython, IronRuby, and managed JavaScript Silverlight applications

Chapter 12

Programming Custom Silverlight Controls and Libraries

S ilverlight is one of the most dynamic languages. It comes with a rich set of controls; however, it is very simple to extend the functionality of existing controls and even create new controls with new functionality. Creating custom controls in Silverlight is a great way to make your Silverlight applications more rich and unique.

One of the most common problems that developers face is how to reuse their code. Typically, the best answer to that is to create some sort of library that can be consumed by multiple applications or at least multiple times in the same application.

Silverlight has a couple of different solutions that allow developers to write reusable code. One solution is to add another Silverlight `UserControl` to a project and then provide the functionality there. A second and better solution is to create a Silverlight class library and implement the UI and functionality there. The following sections describe building and implementing custom Silverlight controls using each of these methods.

Creating Custom Silverlight Controls in Applications

When you build Silverlight applications, you will notice the need to repeat several of the same steps for several controls of the same type. For example, if you create custom buttons you need to either repeat all of the XAML required for the custom button in the XAML file or implement code in the code-behind page to repetitively build the functionality for each button.

375

This can be time consuming. The best way to solve this problem is to create a custom Silverlight `UserControl`. You can build the UI and functionality once in the `UserControl` and then implement that functionality as many times as necessary in your Silverlight application.

> **NOTE**   If you look at the base Silverlight application project created by Visual Studio, you see that `Page.xaml`, `Page.xaml.cs`, and `Page.xaml.vb` are actually `UserControls`. This abstraction allows you to port the functionality from one Silverlight application to another easily.

The following sections take you through the process of building a custom `UserControl` and implementing multiple instances of it in a Silverlight application.

Creating a custom User Control in a Visual Studio project

The first step in creating custom controls in your Silverlight applications it to add a `UserControl` to the project. To add a `UserControl` to a Silverlight project in Visual Studio, right-click on the project in the Solution Explorer and then choose Add➪New Item from the pop-up menu to display the Add New Item window, as shown in Figure 12.1.

From the Add New Item window, select Silverlight User Control. Specify the name of the control in the Name text box. This is the name that you use in your application to reference the control. Click Add and the `UserControl` is added to the project.

FIGURE 12.1

Creating a new Silverlight `UserControl` in Visual Studio

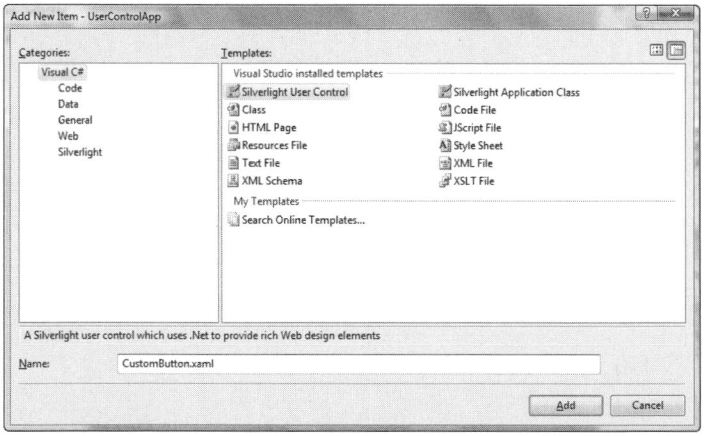

When you add a new `UserControl`, two files are created — an XAML file that is named after the control and either a C# or Visual Basic code-behind file that is also named after the control. The following sections discuss using these files to implement the custom control.

Creating the custom control UI

The first step in implementing a custom control is to add the UI elements to the XAML file. Initially the XAML file created for the custom control contains a simple `UserControl` element and a `Grid` control, as shown in the following code:

```
<UserControl x:Class="UserControlApp.SilverlightControl1"
    xmlns="http://schemas.microsoft.com/client/2007"
    xmlns:x="http://schemas.microsoft.com/winfx/2006/xaml"
    Width="400" Height="300">
    <Grid x:Name="LayoutRoot" Background="White">

    </Grid>
</UserControl>
```

The `x:Class` attribute of the `UserControl` element is set to the control class that has been added to the Namespace of the parent application. You likely want to specify the `Width` and `Height` of the control.

To implement the UI for the control, simply add Silverlight controls to the XAML file. For example, the following code has added a `Button` control to the custom control UI:

```
<UserControl x:Class="UserControlApp.SilverlightControl1"
    xmlns="http://schemas.microsoft.com/client/2007"
    xmlns:x="http://schemas.microsoft.com/winfx/2006/xaml"
    Width="150" Height="50">
    <Grid x:Name="LayoutRoot" Background="White">
        <Button x:Name="btnControl" />
    </Grid>
</UserControl>
```

Notice that the `Height` and `Width` properties of the `UserControl` are set; however, the size of the `Button` is not set. This allows the control to be resized, and the `Button` simply resizes with the control.

Simply adding a single `Button` to the control doesn't make it all that useful. You could have simply added a `Button` control in the XAML of the application. If you are going to take the time to build a custom control, you need to add some reusable functionality to the control's UI.

For example, you could add a `Storyboard` animation that modifies the control in some way. The following code implements a `Storyboard` animation that modifies the size of a `Button` object:

```
<Storyboard x:Name="btnExpand">
    <DoubleAnimationUsingKeyFrames
        Storyboard.TargetName="btnControl"
        Storyboard.TargetProperty=
"(UIElement.RenderTransform).(TransformGroup.Children)[0].
    (ScaleTransform.ScaleX)"
        BeginTime="00:00:00">
        <SplineDoubleKeyFrame KeyTime="00:00:01" Value="1.25"/>
    </DoubleAnimationUsingKeyFrames>
</Storyboard>
```

> **TIP** Remember that you need to add an **x:Name** property for each control that you want to access in the code-behind file.

Coding the functionality

After the UI controls are added to the XAML file, the next step in implementing a custom control in Silverlight is to add functionality to the control in the code-behind file. You can reuse functionality each time you create a new instance of the custom control in your applications.

You can add functionality to the XAML UI by implementing code in the code-behind page. You can access named objects in the XAML because they are part of the namescope.

For example, to attach a MouseEnter event handler for a Button control with the property x:Name="myButton" set, you can use the following C# code in the code-behind file:

```
myButton.MouseLeave +=
    new MouseEventHandler(myButton_MouseLeave);
```

> **CROSS-REF** For more information about adding functionality in the code-behind page, see Chapter 8.

Implementing the custom control in the project

When you finish coding the functionality of the custom control, you can implement it in your Silverlight applications.

You can access the Silverlight application from the managed code in your Silverlight application using the name that you gave the User Control when it was created. For example, if you named the User Control CustomButton, the following C# code creates an instance of the CustomButton User Control in the Silverlight application:

```
CustomButton b = new CustomButton();
```

You should be able to access any elements in the control that have names in the namescope using the instance of the custom control. For example, if a custom control has a TextBox control named x:Name="Title", you should be able to use the following C# code to access and set the Text property of that TextBox:

```
CustomControl ctrl = new CustomControl();
ctrl.Title = "Customized Control";
```

Example of implementing a custom Silverlight User Control

This section takes you through an example to help you understand how to implement a custom `UserControl` in Silverlight applications better. To begin the example, consider the code in Listing 12.1 that implements the UI for a custom `Button` control. The code specifies a `Class` property that specifies the `CustomButton` class in the `UserControlApp` namespace.

The code in Listing 12.1 implements two `Storyboard` controls named `btnExpand` and `btnCollapse` that animate resizing a `Button` control named `btnControl`.

LISTING 12.1

XAML File Containing the UI Elements for a CustomButton Control

```xml
<UserControl x:Class="UserControlApp.CustomButton"
    xmlns="http://schemas.microsoft.com/client/2007"
    xmlns:x="http://schemas.microsoft.com/winfx/2006/xaml"
    Width="150" Height="50">
    <UserControl.Resources>
        <Storyboard x:Name="btnExpand">
            <DoubleAnimationUsingKeyFrames
                Storyboard.TargetName="btnControl"
                Storyboard.TargetProperty=
"(UIElement.RenderTransform).(TransformGroup.Children)[0].
    (ScaleTransform.ScaleX)"
                BeginTime="00:00:00">
                <SplineDoubleKeyFrame KeyTime="00:00:01" Value="1.25"/>
            </DoubleAnimationUsingKeyFrames>
        </Storyboard>
        <Storyboard x:Name="btnCollapse">
            <DoubleAnimationUsingKeyFrames
                Storyboard.TargetName="btnControl"
                Storyboard.TargetProperty=
"(UIElement.RenderTransform).(TransformGroup.Children)[0].
    (ScaleTransform.ScaleX)"
                BeginTime="00:00:00">
                <SplineDoubleKeyFrame KeyTime="00:00:01" Value="1"/>
            </DoubleAnimationUsingKeyFrames>
        </Storyboard>
    </UserControl.Resources>
    <Grid x:Name="LayoutRoot" Background="White">
        <Button x:Name="btnControl"
                RenderTransformOrigin="0.0,0.5">
```

continued

LISTING 12.1 *(continued)*

```
            <Button.RenderTransform>
                <TransformGroup>
                    <ScaleTransform/>
                    <SkewTransform/>
                    <RotateTransform/>
                    <TranslateTransform/>
                </TransformGroup>
            </Button.RenderTransform>
        </Button>
    </Grid>
</UserControl>
```

Now consider the C# code-behind page in Listing 12.2 that adds functionality to the code in Listing 12.1. The code in Listing 12.2 creates a class CustomButton that derives from the UserControl class that matches up the code from Listing 12.1.

The code in Listing 12.2 attaches MouseEnter and MouseLeave event handlers named btnControl_MouseEnter() and btnControl_MouseLeave() to the btnControl Button.

Inside the btnControl_MouseEnter() event handler, the btnExpand Storyboard animation is started. Inside the btnControl_MouseLeave() event handler, the btnCollapse Storyboard animation is started.

Each time the mouse moves over the button, the button expands; when the mouse leaves, the button shrinks. This example uses this UI to implement several instances of the CustomButton class. Each instance retains the expand and collapse functionality.

LISTING 12.2

C# Code-Behind File Containing the Functionality for a CustomButton Control

```
using System;
using System.Collections.Generic;
using System.Windows;
using System.Windows.Controls;
using System.Windows.Input;
using System.Windows.Media;
using System.Windows.Media.Animation;
using System.Windows.Shapes;

namespace UserControlApp
{
    public partial class CustomButton : UserControl
    {
        public CustomButton()
```

```
    {
        InitializeComponent();
        btnControl.MouseEnter +=
            new MouseEventHandler(btnControl_MouseEnter);
        btnControl.MouseLeave +=
            new MouseEventHandler(btnControl_MouseLeave);
    }

    void btnControl_MouseLeave(object sender, MouseEventArgs e)
    {
        btnCollapse.Begin();
    }

    void btnControl_MouseEnter(object sender, MouseEventArgs e)
    {
        btnExpand.Begin();
    }
    }
}
```

To implement the code in a Silverlight application, consider the code in Listings 12.3 and 12.4. The XAML code in Listing 12.3 implements a standard UserControl for a Silverlight application. The code specifies a Class property that specifies the Page class in the UserControlApp namespace. The code defines a Grid as the root element as well as a Canvas control named ButtonBar and a MediaElement named Movie.

LISTING 12.3

XAML File for a Silverlight Application That Implements the CustomButton Control

```
<UserControl x:Class="UserControlApp.Page"
    xmlns="http://schemas.microsoft.com/client/2007"
    xmlns:x="http://schemas.microsoft.com/winfx/2006/xaml"
    Width="580" Height="300">
    <Grid x:Name="LayoutRoot" Background="LightGray">
        <Canvas x:Name="ButtonBar"
                Height="300" Width="150"
                HorizontalAlignment="Left"
                Background="Blue"/>
        <MediaElement x:Name="Movie" Source="/movie.wmv"
                AutoPlay="False"
                Height="300" Width="400"
                HorizontalAlignment="Right"/>
    </Grid>
</UserControl>
```

The code in Listing 12.4 implements the functionality for the Silverlight application. One of the first things the code does is define a string array named `mediaControls` that is used to generate buttons.

The buttons are generated in a `for` loop in the `addButtons()` function. The code uses the following line to create an instance of the button object:

```
CustomButton b = new CustomButton();
```

The code is able to use the following statement to set the `Canvas.Top` property of the `CustomButton` object because it derives from `UserControl`:

```
b.SetValue(Canvas.TopProperty, x * 50);
```

Notice that the code is able use the following code to access the `btnControl Button` control in `CustomButton` to set the `Text` property and attach an event handler to the `Button`:

```
b.btnControl.Content = mediaControls[x];
b.btnControl.Click += new RoutedEventHandler(doControl);
```

The code implements the media controls to play, pause, and stop the `MediaElement Movie` in the `doControl()` event handler function.

LISTING 12.4

C# File Containing the Functionality for a Silverlight Application That Implements Several CustomButton Controls

```
using System;
using System.Collections.Generic;
using System.Windows;
using System.Windows.Controls;
using System.Windows.Input;
using System.Windows.Media;
using System.Windows.Media.Animation;
using System.Windows.Shapes;

namespace UserControlApp
{
    public partial class Page : UserControl
    {
```

```
string[] mediaControls = new string[] {"Play", "Pause", "Stop" };
public Page()
{
    InitializeComponent();
    addButtons();
}
public void addButtons()
{
    for (int x = 0; x < mediaControls.Length; x++)
    {
        CustomButton b = new CustomButton();
        b.SetValue(Canvas.TopProperty, x * 50);
        b.btnControl.Content = mediaControls[x];
        b.btnControl.Click += new RoutedEventHandler(doControl);
        ButtonBar.Children.Add(b);
    }
}

void doControl(object sender, RoutedEventArgs e)
{
    Button b = sender as Button;
    if (b.Content == "Play")
        Movie.Play();
    else if (b.Content == "Pause")
        Movie.Pause();
    else if (b.Content == "Stop")
        Movie.Stop();
}
}
}
```

The result is that when the Silverlight application is run, three CustomButton controls are added to the application. The expand and collapse functionality built into CustomButton is implemented for each instance. Each time the mouse is moved over a button, it expands as shown in Figure 12.2. This allows a developer to implement any number of CustomButton controls without having to reprogram the animations.

FIGURE 12.2

Silverlight application that implements CustomButton controls

Creating Silverlight Class Library Controls

In the previous section, we discussed creating a Silverlight UserControl to implement multiple instances of a custom control. That works well as long as the UserControl is part of the Silverlight application project.

A better method is to create a Silverlight class library that provides the UI and functionality needed in the custom control and can work as a template. Building the custom control into a Silverlight class allows you to import the functionality easily into any number of Silverlight applications.

One of the biggest benefits of implementing Silverlight class library controls is that it is easier to give the Silverlight applications the same look and feel throughout your entire Web site. Another advantage is that it is easier for Web designers to consume the custom control using XAML without the need to understand the code behind the functionality.

The following sections discuss the process of creating a custom control in a Silverlight class library.

Creating the Silverlight library

The first step in building a Silverlight class library in Visual Studio is to create a Silverlight class library project. To create the Silverlight class library project, choose File ➪ New ➪ Project from the main menu to display the New Project window, as shown in Figure 12.3. Next, select Silverlight in either the C# or Visual Basic trees of the Project types pane. Specify the Name, Location, and Solution options for the project, and click OK to create the Silverlight Class Library project.

FIGURE 12.3

FIGURE 12.3

Creating a new Silverlight class library in Visual Studio

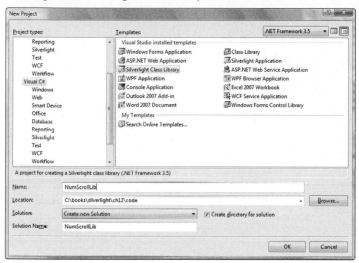

The Silverlight class library project initially contains only one source file named Class.cs if you create a C# Silverlight class library or Class.vb if you create a Visual Basic Silverlight class library. Typically, you want to remove this file from the project and create your own class file.

To remove the class file, simply right-click on it in the Solution Explorer and select Delete from the pop-up menu. Then right-click on the project in the Solution Explorer and choose Add ➪ Class from the pop-up menu to display the Add New Item window, as shown in Figure 12.4. Specify the Name of the class and click Add to add the new class to the control. Use a name that is meaningful to the library, because it is the class name that is referenced when using the library.

After the new class is created, you need to create an XAML file that contains the UI definitions for the class. The XAML file should be named generic.xaml. To create the generic.xaml file, right-click on the project in Solution Explorer and choose Add ➪ New Item from the pop-up menu to display the Add New Item window. Select XML File from the list of templates. Then specify generic.xaml as the Name of the XML file.

NOTE   You need to add references to the System.Windows.Controls and System.Windows.Controls.Extended namespaces if you are going to use them in the custom control. They are not added by default.

FIGURE 12.4

Adding new items to a project in Visual Studio

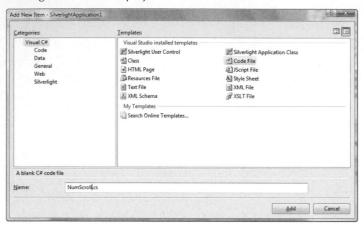

Defining the UI for the custom control

After creating and configuring the Silverlight class library project as described in the previous section, you can begin adding UI elements to the generic.xaml file. This can be done in one of two ways.

The first way is to simply add the XAML necessary for the library. The second way is to implement a ResourceDictionary element that contains a Style element that can be used as a custom template control. The second method takes a bit more code, but it enables application developers who use the control to change the appearance without having to write code or change functionality.

Defining a control template

To create a control that can be used with templates, add the following code to implement the ResourceDictionary, Style, Setter, and ControlTemplate elements to the generic.xaml file:

```
<ResourceDictionary
    xmlns="http://schemas.microsoft.com/client/2007"
    xmlns:x="http://schemas.microsoft.com/winfx/2006/xaml"
    xmlns:custom="clr-namespace:NumScrollLib;assembly=NumScrollLib">
    <Style TargetType="custom:NumScroll">
        <Setter Property="Template">
            <Setter.Value>
                <ControlTemplate TargetType="src:NumScroll">
                </ControlTemplate>
```

```
            </Setter.Value>
        </Setter>
    </Style>
</ResourceDictionary>
```

You need to specify the namespaces that are used by the XAML elements in the library in the `ResourceDictionary` element. Included in those namespaces should be the class that you created when configuring the Silverlight class library. For example, if you add a class named `NumScroll`, then the following line of code adds that namespace:

```
xmlns:custom="clr-namespace:NumScrollLib;assembly=NumScrollLib">
```

The `TargetType` property of the `Style` element should be set using the namespace defined for the custom class; for example:

```
<Style TargetType="custom:NumScroll">
```

The `Property` property of the `Setter` element should be set to `Template` to designate that this is a template. The `TargetType` property of the `ControlTemplate` element should also be set using the namespace defined for the custom class.

Adding UI elements to the control template

After you set up the control template, you can add Silverlight controls to the `ControlTemplate` element to implement the UI. For example, the following code adds a `Grid` element that contains a `TextBlock` and a `Button` control:

```
<ControlTemplate TargetType="src:NumScroll">
    <Grid x:Name="RootElement"
          Background="{TemplateBinding Background}">
        <TextBlock x:Name="txtControl" Text="text"/>
        <Button Content="+" x:Name="btnControl" />
    </Grid>
</ControlTemplate>
```

Notice that the `Background` property of the `Grid` control implements a `TemplateBinding` statement. This binds the value of the `Background` property to the Background member of the control class. This is necessary if you desire the attribute to be set using XAML when a developer implements the control library in another Silverlight application.

> **TIP** When you name the UI elements of a custom control library using `x:Name`, use meaningful names. Remember to name every control and element that is needed to implement the functionality of the control.

You can also implement a `ContentPresenter` element as part of the UI definition. This allows the developer a much more dynamic set of options when implementing the custom control. For example, to implement a `ContentPresenter` that binds the `Content`, `FontSize`, and `FontFamily` properties to the template, you could add the following code to the previous `Grid`:

```
<ContentPresenter Content="{TemplateBinding Content}"
                  FontSize="{TemplateBinding FontSize}"
                  FontFamily ="{ TemplateBinding FontFamily}"/>
```

Implementing the custom control functionality

After you add the UI elements to the `generic.xaml` file, you can begin implementing the functionality of the control in the control class file. The first step is to modify the class definition to specify that the class derives from the `Control` class. The following C# code illustrates setting the `NumScroll` class to derive from `Control`:

```
namespace NumScrollLib
{
    public class NumScroll : Control
    {
. . .
```

After you specify that the custom control class derives from `Control`, you can begin implementing properties and event handling to add functionality to the control.

Adding dependency properties

When implementing custom controls, you are likely adding properties to the control that can be accessed and set. It is recommended that when you create properties in a custom control, that they be defined as `DependencyProperty` objects. For example, you can use the following code to create a `DependencyProperty` named `BackgroundProperty` for the `Background` property of a custom control:

```
public static readonly DependencyProperty BackgroundProperty =
        DependencyProperty.Register("Background", typeof(Brush),
        typeof(NumScroll), null);
```

After you add the `DependencyProperty` objects, specify the `Get` and `Set` accessors that retrieve and set the value of the property. For example, for the `BackgroundProperty` dependency defined previously, the following code implements the `Get` and `Set` accessors:

```
public Brush Background
{
    get { return (Brush)GetValue(BackgroundProperty); }
    set { SetValue(BackgroundProperty, value); }
}
```

Assigning references to elements

You also likely need to assign references to some of the controls that are defined in the `ControlTemplate` element of the `generic.xaml` file using the `GetTemplateChild()` function. This is best done by overidding the `OnApplyTemplate()` method of the `Control` class. For

Programming Custom Silverlight Controls and Libraries

example, the following code snippet overrides the OnApplyTemplate() method to add references to the RootElement and btnControl controls that are defined in the generic.xaml file:

```
protected override void OnApplyTemplate()
{
    RootElement = (FrameworkElement)GetTemplateChild("RootElement");
    btnControl = (TextBlock)GetTemplateChild("btnControl");
}
```

Using the OnApplyTemplate() method ensures that the references to the needed objects are available every time the template is applied. With the references added, you can access the elements to modify values and implement event handling.

Implementing events

To implement event handling on elements that are defined in the template, you need to define a private reference in the class that you can use to interface with the object in the Get and Set accessors. For example, to implement a button Click event for a Button control btnControl that is defined in the generic.xaml file, you can use the following code:

```
private RepeatButton myButton;
private RepeatButton btnControl
{
    get { return myButton; }
    set
    {
        myButton.Click +=
                new RoutedEventHandler(myButton_Click);
    }
}
```

After the event is wired up, you can implement the event handler to handle the event. For example, the following event handler sets the Text property of TextBlock control named txtControl:

```
void addButton_Click(object sender, RoutedEventArgs e)
{
    txtControl.Text = "Clicked";
}
```

Publishing the template parts of the control

After you implement the functionality in the custom control, you should define what parts your code expects to find in the ControlTemplate. This is done by using TemplatePart attribute for each part in the template that your code expects.

For example, the following TemplatePart attributes specify the RootElement and btnControl elements:

```
namespace NumScrollLib
{
    [TemplatePart(Name="RootElement", Type=typeof(FrameworkElement))]
    [TemplatePart(Name = "btnControl", Type = typeof(Button))]
    public class NumScroll : Control
    {
        . . .
```

Example of a custom control Silverlight class library

This section takes you through an example to help you understand how to implement a custom control class library better. To begin the example, consider the code in Listing 12.5 that implements the UI for a custom numeric scrolling control.

The code in Listing 12.5 defines a ResourceDictionary that includes the Style, Setter, and ControlTemplate elements to implement a template for a NumScroll class that is implemented in the code in Listing 12.6.

The ResourceDictionary adds the NumScrollLib assembly as the custom namespace using the following code:

```
xmlns:custom="clr-namespace:NumScrollLib;assembly=NumScrollLib"
```

The code in Listing 12.5 defines a TextBlock named txtControl, and two RepeatButton controls named addControl and subControl. It also defines a Grid control named RootElement and implements a TemplateBinding to the background property using the following code:

```
<Grid x:Name="RootElement" Margin="5"
    Background="{TemplateBinding Background}">
```

These controls are used to implement the UI for a custom numeric scroll control.

LISTING 12.5

XAML File Contents of a Generic.xaml File That Implements the UI Components for a Custom Silverlight Template Control

```
<ResourceDictionary
    xmlns="http://schemas.microsoft.com/client/2007"
    xmlns:x="http://schemas.microsoft.com/winfx/2006/xaml"
    xmlns:custom="clr-namespace:NumScrollLib;assembly=NumScrollLib"
    >
    <Style TargetType="custom:NumScroll">
        <Setter Property="Template">
            <Setter.Value>
                <ControlTemplate TargetType="custom:NumScroll">
```

```
                  <Grid x:Name="RootElement" Margin="5"
                        Background="{TemplateBinding Background}">
                      <Border BorderThickness="2"
                              BorderBrush="Black"
                              Margin="5,1,50,1"
                              Background="White"
                              VerticalAlignment="Center"
                              HorizontalAlignment="Stretch">
                          <TextBlock x:Name="txtControl"
                                     TextAlignment="Center"
                                     Padding="1"/>
                      </Border>
                      <RepeatButton Content="+"
                                    Margin="1,5,5,0"
                                    x:Name="addControl"
                                    Height="15" Width="30"
                                    VerticalAlignment="Top"
                                    HorizontalAlignment="Right"/>
                      <RepeatButton Content="-"
                                    Margin="1,0,5,5"
                                    x:Name="subControl"
                                    Height="15"  Width="30"
                                    VerticalAlignment="Bottom"
                                    HorizontalAlignment="Right"/>
                  </Grid>
              </ControlTemplate>
          </Setter.Value>
      </Setter>
  </Style>
</ResourceDictionary>
```

The code in Listing 12.6 implements the necessary functionality for the custom numeric scroll control. The code implements a class named NumScroll in the namespace NumScrollLib and derives from Control.

The code first uses the TemplatePart attribute to publish the required elements for the code. Next, the code defines two DependencyProperty properties. The ValueProperty registers the name Value and BackgroundProperty registers the name Background.

The ValueProperty is used to track the value of the numeric control and set the value of the TextBlock txtControl in the UI as you see later.

The ValueProperty definition attaches the ValueChangedCallback() handler function to the ValueProperty property. To implement ValueChangedCallBack, the code creates an event handler function named ValueChangedEventHandler() and defines ValueChangedEventArgs to provide the Value property in the event handler.

The BackGround DependencyProperty is implemented so that the value Background property of the NumScroll control can be retrieved and set when the control is added to an application. The following code handles getting and setting the BackgroundProperty:

```
public Brush Background
{
    get { return (Brush)GetValue(BackgroundProperty); }
    set { SetValue(BackgroundProperty, value); }
}
```

Then the NumScroll class overrides the OnApplyTemplate() function to provide access to the RootElement, txtControl, addControl, and subControl controls from the code in Listing 12.5.

```
protected override void OnApplyTemplate()
{
    RootElement = (FrameworkElement)GetTemplateChild("RootElement");
    txtControl = (TextBlock)GetTemplateChild("txtControl");
    addControl = (RepeatButton)GetTemplateChild("addControl");
    subControl = (RepeatButton)GetTemplateChild("subControl");
}
```

Next, the NumScroll class implements the Get and Set accessors for each of the controls. In the case of the button controls, the Set accessor implements mouse Click events using the following code. If the button has already been set up, then the old handler is removed and a new one is added:

```
private RepeatButton subControl
{
    get { return subButton; }
    set
    {
        if (subButton != null)
        {
            subButton.Click -=
                    new RoutedEventHandler(subButton_Click);
        }
        subButton = value;

        subButton.Click +=
                new RoutedEventHandler(subButton_Click);
    }
}
```

The Set accessor for the txtControl control sets the Text attribute from the Value property using the following code:

```
private TextBlock txtControl
```

```
    {
        get { return valueText; }
        set
        {
            valueText = value;
            valueText.Text = Value.ToString();
        }
    }
}
```

LISTING 12.6

C# File Containing the Functionality for a Custom Silverlight Class Library Control

```csharp
using System;
using System.Windows;
using System.Windows.Controls;
using System.Windows.Controls.Primitives;
using System.Windows.Input;
using System.Windows.Media;
using System.Windows.Media.Animation;
using System.Windows.Shapes;

namespace NumScrollLib
{
    [TemplatePart(Name = "RootElement", Type = typeof(FrameworkElement))]
    [TemplatePart(Name = "txtControl", Type = typeof(TextBlock))]
    [TemplatePart(Name = "addControl", Type = typeof(RepeatButton))]
    [TemplatePart(Name = "subControl", Type = typeof(RepeatButton))]
    public class NumScroll : Control
    {
        public static readonly DependencyProperty ValueProperty =
            DependencyProperty.Register("Value", typeof(int),
                typeof(NumScroll),
                new PropertyChangedCallback(ValueChangedCallback));

        public static readonly DependencyProperty BackgroundProperty =
            DependencyProperty.Register("Background", typeof(Brush),
                typeof(NumScroll), null);

        public int Value
        {
            get { return (int)GetValue(ValueProperty); }
            set { SetValue(ValueProperty, value); }
        }

        public Brush Background
        {
```

continued

393

LISTING 12.6   *(continued)*

```csharp
        get { return (Brush)GetValue(BackgroundProperty); }
        set { SetValue(BackgroundProperty, value); }
    }

    protected override void OnApplyTemplate()
    {
        RootElement = (FrameworkElement)GetTemplateChild("RootElement");
        txtControl = (TextBlock)GetTemplateChild("txtControl");
        addControl = (RepeatButton)GetTemplateChild("addControl");
        subControl = (RepeatButton)GetTemplateChild("subControl");
    }

    private RepeatButton addButton;
    private RepeatButton subButton;
    private TextBlock valueText;
    private FrameworkElement rootElement;

    private RepeatButton addControl
    {
        get { return addButton; }
        set
        {
            if (addButton != null)
            {
                addButton.Click -=
                    new RoutedEventHandler(addButton_Click);
            }
            addButton = value;

            addButton.Click +=
                    new RoutedEventHandler(addButton_Click);
        }
    }

    private RepeatButton subControl
    {
        get { return subButton; }
        set
        {
            if (subButton != null)
            {
                subButton.Click -=
                        new RoutedEventHandler(subButton_Click);
            }
            subButton = value;

            subButton.Click +=
                    new RoutedEventHandler(subButton_Click);
        }
```

```
}

private TextBlock txtControl
{
    get { return valueText; }
    set
    {
        valueText = value;
        valueText.Text = Value.ToString();
    }
}

private FrameworkElement RootElement
{
    get{ return rootElement; }
    set{ rootElement = value;}
}

void addButton_Click(object sender, RoutedEventArgs e)
{
    Value++;
}

void subButton_Click(object sender, RoutedEventArgs e)
{
    Value--;
}

private static void ValueChangedCallback(DependencyObject obj,
                    DependencyPropertyChangedEventArgs args)
{
    NumScroll nsControl = (NumScroll)obj;
    int oldValue = (int)args.OldValue;
    int newValue = (int)args.NewValue;

    nsControl.txtControl.Text = newValue.ToString();

    ValueChangedEventArgs e = new ValueChangedEventArgs(newValue);
    nsControl.OnValueChanged(e);
}

public event ValueChangedEventHandler ValueChanged;
protected virtual void OnValueChanged(ValueChangedEventArgs e)
{
    ValueChangedEventHandler handler = ValueChanged;
    if (handler != null)
        handler(this, e);
}
}
```

continued

LISTING 12.6 *(continued)*

```
//Implement ValueChangedEventArgs class
public delegate void ValueChangedEventHandler(object sender,
                    ValueChangedEventArgs e);
public class ValueChangedEventArgs : EventArgs
{
    private int numValue;

    public ValueChangedEventArgs(int num)
    {
        numValue = num;
    }

    public int Value
    {
        get { return numValue; }
    }
}
}
```

The result of the code in Listing 12.5 and Listing 12.6 is that a custom control is defined with a UI similar to the one in Figure 12.5. That control can be added as a class library to several Silverlight applications and then implemented in each.

FIGURE 12.5

UI for a numeric scroll custom Silverlight control

Adding a Silverlight Class Library Control to an Application

After you create a Silverlight class library, you can easily add it to existing as well as new Silverlight applications. This allows you to create controls that can be consumed in several applications on the Web site, giving the entire site a uniform look and feel as well as saving time coding the functionality to each application.

To add a Silverlight class library to an existing Silverlight application project in Visual Studio, right-click on the solution in Solution Explorer and choose Add ➪ New Project from the pop-up menu. Navigate to the Silverlight class library project and click Add to add the project to the solution.

Once the library is added to the solution, you need to add a reference to it in the Silverlight application project. To add the reference, right-click on the project in the Solution Explorer and then select Add Reference from the pop-up menu to display the Add Reference dialog box, as shown in Figure 12.6.

Adding a reference to a custom control Silverlight class library

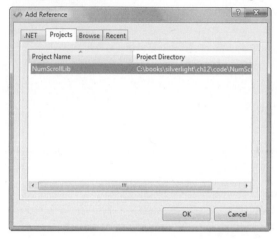

In the Add Reference dialog box, click the Projects tab and select the Silverlight class library project. Click OK to add the reference. After you add the reference, you can implement the controls in the custom class library in the application.

CAUTION Once you add the Silverlight class library to a project, the project appears in the Solution Explorer. You can access the source files of the library. This is the actual class library project. If you change the source files in the current solution, they are changed in the project.

To add items from the custom class library in the XAML, you need to add the namespace of the custom control to the Application or UserControl element. For example, to add the NumScrollLib custom library namespace defined in Listings 12.5 and 12.6, you would add an xmlns entry, as shown in the following XAML code:

```
<UserControl x:Class="SilverlightApplication1.Page"
    xmlns="http://schemas.microsoft.com/client/2007"
    xmlns:x="http://schemas.microsoft.com/winfx/2006/xaml"
    xmlns:custom="clr-namespace:NumScrollLib;assembly=NumScrollLib"
    Width="400" Height="300">
```

After the namespace is added by setting the xmlns property, you can add the custom controls to the XAML code using the namespace name. For example, the following line of XAML adds a NumScroll element using the xmlns:custom namespace defined previously:

```
<custom:NumScroll Background="Gray" Height="50" Width="300"/>
```

You also need to add a reference to the custom control class library to be able to add the custom control in managed code. For example, the following C# using statement adds a reference to the NumScrollLib namespace:

```
using NumScrollLib;
```

After the reference is added to the managed code, you can create instances of the control. For example, the following lines of C# code create a new NumScroll control object and set the Background property:

```
NumScroll nScroll = new NumScroll();
nScroll.Background = new SolidColorBrush(Colors.Black);
```

The code in Listings 12.7 and 12.8 shows an example XAML and C# file from a Silverlight application that implements the custom control NumScroll from Listings 12.5 and 12.6. The Silverlight application implements two NumScroll controls, one in the XAML file and one in the managed code.

LISTING 12.7

XAML File That Implements a Custom Control from a Silverlight Class Library

```
<UserControl x:Class="SilverlightApplication1.Page"
    xmlns="http://schemas.microsoft.com/client/2007"
    xmlns:x="http://schemas.microsoft.com/winfx/2006/xaml"
    xmlns:custom="clr-namespace:NumScrollLib;assembly=NumScrollLib"
    Width="400" Height="300">
    <Grid x:Name="LayoutRoot" Background="White">
        <TextBlock Text="Custom Silverlight Numberic Scroller"
  FontSize="20"/>
        <Canvas x:Name="controlCanvas" Background="LightGray"
                Height="200" Width="350">
            <TextBlock Text="XAML Control"
                    FontSize="20"
                    Canvas.Left="5"/>
            <custom:NumScroll
                Background="Gray"
                Canvas.Left="150"
                Height="50" Width="200"/>
        </Canvas>
    </Grid>
</UserControl>
```

LISTING 12.8

C# File That Implements a Custom Control from a Silverlight Class Library

```csharp
using System;
using System.Collections.Generic;
using System.Windows;
using System.Windows.Controls;
using System.Windows.Input;
using System.Windows.Media;
using System.Windows.Media.Animation;
using System.Windows.Shapes;

using NumScrollLib;

namespace SilverlightApplication1
{
    public partial class Page : UserControl
    {
        public Page()
        {
            InitializeComponent();
            NumScroll nScroll = new NumScroll();
            nScroll.Background = new SolidColorBrush(Colors.Black);
            nScroll.Height = 50;
            nScroll.Width = 200;
            nScroll.SetValue(Canvas.LeftProperty, 150);
            nScroll.SetValue(Canvas.TopProperty, 100);
            TextBlock t = new TextBlock();
            t.Text = "Code Control";
            t.SetValue(Canvas.LeftProperty, 5);
            t.SetValue(Canvas.TopProperty, 100);
            t.FontSize = 20;
            controlCanvas.Children.Add(t);
            controlCanvas.Children.Add(nScroll);

        }
    }
}
```

The XAML code in Listing 12.7 adds the NumScrollLib namespace to the file using the name custom, as shown in the following code:

```
xmlns:custom="clr-namespace:NumScrollLib;assembly=NumScrollLib"
```

The code in Listing 12.7 then implements a Canvas control named controlCanvas that is used to place the custom NumScroll controls. A custom NumScroll control is added using the following XAML code from Listing 12.7:

```
<custom:NumScroll
    Background="Gray"
    Canvas.Left="150"
    Height="50" Width="200"/>
```

The code in Listing 12.8 also adds a reference to the `NumScrollLib` namespace using the following `using` statement:

```
using NumScrollLib;
```

Then the code creates an instance of the `NumScroll` control using the following line of code:

```
NumScroll nScroll = new NumScroll();
```

The code in Listing 12.8 then sets the `Background`, `Height`, `Width`, `Canvas.Left`, and `Canvas.Top` properties of the `NumScroll` control and adds it to the `controlCanvas` control defined in Listing 12.8.

When the Silverlight application from Listings 12.7 and 12.8 is run, a page similar to the one in Figure 12.7 is displayed. Two custom `NumScroll` controls are displayed — one created in the XAML file and one created in the managed source.

FIGURE 12.7

Silverlight application that implements a custom numeric scroll control in XAML and in managed source

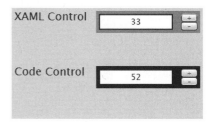

Summary

Silverlight provides an infinite number of ways to create customized controls that provide rich and unique functionality. This chapter covered methods to create and implement custom controls in your Silverlight applications.

Custom Silverlight controls can be implemented in applications either as a `UserControl` that is part of the application or as a Silverlight class library that is referenced by the application.

In this chapter, you learned how to:

- Build custom `UserControl` controls
- Add custom `UserControl` controls to Silverlight applications
- Add a reference to a Silverlight class library control in XAML and managed code
- Implement classes from class libraries in Silverlight applications
- Make a custom control that can work as a template control

Part IV

Understanding Silverlight Frameworks

Chapter 13

Using the Silverlight Presentation Framework

The Silverlight presentation framework consists of several libraries that provide most of the functionality for Silverlight applications. Parts II and III of this book cover much of the presentation framework, as we discuss the various techniques to program Silverlight applications. For example, all of the Silverlight controls you learn about in Chapter 3 are part of the presentation framework, as are the media and animation controls discussed in Chapter 8.

Because most of the UI functionality of the presentation framework has already been discussed, this chapter focuses on helping you understand how to use the presentation framework to interact with the browser, access the client file system, and implement threading.

Understanding the Silverlight Presentation Framework

The main purpose of the Silverlight presentation framework is to provide you with the UI controls and functionality to implement rich Internet applications. However, the presentation framework is much more than just the UI controls; it also encompasses browser interaction, threading, and system calls. Table 13.1 lists the namespaces that are part of the Silverlight presentation framework.

TABLE 13.1

Silverlight Presentation Foundation Namespaces

Library	Description
`System.Windows`	Provides the general presentation and base classes for Silverlight development. For example, the `Application`, `UIElement`, `EventTrigger`, and `FontStyles`.
`System.Windows.Browser`	Provides the classes used to interact with the browser. For example, the `HtmlDocument`, `HtmlElement`, `HtmlPage`, and `ScriptObject`.
`System.Windows.Controls`	Provides most of the UI controls. For example, `TextBlock`, `Image`, `Grid`, and `UserControl`.
`System.Windows.Documents`	Provides the classes that support basic document concepts. For example, `Fontsource`, `LineBreak`, `Inline`, and `Run`.
`System.Windows.Markup`	Provides the classes that support XAML processing. For example, `XamlReader`, `ContentPropertyAttribute`, and `XmlLanguage`.
`System.Windows.Media`	Provides the classes that enable you to apply rich functionality to your applications. For example, `GradientBrush`, `ScaleTransform`, `Colors`, `FontFamily`, and `PathGeometry`.
`System.Windows.Media.-Animation`	Provides the classes used to animate Silverlight controls. For example, `Begin Storyboard`, `Storyboard`, `DoubleAnimation`, `SplinePointKeyFrame`, `Timeline`, and `TimeLineMarker`.
`System.Windows.Shapes`	Provides the classes used to implement basic XAML shapes. For example, `Ellipse`, `Path`, and `Rectangle`.
`System.Windows.Threading`	Provides the classes used to implement threads in your Silverlight applications. For example, `Dispatcher`, `DispatcherOperation`, and `DispatcherTimer`.
`System.ComponentModel`	Provides the classes used to implement runtime and design-time behavior of components and controls. For example, `ProgressChangedEventArgs`, `PropertyChangedEventArgs`, `BackgroundWorker`, `AsyncCompletedEventArgs`, and `TypeConverter`.

Interacting with the HTML DOM

Because Silverlight applications are implemented as embedded objects in the HTML DOM of Web pages, it makes sense to be able to have some interaction between the DOM and Silverlight application. Silverlight provides the ability to interact between the DOM elements and Silverlight controls.

Providing interactions between your Silverlight code and HTML code allows you to easily integrate Silverlight applications into existing Web pages. You can also use Silverlight managed code to implement client-side functionality that is more difficult in JavaScript.

The following sections discuss how to implement managed Silverlight code that accesses and modifies DOM elements as well as how to implement JavaScript that can access Silverlight controls and managed code.

Accessing the HTML DOM from managed code

Silverlight provides the `System.Windows.Browser` library that allows you to access the HTML DOM from managed Silverlight code. Using the `Browser` library, you can access the HTML document, individual DOM elements, and invoke scripts.

Using Silverlight to access and modify elements in the DOM allows you to modify the Web page UI using managed Silverlight code without the need to refresh the browser and retrieve an updated page from the server. This eliminates client-to-server traffic and makes for a much better experience for the user.

The easiest way to access DOM elements from Silverlight managed code is to first access the HTML document itself. This is done by creating an instance of the `HtmlDocument` class provided in the `Browser` library and setting it to the value of the `HtmlPage.Document` object that is exposed by the Silverlight application. For example:

```
HtmlDocument doc;
doc = HtmlPage.Document;
```

Using the `HtmlDocument` object, you can access elements in the DOM using the `GetElementById()` function that is similar to the one provided in JavaScript. `GetElementById()` accepts a `String` that points to the `id` of a DOM element as the only argument and returns an `HtmlElement` object.

The `id` argument of the `GetElementById()` function points to the id property of the element in the DOM. For example, consider the following `div` element in the DOM with an `id` property set to `TitleBar`:

```
<div id=TitleBar>
```

The following code in the Silverlight application creates an `HtmlElement` object that points to the `div` element:

```
HtmlElement divElement = doc.GetElementById("TitleBar");
```

The `HtmlElement` class exposes several properties and functions that allow you to interact with the DOM element from managed code. For example, the following code implements the `SetProperty()` function that allows you to set the properties of the DOM object. The following code sets the `visible` property of the `div` element:

```
divElement.SetProperty("visible", "false");
```

You can use the `HtmlPage.Window.Invoke()` function exposed in Silverlight to run JavaScript functions that are available in the DOM. The `HtmlPage.Window.Invoke()` function accepts two arguments. The first argument is the name of the JavaScript Function. The second argument is the `args[]` array that includes any arguments required by the function.

The code in Listings 13.1, 13.2, and 13.3 shows example Silverlight applications that implement managed code that interacts with the HTML elements in the browser.

The code in Listing 13.1 is a fairly straightforward HTML document. The code embeds the Silverlight application in a div tag. Also included in the HTML page are an h1 heading with id set to docTitle and an img tag with the id set to docImage.

The code in Listing 13.1 also implements a JavaScript function, setTitle(), that changes the text docTitle heading. The setTitle() function accepts a string named newTitle as an argument, then finds the docTitle element and sets the innerHTML property to the value of newTitle.

LISTING 13.1

HTML Code That Implements Some JavaScript Functionality and Embeds the Silverlight Application

```
<!DOCTYPE html PUBLIC "-//W3C//DTD XHTML 1.0 Transitional//EN"
"http://www.w3.org/TR/xhtml1/DTD/xhtml1-transitional.dtd">
<html xmlns="http://www.w3.org/1999/xhtml" >

<head>
    <title>Silverlight Controlling DOM Application</title>

    <script type="text/javascript">
        function setTitle(newTitle) {
            var titleBlock = document.getElementById("docTitle");
            titleBlock.innerHTML = newTitle;
        }
    </script>
</head>

<body>
    <div id="silverlightControlHost">
        <object id="silverlightControl"
                data="data:application/x-silverlight,"
                type="application/x-silverlight-2 "
                width="350" height="200">
            <param name="source" value="ClientBin/SLToDOM.xap"/>
            <param name="background" value="white" />
        </object>
        <iframe style='visibility:hidden;height:0;width:0;border:0px'>
        </iframe>
    </div>
    <hr /><h1 id="docTitle">Image</h1>
    <hr /><img id="docImage" src="imageA.jpg" width="100" />
</body>
</html>
```

The code in Listing 13.2 implements three Image controls named imgA, imgB, and imgC; a Button control named myButton; a TextBox control named myText; and a Slider control named sizeSlider. The code in Listing 13.3 implements the functionality to use these Silverlight controls to modify the h1 and img elements defined in Listing 13.1.

LISTING 13.2

XAML Code That Implements a Button, TextBox, Slider, and Three Image Controls That Control HTML DOM Elements

```
<UserControl x:Class="SLToDOM.Page"
    xmlns="http://schemas.microsoft.com/client/2007"
    xmlns:x="http://schemas.microsoft.com/winfx/2006/xaml"
    Width="350" Height="200">
    <Grid x:Name="LayoutRoot" Background="LightGray">
        <Image x:Name="imgA" Source="imageA.jpg"
                VerticalAlignment="Top" HorizontalAlignment="Left"
                Margin="10,10,0,0"
                Height="100" Width="100"/>
        <Image x:Name="imgB" Source="imageB.jpg"
                VerticalAlignment="Top" HorizontalAlignment="Left"
                Margin="120,10,0,0"
                Height="100" Width="100"/>
        <Image x:Name="imgC" Source="imageC.jpg"
                VerticalAlignment="Top" HorizontalAlignment="Left"
                Margin="230,10,0,0"
                Height="100" Width="100"/>
        <Button x:Name="myButton" Content="Set Title"
                VerticalAlignment="Top" HorizontalAlignment="Left"
                Margin="10,100,0,0"
                Height="30" Width="100"/>
        <TextBox x:Name="myText"
                VerticalAlignment="Top" HorizontalAlignment="Left"
                Margin="120,100,0,0"
                Height="30" Width="200"/>
        <Slider x:Name="sizeSlider"
                Minimum="100" Maximum="500"
                Height="50" Width="300"
                VerticalAlignment="Bottom" HorizontalAlignment="Center"
                Margin="0,0,10,0" />
    </Grid>
</UserControl>
```

The code in Listing 13.3 adds the System.Windows.Browser library to the application that provides access to the tools to interact with the HTML DOM. An HtmlDocument object named doc is defined as a class member.

Inside the Page() constructor function, the doc object is initialized to the value of HtmlPage. Document. The Page() constructor also wires up the MouseLeftButtonUp event handlers for the Image controls, a Click event handler for the Button control, and a ValueChanged event handler for the Slider control.

Inside the Image MouseLeftButtonUp event handlers, the doc object is used to get the docImage element from the DOM and set the src attribute using the following lines of code:

```
HtmlElement dImage = doc.GetElementById("docImage");
dImage.SetProperty("src", "imageB.jpg");
```

Inside the sizeSlider_ValueChanged() event handler function, the value of the slider is used to set the width attribute of the docImage in the DOM using the following lines of code:

```
HtmlElement dImage = doc.GetElementById("docImage");
dImage.SetAttribute("width", sizeSlider.Value.ToString());
```

Inside the myButton_Click() event handler, the HtmlPage.Window.Invoke() function is used to invoke the setTitle() JavaScript function in the DOM to set the text of the docTitle element to the value of myText.Text using the following line of code:

```
HtmlPage.Window.Invoke("setTitle", myText.Text);
```

The result is that the user can dynamically change the image file that is displayed in the Web page by clicking on one of the images in the Silverlight application, as shown in Figure 13.1. The size of the image is controlled by the Silverlight slider control. The user can also type text in the Silverlight application and click Set Title to change the value in the HTML document, as shown in Figure 13.1.

LISTING 13.3

C# Code That Implements a Functionality to Use the Silverlight Application to Control HTML DOM Elements

```csharp
using System;
using System.Windows;
using System.Windows.Controls;
using System.Windows.Documents;
using System.Windows.Input;
using System.Windows.Media;

using System.Windows.Browser;

namespace SLToDOM
{
    public partial class Page : UserControl
    {
        HtmlDocument doc;
```

```
public Page()
{
    InitializeComponent();

    //Get HTML Document object
    doc = HtmlPage.Document;

    myButton.Click += new RoutedEventHandler(myButton_Click);
    imgA.MouseLeftButtonUp +=
            new MouseButtonEventHandler(imgA_Click);
    imgB.MouseLeftButtonUp +=
            new MouseButtonEventHandler(imgB_Click);
    imgC.MouseLeftButtonUp +=
            new MouseButtonEventHandler(imgC_Click);
    sizeSlider.ValueChanged +=
            new RoutedPropertyChangedEventHandler<double>(
                    sizeSlider_ValueChanged);
}

void sizeSlider_ValueChanged(object sender,
                    RoutedPropertyChangedEventArgs<double> e)
{
    HtmlElement dImage = doc.GetElementById("docImage");
    dImage.SetAttribute("width", sizeSlider.Value.ToString());
}

void imgA_Click(object sender, MouseButtonEventArgs e)
{
    HtmlElement dImage = doc.GetElementById("docImage");
    dImage.SetProperty("src", "imageA.jpg");
}
void imgB_Click(object sender, MouseButtonEventArgs e)
{
    HtmlElement dImage = doc.GetElementById("docImage");
    dImage.SetProperty("src", "imageB.jpg");
}
void imgC_Click(object sender, MouseButtonEventArgs e)
{
    HtmlElement dImage = doc.GetElementById("docImage");
    dImage.SetProperty("src", "imageC.jpg");
}

void myButton_Click(object sender, RoutedEventArgs e)
{
    HtmlPage.Window.Invoke("setTitle", myText.Text);
}
    }
}
```

FIGURE 13.1

HTML page dynamically controlled by a Silverlight application

Accessing managed code from HTML JavaScript

The previous section discussed using Silverlight applications to interact with UI elements in the HTML DOM. You can also access functions in your Silverlight applications from JavaScript functions located in the HTML page.

To access functions in your Silverlight applications from JavaScript, the functions need to be scriptable and the class needs to be registered as a scriptable object. The JavaScript code can access the scriptable object using the DOM and execute any functions that are designated as scriptable.

You need to use the `System.Windows.Browser` library in order to access the tools necessary to make the class and methods scriptable. The best way to do this is to add a `using` statement to the code — for example:

```
using System.Windows.Browser;
```

Use the `HtmlPage.RegisterScriptableObject()` function to register the class as a scriptable object. The `RegisterScriptableObject()` function accepts two parameters. The first parameter is a string that is used to identify the scriptable class in the DOM. The second is the object that is associated with that name. The following line of code registers the current class object in the DOM as `SilverlightApp`:

```
HtmlPage.RegisterScriptableObject("SilverlightApp", this);
```

You also need to designate the Silverlight class as scriptable. This is done by adding the `ScriptableType` decorator to the class definition, as shown in the following code:

```
[ScriptableType]
public partial class Page : UserControl
{
```

Once the class is designated as a scriptable type you can designate methods in the class as scriptable methods by adding the `ScriptableMember` decorator to the function definition. For example:

```
[ScriptableMember]
public void updateTextBlock(string text)
{
```

Scriptable member functions can then be accessed in the JavaScript code from the Silverlight object in the DOM. For example, if the Silverlight object is created with the `id` set to `silverlight-Control`, the following JavaScript function could access a scriptable function named `update-TextBlock()` in the Silverlight managed code:

```
<script type="text/javascript">
    function doClick() {
        var slCntrl = document.getElementById("silverlightControl");
        slCntrl.content.slPage.updateTextBlock("New Text");
    }
</script>
```

The code in Listings 13.4, 13.5, and 13.6 shows example Silverlight applications that contain a scriptable function in managed code that is executed by a JavaScript function in HTML.

The code in Listing 13.4 is a fairly straightforward HTML document that implements three `text input` and one `button input` elements. The code also embeds a Silverlight application in an `object` tag with the `id` set to `silverlightControl`.

The code in Listing 13.4 also implements a JavaScript function `doClick()` that is attached as an `onclick` event handler to the `button input` element. The `doClick()` function retrieves the `silverlightControl` object from the DOM. It then gets the values from the `text input` elements in the DOM and uses those values to call the `setBall()` scriptable method in the Silverlight application.

LISTING 13.4

HTML Code That Implements a JavaScript Function That Invokes a Method in the Managed Code of a Silverlight Application

```
<!DOCTYPE html PUBLIC "-//W3C//DTD XHTML 1.0 Transitional//EN"
"http://www.w3.org/TR/xhtml1/DTD/xhtml1-transitional.dtd">
<html xmlns="http://www.w3.org/1999/xhtml" >

<head>
    <title>HTML Accessing Silverlight Page </title>

 <script type="text/javascript">
    function doClick() {
      var silverLightControl = document.getElementById("silverlightControl");
```

continued

413

LISTING 13.4 *(continued)*

```
        var size = document.getElementById("ballSize").
    getAttribute("value");
        var X = document.getElementById("ballX").getAttribute("value");
        var Y = document.getElementById("ballY").getAttribute("value");
        silverLightControl.content.slPage.setBall(size, X, Y);
    }
 </script>
</head>

<body>
<h1 id="docTitle">Set Silverlight</h1>
X: <input id="ballX" type="text" /><br />
Y: <input id="ballY" type="text" /><br />
Size: <input id="ballSize" type="text" /><br />
<input id="docButton" type="button" value="Set Ball" onclick="doClick()"
    />
    <hr />
    <div id="silverlightControlHost">
        <object id="silverlightControl"
                data="data:application/x-silverlight,"
                type="application/x-silverlight-2 "
                width="400" height="300">
            <param name="source" value="ClientBin/Dom2SL.xap"/>
            <param name="background" value="white" />
        </object>
        <iframe style='visibility:hidden;height:0;width:0;border:0px'>
        </iframe>
    </div>
</body>
</html>
```

The code in Listing 13.5 is a basic XAML file that contains a Canvas root control and a single Ellipse control named Ball that acts as an object that is controlled using HTML DOM elements.

LISTING 13.5

XAML Code That Implements a Canvas Root Control and an Ellipse

```
<UserControl x:Class="Dom2SL.Page"
    xmlns="http://schemas.microsoft.com/client/2007"
    xmlns:x="http://schemas.microsoft.com/winfx/2006/xaml"
    Width="400" Height="300">
    <Canvas x:Name="LayoutRoot" Background="Blue">
        <Ellipse x:Name="Ball"
                MaxHeight="100" MaxWidth="100"
```

```
            Height="100" Width="100">
        <Ellipse.Fill>
            <RadialGradientBrush x:Name="pulse"
                            RadiusX="0.5" RadiusY="0.5"
                            GradientOrigin="0.5,0.5">
                <GradientStop Color="Blue"/>
                <GradientStop Color="White"
                        Offset="0.5"/>
                <GradientStop Color="Blue"
                        Offset="1"/>
            </RadialGradientBrush>
        </Ellipse.Fill>
    </Ellipse>
  </Canvas>
</UserControl>
```

The code in Listing 13.6 adds the `ScriptableType` decorator to the `Page` class definition and the `ScriptableMember` decorator to the `setBall()` function. The code also registers the class as a scriptable object to expose it to the HTML DOM using the following line of code:

```
HtmlPage.RegisterScriptableObject("slPage", this);
```

The `setBall()` function accepts three parameters — `size`, `X`, and `Y` — and uses them to set the position and size of the `Ball Ellipse` control. The result is that the user can type values into the HTML input elements and then use the HTML button input to set the size and position of the `Ellipse` control, as shown in Figure 13.2.

LISTING 13.6

C# Code That Implements a Scriptable Member Method That Can Be Accessed from JavaScript to Set the Size and Location of an Ellipse Control

```
using System;
using System.Windows;
using System.Windows.Controls;
using System.Windows.Shapes;

using System.Windows.Browser;

namespace Dom2SL
{
    [ScriptableType]
    public partial class Page : UserControl
    {
```

continued

LISTING 13.6   *(continued)*

```
public Page()
{
    InitializeComponent();
    HtmlPage.RegisterScriptableObject("slPage", this);
}

[ScriptableMember]
public void setBall(string sizeStr, string xStr, string yStr)
{
    int size = Convert.ToInt16(sizeStr);
    int X = Convert.ToInt16(xStr);
    int Y = Convert.ToInt16(yStr);
    Ball.Height = size;
    Ball.Width = size;
    Ball.SetValue(Canvas.LeftProperty, X);
    Ball.SetValue(Canvas.TopProperty, Y);
}
}
}
```

FIGURE 13.2

HTML page dynamically controlling an ellipse size and position in a Silverlight application

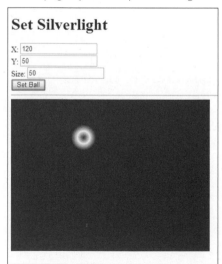
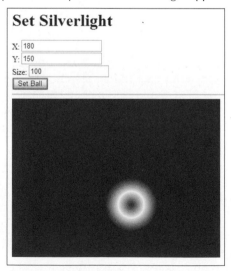

Accessing the Local File System from Silverlight Applications

Silverlight applications can access the browser's local file system in two ways. One way is to use a native open and read functionality to read files. Using the native open and read functionality is limited to reading files only.

Another way to access the browser's local file system is to use the isolated local storage that is assigned to Silverlight applications. The isolated local storage is a small amount of disk space that is isolated based on user and assembly credentials. Silverlight applications can read and write to isolated local storage areas.

> **NOTE** Accessing files locally cannot be guaranteed because the browser or other security applications may not allow access. You should provide functionality in your applications to notify the user and gracefully handle these situations.

Using the operating system's native open for read-only

Silverlight applications cannot directly access files in the local file system for obvious security reasons. However, it is possible to prompt the user to access the file system using an `OpenFileDialog` object.

By asking the user to open the file for you, you are involving the user in making the determination to access the file system. The `SelectedFile` property of the `OpenFileDialog` object can be used to access files that are selected by the user.

> **NOTE** The user must select the file to be opened and read. That means that the results may be unreliable. However, using the `OpenFileDialog` option is great for developing Silverlight applications that allow users to load their own local files.

For example, the following code snippet from a Silverlight application creates and displays an `OpenFileDialog` object and then uses the user `OpenRead()` function on the selected results to create a `System.IO.Stream` object:

```
OpenFileDialog fDialog = new OpenFileDialog();
if (fDialog.ShowDialog() == DialogResult.OK)
{
    System.IO.Stream fileStream =
        fDialog.SelectedFile.OpenRead();
```

To better illustrate using the `OpenFileDialog` object in Silverlight applications, consider the code in Listings 13.7 and 13.8. The code in these listings implements a simple Silverlight application that uses the `OpenFileDialog` to allow the user to select a text file and load it in the application.

The code in Listing 13.7 simply creates a `Button` control named `openBtn` and a `TextBox` control named `readText`. The `TextBox` control is nested in a `ScrollViewer` control so that a large amount of text can be placed in the `TextBox`. The `Button` control is used in Listing 13.8 to launch an `OpenFileDialog` object.

LISTING 13.7

XAML Code That Displays a Button and TextBox Control Nested in a ScrollViewer

```
<UserControl x:Class="slFileDialog.Page"
    xmlns="http://schemas.microsoft.com/client/2007"
    xmlns:x="http://schemas.microsoft.com/winfx/2006/xaml"
    Width="400" Height="300">
    <Grid x:Name="LayoutRoot" Background="LightBlue">
        <Button x:Name="openBtn" Content="Read File"
                VerticalAlignment="Top" HorizontalAlignment="Left"
                Margin="10,10,0,0"
                Height="30" Width="100" />
        <ScrollViewer HorizontalScrollBarVisibility="Auto"
                VerticalScrollBarVisibility="Auto"
                VerticalAlignment="Top" HorizontalAlignment="Left"
                Margin="30,60,0,0"
                Height="220" Width="350" >
            <ScrollViewer.Content>
                <TextBox x:Name="readText"
                        FontSize="15"
                        AcceptsReturn="True"/>
            </ScrollViewer.Content>
        </ScrollViewer>
    </Grid>
</UserControl>
```

The code in Listing 13.8 defines an `OpenFileDialog` object named `fDialog`. The `Click` event handler for the `openBtn` control uses `fDialog` to display an `OpenFileDialog` box that allows the user to select text files. The text file filter is set up using the `Filter` and `FilterIndex` properties of the `OpenFileDialog` box, as shown in Listing 13.8.

After the user selects a file in the `OpenFileDialog` object, the `OpenRead()` function of the `SelectedFile` property is used to create a `System.IO.Stream` object named `fileStream`. The code then reads the data in the `fileStream` `Stream` one line at a time and appends it to the `readText` `TextBox` control.

The results are shown in Figure 13.3. When the user clicks Read File and selects a TXT file, the file is loaded into the `TextBox` of the Silverlight application.

LISTING 13.8

C# Code That Launches an Open File Dialog Box to Access Files on the Client

```csharp
using System;
using System.Windows;
using System.Windows.Controls;
using System.Windows.Documents;
using System.Windows.Input;


namespace slFileDialog
{
    public partial class Page : UserControl
    {
        OpenFileDialog fDialog;
        public Page()
        {
            InitializeComponent();
            openBtn.Click += new RoutedEventHandler(openBtn_Click);
        }

        void openBtn_Click(object sender, RoutedEventArgs e)
        {
            fDialog = new OpenFileDialog();
            fDialog.Filter =
                "Text Files (*.txt)|*.txt | All Files (*.*) | *.*";
            fDialog.FilterIndex = 1;

            if (fDialog.ShowDialog() == DialogResult.OK)
            {
                System.IO.Stream fileStream =
                    fDialog.SelectedFile.OpenRead();

                using (System.IO.StreamReader sReader =
                    new System.IO.StreamReader(fileStream))
                {
                    string line;
                    readText.Text = "";

                    while ((line = sReader.ReadLine()) != null)
                    {
                        readText.Text += String.Format("{0}\r\n", line);
                    }
                }
                fileStream.Close();
            }
        }
    }
}
```

FIGURE 13.3

Silverlight application that allows users to load text files from the local file system and displays them in the Silverlight application

Accessing the isolated local storage

Isolated local storage is a small section of local storage that is isolated to a specific application and user. The idea behind isolated local storage is that web applications can save small amounts of persistent data there for their own purposes. The storage cannot be accessed by other applications or users so it is fairly secure.

CROSS-REF The location of the isolated local storage in the local file system depends on which OS the user is running. For more information about isolated local storage, including its location, go to `http://msdn.microsoft.com/en-us/library/3ak841sy.aspx`.

The isolated local storage is automatically created for the Silverlight application as it is needed. The size of the isolated local storage for Silverlight applications is a maximum of 1MB. That size should be enough to store most of the persistent settings that you need for your applications.

TIP The isolated local storage is not enough to be able to store large files such as graphics or media. You can still customize those types of things to the user by storing them at the server and then using data from the isolated local storage to point to them.

The isolated local storage is accessed using the `IsolatedStorageFile` class from the `System.IO.IsolatedStorage` library. The `IsolatedStorageFile` class contains a member function named `GetUserStoreForApplication()`. The `GetUserStoreForApplication()` function returns an `IsolatedStorageFile` object that you can use to access the local storage. For example:

```
IsolatedStorageFile localStore =
    IsolatedStorageFile.GetUserStoreForApplication();
```

Using the GetFileNames() function of the IsolatedStorageFile object you can get a string array of filenames. If GetFileNames() is called without any arguments then it returns all files in the local storage. You can also specify a search pattern string to filter on a specific subset of files. For example, the following code retrieves only TXT files:

```
string[] files = localStore.GetFileNames("*.txt");
```

You can use the IsolatedStorageFileStream class to access a specific file in the local storage. To create an IsolatedStorageFileStream object, you need to pass the following arguments in order to the constructor function:

- **file name:** Specifies the name of the file.
- **file mode:** Specifies the mode that is used to open the file using the FileMode class. Options are Append, Create, CreateNew, Open, OpenOrCreate, and Truncate.
- IsolatedStorageFile: Specifies the instance of the IsolatedStorageFile that was returned by GetUserStoreForApplication().

The following code shows an example of opening a file named settings.txt in the isolated local storage:

```
IsolatedStorageFileStream stream =
    new IsolatedStorageFileStream("settings.txt",
                                    FileMode.Open, localStore);
```

Data can be read from the IsolatedStorageFileStream object using a StreamReader object. Data can be written to the IsolatedStorageFileStream using a StreamWriter object. For example, the following code reads a single line from an IsolatedStorageFileStream:

```
StreamReader sReader = new StreamReader(stream);
getText.Text = sReader.ReadLine();
```

To better illustrate using the isolated local storage in Silverlight applications, consider the code in Listings 13.9 and 13.10. These listings implement a simple Silverlight application that uses an IsolatedStorageFile object to allow a user to save and retrieve text in the isolated local storage. After the user saves the text, it can be retrieved even if the Web browser is closed and reopened.

The code in Listing 13.9 simply creates a Button control named saveBtn, a Button control named getBtn, a TextBox control named saveText, and a TextBlock control named getText. The Button controls are used in Listing 13.10 to save text from the TextBox to the isolated local storage and then retrieve the text from the isolated local storage into the TextBlock.

LISTING 13.9

XAML Code That Displays a Button and TextBox Control to Allow a User to Add Text to a File in the Isolated Local Storage as Well as a Button Control That Retrieves That Saved Text

```
<UserControl x:Class="SLIsolatedStorage.Page"
    xmlns="http://schemas.microsoft.com/client/2007"
    xmlns:x="http://schemas.microsoft.com/winfx/2006/xaml"
    Width="400" Height="300">
    <Grid x:Name="LayoutRoot" Background="LightBlue">
        <Button x:Name="saveBtn" Content="Save"
                HorizontalAlignment="Left" VerticalAlignment="Top"
                Margin="10,10,0,0"
                Height="20" Width="100"/>
        <TextBox x:Name="saveText"
                HorizontalAlignment="Left" VerticalAlignment="Top"
                Margin="120,10,0,0"
                Height="100" Width="220"/>
        <Button x:Name="getBtn" Content="Retrieve"
                HorizontalAlignment="Left" VerticalAlignment="Top"
                Margin="10,150,0,0"
                Height="20" Width="100"/>
        <TextBlock x:Name="getText" TextWrapping="Wrap"
                HorizontalAlignment="Left" VerticalAlignment="Top"
                Margin="120,150,0,0"
                Height="100" Width="200"/>
    </Grid>
</UserControl>
```

The code in Listing 13.10 defines an `IsolatedStorageFile` object named `localStore`. Inside the constructor for the class, the code creates an instance of the `IsolatedStorageFile` object using the `GetUserStoreForApplication()` function as shown in the following code:

```
localStore = IsolatedStorageFile.GetUserStoreForApplication();
```

The code in Listing 13.10 also implements `Click` event handlers for the `saveBtn` and `getBtn` controls named `saveBtn_Click()` and `getBtn_Click()`. Inside the `saveBtn_Click()` handler function, the code first retrieves all files with the .dat extension using the `GetFileNames()` function of the `IsolatedStorageFile` object. Then those files are deleted from the isolated local storage using the `DeleteFile()` function.

 **TIP**   **Because disk space is limited, it is a good idea to keep the isolated local storage as clean as possible so that you do not run out of disk space.**

Then the code creates a new `IsolatedStorageFileStream` object named `stream` using the following code:

```
IsolatedStorageFileStream stream =
    new IsolatedStorageFileStream("test.dat",
                                  FileMode.Create, localStore);
```

The `IsolatedStorageFileStream` implements the `FileMode.Create` mode on a file named `test.dat` using the `localStore` object. Using the `stream` object, the code then creates a `StreamWriter` object that writes the text in the `saveText` TextBox to the `test.dat` file in the local storage using the following code:

```
StreamWriter sWriter = new StreamWriter(stream);
sWriter.WriteLine(saveText.Text);
```

Inside the `getBtn_Click()` handler function, the code first creates a new `IsolatedStorageFileStream` object named `stream` using the following code:

```
IsolatedStorageFileStream stream =
    new IsolatedStorageFileStream("test.dat",
                                  FileMode.Open, localStore);
```

The `IsolatedStorageFileStream` implements the `FileMode.Open` mode on a file named `test.dat` so that the file can be read from. Using the `stream` object, the code then creates a `StreamReader` object that reads a line of text from the `test.dat` file in the isolated local storage and uses the text to set the `Text` property of the `getText` TextBlock using the following code:

```
StreamReader sReader = new StreamReader(stream);
getText.Text = sReader.ReadLine();
```

The results are shown in Figure 13.4. When the user clicks Save, the text in the `saveText` TextBox control is stored in the isolated local storage. When the user clicks Retrieve, the text is loaded in the `getText` textBlock control even if the browser has been closed and the application completely reloaded.

LISTING 13.10

C# Code That Displays a Button and TextBox Control Nested in a ScrollViewer

```
using System;
using System.Windows;
using System.Windows.Controls;
using System.Windows.Documents;
using System.Windows.Input;


//Add Isolated Storage Library
using System.IO;
using System.IO.IsolatedStorage;

namespace SLIsolatedStorage
```

continued

LISTING 13.10 *(continued)*

```
{
    public partial class Page : UserControl
    {
        IsolatedStorageFile localStore;

        public Page()
        {
            InitializeComponent();

            //Initialize Handlers
            saveBtn.Click += new RoutedEventHandler(saveBtn_Click);
            getBtn.Click += new RoutedEventHandler(getBtn_Click);

            localStore = IsolatedStorageFile.GetUserStoreForApplication();
        }

        void saveBtn_Click(object sender, RoutedEventArgs e)
        {
            //Remove any existing data files
            string[] files = localStore.GetFileNames("*.dat");
            if (files.Length != 0)
                foreach (string name in files)
                    localStore.DeleteFile(name);

            //Write a new data file
            IsolatedStorageFileStream stream =
                new IsolatedStorageFileStream("test.dat",
                                              FileMode.Create, localStore);
            StreamWriter sWriter = new StreamWriter(stream);
            sWriter.WriteLine(saveText.Text);
            sWriter.Close();
            stream.Close();
        }
        void getBtn_Click(object sender, RoutedEventArgs e)
        {
            //Open and read Isolated Storage data file
            IsolatedStorageFileStream stream =
                new IsolatedStorageFileStream("test.dat",
                                              FileMode.Open, localStore);

            StreamReader sReader = new StreamReader(stream);
            getText.Text = sReader.ReadLine();
            sReader.Close();
            stream.Close();
        }
    }
}
```

FIGURE 13.4

Silverlight application that allows users to save and retrieve text from the isolated local storage

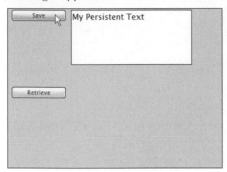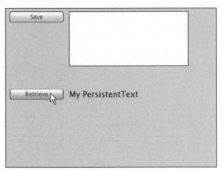

Implementing Threading in Silverlight Applications

Silverlight provides the ability for you to add threading functionality to your applications. Threading enables you to work in the background on the client without affecting the functionality of the Silverlight application. This can be very useful if you need to do time-consuming tasks such as downloading resources or complex calculations.

There are a couple of different methods to implement threads. One method is to implement a timer thread that sleeps and wakes up at a defined interval to process work. Timer threads are very useful to implement time-critical events.

Another method is to implement a background worker thread that simply runs from start to completion. Background threads are great for taking away heavy workload from the UI thread so that the Silverlight controls are updated quickly.

Implementing a timer thread

Timer threads are implemented in Silverlight applications using the `DispatchTimer` class, which is part of the `System.Windows.Threading` library. The `DispatcherTimer` implements threads that wake up on a specific interval and execute a defined function in the Silverlight application and then sleep. The UI thread in the Silverlight application is responsible for starting and stopping the `DispatchTimer` thread.

To implement a `DispatchTimer` thread, you need to create an instance of the class and then set the `Interval` property and `Tick` event handler of the `DispatcherTimer` object. The `Interval` property is a `TimeSpan` object that defines at what interval to wake up the thread.

The `Tick` event handler is a `RoutedEvent` handler that points to a Silverlight function to run when the timer wakes up.

For example, the following code creates a `DispatcherTimer` thread named `alarm` that wakes up every 5 seconds and calls a function named `WakeUp()`:

```
DispatcherTimer alarm = new DispatcherTimer();
alarm.Interval = new TimeSpan(0, 0, 0, 5, 0);
alarm.Tick += new EventHandler(WakeUp);
```

The `DispatchTimer` object also contains a `Start()` and `Stop()` method. The `Start()` method creates a timer thread and begins the interval wait. Each time the interval is reached, the `Tick` event handler is called. The thread continues to run until the `Stop()` method is executed.

> **NOTE** The `DispatchTimer` thread actually runs on a UI thread and is able to directly access Silverlight controls without using `BeginInvoke()`.

The code in Listings 13.11 and 13.12 shows Silverlight application examples that implement a `DispatchTimer` thread. The code in Listing 13.11 implements a `TextBlock` control to display the current time and a `Button` control that will be used to start the clock.

LISTING 13.11

XAML Code That Defines a TextBlock and Button Control That Creates a Clock in the Browser

```
<UserControl x:Class="TimerApp.Page"
    xmlns="http://schemas.microsoft.com/client/2007"
    xmlns:x="http://schemas.microsoft.com/winfx/2006/xaml"
    Width="500" Height="180">
    <Grid x:Name="LayoutRoot" Background="Black">
        <TextBlock x:Name="myText"
                    Foreground="Red"
                    FontFamily="Arial Black"
                    FontSize="80"  FontWeight="Bold"
                   VerticalAlignment="Center" HorizontalAlignment="Center"/>
        <Button x:Name="myButton" Content="Start Clock"
                VerticalAlignment="Bottom"
                Margin="0,0,0,20"
                Height="20" Width="100"/>
    </Grid>
</UserControl>
```

The code in Listing 13.12 imports the System.Windows.Threading library and defines a DispatchTimer class named timer. In the Page() constructor function the timer object is instantiated and the Interval is set to 1 second. The UpdateClock() Tick event handler is also attached to the timer object.

A Click event handler named StartClock() is attached to the Button control. Inside the StartClock() event handler the Start() and Stop() functions are used to begin and end the timer thread.

The results are shown in Figure 13.5. When the user clicks Start Clock, the timer thread launches and the Silverlight application begins to update the time. When Stop Clock is clicked, the timer thread stops and the clock stops updating.

LISTING 13.12

C# Code That Implements a DispatchTimer Thread to Start and Stop a Clock in the Browser

```
using System;
using System.Windows;
using System.Windows.Controls;
using System.Windows.Media;
using System.Windows.Media.Animation;

using System.Windows.Threading;

namespace TimerApp
{
    public partial class Page : UserControl
    {
        DispatcherTimer timer;
        bool isTicking;
        public Page()
        {
            InitializeComponent();
            isTicking = false;

            timer = new DispatcherTimer();
            timer.Interval = new TimeSpan(0, 0, 0, 1, 0); // 1 Second
            timer.Tick += new EventHandler(UpdateClock);

            myButton.Click += new RoutedEventHandler(StartClock);
        }

        public void StartClock(object o, RoutedEventArgs sender)
        {
```

continued

LISTING 13.12   *(continued)*

```
        if (isTicking)
        {
            myButton.Content = "Start Clock";
            timer.Stop();
            isTicking = false;
        }
        else
        {
            myButton.Content = "Stop Clock";
            timer.Start();
            isTicking = true;
        }
    }

    public void UpdateClock(object o, EventArgs sender)
    {
        this.myText.Text = String.Format("{0:T}", DateTime.Now);
    }
  }
}
```

FIGURE 13.5

Silverlight application that implements a basic clock

Adding background threads to Silverlight applications

Background worker threads are implemented in Silverlight applications using the `BackgroundWorker` class, which is part of the `System.ComponentModel` namespace. The `BackgroundWorker` implements threads that are started, run to completion, and then self-terminate. The UI thread in the Silverlight application is only responsible for starting the `BackgroundWorker` thread.

NOTE   `BackgroundWorker` threads are basically the same as a .NET `System.Windows.Thread`, except that it includes additional event handlers to handle progress update and completion events.

Creating a BackgroundWorker thread

To create a `BackgroundWorker` thread, you need to create an instance of the class. You also need to specify the `DoWork` event handler of the `BackgroundWorker` object. The `BackgroundWorker` event handler is a `DoWorkEvent` handler that points to a Silverlight function that is called when the thread is started. For example:

```
BackgroundWorker worker = new BackgroundWorker();
worker.DoWork +=new DoWorkEventHandler(DoBackground);
```

Starting a BackgroundWorker thread

`BackgroundWorker` threads are started by calling the `RunWorkerAsync()` function of the object. The `RunWorkerAsync()` function creates a new thread that begins executing the Silverlight function attached to the `DoWork` event handler of the object.

`BackgroundWorker` threads support the ability to pass arguments to the `DoWork` event handler. This is done by passing one object as an argument to the `RunWorkerAsync()` function. For example:

```
worker.RunWorkerAsync(someNum);
```

The `RunWorkerAsync()` function supports only zero or one argument. The argument is passed to the background as the Argument property of the `DoWorkEventArgs` object. For example, the following code accesses the argument from the `DoWork` event handler:

```
void DoBackground(object sender, DoWorkEventArgs e)
{
    int num = Convert.ToInt32(e.Argument);
    . . .
```

Accessing the UI from a BackgroundWorker thread

Silverlight requires that UI objects be updated on a UI thread. The `BackgroundWorker` thread is not a UI thread and therefore cannot directly access the UI objects. To access UI objects from the `BackgroundWorker` thread, you need to implement a `delegate` method that can be invoked by the `BackgroundWorker` thread to perform work on the UI thread on its behalf.

To implement a `delegate` function, first define the `delegate` as a member of the Silverlight application class. For example:

```
delegate void UpdateUIDelegate(int num, String str);
```

Then, inside the worker thread, you can create an instance of the `delegate` function that points to a function in the Silverlight application that can update the UI. For example, the following code creates an instance of the `UpdateUIDelegate()` function, defined previously, that points to a Silverlight function named `UpdateUI()`:

```
UpdateUIDelegate doUpdate = new UpdateUIDelegate(UpdateUi);
```

The Silverlight function can then be called using the `Dispatcher.BeginInvoke()` function of the Silverlight application class. The `BeginInvoke()` function accepts the `delegate` function as the first parameter. If there are arguments that need to be passed to the Silverlight function they are passed as a `params object[]` following the delegate. For example, the following code invokes the `delegate` object `doUpdate` and passes two arguments to the `UpdateUI()` Silverlight function:

```
this.Dispatcher.BeginInvoke(doUpdate, num, str);
```

The `UpdateUI()` Silverlight function is executed on the UI thread and passed the `num` and `str` parameters.

Silverlight controls provide the `CheckAccess()` function to determine if the control is accessible from the current thread. The `CheckAccess()` function returns `true` if the current thread can update the control and `false` if it cannot. For example, the following code checks to see if a TextBlock control can be accessed by the current thread before updating it:

```
if (myText.CheckAccess())
    myText.Text = "Updated";
```

Updating progress of a BackgroundWorker thread

`BackgroundWorker` threads also support the ability to update the Silverlight application of their progress. This is done by setting the `WorkerSupportsProgress` property of the `BackgroundWorker` object to true and then attaching a `ProgressChanged` event handler to the object before the `BackgroundWorker` thread is started. For example:

```
worker.WorkerReportsProgress = true;
worker.ProgressChanged +=
        new ProgressChangedEventHandler(UpdateProgress);
```

The `ProgressChanged` event handler is triggered inside the `BackgroundWorker` thread code by calling the `ReportProgress()` function of the object. `ReportProgress()` accepts an integer, representing the percentage complete that should range from 0 to 100, as an argument. For example, to report back a progress of 50 percent, use the following code:

```
worker.ReportProgress(50);
```

The `ProgressChanged` event handler actually runs on a UI thread, so you can access the Silverlight controls in the application and update them. The `ProgressChanged` event hander is a great way to implement a progress bar.

Cancelling a BackgroundWorker thread

An important feature of `BackgroundWorker` threads is the ability to cancel them if necessary. This feature must be enabled before the thread is started.

To enable cancelling a `BackgroundWorker` thread, set the `WorkerSupportsCancellation` property of the object to `true`. For example:

```
worker.WorkerSupportsCancellation = true;
```

Then the BackgroundWorker thread can be cancelled from the UI thread using the
CancelAsync() function of the object. For example:

```
worker.CancelAsync();
```

The CancelAsync() function sets the CancellationPending property of the
BackgroundWorker object to true. It does not halt the thread for you. This gives you the ability to gracefully end the thread. To gracefully end the thread, monitor the
CancellationPending property and if it is true, clean up and return from the thread. On the
way out, you need to set the Cancel property of the DoWorkEventArgs to true. For example,
the following code shows a basic way to cancel a BackgroundWorker thread:

```
if (worker.CancellationPending)
{
    e.Cancel = true;
    return;
}
```

Handling completion of a BackgroundWorker thread

The BackgroundWorker class also provides a completion event that enables you to clean up
after the thread and handle any errors. This is done attaching a RunWorkerCompleted event
handler to the object before the BackgroundWorker thread is started. For example:

```
worker.RunWorkerCompleted +=
        new RunWorkerCompletedEventHandler(DoBackgroundCompleted);
```

The RunWorkerCompleted event handler is triggered upon returning from the DoWork event
handler function. The status of the thread can be determined by the Cancel, Error, and
Result attributes of the RunWorkerCompletedEventArgs passed to the handler. Cancel is
a boolean type, Error is an error type, and Result is an object type.

The Cancel and Result properties can be set in the BackgroundWorker code prior to returning from the handler. The Error property is set if the worker thread returns an unhandled error.

Example: BackgroundWorker thread application

Listings 13.13 and 13.14 show an example of implementing BackgroundWorker threads in a
Silverlight application. The XAML code in Listing 13.13 implements a Canvas control named sky
on which the application places stars.

The TextBox control numText allows users to specify the number of stars. The Button controls
loadButton and cancelButton are used to begin and cancel a BackgroundWorker thread.
The Canvas control progressIndicator contains a TextBlock control named
progressText, and a Rectangle control named progressBar, that are used to implement a
status bar showing percentage complete.

LISTING 13.13

XAML Code That Defines a Black Canvas Control That Is Used as a Night Sky and Two Button Controls to Start and Cancel a BackgroundWorker Thread

```xml
<UserControl x:Class="backgroundthread.Page"
    xmlns="http://schemas.microsoft.com/client/2007"
    xmlns:x="http://schemas.microsoft.com/winfx/2006/xaml"
    Width="400" Height="300">
    <Grid x:Name="LayoutRoot" Background="DarkBlue">
        <Canvas x:Name="sky"
                Background="Black"
                VerticalAlignment="Top"
                Width="400" Height="250" />
        <TextBox x:Name="numText" Text="100"
                BorderThickness="2"
                Height="30" Width="75"
                Margin="-250,0,0,10"
                VerticalAlignment="Bottom"/>
        <Button x:Name="loadButton" Content="Load Stars"
                Height="30" Width="100"
                Margin="-50,0,0,10"
                VerticalAlignment="Bottom"/>
        <Button x:Name="cancelButton" Content="Cancel"
                Height="30" Width="100"
                Margin="220,0,0,10"
                VerticalAlignment="Bottom"/>
        <Canvas x:Name="progIndicator"
                Opacity=".5"
                Background="Gray"
                Height="25" Width="100"
                VerticalAlignment="Center"
                HorizontalAlignment="Center">
            <Rectangle x:Name="progressBar"
                    Height="25" Width="0"
                    Fill="Blue" />
            <TextBlock x:Name="progressText"
                    Foreground="White"
                    Canvas.Left="4" />
        </Canvas>
    </Grid>
</UserControl>
```

The code in Listing 13.14 imports the `System.Windows.Threading` library and defines a `BackgroundWorker` class named `bgWork`. In the `Page()` constructor function, the `bgWork` object is instantiated and the `WorkerReportsProgress` and `WorkerSupportsCancellation` properties are set to `true`.

The constructor function also attaches `DoWork`, `ProgressChanged`, and `RunWorkerCompleted` event handlers to the `bgWork` object. A `Click` event handler named `loadButton_Click()` is attached to the `loadButton` Button control and a `Click` event handler named `cancelButton_Click()` is attached to the `cancelButton` Button control.

Inside the `loadButton_Click()` event handler, the code gets the number of stars from the `numText TextBlock` and calls the `RunWorkerAsync()` function of the `bgWorker` object to begin thread execution.

Inside the `cancelButton_Click()` event handler, the code calls the `CancelAsync()` function of the `bgWorker` object to notify the `bgWorker` thread to halt execution.

The `bgWorker` object's `DoWork` event handler `DoBackground()` creates a `delegate` object that points to the `AddStar()` function using the following line of code:

```
AddStarDelegate updateUI = new AddStarDelegate(AddStar);
```

Then the code implements a `for` loop that randomly sets `X` and `Y` coordinates and invokes the delegate function `AddStar()` to add an `Ellipse` to the `sky Canvas` at coordinates `X` and `Y` using the following line of code:

```
this.Dispatcher.BeginInvoke(updateUI, X, Y);
```

In each pass through the `for` loop, the code calls the `ReportProgress()` function of the `bgWorker` object. When the progress is reported, the `DoBackgroundProgressChanged()` event handler function is called, which updates the `progressBar` and `progressText` objects in the status bar UI.

The `DoBackgroundCompleted()` event handler is called when the `DoWorker()` event handler finishes. The `DoBackgroundCompleted()` checks the `Cancelled` and `Error` properties of the `RunWorkerCompletedEventArgs` object and updates the `progressText` control.

The results are shown in Figure 13.6. When the user clicks Load Stars, the `bgworker` thread launches and begins adding stars to the `Canvas`. If the user clicks Cancel, the `bgWorker` thread stops adding stars and returns. The progress bar is updated each time a star is added to the canvas.

LISTING 13.14

**C# Code That Implements a BackgroundWorker Thread to Add Stars to a Black Canvas
Control**

```csharp
using System;
using System.Windows;
using System.Windows.Controls;
using System.Windows.Media;
using System.Windows.Media.Animation;
using System.Windows.Shapes;

//Add Background thread support
using System.Windows.Threading;

namespace backgroundthread
{
    public partial class Page : UserControl
    {
        delegate void AddStarDelegate(int X, int Y);
        BackgroundWorker bgWork;

        public Page()
        {
            InitializeComponent();

            //Setup Background Worker Thread
            bgWork = new BackgroundWorker();
            bgWork.WorkerReportsProgress = true;
            bgWork.WorkerSupportsCancellation = true;
            bgWork.DoWork +=new DoWorkEventHandler(DoBackground);
            bgWork.ProgressChanged +=
                new ProgressChangedEventHandler(DoBackgroundProgressChanged);
            bgWork.RunWorkerCompleted +=
                new RunWorkerCompletedEventHandler(DoBackgroundCompleted);

            loadButton.Click += new RoutedEventHandler(loadButton_Click);
            cancelButton.Click +=
                new RoutedEventHandler(cancelButton_Click);
        }

        void cancelButton_Click(object sender, RoutedEventArgs e)
        {
            bgWork.CancelAsync();
        }
```

```csharp
void loadButton_Click(object sender, RoutedEventArgs e)
{
    int numStars = Convert.ToInt32(numText.Text);

    //Start Background Worker
    bgWork.RunWorkerAsync(numStars);
}

void DoBackground(object sender, DoWorkEventArgs e)
{
    BackgroundWorker worker = sender as BackgroundWorker;
    AddStarDelegate updateUI = new AddStarDelegate(AddStar);
    int X, Y, wait, starCount, percent;

    starCount = Convert.ToInt32(e.Argument);
    for (int cnt = 1; cnt <= starCount; cnt++)
    {
        //Check for Cancel
        if (worker.CancellationPending)
        {
            e.Cancel = true;
            return;
        }

        X = new Random().Next(10, 390);
        wait = new Random().Next(100, 500);
        System.Threading.Thread.Sleep(wait);
        Y = new Random().Next(10, 240);

        //Invoke Delegate Function to Update UI
        this.Dispatcher.BeginInvoke(updateUI, X, Y);

        //Notify Progress Event Handler
        percent = Convert.ToInt32(((double)cnt /
                                   (double)starCount) * 100);
        worker.ReportProgress(percent);
    }
}

protected void DoBackgroundProgressChanged(object sender,
                                  ProgressChangedEventArgs e)
{
    progressText.Text = String.Format("Loading {0}%",
                            e.ProgressPercentage.ToString());
    progressBar.Width = e.ProgressPercentage;
}
```

continued

LISTING 13.14   *(continued)*

```
void DoBackgroundCompleted(object sender,
                           RunWorkerCompletedEventArgs e)
{
    if (e.Cancelled)
        progressText.Text = "Cancelled";
    else if (e.Error != null)
        progressText.Text = "Error";
    else
        progressText.Text = "Completed";
}

void AddStar(int X, int Y)
{
    Ellipse star = new Ellipse();

    star.Height = 3;
    star.Width = 3;
    star.SetValue(Canvas.LeftProperty, X);
    star.SetValue(Canvas.TopProperty, Y);
    star.Fill = new SolidColorBrush(Colors.White);
    sky.Children.Add(star);
}
  }
}
```

FIGURE 13.6

Silverlight application that implements a `BackgroundWorker` thread that adds stars to a `Canvas` control and updates a progress bar

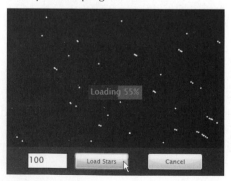

Summary

This chapter focused on using Silverlight's presentation framework to interact with the HTML DOM. Using the `Browser` library, you can access elements in the DOM directly from Silverlight applications. Also, by exposing Silverlight applications as scriptable, you can access Silverlight functions from HTML JavaScript.

Silverlight provides the `OpenFileDialog` class to provide read-only access to client-side files. Silverlight also provides the `IsolatedStorageFile` class to access the isolated local storage on the client. Data can be written to the isolated local storage as well as read.

Using the `DispatchTimer` class makes it simple to add timer threads to Silverlight applications. Silverlight also provides the `BackgroundWorker` class to implement multiple threads in Silverlight applications. The `BackgroundWorker` class supports progress update and completion handling events that make it easy to implement.

In this chapter, you learned how to:

- Access and change elements in the HTML DOM from managed code in Silverlight applications
- Use JavaScript functions to access and call methods in Silverlight managed code
- Use the `OpenFileDialog` class to retrieve files from the client
- Create and read files that are stored in the isolated local storage of the client
- Create, start, and stop a `Timer` thread
- Add `BackgroundWorker` threads to Silverlight applications
- Invoke functions on the UI thread from a `BackgroundWorker` thread

Chapter 14

Using the Silverlight Communication Framework

S ilverlight 2 provides a fairly robust communication framework to communicate with Web services and retrieve remote resources. The combination of the Silverlight communication framework and data framework, discussed in the next chapter, provides Silverlight applications with the ability to interact with a wide variety of Web services based on RSS, JSON, REST, SOAP, and other technologies.

The Silverlight communication framework can be broken down into three pieces: the WebClient class, HTTP classes, and sockets. Each of these frameworks has advantages over the others and is used for different purposes.

The WebClient interface is the simplest to implement and can be used to download remote resources or data from Web services. The Socket library provides the tools necessary for Silverlight applications to interact with TCP-based Web services. The HttpWebRequest and HttpWebResponse classes are more complex; however, they provide much more control when interacting with Web services.

CROSS-REF In Chapter 10, we discuss setting up ASP.NET Web services to work with Silverlight applications and how to access them using a SOAP client. That is part of the communication framework; however, we don't discuss it in this chapter because it has already been covered.

The Silverlight communication framework does support cross-domain access to Web services and resources. However, cross-domain access is tightly governed using access policies. This protects Web services and resources from network threats by allowing the remote services to implement policies to restrict access.

IN THIS CHAPTER

Implementing a network security access policy to enable Silverlight client access

Downloading content on demand

Accessing RSS and Atom Syndication feeds

Implementing sockets in Silverlight applications

Using HttpWebRequest and HttpWebResponse to build and send a Web request

> **TIP** There is a very useful tool named Fiddler that tracks the communication going out of the client. This tool is very useful when debugging Silverlight applications that implement the communication framework. The utility can be downloaded from `www.fiddlertool.com/fiddler/`.

This chapter discusses the different components of the Silverlight application and how to use them to access Web services and remote resources. We also discuss using the Syndication framework to access RSS and Atom feeds. The Silverlight communication framework is so extensive that we cannot cover everything; however, this chapter should give you a good feel for what is possible with the Silverlight communication framework.

> **TIP** If you want your Silverlight applications to be able to call existing Web services, you should select the option to create a Web project in the solution when you create the Silverlight application project. If you don't, you get a security exception when the application tries to call a Web service from the dynamically created HTML test page.

Enabling Network Security Access for Silverlight Applications

Whenever you are dealing with network communication, especially for Web applications, you should be concerned with security. The Silverlight framework implements a rigid security scheme to protect services from network threats such as denial of service, DNS rebinding, and reverse tunneling.

The simplest way to protect against such attacks is to prevent any cross-domain access to services and to limit access to the host or at least the site of origin. This works well for many services; however, a large number of services require the ability to communicate across multiple domains.

To solve this problem, Silverlight has implemented a security policy system that allows you to implement cross-domain access using the Silverlight `WebClient`, HTTP classes, `System.Net` namespace, and `System.Net.Sockets` namespace.

The security policy is implemented by providing a policy file at the root of the Web server that handles the request. If a policy file does not exist, then the Silverlight application receives an exception and the request fails.

> **NOTE** If you want your Silverlight application to talk across multiple domains, each domain needs to implement a cross-domain policy file that grants permission to the Silverlight application. The policy file *must* reside in the root path of the remote Web server.

Silverlight supports the following two types of policy files to provide cross-domain access to Silverlight applications:

- **Flash policy file** — `crossdomain.xml`: Policy file used by Adobe Flash. Supports `WebClient`, HTTP classes, and `System.Net` namespace communication.

- **Silverlight policy file** — `clientaccesspolicy.xml`: Silverlight policy file, similar to the Flash policy but with a different format. Supports `WebClient`, HTTP classes, and `System.Net` namespace, and `System.Net.Sockets` namespace communication.

When a Silverlight `WebClient` or HTTP class request is made to a cross-domain URI, Silverlight tries to download the `clientaccesspolicy.xml` file. If that file is not present, it tries to download the `crossdomain.xml` file. If the policy file configuration provides access, the communication continues. If Silverlight cannot access either of those files or the policy does not grant the appropriate permissions, the request throws an exception.

Socket applications behave a little bit differently. The socket application first tries to connect to the servers using port 943. Once connected, it sends a special string, `<policy-file-request/>`, to the server that requests the Silverlight policy file.

NOTE To deploy a Silverlight policy that provides cross-domain access to Windows services, you need to configure a separate authenticate service on port 943 for each IP address that will provide the Silverlight policy file.

The Silverlight policy file is an XML document that describes security access for the domain. Table 14.1 shows a list of elements that can be added to the Silverlight policy file.

TABLE 14.1

Silverlight Policy File Elements

Element	Parent	Required	Description
access-policy	none (root)	YES	Root element of a Silverlight policy file.
cross-domain-access	access-policy	YES	Specifies cross-domain policies for entire site.
policy	cross-domain-access	YES	Specifies a specific cross-domain policy for a set of one or more domains. (More than one policy can be defined in the same file.)
allow-from	policy	YES	Specifies (from) domains that are affected by this policy. If `allow-from` is used, only listed domains can gain access. If `allow-from` is not specified, then the policy grants access to all domains.
domain	allow-from	YES	Specifies a domain or Silverlight application that is affected by the policy.

continued

TABLE 14.1   *(continued)*

Element	Parent	Required	Description
grant-to	policy	YES	Specifies all the server's resources that are affected by this policy.
resource	grant-to	YES (WebClient & HTTP)	Specifies the resources that can be accessed using this policy.
socket-resource	grant-to	YES (sockets)	Specifies the socket resources that can be accessed using this policy. (Only for socket access)

Table 14.2 shows a list of possible attributes that can be added to elements in the Silverlight policy file.

TABLE 14.2

Attributes of Silverlight Policy File Elements

Attribute	Element	Required	Description
HTTP-request-headers	access-policy	NO	Specifies a case-insensitive, comma-separated list of allowed headers for the domain. If this attribute is missing, no headers will be allowed.
include-subpaths	resource	NO	Specifies whether to grant access to subpaths of the `path` attribute.
path	resource	YES (WebClient & HTTP)	Specifies the URI relative to the root of the domain that refers to the path of the Web service or file. (For `WebClient` and HTTP requests only.)
port	socket-resource	YES (sockets)	Specifies the port or port range that applications are allowed to connect to. (Only for socket access)
protocol	socket-resource	YES (sockets)	Specifies the protocols that applications are allowed to use when connecting. Currently only supports `tcp`. (Only for socket access)
URI	domain	YES	Specifies a list of allowed domains and Silverlight applications that can access the granted paths.

 **TIP**   You can include the elements specific to sockets and HTTP classes in the same policy file. That way you can provide access to both types of resources on the same site.

The code in Listing 14.1 shows an example `clientaccesspolicy.xml` policy file that grants access to the entire domain to everyone.

LISTING 14.1

Silverlight clientaccesspolicy.xml File That Grants Rights to the Root Path and Subpaths to Everyone

```
<?xml version="1.0" encoding="utf-8" ?>
<acces-policy>
  <cross-domain-access>
    <policy>
      <allow-from>
        <domain uri="*" />
      </allow-from>
      <grant-to>
        <resource path="/" include-subpaths="true"/>
      </grant-to>
    </policy>
  </cross-domain-access>
</acces-policy>
```

The code in Listing 14.1 is good for testing, but it leaves your Web site vulnerable. When you go to production, you will want to provide more security. Listing 14.2 shows a more restrictive Silverlight `clientaccesspolicy.xml` policy file.

LISTING 14.2

Silverlight clientaccesspolicy.xml File That Grants Access for Specific Directories to Specific Domains

```
<?xml version="1.0" encoding="utf-8" ?>
<acces-policy>
  <cross-domain-access>
    <policy>
      <allow-from http-request-headers="X-API-*">
        <domain uri="http://www.myserver.com:0000" />
        <domain uri="http://www.amazon.com" />
        <domain uri="http://www.microsoft.com" />
      </allow-from>
      <grant-to>
        <resource path="/http-apps" include-subpaths="false"/>
      </grant-to>
    </policy>
    <policy>
      <allow-from>
        <domain uri="http://www.myserver.com:8080" />
```

continued

443

LISTING 14.2   *(continued)*

```
      </allow-from>
      <grant-to>
        <socket-resource port="4501-4504" protocol="tcp" />
      </grant-to>
    </policy>
  </cross-domain-access>
</acces-policy>
```

The policy in Listing 14.2 limits access to the `http://www.myserver.com:8080`, `http://www.amazon.com`, and `http://www.microsoft.com` domains. The listing specifies the `http-request-headers` attribute that allows only headers beginning with `X-API` to be sent.

Listing 14.2 also implements a policy for access from socket applications. That policy limits access to only the `http://www.myserver.com:8080` domain. It also uses the `port` attribute of the `socket-resource` element to limit access to ports between 4501 and 4504.

Using a WebClient to Download Resources on Demand

One of the most useful features of the Silverlight communication framework is the `System.Net.WebClient` class. The `WebClient` class provides the framework necessary to download content from a server in response to an application request.

Downloading content dynamically allows your XAP packages to be much smaller and provides an abstraction layer that can be useful when dealing with resources that need to be packaged together.

The communication between the `WebClient` class and server is all done asynchronously. This is a necessity for Web applications so that requests do not impact the responsiveness of the rest of the Silverlight application.

CAUTION   Only one `WebClient` request can be initiated at a time. If a second request is made before the Completed event is triggered for the first, a `NotSupportedException` is thrown in the second request.

To access the functionality of the `WebClient` class, you need to add a reference to the `System.Net` library in your application and add a `using` statement that includes the namespace in the code. Then you will need to create an instance of the `WebClient` using the following line of code:

```
WebClient client = new WebClient();
```

The WebClient class exposes two functions that can be used to access and download resources from the server, DownloadStringAsync() and OpenReadAsync().

Using a WebClient to download a text file

The DownloadStringAsync() function of the WebClient class can be used to download the contents of files as a string. The DownloadStringAsync() accepts a Uri object as an argument and sends the equivalent of a GET request to the server to retrieve the content of the file specified by the Uri. For example:

```
client.DownloadStringAsync(new Uri("afile.txt", UriKind.
    Relative));
```

To access the result of the DownloadStringAsync() function, you need to attach a DownloadStringCompleted event handler function to the WebClient object. For example, the following line of code attaches a DownloadStringCompleted event handler function doDownloadCompleted() to a WebClient object named client.

```
client.DownloadStringCompleted +=
    new DownloadStringCompletedEventHandler(doDownloadCompleted);
```

The DownloadStringCompleted event handler function must accept an object, the sender, as the first argument and a DownloadStringCompletedEventArgs as the second argument.

Inside the DownloadStringCompleted event handler function, the contents of the file downloaded can be accessed using the result property of the DownloadStringCompleted EventArgs argument. The result property is of string type and contains the contents of the downloaded file.

Listings 14.3 and 14.4 show a simple example of using a WebClient object to download a text file and display it in a Silverlight application. The code in Listing 14.3 defines a simple interface with a Button control to initiate a file download and a TextBlock in a ScrollViewer to display the contents of the downloaded file.

LISTING 14.3

Page.xaml File That Defines a Button Control to Initiate a File Download and a TextBlock Control in a ScrollViewer to Display the Results

```
<UserControl x:Class="DownloadStringApp.Page"
    xmlns="http://schemas.microsoft.com/client/2007"
    xmlns:x="http://schemas.microsoft.com/winfx/2006/xaml"
    Width="400" Height="300">
    <Grid x:Name="LayoutRoot" Background="White">
        <ScrollViewer HorizontalScrollBarVisibility="Auto"
```

continued

LISTING 14.3 *(continued)*

```
                         Height="200" Width="300"
                         VerticalAlignment="Top"
                         Margin="20">
            <TextBlock x:Name="downloadText"/>
        </ScrollViewer>
        <Button x:Name="downloadBtn" Content="Download Dynamic Content"
                VerticalAlignment="Bottom" Margin="20"
                Height="30" Width="200" />
    </Grid>
</UserControl>
```

The code in Listing 14.4 implements the System.Net library and then attaches a Click event handler, doGetContent(), to the Button control defined in Listing 14.3. Inside the doGet-Content() event handler, the WebClient object, client, is created.

A DownloadStringCompleted event handler, doDownloadCompleted(), is attached to the client object. Then the following line of code is used to create a Uri object for the readme.txt file and initiate the file download:

```
    client.DownloadStringAsync(new Uri(filename, UriKind.Relative));
```

Inside the handler doDownloadCompleted() function, the result property of the DownloadStringCompletedEventArgs argument is used to set the Text property of the downloadText TextBlock defined in Listing 14.3.

LISTING 14.4

Page.xaml.cs File That Creates a WebClient and Uses It to Download the Contents of a File Named readme.txt

```
using System;
using System.Windows;
using System.Windows.Controls;
using System.Windows.Input;

using System.Net;

namespace DownloadStringApp
{
    public partial class Page : UserControl
```

```
    {
        public Page()
        {
            InitializeComponent();

            downloadBtn.Click += new RoutedEventHandler(doGetContent);
        }

        void doGetContent(object sender, RoutedEventArgs e)
        {
            string filename = "readme.txt";

            WebClient client = new WebClient();
            client.DownloadStringCompleted +=
                new DownloadStringCompletedEventHandler(doDownloadCompleted);
            client.DownloadStringAsync(new Uri(filename, UriKind.Relative));
        }

        void doDownloadCompleted(object sender,
                                 DownloadStringCompletedEventArgs e)
        {
            downloadText.Text = e.Result;
        }
    }
}
```

The results of the application defined by Listings 14.3 and 14.4 are shown in Figure 14.1. When the user clicks Download Dynamic Content, the contents of the file are displayed in the text block.

FIGURE 14.1

Silverlight application that dynamically downloads a text file and displays it

Using a WebClient to download and access a ZIP package

The `OpenReadAsysc()` function of the `WebClient` class is similar to the `DownloadStringAsync()` function, except it opens a `Uri` object as a stream. The `OpenReadAsysc()` accepts a `Uri` object as an argument and retrieves the contents of the path specified by the `Uri` as a stream. For example:

```
client.OpenReadAsync(new Uri("image.jpg", UriKind.Relative));
```

To access the result of the `OpenReadAsysc()` function, you need to attach an `OpenReadCompleted` event handler function to the `WebClient` object. For example, the following line of code attaches an `OpenReadCompleted` event handler function `doDownload Completed()` to a `WebClient` object named `client`.

```
client.DownloadStringCompleted +=
    new DownloadStringCompletedEventHandler(doDownloadCompleted);
```

The `OpenReadCompleted` event handler function must accept an object, the sender, as the first argument and an `OpenReadCompletedEventArgs` as the second argument.

Inside the `OpenReadCompleted` event handler function the downloaded file stream can be accessed using the `result` property of the `OpenReadCompletedEventArgs` argument. The `result` property is of `Stream` type and can be used to access the contents of the downloaded file.

For example, the following `OpenReadCompleted` event handler function uses the `result` property to access the file stream of an image file and uses it to set the `Source` property of an `Image` control named `img`:

```
void doDownloadCompleted(object sender,
    OpenReadCompletedEventArgs e)
{
    StreamResourceInfo imageStream =
            new StreamResourceInfo(e.Result as Stream, null);
    BitmapImage imgsrc = new BitmapImage();
    imgsrc.SetSource(imageInfo.Stream);
    img.Source = imgsrc;
}
```

Listings 14.5 and 14.6 show an example of using a `WebClient` object to download a ZIP file from the server. The code then uses the contents of the ZIP file to set various controls in a Silverlight application.

The code in Listing 14.5 defines a simple interface with a Button control, downloadBtn, to initiate a file download, a TextBlock control, titleText , and a Grid control, imageGrid.

LISTING 14.5

Page.xaml File That Defines a Button Control to Initiate a File Download and a TextBlock Control and Grid Control Used to Display the Results

```
<UserControl x:Class="DownloaderApp.Page"
    xmlns="http://schemas.microsoft.com/client/2007"
    xmlns:x="http://schemas.microsoft.com/winfx/2006/xaml"
    Width="400" Height="400">
    <Grid x:Name="LayoutRoot" Background="Black">
        <TextBlock x:Name="titleText"
                   FontSize="50" Foreground="White"
                   HorizontalAlignment="Center"/>
        <Grid    x:Name="imageGrid"
                 HorizontalAlignment="Center"
                 VerticalAlignment="Center"
                 Height="240" Width="300" />
        <Button x:Name="downloadBtn" Content="Download Content"
                Height="30" Width="150"
                VerticalAlignment="Bottom"
                Margin="10" />
    </Grid>
</UserControl>
```

The code in Listing 14.6 first implements the System.Net library for the WebClient class, the System.IO library for the StreamReader and Stream classes, the System.Windows. Resources library for the StreamResourceInfo class and the System.Windows.Media. Imaging library for the BitmapImage class.

Inside the Page() constructor, the code attaches a Click event handler, doDownload(), to the downloadBtn control defined in Listing 14.5. Inside the doDownload ()event handler, the WebClient object, client, is created.

An OpenAsyncCompleted event handler, DownloadZipCompleted(), is attached to the client object. Then the following line of code is used to create a Uri object for the content.zip file, shown in Figure 14.2, and initiates the file download:

```
client.OpenReadAsync(new Uri(filename, UriKind.Relative));
```

LISTING 14.6

Page.xaml.cs File That Creates a WebClient and Uses It to Download the Contents of a File Named readme.txt

```csharp
using System;
using System.Windows;
using System.Windows.Controls;
using System.Windows.Documents;
using System.Windows.Media;

using System.Net;
using System.IO;
using System.Windows.Resources;
using System.Windows.Media.Imaging;

namespace DownloaderApp
{
    public partial class Page : UserControl
    {
        public Page()
        {
            InitializeComponent();
            downloadBtn.Click += new RoutedEventHandler(doDownload);
        }

        void doDownload(object sender, RoutedEventArgs e)
        {
            string filename ="content.zip";

            WebClient client = new WebClient();
            client.OpenReadCompleted +=
                new OpenReadCompletedEventHandler(DownloadZipCompleted);
            client.OpenReadAsync(new Uri(filename, UriKind.Relative));
        }

        void DownloadZipCompleted(object sender,
                            OpenReadCompletedEventArgs e)
        {
            StreamResourceInfo zipInfo =
                new StreamResourceInfo(e.Result, null);

            //Get Image from ZIP
```

```
StreamResourceInfo imageInfo = Application.GetResourceStream(
        zipInfo, new Uri("image.jpg", UriKind.Relative));
Image img = new Image();
img.Height = 240;
BitmapImage imgsrc = new BitmapImage();
imgsrc.SetSource(imageInfo.Stream);
img.Source = imgsrc;
imageGrid.Children.Clear();
imageGrid.Children.Add(img);

//Get Audio from ZIP
StreamResourceInfo audioInfo = Application.GetResourceStream(
        zipInfo, new Uri("music.mp3", UriKind.Relative));
MediaElement music = new MediaElement();
music.SetSource(audioInfo.Stream);
LayoutRoot.Children.Add(music);
music.Play();

//Get Font from ZIP
StreamResourceInfo fontInfo = Application.GetResourceStream(
        zipInfo, new Uri("font.ttf", UriKind.Relative));
FontSource newFont = new FontSource(fontInfo.Stream);
titleText.FontSource = newFont;
StreamResourceInfo fontName = Application.GetResourceStream(
        zipInfo, new Uri("fontinfo.txt", UriKind.Relative));
StreamReader reader = new StreamReader(fontName.Stream);
titleText.FontFamily = new FontFamily(reader.ReadLine());

//Get Text from ZIP
StreamResourceInfo dataInfo = Application.GetResourceStream(
        zipInfo, new Uri("data.txt", UriKind.Relative));
StreamReader dataReader = new StreamReader(dataInfo.Stream);
titleText.Text = dataReader.ReadToEnd();
    }
  }
}
```

Inside the handler DownloadZipCompleted () function, the following line of code uses the result property of the DownloadStringCompletedEventArgs argument to create a StreamResourceInfo object that can access the downloaded ZIP file stream:

```
StreamResourceInfo zipInfo = new StreamResourceInfo(e.Result, null);
```

Using the `zipInfo` `SreamResourceInfo` object, the code is then able to access the individual components of the ZIP file. For example, the following line of code is used to access an MP3 file stored in the ZIP file:

```
StreamResourceInfo audioInfo = Application.GetResourceStream(
        zipInfo, new Uri("music.mp3", UriKind.Relative));
```

The code in the `DownloadZipCompleted()` function of Listing 14.6 uses this same technique to access each of the different files in the `content.zip` file shown in Figure 14.2. The `image.jpg` file is read and used to create a new `Image` object that is added as a child to the `imageGrid` control.

The `music.mp3` file is read and used to create a new `MediaElement` control that is added to the `LayoutRoot` control. The `Play()` function of the `MediaElement` control is used to start playback of the music file.

The `font.ttf` file is used to set the `FontSource` property of the `titleText` control. To set the `FontFamily` property, the typeface name is read from the `fontinfo.txt` file.

The `data.txt` file is read using a `StreamReader`, and the contents are applied as the `Text` property of the `titleText` control.

FIGURE 14.2
_____

Contents of the `content.zip` file used in Listing 14.6

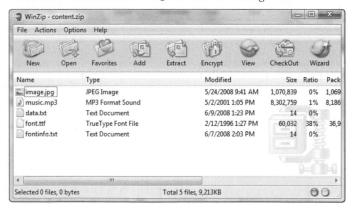

The results of the application defined by Listings 14.5 and 14.6 are shown in Figure 14.3. When the user clicks Download Content, the contents of the `content.zip` file are downloaded and the contents are used to add an image and music, and set the typeface and text of the Silverlight application dynamically.

FIGURE 14.3

Silverlight application that dynamically downloads a ZIP file and uses the contents to dynamically change several controls

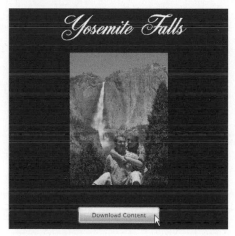

Accessing RSS Services

Another very useful feature of the Silverlight communication framework is the `System.ServiceModel.Syndication` library. The `Syndication` library included with Silverlight provides most of the functionality available in the .NET framework. The `Syndication` library provides a rich set of functionality that enables you to implement RSS or Atom feeds in your Silverlight applications.

The three main classes you use from the `Syndication` library are the `SyndicationFeed`, `SyndicationItem`, and `SyndicationContent` classes.

The `SyndicationFeed` class provides the necessary utilities that you need to interact with RSS and Atom feeds. `SyndicationFeed` object properties contain information about the feed. Table 14.3 lists some of the important property variables of `SyndicationFeed` class objects.

TABLE 14.3

Properties of the SyndicationFeed Class

Property	Description
AttributeExtensions	Dictionary. Specifies additional attributes for the feed.
BaseUri	Uri. Specifies the base URI for the feed.
Description	String. Provides a description of the feed.
ElementExtensions	Dictionary. Specifies additional attributes for the feed.
Items	List<SyndicationItem>. List of SyndicationItem objects in the feed.
LastUpdateTime	DateTimeOffset. Specifies the last time the feed was updated.
Links	Collection<SyndicationLink>. Collection of SyndicationLink objects.
Title	String. Specifies the title of the feed.

The SyndicationItem class provides functionality to work with individual items in the feed. SyndicationItem classes represent an RSS <item> or an Atom <entry> element. Table 14.4 lists some of the important property variables of SyndicationItem class objects.

TABLE 14.4

Properties of the SyndicationItem Class

Property	Description
AttributeExtensions	Dictionary. Specifies additional attributes for the feed item.
BaseUri	Uri. Specifies the base URI for the feed item.
Content	String. Specifies the SyndicationContent object that is associated with this item.
ElementExtensions	Dictionary. Specifies additional attributes for the feed item.
Links	Collection<SyndicationLink>. Collection of SyndicationLink objects associated with the item.
PublishedDate	DateTimeOffset. Specifies the date that the item was published.
SourceFeed	SyndicationFeed. Specifies the SyndicationFeed object this item belongs to.
Summary	TextSyndicationContent. Specifies a summary of the content of the item.

The SyndicationContent class is actually an abstract for the following content classes:

- **TextSyndicationContent**: SyndicationContent class that provides content to SyndicationItem classes as HTML, XHTML, or plain text.

- **UrlSyndicationContent**: SyndicationContent class that provides content to SyndicationItem classes as a URL that points to another resource.

- **XmlSyndicationContent**: SyndicationContent class that provides content to SyndicationItem classes as XML data. This type of content is not intended to be displayed in a Web browser.

The code in Listings 14.7 and 14.8 shows an example Silverlight application that implements an RSS feed. The code in Listing 14.7 defines a simple interface with a Button control, getBtn, to initiate retrieval of the RSS feed. A ListBox control, titleList, is defined in a ScrollViewer to store a list of feed item titles. A TextBlock, feedSummary is defined in a ScrollViewer to display the Summary attribute of a list item. A TextBlock, dateText is defined to display the publication date of the feed item.

LISTING 14.7

Page.xaml File That Defines an Interface to Retrieve and Display the Summaries of Items in an RSS Feed

```xml
<UserControl x:Class="RssFeedsApp.Page"
    xmlns="http://schemas.microsoft.com/client/2007"
    xmlns:x="http://schemas.microsoft.com/winfx/2006/xaml"
    Width="640" Height="300">
    <Grid x:Name="LayoutRoot" Background="LightBlue">
        <TextBlock Text="RSS Feed Items"
                    HorizontalAlignment="Left" Margin="100,10"/>
        <TextBlock Text="Item Summary"
                    HorizontalAlignment="Right" Margin="110,10"/>
        <ScrollViewer Background="White"
                    Height="200" Width="280"
                    VerticalAlignment="Top"
                    HorizontalAlignment="Left"
                    Margin="20, 40">
            <ListBox x:Name="titleList"/>
        </ScrollViewer>
        <ScrollViewer Background="White"
                    Height="200" Width="280"
                    VerticalAlignment="Top"
                    HorizontalAlignment="Right"
                    Margin="0,40,20,0">
            <TextBlock x:Name="feedSummary"
                    TextWrapping="Wrap"/>
        </ScrollViewer>
        <Button x:Name="getBtn" Content="Get Feed"
                VerticalAlignment="Bottom"
                HorizontalAlignment="Left"
```

continued

LISTING 14.7 *(continued)*

```
                Margin="20" Height="30" Width="100" />
        <TextBlock x:Name="dateText" Text="Published: "
                VerticalAlignment="Bottom"
                HorizontalAlignment="Left"
                Margin="340, 0, 0, 30" />
    </Grid>
</UserControl>
```

The code in Listing 14.6 first implements the `System.Net` library for the `HttpWebRequest` class, the `System.Xml library` for the `XmlReader` class, and the `System.ServiceModel. Syndication` library for the `SyndicationFeed` and `SyndicationItem` classes.

Inside the `Page()` constructor, the code attaches a `Click` event handler, `doGetFeed()`, to the `getBtn` control defined in Listing 14.7. The code also attaches a `SelectionChanged` event handler, `doShowSummary()`, to the `titleList` Listbox.

Inside the `doGetFeed()` event handler, an `HttpWebRequest` object, `request`, is created using the following code:

```
HttpWebRequest request =
    (HttpWebRequest)HttpWebRequest.Create(new Uri(feedURL));
```

> **NOTE** The URL specified by the `feedURL` argument when creating the `HttpWebRequest` points to an `aspx` file located in the same project as the code in Listings 14.7 and 14.8. If you try to access an RSS feed that is across domains, the RSS server needs to implement a cross-domain policy as discussed earlier in this chapter.

Once the `HttpWebRequest` object is created, the code uses the following code to send the request and wait for the response in the `AsyncCallback` handler function `responseHandler()`:

```
request.BeginGetResponse(new AsyncCallback(responseHandler),
                        request);
```

Inside the `responseHandler()` function, the code uses the following lines of code to get the request from the `IAsyscResult` argument `asyncResult` and create an `HttpWebResponse` object `response`:

```
HttpWebRequest request =
    (HttpWebRequest)asyncResult.AsyncState;
HttpWebResponse response =
    (HttpWebResponse)request.EndGetResponse(asyncResult);
```

The code uses the `GetResponseStream()` function of the `response` object to read the XML data from the RSS feed into an `XmlReader` object `reader`. The contents of the RSS feed are read as XML and loaded into the `SyndicationFeed` object `rssFeed` using the following code:

```
XmlReader reader =
    XmlReader.Create(response.GetResponseStream());
rssFeed = SyndicationFeed.Load(reader);
```

Next, the code uses the Items property of the rssFeed object to access the list of SyndicationItem objects contained in the feed. The titles of the items in the feed are added to the titleList ListBox defined in Listing 14.7 using the following code:

```
foreach (SyndicationItem item in rssFeed.Items)
{
    titleList.Items.Add(item.Title.Text);
}
```

Inside the doShowSummary() handler function, the code gets the SyndicationItem associated with the index of the list selection and displays the Summary.Text property of the item in the feedSummary control and the PublishedDate property in the dateText control.

LISTING 14.8

Page.xaml.cs File That Retrieves an RSS Feed into a SyndicationFeed Object and Implements the Functionality to View Summaries of the Feed Items

```csharp
using System;
using System.Collections.Generic;
using System.Linq;
using System.Windows;
using System.Windows.Controls;
using System.Windows.Documents;
using System.Windows.Input;


using System.ServiceModel.Syndication;
using System.Net;
using System.Xml;

namespace RssFeedsApp
{
    public partial class Page : UserControl
    {
        SyndicationFeed rssFeed;

        public Page()
        {
            InitializeComponent();

            getBtn.Click += new RoutedEventHandler(doGetFeed);
```

continued

LISTING 14.8 *(continued)*

```
            titleList.SelectionChanged +=
                new SelectionChangedEventHandler(doShowSummary);
        }

        void doShowSummary (object sender, SelectionChangedEventArgs e)
        {
            SyndicationItem item =
                rssFeed.Items.ElementAt(titleList.SelectedIndex);
            dateText.Text = "Published: "+ item.PublishDate.Date.ToString();
            feedSummary.Text = item.Summary.Text.ToString();
        }

        void doGetFeed(object sender, RoutedEventArgs e)
        {
            string feedURL =
            "http://localhost:3333/RssFeedsApp_Web/ClientBin/MainFeed.aspx";
            HttpWebRequest request =
                (HttpWebRequest)HttpWebRequest.Create(new Uri(feedURL));
            request.BeginGetResponse(new AsyncCallback(responseHandler),
                request);
        }

        void responseHandler(IAsyncResult asyncResult)
        {
            HttpWebRequest request =
                (HttpWebRequest)asyncResult.AsyncState;
            HttpWebResponse response =
                (HttpWebResponse)request.EndGetResponse(asyncResult);

            XmlReader reader =
                XmlReader.Create(response.GetResponseStream());
            rssFeed = SyndicationFeed.Load(reader);

            foreach (SyndicationItem item in rssFeed.Items)
            {
                titleList.Items.Add(item.Title.Text);
            }
        }
    }
}
```

The results of the application defined by Listings 14.7 and 14.8 are shown in Figure 14.4. When the user clicks Get Feed, the contents of the feed are retrieved via an `HttpWebRequest` and loaded into a `SyndicationFeed` object. The titles of the list are displayed in the list box. When an item in the list box is selected, the RSS item summary and publication date are displayed.

FIGURE 14.4

Silverlight application that downloads an RSS feed and displays it in a list

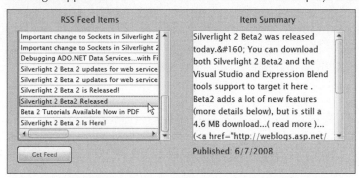

Implementing Sockets in Silverlight Applications

The Silverlight communication framework provides the ability to implement sockets in your Silverlight applications. The `System.Net.Sockets` library provides the functionality to open duplex communication back to the host server or across domains to other socket services. This allows your Silverlight applications to integrate with existing TCP services.

 **The Silverlight socket framework is currently limited to ports 4502-4534, although this may change in the future.**

The Silverlight socket framework is based on the .NET socket framework with the following additional classes:

- **DnsEndPoint**: Defines a host name or a string representation of an IP address and a port number that specify a network endpoint
- **EndPoint**: Defines a network address (abstract class)
- **IPAddress**: Defines an IP address
- IPEndPoint: Defines an IP address and a port number that represents a network endpoint
- **SocketAddress**: Defines serialized information from the `System.Net.EndPoint` derived classes

The main class that you work with in socket programming is the `Socket` class. The `Socket` class provides all of the functionality to actually connect as well as send and receive data on a socket.

All of the socket communication in Silverlight applications must be done asynchronously. This allows the communication to run in the background on a non-UI thread that does not impact the responsiveness of the controls.

Table 14.5 shows a list of the Socket object methods that you use for asynchronous communication. Each of these methods triggers the `Completed` event of the `SocketAsyncEventArgs` object associated with the `Socket` object.

TABLE 14.5

Asynchronous Communication Methods of Socket Objects

Method	Description
ConnectAsync	Opens a socket connection to the remote host
SendAsync	Writes data to the socket connection of the remote host
ReceiveAsync	Reads data from the socket connection
Shutdown	Finalizes any pending operations on the socket and then signals the remote host at the endpoint that the connection should be closed
Close	Closes the socket to the remote host and then releases all resources associated with it

TIP You need to use the host name when implementing Silverlight sockets; the application throws an exception if you try to use the IP address. When testing using the local host, make certain that `localhost` is defined in your host file. For example, c:\Windows\System32\etc\host.

Opening a socket to a remote host

To open a socket to a remote host, first create an endpoint object that defines the address of the remote host. For example, the following line of code creates a `DnsEndPoint` object that points to port 4510 on host www.MySocketServer.com:

```
DnsEndPoint ePoint = new DnsEndPoint("www.MySocketServer.com", 4510);
```

You also need to create a `Socket` object. To create a `Socket` object, use the constructor of the `Socket` class. The `Socket` class constructor takes three arguments — an `AddressFamily`, `SocketType`, and `ProtocolType`.

The `AddressFamily` argument supports both the `InterNetwork` (IPv4) and `InterNetworkV6` (IPv6) protocols. The `SocketType` argument only supports `Stream`. The `ProtocolType` argument only supports the `Tcp` protocol. The following code shows an example of creating a `Socket` object:

```
Socket socket = new Socket(AddressFamily.InterNetwork,
```

```
                              SocketType.Stream, ProtocolType.Tcp);
```

After you create the endpoint object and the `Socket` object, you need to set up the `SocketAsyncEventArgs` object that will be used to connect the socket to the remote host. Specifically, you need to set the `UserToken` property to the `Socket` object and the `RemoteEndPoint` property to the endpoint object. For example:

```
SocketAsyncEventArgs sArgs = new SocketAsyncEventArgs();
sArgs.UserToken = socket;
sArgs.RemoteEndPoint = ePoint;
```

Next, attach an event handler to handle the completed connection event. The `Socket` object itself does not have any event handlers associated with it, so you will need to use the `Completed` event handler with the `SocketAsyncEventArgs` object. For example, the following code adds an `OnSocketConnectCompleted()` event handler to the `SocketAsyncEventArgs` object created previously:

```
sArgs.Completed +=
    new EventHandler<SocketAsyncEventArgs>(OnSocketConnectCompleted);
```

When the connection is opened to the remote host, the `OnSocketConnectCompleted()` event handler is called. To open the connection to the remote host, use the `ConnectAsync()` method of the `Socket` object and pass the `SocketAsyncEventArgs` object as shown in the following line:

```
socket.ConnectAsync(sArgs);
```

Sending data on a socket

To send data on a socket, use the `SendAsync()` method. As with the `ConnectAsync()` method, you need to set up a `SocketAsyncEventArgs` object again. The `UserToken` property must be set to the `Socket` object and the `RemoteEndPoint` property must be set to the endpoint object.

If you are sending data in the connection completed event handler function, you can use the `SocketAsyncEventArgs` object that is passed as the second argument to the handler. The `UserToken` and `RemoteEndPoint` properties are already set to the `Socket` and endpoint objects.

You also need to provide the data that is sent on the socket. This is done by encoding the data into a byte buffer, as shown in the following line:

```
Byte[] bytes = Encoding.UTF8.GetBytes("My Data");
```

The encoded data can then be attached to the `SocketAsyncEventArgs` object using the `SetBuffer()` function. The `SetBuffer()` function accepts a byte array as the first parameter, an `int` offset as the second, and an `int` length as the third. The following code shows an example of adding the `byte` array `bytes` from the earlier line into a `SocketAsyncEventArgs` object `args`:

```
args.SetBuffer(bytes, 0, bytes.Length);
```

Next, attach an event handler to handle the send completed event. Because the `Socket` object itself does not have any event handlers associated with it, you need to use the `Completed` event handler with the `SocketAsyncEventArgs` object.

For example, the following code adds an `OnSendCompleted()` event handler to a `SocketAsyncEventArgs` object `args`:

```
args.Completed +=
    new EventHandler<SocketAsyncEventArgs>(OnSendCompleted);
```

If the connection completed event handler is still attached to the `SocketAsyncEventArgs` object, remove it before adding the send event handler.

To send the data to the remote host, use the `SendAsync()` method of the Socket object and pass the `SocketAsyncEventArgs` object, as shown in the following line of code. When data is sent to the remote host, the `OnSendCompleted()` event handler is called:

```
socket.SendAsync(args);
```

Receiving data from a socket

To receive data from a Socket, use the `ReceiveAsync()` method. Just as with the `SendAsync()` method, you need to set up a `SocketAsyncEventArgs` object again. The `UserToken` property must be set to the `Socket` object and the `RemoteEndPoint` property must be set to the endpoint object.

If you send data in a connection completed or send completed event handler function, you can use the `SocketAsyncEventArgs` object that is passed as the second argument to the handler. The `UserToken` and `RemoteEndPoint` properties already are set to the `Socket` and endpoint objects.

You also need to provide `SocketAsyncEventArgs` object with a data buffer that can store data that is received on the socket. This is done by creating a byte array and attaching it to the `SocketAsyncEventArgs` object using the `SetBuffer()` function.

The `SetBuffer()` function accepts a byte array as the first parameter, an `int` offset as the second, and an `int` length as the third. The following code shows an example of creating a `byte` array and adding it to a `SocketAsyncEventArgs` object `args`:

```
byte[] response = new byte[1024];
arg.SetBuffer(response, 0, response.Length);
```

Next, attach an event handler to handle the `ReceiveCompleted` event. The `Socket` object itself does not have any event handlers associated with it. Use the `Completed` event handler with the `SocketAsyncEventArgs` object.

For example, the following code adds an `OnReceiveCompleted()` event handler to a `SocketAsyncEventArgs` object `args`:

```
args.Completed +=
    new EventHandler<SocketAsyncEventArgs>(OnReceiveCompleted);
```

If the connection completed or send completed event handler is still attached to the `SocketAsyncEventArgs` object, you can remove it before adding the receive event handler.

To receive the data to the remote host, use the `ReceiveAsync()` method of the `Socket` object and pass the `SocketAsyncEventArgs` object as shown in the following line of code. When data is received from the remote host, the `OnReceiveCompleted()` event handler is called:

```
socket.ReceiveAsync(args);
```

Closing a socket

To close a socket, first call the `Shutdown()` method of the `Socket` object. The `Shutdown()` method finalizes any pending operations on the socket and then signals the remote host at the endpoint that the connection should be closed. This way, any data that isn't sent or received can be flushed before the socket is closed.

Check the `Connected` attribute of the `Socket` object to verify if the socket is actually connected prior to calling the `Close()` method to close the connection. For example:

```
if (socket.Connected)
{
    socket.Shutdown();
    socket.Close();
}
```

Example of a Silverlight socket application

The code in Listings 14.9 and 14.10 shows an example Silverlight application that opens a socket connection to a basic Windows service that accepts a format string then periodically writes a formatted string representing the server timeout on the socket.

The code in Listing 14.9 defines a simple interface with three `Button` controls — `dateBtn`, `timeBtn`, and `fullBtn`. Each of these buttons initiates a request to open a socket and send a specific format string to the service. A `TextBlock`, `serverText`, is defined to display the text string returned on the socket.

LISTING 14.9

Page.xaml File That Defines an Interface with Three Buttons to Initiate Socket Connections to a Socket Service

```xaml
<UserControl x:Class="SocketApp.Page"
    xmlns="http://schemas.microsoft.com/client/2007"
    xmlns:x="http://schemas.microsoft.com/winfx/2006/xaml"
    Width="500" Height="200">
    <Grid x:Name="LayoutRoot" Background="White">
        <Button x:Name="timeBtn" Content="Server Time"
                Height="30" Width="100"
                VerticalAlignment="Bottom"
                HorizontalAlignment="Left"
                Margin="80,0,0,20"/>
        <Button x:Name="dateBtn" Content="Server Date"
                Height="30" Width="100"
                VerticalAlignment="Bottom"
                HorizontalAlignment="Left"
                Margin="200,0,0,20"/>
        <Button x:Name="fullBtn" Content="Server Full"
                Height="30" Width="100"
                VerticalAlignment="Bottom"
                HorizontalAlignment="Left"
                Margin="320,0,0,20"/>
        <TextBlock Text="Server Date / Time"
                VerticalAlignment="Top"
                HorizontalAlignment="Center"
                Margin="20"/>
        <TextBlock x:Name="serverText"
                VerticalAlignment="Top"
                HorizontalAlignment="Center"
                FontSize="40"
                Margin="0,30,0,0"/>
    </Grid>
</UserControl>
```

The code in Listing 14.10 first implements the `System.Net` library for the `DnsEndPoint` class, the `System.Net.Sockets` library for the `Socket` and `SocketAsyncEventArgs` classes, and the `System.Text` library for the `Encoding` class.

Inside the `Page()` constructor, the code attaches `Click` event handler functions to the `timeBtn`, `dateBtn`, and `fullBtn` controls. Each of these handlers simply sets the `timeDateFormat` variable and then calls the `doGetData()` function.

Inside the doGetData() function, the code creates a DnsEndPoint object — ePoint. The host of ePoint is set to Application.Current.Host.Source.DnsSafeHost, which is the unescaped host name of the Silverlight application. We can use this address because the socket service project is part of the solution in Visual Studio. Next, the code creates a Socket object, using the following code:

```
DnsEndPoint ePoint =
    new DnsEndPoint(Application.Current.Host.Source.DnsSafeHost,
                    4510);
Socket socket = new Socket(AddressFamily.InterNetwork,
                    SocketType.Stream, ProtocolType.Tcp);
```

The code then creates a SocketAsyncEventArgs object, sArgs, and sets the UserToken property to the Socket object socket and the RemoteEndPoint property to the DnsEndPoint object ePoint.

Next, the code attaches the OnConnectCompleted() event to the Connected event property of the sArgs object. Finally, the ConnectAsync() function of the Socket object is called using the sArgs object to open the socket.

When the Socket connect returns, the OnConnectCompleted() event handler is called. Typically, you should verify the connection opened successfully by checking the SocketError property of the SocketAsyncEventArgs argument passed to the handler. We don't implement error handling in this example to keep it simple.

Inside the OnConnectCompleted() function, a byte array is created and encoded with the value of the timeDateFormat string. Next, the byte array is attached to the SocketAsyncEventArgs argument using the following code:

```
Byte[] bytes = Encoding.UTF8.GetBytes(timeDateFormat);
e.SetBuffer(bytes, 0, bytes.Length);
```

The code then removes the OnConnectedCompleted() event handler from the Completed property of the SocketAsyncEventArgs argument and attaches the OnSocketSendCompleted() event handler using the following lines of code. This sets up the socket to be able to send data and the Silverlight application to be able to respond to the send completion event:

```
e.Completed =
    new EventHandler<SocketAsyncEventArgs>(OnConnectCompleted);
e.Completed +=
    new EventHandler<SocketAsyncEventArgs>(OnSocketSendCompleted);
```

Next, the code gets the Socket object from the UserToken property of the SocketAsyncEventArgs argument and sends the data using the following lines of code. The UserToken and RemoteEndPoint properties are still set to the values used to open the socket:

```
Socket socket = (Socket)e.UserToken;
socket.SendAsync(e);
```

Inside the OnSocketSendCompleted() function, a byte array defined to store data received on the socket and attached to the SocketAsyncEventArgs argument using the following code:

```
byte[] response = new byte[1024];
e.SetBuffer(response, 0, response.Length);
```

The code then removes the OnSocketSendCompleted() event handler from the Completed property of the SocketAsyncEventArgs argument and attaches the OnSocketReceiveCompleted() event handler using the following lines of code. This sets up the socket to be able to receive data and the Silverlight application to be able to respond to the receive completion event:

```
e.Completed -=
  new EventHandler<SocketAsyncEventArgs>(OnSocketSendCompleted);
e.Completed +=
  new EventHandler<SocketAsyncEventArgs>(OnSocketReceive);
```

Next, the code gets the Socket object from the UserToken property of the SocketAsyncEventArgs argument and tells the socket to begin receiving data by calling the ReceiveAsync() function as shown in the following lines of code:

```
Socket socket = (Socket)e.UserToken;
socket.ReceiveAsync(e);
```

Inside the OnSocketSendCompleted() function, the code gets a string from the encoded data stored in the Buffer attribute of the SocketAsyncEventArgs argument using the following code. The Offset property points to the current offset inside the buffer and the BytesTransferred property specifies the length of data transferred in the buffer.

```
string data = Encoding.UTF8.GetString(e.Buffer, e.Offset,
                                      e.BytesTransferred);
```

Next, the UI is updated with the string received on the socket by setting the Text property of the serverText control. The receive event will not be running on a UI thread, so this needs to be done using the following Dispatcher call:

```
this.Dispatcher.BeginInvoke(delegate { serverText.Text = data; });
```

The code then gets the Socket object from the SocketAsyncEventArgs argument and requests more data on the socket by calling the ReceiveAsync() function again.

LISTING 14.10

Page.xaml.cs File That Opens a Socket and Writes a Format Request to a Windows Service That Periodically Writes a Formatted Date or Time String to the Socket

```
using System;
using System.Windows;
using System.Windows.Controls;
using System.Windows.Documents;
using System.Windows.Input;

using System.Net;
using System.Net.Sockets;
using System.Text;

namespace SocketApp
{
    public partial class Page : UserControl
    {
        string timeDateFormat;
        public Page()
        {
            InitializeComponent();
            timeDateFormat = "Full";

            timeBtn.Click += new RoutedEventHandler(doGetTime);
            dateBtn.Click += new RoutedEventHandler(doGetDate);
            fullBtn.Click += new RoutedEventHandler(doGetFull);
        }
        void doGetTime(object sender, RoutedEventArgs e)
        {
            timeDateFormat = "Time";
            doGetData();
        }
        void doGetDate(object sender, RoutedEventArgs e)
        {
            timeDateFormat = "Date";
            doGetData();
        }
        void doGetFull(object sender, RoutedEventArgs e)
        {
            timeDateFormat = "Full";
            doGetData();
        }

        //Create and Open Socket
```

continued

LISTING 14.10   *(continued)*

```
void doGetData()
{
    DnsEndPoint ePoint =
        new DnsEndPoint(Application.Current.Host.Source.DnsSafeHost,
                        4510);
    Socket socket = new Socket(AddressFamily.InterNetwork,
                               SocketType.Stream, ProtocolType.Tcp);

    SocketAsyncEventArgs sArgs = new SocketAsyncEventArgs();
    sArgs.UserToken = socket;
    sArgs.RemoteEndPoint = ePoint;
    sArgs.Completed +=
      new EventHandler<SocketAsyncEventArgs>(OnConnectCompleted);
    socket.ConnectAsync(sArgs);
}

//On Completed Connection Send Data
private void OnConnectCompleted(object sender,
                               SocketAsyncEventArgs e)
{
    Byte[] bytes = Encoding.UTF8.GetBytes(timeDateFormat);
    e.SetBuffer(bytes, 0, bytes.Length);
    e.Completed -=
      new EventHandler<SocketAsyncEventArgs>(OnConnectCompleted);
    e.Completed +=
      new EventHandler<SocketAsyncEventArgs>(OnSocketSendCompleted);
    Socket socket = (Socket)e.UserToken;
    socket.SendAsync(e);
}

//On Send Complete Receive Data
private void OnSocketSendCompleted(object sender,
                                  SocketAsyncEventArgs e)
{
    byte[] response = new byte[1024];
    e.SetBuffer(response, 0, response.Length);
    e.Completed -=
      new EventHandler<SocketAsyncEventArgs>(OnSocketSendCompleted);
    e.Completed +=
      new EventHandler<SocketAsyncEventArgs>(OnSocketReceive);
    Socket socket = (Socket)e.UserToken;
    socket.ReceiveAsync(e);
}
```

```
//On Receive Data Update UI and Receive More Data
private void OnSocketReceive(object sender, SocketAsyncEventArgs e)
{

    string data = Encoding.UTF8.GetString(e.Buffer, e.Offset,
                                        e.BytesTransferred);
    this.Dispatcher.BeginInvoke(delegate {
                                    serverText.Text = data;
                                });

    Socket socket = (Socket)e.UserToken;
    socket.ReceiveAsync(e);
}
}
}
```

The results of the application defined by Listings 14.9 and 14.10 are shown in Figure 14.5. When the user clicks Server Time, a socket opens to the service, the string "Time" is sent, and the UI is updated with the current time of the server, as shown in Figure 14.5.

When the user clicks Server Date, a socket opens to the service, the string "Date" is sent, and the UI is updated with the current date of the server, as shown in Figure 14.5.

When the user clicks Server Full, a socket opens to the service, the string "Full" is sent and the UI is updated with the current date and time, as shown in Figure 14.5.

For those who are interested, the service code that responds to the socket requests in Listing 14.10 is included in Listing 14.11. We did not include setting up the service as part of the example to keep it simple and because it was a bit out of the scope of the book. The following is a brief list of steps we took to set up the service. If you are familiar with setting up Windows services in .NET, these steps should make sense; if they don't, you should at least be able to follow the code in Listing 14.11 to see how the service responds to the requests from the Silverlight client.

1. Add a new application to the Silverlight socket solution in Visual Studio.
2. Add the `DataSocketServer` class code from Listing 14.11 to the new project.
3. Add a Windows service to the new project.
4. Add an installer to the Windows service (right-click on the Design view of the Windows service).
5. Set the `DisplayName` and `ServiceName` properties of the installer object to the same value.
6. Add the Windows service as a `ServiceBase` to run in the main class of the new project.

469

7. Create a test class that creates an instance of the `DataSocketServer` class and then start it.

8. Add the test class as the Startup object in the Application tab of the new project properties.

Silverlight application that uses sockets to request the time, date, or date/time strings from a service

DataSocketServer.cs File That Opens a Socket and Writes a Format Request to a Windows Service That Periodically Writes

```
using System;
using System.Collections.Generic;
using System.Text;
using System.Net;
using System.Net.Sockets;
using System.IO;
```

```csharp
using System.Timers;
using System.Threading;

namespace SocketServer
{

    public class DataSocketServer
    {
        TcpListener sListener = null;
        System.Timers.Timer sTimer = null;
        static ManualResetEvent sTcpClientConnect =
                                    new ManualResetEvent(false);
        List<StreamWriter> sClientStreams = new List<StreamWriter>();
        string timeDateFormat;

        private void InitializeData()
        {
            timeDateFormat = "Full";
        }

        public void StartSocketServer()
        {
            InitializeData();
            sTimer = new System.Timers.Timer();
            sTimer.Enabled = false;
            sTimer.Interval = 1000;
            sTimer.Elapsed += new ElapsedEventHandler(doTimer);

            try
            {
                sListener = new TcpListener(IPAddress.Any, 4510);
                sListener.Start();
                while (true)
                {
                    sTcpClientConnect.Reset();
                    sListener.BeginAcceptTcpClient(
                            new AsyncCallback(OnBeginAccept), null);
                    sTcpClientConnect.WaitOne();
                }
            }
            catch (Exception e)
            {

            }
        }

        private void OnBeginAccept(IAsyncResult result)
        {
```

continued

LISTING 14.11   *(continued)*

```
        sTcpClientConnect.Set();
        TcpListener listener = sListener;
        TcpClient client = listener.EndAcceptTcpClient(result);
        if (client.Connected)
        {
            char[] bytes = new char[5];
            StreamReader reader = new StreamReader(client.GetStream());
            int size = reader.ReadBlock(bytes,0,4);
            timeDateFormat = new String(bytes,0,4);

            StreamWriter writer = new StreamWriter(client.GetStream());
            writer.AutoFlush = true;
            sClientStreams.Add(writer);
            SendData();
            if (sTimer.Enabled == false)
            {
                sTimer.Start();
            }
        }
    }

    public void StopSocketServer()
    {
        foreach (StreamWriter writer in sClientStreams)
        {
            writer.Dispose();
        }
        sClientStreams.Clear();
        sListener.Stop();
        sListener = null;
    }

    private void doTimer(object sender, ElapsedEventArgs e)
    {
        SendData();
    }

    private void SendData()
    {
        if (sClientStreams != null)
        {
            foreach (StreamWriter writer in sClientStreams)
            {
                if (writer != null)
                {
```

```
                        string data;
                        if (timeDateFormat == "Date")
                            data = DateTime.Now.ToLongDateString();
                        else if(timeDateFormat == "Time")
                            data = DateTime.Now.ToLongTimeString();
                        else
                            data = DateTime.Now.ToString();
                        writer.Write(data);
                    }
                }
            }
        }
    }
}
```

Using the HttpWebRequest and HttpWebResponse Objects

The Silverlight communication framework also includes the HttpWebRequest and HttpWebResponse classes as part of the System.Net library. These classes provide a similar functionality to the WebClient class. In fact, the WebClient class implements the HttpWebRequest and HttpWebResponse classes behind the scenes.

The WebClient class is much easier to use for simple communications. However, use the HttpWebRequest and HttpWebResponse classes if you need to send headers as part of the request or if you need more control over the Web service request.

Using the HttpWebRequest to send requests

The HttpWebRequest class provides the functionality to create Web client requests and send them to Web services. The HttpWebRequest has no constructor, so to implement an HttpWebRequest you need to create an instance using the Create() function as shown in the following code. Create() accepts the Uri object specifying the Web service to connect to as its only argument:

```
HttpWebRequest request =
    (HttpWebRequest)HttpWebRequest.Create(new Uri(serviceUrl));
```

You can set the method and the ContentType header of the request using the Method and ContentType properties of the HttpWebRequestObject. The default method is GET. Table 14.6 lists the properties and methods associated with the HttpWebRequest class.

TABLE 14.6

Properties and Methods of the HttpWebRequest Class

Property/Method	Description
Abort()	Cancels an outstanding HttpWebRequest.
BeginGetRequestStream()	Starts an asynchronous request to get an IO stream that can be used to write data into the request.
BeginGetResponse()	Starts an asynchronous request to an Internet resource.
ContentType	String. Specifies the ContentType header of the request.
Create()	Creates an instance of the HttpWebRequest class.
EndGetRequestStream()	Finalizes the request for an IO stream and returns the Stream object.
EndGetResponse()	Finalizes the response to the request and returns an HttpWebResponse object.
HaveResponse	Boolean. Specifies whether there is a response associated with the request.
Headers	WebHeader collection. Specifies a collection of custom headers that will be included with the request.
Method	String. Specifies the method of the request.
RequestURI	Uri. Specifies the URI of the request.

CAUTION If you set the ContentType property of the HttpWebRequest object when the method is GET, an exception is thrown.

The BeginGetResponse() method of the HttpWebRequest sends the asynchronous request to the Web services. The BeginGetResponse() method accepts an AsyncCallback object as the first argument and the HttpWebRequestObject as the second. For example, the following code starts the request and specifies the responseHandler() function:

```
request.BeginGetResponse(new AsyncCallback(responseHandler),
                         request);
```

The handler specified in the AsyncCallback object should accept an IAsyncResult object as an argument as shown in the following definition:

```
void responseHandler(IAsyncResult asyncResult)
```

When the Web request is completed, the handled request and response data are returned in the IAsyncResult argument to the AsyncCallback handler function.

If you are implementing a POST method, you will likely want to write data out with the request. This is done by calling the BeginGetRequestStream() function to get an IO stream for the request. The BeginGetRequestStream() method accepts an AsyncCallback object as the first argument and the HttpWebRequestObject as the second. For example, the following code requests the IO stream and specifies the requestHandler() function:

```
request.BeginGetRequestStream(new AsyncCallback(requestHandler),
                              request);
```

The handler specified in the AsyncCallback object for the BeginGetRequestStream() call should accept an IAsyncResult object as an argument as shown in the following definition:

```
void requestHandler(IAsyncResult asyncResult)
```

When the request for the IO stream is completed the AsyncCallback handler function is called and the updated request object is passed as the AsyncState property of the IAsyncResult argument. The IO stream is available by calling the EndGetRequestStream() function of the request object as shown in the following code:

```
HttpWebRequest request = (HttpWebRequest)asyncResult.AsyncState;
Stream requestStream = request.EndGetRequestStream(asyncResult);
```

Post data can be written into the request by writing to the IO stream returned by EndGetRequestStream(). After the data is written to the stream, you can call the BeginGetResponse() function to send the data to the server and wait for the response.

> **TIP** It is a good idea to flush the data being written to the IO stream of the request before sending it to the server using the BeginGetResponse() function.

Using the HttpWebResponse class to handle responses

The HttpWebResponse class provides the functionality to handle the response to an HttpWebRequest. The HttpWebResponse class has no constructor, so to implement an HttpWebResponse object you need to get it from the HttpWebRequest object that is passed to the BeginGetResponse() completed event handler function.

When the request is completed and returned by the server, the AsyncCallback handler specified in the BeginGetResponse() function is called. The updated request object is passed as the AsyncState property of the IAsyncResult argument. The EndGetResponse() function of the HttpWebRequest object can be used to get the HttpWebResponse object, as shown in the following code:

```
HttpWebRequest request = (HttpWebRequest)asyncResult.AsyncState;
HttpWebResponse response =
    (HttpWebResponse)request.EndGetResponse(asyncResult);
```

The status of the response can be retrieved from the `StatusCode` property of the `HttpWeb Response` object. The actual response data can be retrieved using the `GetResponseStream()` function of the `HttpWebResponse` object, as shown in the following code:

```
StreamReader reader = new StreamReader(response.GetResponseStream());
StatusText.Text = reader.ReadToEnd();
```

Table 14.7 lists the properties and methods associated with the `HttpWebResponse` class.

TABLE 14.7

Properties and Methods of the HttpWebResponse Class

Property/Method	Description
Close()	Closes the HttpWebResponse.
ContentType	String. Specifies the ContentType header of the response.
ContentLength	Long. Specifies the ContentLength header of the response.
GetResponseStream()	Returns the data Stream object associated with the response.
Method	String. Specifies the method of the response.
RequestURI	Uri. Specifies the URI of the response.
StatusCode	HttpStatusCode. Specifies the status of the response.
StatusDescription	String. String associated with the StatusCode.

Example of using HttpWebRequest and HttpWebResponse to send POST data

The code in Listings 14.12 and 14.13 shows an example Silverlight application that uses an `HttpWebRequest` object to send a `POST` request to a simple PHP Web service and uses an `HttpWebResponse` object to get the response and update the UI.

The code in Listing 14.12 defines a simple e-mail form that collects the To, From, Subject, and Message data in four `TextBox` controls: `To`, `From`, `Subject`, and `Message`. A `Button` control, `SendBtn`, is implemented to initiate the `HttpWebRequest` to send the data from the form as a `POST` request to the service. A `TextBlock`, `StatusText`, is defined to display the response from the request.

LISTING 14.12

Page.xaml File That Defines an E-mail Form That Is Used to Send E-mail Data to a Web Service Using an HttpWebRequest

```xml
<UserControl x:Class="WebRequestApp.Page"
    xmlns="http://schemas.microsoft.com/client/2007"
    xmlns:x="http://schemas.microsoft.com/winfx/2006/xaml"
    Width="640" Height="400">
    <Grid x:Name="LayoutRoot" Background="LightBlue">
        <TextBlock Text="To:" Margin="10,10,0,0"
                VerticalAlignment="Top"
                HorizontalAlignment="Left" />
        <TextBox x:Name="To"
                VerticalAlignment="Top"
                HorizontalAlignment="Left"
                Margin="100,10,0,0" Width="200"/>
        <TextBlock Text="From:" Margin="10,50,0,0"
                VerticalAlignment="Top"
                HorizontalAlignment="Left" />
        <TextBox x:Name="From"
                VerticalAlignment="Top"
                HorizontalAlignment="Left"
                Margin="100,50,0,0" Width="200"/>
        <TextBlock Text="Subject:" Margin="10,90,0,0"
                VerticalAlignment="Top"
                HorizontalAlignment="Left" />
        <TextBox x:Name="Subject"
                VerticalAlignment="Top"
                HorizontalAlignment="Left"
                Margin="100,90,0,0" Width="500"/>
        <TextBlock Text="Message:" Margin="10,130,0,0"
                VerticalAlignment="Top"
                HorizontalAlignment="Left" />
        <TextBox x:Name="Body"
                VerticalAlignment="Top"
                HorizontalAlignment="Left"
                Margin="100,130,0,0"
                Height="200" Width="500"
                AcceptsReturn="True" />
        <Button x:Name="SendBtn" Content="Send"
                Height="30" Width="100"
                VerticalAlignment="Bottom"
                Margin="20"/>
        <TextBlock x:Name="StatusText"
                VerticalAlignment="Bottom"
                Margin="20"/>
    </Grid>
</UserControl>
```

The code in Listing 14.13 first implements the `System.Net` library for the `HttpWebRequest` and `HttpWebResponse` classes and the `System.IO library` for the `Stream`, `StreamReader`, and `StreamWriter` classes.

Inside the `Page()` constructor, the code attaches a `Click` event handler, `DoRequest()`, functions to the `SendBtn` control. Inside the `DoRequest()` function, the code creates an `HttpRequest` object, `request`, using the following line of code:

```
HttpWebRequest request =
    (HttpWebRequest)HttpWebRequest.Create(new Uri(serviceUrl));
```

The `Method` property of the request is set to `POST` and the `ContentType` is set to `application/x-form-urlencoded` to define a POST request, as shown in the following line of code:

```
request.Method = "POST";
request.ContentType = "application/x-form-urlencoded";
```

Because this is a `POST` request, the `BeginGetRequestStream()` function is called to get an IO stream to send the `POST` data on. The `AsyncCallback` handler `requestHandler()` is attached to handle the get request stream completed event.

Inside the `requestHandler()` function, the code first creates a `POST` data string from the UI form elements. Then it gets the request from the `AsyncState` of the `IAsyncResult` argument and uses the `EndGetRequstStream()` function of the request object to get the IO stream using the following lines of code: ·

```
HttpWebRequest request = (HttpWebRequest)asyncResult.AsyncState;
Stream requestStream = request.EndGetRequestStream(asyncResult);
```

The `POST` data is written to the `HttpWebRequest` using a `StringWriter` object. The data is flushed to the stream and the stream is closed. After the data is written, the code uses the `BeginGetResponse()` function of the request object to send the request to the server. The `AsyncCallback` handler `responseHandler()` is attached to handle the get response completed event using the following line of code:

```
request.BeginGetResponse(new AsyncCallback(responseHandler),request);
```

Inside the `responseHandler()` function, the code gets the request from the `AsyncState` of the `IAsyncResult` argument and uses the `EndGetResponse()` function of the request object to get the `HttpWebResponse` object from the request.

The code checks the `HaveResponse` property of the request object to verify that there is a response and then checks the `StatusCode` property of the response object to verify that the service was successful. Then the code uses the `GetResponseStream()` function of the `HttpWebResponse` object to get the response stream and update the `Text` property of the `StatusText` control using the following code:

```
        StreamReader reader =
            new StreamReader(response.GetResponseStream());
        StatusText.Text = reader.ReadToEnd();
```

The code then removes the SendBtn from the control so that the status of the request takes its place.

LISTING 14.13

Page.xaml.cs File That Implements an HttpWebRequest to Send a POST Request to a Remote Web Service

```csharp
using System;
using System.Windows;
using System.Windows.Controls;
using System.Windows.Documents;
using System.Windows.Input;

using System.Net;
using System.IO;

namespace WebRequestApp
{
    public partial class Page : UserControl
    {
        public Page()
        {
            InitializeComponent();

            SendBtn.Click += new RoutedEventHandler(DoRequest);
        }

        void DoRequest(object sender, RoutedEventArgs e)
        {
            string serviceUrl =
                "http://www.myserver.com/mailservice.php";
            HttpWebRequest request =
                (HttpWebRequest)HttpWebRequest.Create(new Uri(serviceUrl));
            request.Method = "POST";
            request.ContentType = "application/x-form-urlencoded";
            request.BeginGetRequestStream(new AsyncCallback(requestHandler),
                                          request);

        }

        void requestHandler(IAsyncResult asyncResult)
```

continued

LISTING 14.13   *(continued)*

```
        {
            string postData =
               String.Format("ToAddr={0}&FromAddr={1}&Subject={2}&Body={3}",
                             To.Text, From.Text, Subject.Text, Body.Text);

        HttpWebRequest request = (HttpWebRequest)asyncResult.AsyncState;
        Stream requestStream = request.EndGetRequestStream(asyncResult);

         StreamWriter writer = new StreamWriter(requestStream);
         writer.Write(postData);
         writer.Flush();
         writer.Close();

         request.BeginGetResponse(new AsyncCallback(responseHandler),
                                  request);
        }

    void responseHandler(IAsyncResult asyncResult)
    {
        HttpWebRequest request = (HttpWebRequest)asyncResult.AsyncState;
        HttpWebResponse response =
             (HttpWebResponse)request.EndGetResponse(asyncResult);
        if (request.HaveResponse &&
            response.StatusCode == HttpStatusCode.OK)             {

            StreamReader reader =
                new StreamReader(response.GetResponseStream());

            StatusText.Text = reader.ReadToEnd();
            reader.Close();
        }
        else
        {
            StatusText.Text = "No Response From Mail Server";
        }

        LayoutRoot.Children.Remove(SendBtn);
        }
    }
}
```

The results of the application defined by Listings 14.12 and 14.13 are shown in Figure 14.6. When the user clicks Send, an `HttpWebRequest` is initiated that gets data from a form and sends a `POST` request to a remote Web service to send the e-mail. The status of the request is displayed in the bottom of the form after the message is sent.

FIGURE 14.6

Silverlight application that collects e-mail data from a form and uses an `HttpWebRequest` to post the data to a remote Web service

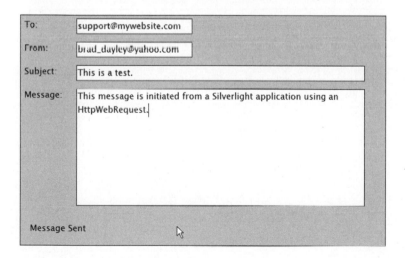

Summary

Silverlight 2 provides a communication framework that allows Silverlight applications to communicate with Web services and retrieve remote resources. The basic components of the Silverlight communication framework are the WebClient class, HTTP classes, and sockets.

The Silverlight communication framework supports cross-domain access to Web services and resources through the use of network access policies. These policies must be implemented on the remote server or Silverlight applications will not be able to access Web services and resources.

The WebClient interface is the simplest to implement and can be used to download remote resources. The HttpWebRequest and HttpWebResponse classes are more complex; however, they allow you to implement headers and implement more control of the request. The Socket library provides the tools necessary for Silverlight applications to interact with TCP based Web services.

In this chapter, you learned how to:

- Create a network access policy that grants rights to Web services and resources to cross-domain Silverlight applications

- Implement a WebClient request that dynamically downloads a ZIP file, unpackages the contents, and uses it to update the UI

- Use an HttpWebRequest object to access an RSS feed

- Use the Syndication library to parse and access items in an RSS feed

- Open a Socket client to a remote server

- Send and receive data on a socket

- Use an HttpWebRequest object to send a POST request to a remote Web service

Chapter 15

Using the Silverlight Data Framework

S ilverlight implements much of the .NET data framework to allow developers a means of delivering data content that can be modified and displayed from a rich UI. Silverlight provides several methods to implement data from a wide variety of sources such as XML files and SQL databases. Silverlight also provides interfaces to consume and display data from those sources.

This chapter discusses how to use Silverlight XML libraries, data binding, DataGrid controls, and LINQ queries to access and implement data in your Silverlight applications.

Using XmlReader and XmlWriter

Silverlight provides a subset of the System.Xml .NET framework for reading and writing XML data. The ability to read and write XML data allows you to easily implement Silverlight applications that interface with services that send and receive data in XML form.

The XmlReader class and the XmlWriter classes allow you to parse, edit, and write XML data in the memory of your Silverlight applications. These classes are part of the System.Xml library provided with Silverlight.

Implementing XmlReader to parse XML data

The `XmlReader` class is similar to the `XmlDocument` class provided with the .NET framework. It provides an interface to read and parse XML data.

To implement `XmlReader` in your Silverlight applications, you need to create an instance of the `XmlReader` class that has access to the XML data. This is done by calling the `XmlReader.Create()` function and passing in the source of the XML data.

The `XmlReader.Create()` function accepts the source of the XML data as the first argument and an `XmlReaderSettings` object as an optional second argument. The source of the XML data can be a `Stream` object type, `TextReader` object, or a `string` with the URI of an XML file.

For example, the following code creates an `XmlReader` object that accesses XML data that is stored in a `StringReader` object:

```
StringReader xmlString = new StringReader(XmlDataString);
XmlReader reader = XmlReader.Create(xmlString);
```

The `XmlReaderSettings` argument provides you with the ability to set specific settings when accessing the XML source location. Table 15.1 lists the properties that can be applied to `XmlReaderSettings` objects.

TABLE 15.1

Properties of the XmlReaderSettings Class

Property	Description
CheckCharacters	Specifies whether to do character checking.
CloseInput	Specifies whether the underlying stream or `TextReader` should be closed when the reader is closed.
ConformanceLevel	Specifies the level of conformance with which the `XmlReader` will comply.
DtdProcessing	Specifies the `DtdProcessing` enumeration.
IgnoreComments	Specifies whether to ignore comments.
IgnoreProcessing Instructions	Specifies whether to ignore processing instructions.
IgnoreWhitespace	Specifies whether to ignore insignificant white space.
LineNumberOffset	Specifies a line number offset of the `XmlReader` object to begin reading from.
LinePositionOffset	Specifies a line position offset of the `XmlReader` object to begin reading from.
MaxCharacters FromEntities	Specifies the maximum allowable number of characters in a document that result from expanding elements.
MaxCharactersIn Document	Specifies the maximum allowable number of characters in an XML document. 0 means no limit on the size of the XML document.
NameTable	Specifies the `XmlNameTable` used for atomized string comparisons.
XmlResolver	Sets the `XmlResolver` used to access external documents.

Silverlight supports reading XML files that are stored in the application's XAP package using the XmlXapResolver class. To access files stored in the XAP, you need to specify the XML file URI as the source argument and pass in an XmlReaderSettings object with the XmlResolver set to an instance of the XmlXapResolver class. For example:

```
XmlReaderSettings rSettings = new XmlReaderSettings();
rSettings.XmlResolver = new XmlXapResolver();
XmlReader reader = XmlReader.Create("data.xml", rSettings);
```

After the XmlReader object is created, data can be read from the XML source using Read() function of the object. The Read() function reads the next node in the file and returns a null when there are no more nodes left.

After the Read() function has been executed, several attributes of the XmlReader object are updated to describe the node that has been read. Table 15.2 describes some of the properties of the XmlReader class that apply to the node that has just been read.

TABLE 15.2

Node Properties of the XmlReader Class

Property	Description
Attribute Count	Integer. Indicates the number of attributes on the current node.
Has Attributes	Boolean. Indicates whether the current node has any attributes.
HasValue	Boolean. Indicates whether the current node can have a value.
Name	String. Specifies the qualified name of the current node.
NodeType	XmlNodeType. Specifies the type of the current node.
Value	String. Specifies the text value of the current node.
ValueType	Type. Specifies the Common Language Runtime (CLR) type for the current node.

The following code snippet reads the current node, then checks to see if the NodeType is an Element type; if so, it sets a value to the Name property of the node:

```
reader.Read();
if (reader.NodeType == XmlNodeType.Element)
    myText = reader.Name;
```

CROSS-REF There are numerous XmlReader functions that can be implemented to read XML files. For a list of those functions, refer to the MSDN documentation at http://msdn.microsoft.com/en-us/library/system.xml.xmlreader_members(VS.95).aspx.

Implementing XmlWriter to write XML data

The XmlWriter class is similar to the XmlWriter class provided with the .NET framework. It provides an interface to write data in XML format to an XML destination.

To implement XmlWriter in your Silverlight applications, you first need to create an instance of the XmlWriter class that can write to the XML destination. This is done by calling the XmlWriter.Create() function and passing in the destination location of the XML data.

The XmlWriter.Create() function accepts the destination of the XML data as the first argument and an XmlWriterSettings object as an optional second argument. The source of the XML data can be a Stream object type, TextWriter object, or a StringBuilder object.

For example, the following code creates an XmlWriter object that writes XML data to a StringBuilder object:

```
StringBuilder xmlData = new StringBuilder();
XmlWriter writer = XmlWriter.Create(xmlData);
```

The XmlWriterSettings argument provides you with the ability to set specific settings when writing to the XML destination location. Table 15.3 lists the properties that can be applied to XmlWriterSettings objects.

TABLE 15.3

Properties of the XmlWriterSettings Class

Properties	Description
CheckCharacters	Boolean. Specifies whether to do character checking.
CloseOutput	Boolean. Specifies whether the XmlWriter should also close the underlying stream or TextWriter when the Close method is called.
ConformanceLevel	Specifies level of conformance with which the XmlWriter complies.
Encoding	Specifies the text encoding to use when writing XML data.
Indent	Boolean. Specifies whether to indent elements.
IndentChars	String. Specifies the character string to use when indenting. This setting is used when the Indent property is set to true.
NewLineChars	String. Specifies the character string to use for line breaks.
NewLineHandling	Specifies whether to normalize line breaks in the output.
NewLineOn Attributes	Boolean. Specifies whether to write attributes on a new line.
OmitXml Declaration	Boolean. Specifies whether to write an XML declaration.
ReadOnly	Specifies whether this XmlWriterSettings is read-only.

The following code implements an `XmlWriterSettings` object to create an `XmlWriter` object that implements indentation and line handling:

```
StringBuilder xmlData = new StringBuilder();
XmlWriterSettings wSettings = new XmlWriterSettings();
wSettings.Indent = true;
wSettings.NewLineHandling = NewLineHandling.Replace;
wSettings.NewLineChars = "\r\n";
XmlWriter writer = XmlWriter.Create(xmlData, wSettings);
```

After the `XmlWriter` object is created, data can be written to the XML destination. The simplest way to write an element to the XML destination is to use the `WriteStartElement()`, `WriteEndElement()`, `WriteStartAttribute()`, `WriteEndAttribute()`, and `WriteString()` functions. The `WriteStartElement()` and `WriteEndElement()` functions write the start and end tags for an XML element. The `WriteStartAttribute()` and `WriteEndAttribute()` functions write the start and end tags for an XML attribute of an element. The `WriteString()` function writes the text value of the XML element.

For example, the following code writes an XML element with the syntax `<UserName type="Home">BDayley</User>`:

```
writer.WriteStartElement("UserName");
writer.WriteStartAttribute("Type");
writer.WriteEndElement();
writer.WriteString("Brad");
writer.WriteEndElement();
```

The data will not actually be written to the XML destination until you call the `Flush()` or `Close()` function of the `XmlWriter` object.

CROSS-REF There are numerous `XmlWriter` functions that can be implemented to write XML files. For a list of those functions, refer to the MSDN documentation at `http://msdn.microsoft.com/en-us/library/system.xml.xmlwriter_members(VS.95).aspx`.

Example: Reading and writing XML data in memory

The code in Listings 15.1 and 15.2 shows an example Silverlight application that accepts data from `TextBox` and `RadioButton` controls, writes that data to XML format, and then parses that XML data.

The code in Listing 15.1 implements a simple form with two `TextBox` controls — `NameText` and `PhoneText` — as well as three `RadioButton` controls — `HomeBtn`, `OfficeBtn`, and `CellBtn`.

The code also implements two `Button` controls — `XMLReadBtn` and `XMLWriteBtn` — that are used to initiate an `XmlReader` and `XmlWriter`. A `TextBlock` control — `myText` — is nested inside a `ScrollViewer` control to display the results of the `XmlReader` and `XmlWriter`.

LISTING 15.1

XAML Code That Implements a Simple Form with Button Controls to Collect Data That Will Be Written to XML and Read Back

```xml
<UserControl x:Class="XMLParserApp.Page"
    xmlns="http://schemas.microsoft.com/client/2007"
    xmlns:x="http://schemas.microsoft.com/winfx/2006/xaml"
    Width="600" Height="400">
    <Grid x:Name="LayoutRoot" Background="LightGray">
        <TextBox x:Name = "NameText"
                            Text="Full Name"
                            VerticalAlignment="Top"
                            HorizontalAlignment="Left"
                            Margin="20,20"
                            Width="200" Height="30"/>
        <TextBox x:Name = "PhoneText"
                            Text="Phone Number"
                            VerticalAlignment="Top"
                            HorizontalAlignment="Left"
                            Margin="20,70"
                            Width="200" Height="30"/>
        <StackPanel Orientation="Horizontal"
                    VerticalAlignment="Top"
                    HorizontalAlignment="Left"
                    Margin="20,110"
                    Width="300" Height="30">
            <RadioButton x:Name="HomeBtn" Content="Home" />
            <RadioButton x:Name="OfficeBtn" Content="Office" />
            <RadioButton x:Name="CellBtn" Content="Cell" />
        </StackPanel>
        <Button x:Name="XMLWriteBtn" Content="Write XML"
                VerticalAlignment="Top"
                HorizontalAlignment="Left"
                Margin="20,180"
                Height="30" Width="100" />
        <Button x:Name="XMLReadBtn" Content="Read XML"
                VerticalAlignment="Top"
                HorizontalAlignment="Left"
                Margin="140,180"
                Height="30" Width="100" />
        <ScrollViewer Background="White"
                    HorizontalScrollBarVisibility="Auto"
                    HorizontalAlignment="Right"
                    Margin="10" Width="300" Height="350">
            <TextBlock x:Name="myText" Margin="5"/>
        </ScrollViewer>
    </Grid>
</UserControl>
```

The code in Listing 15.2 adds a reference to the System.Xml library that includes the Silverlight XmlReader and XmlWriter classes. It also adds references to the System.IO and System.Text libraries to provide access to the StringReader and StringWriter classes.

Inside the Page() constructor, the code attaches the doRead() and doWrite() Click event handlers to the XMLReadBtn and XmlWriteBtn controls, respectively.

Inside the doWrite() event handler, the code first creates a StringBuilder object — xmlData — that is used as a destination to write XML output. Then an XmlWriterSettings object — wSettings — is created and the Indent property is set to true.

The xmlData StringBuilder and wSettings XmlWriterSettings objects are used in the following line of code to create an XmlWriter object named writer:

```
XmlWriter writer = XmlWriter.Create(xmlData, wSettings);
```

The code can then use the writer object to write XML tags to the xmlData object. Using the WriteStartElement() function of the writer object Contact, FullName and Phone elements are created. Using the WriteString() function, the values of NameText.Text and PhoneText.Text are written. The code also uses the WriteStartAttribute() function to add a Type attribute to the Phone element based on which RadioButton control is selected.

The code uses the WriteEndElement() and WriteEndAttribute tags to close the tags. Then the code calls the Close() function of writer to flush the data to the xmlData object. The xmlData object is then converted to a string and displayed in the myText TextBlock.

Inside the doRead() event handler, the code first creates a StringBuilder object — textData — that is used to store parsed XML data. Then a StringReader object — sReader — is created that points to the value of myText.Text as the XML source.

The sReader StringReader object is used in the following line of code to create an XmlReader object named reader:

```
XmlReader reader = XmlReader.Create(sReader);
```

The code is then able to use the Read() function of the reader XmlReader object to parse XML tags from the sReader object. The code implements a switch statement using the reader.NodeType value to parse the different tags in the XML data.

As each tag is parsed, the Name and/or Value attributes of the tag are written to the textData StringBuilder. The code also uses the GetAttribute() function of the reader object to get the Type attribute of the Phone element.

The code calls the Close() function of the reader object to close the XML source. The textData object is then converted to a string and displayed in the myText TextBlock.

The results of the code in Listings 15.1 and 15.2 are shown in Figure 15.1. The user types a name and phone number in the text boxes and sets the type of phone number. When the Write XML button is clicked, the data that is input by the user is converted to XML and displayed in the scroll viewer. Then when the user clicks Read XML, the XML data is parsed and displayed in the scroll viewer.

LISTING 15.2

C# Code That Implements an XmlReader and XmlWriter to Read and Write XML Data

```csharp
using System;
using System.Windows;
using System.Windows.Controls;
using System.Windows.Documents;

using System.Xml;
using System.IO;
using System.Text;


namespace XMLParserApp
{
    public partial class Page : UserControl
    {
        public Page()
        {
            InitializeComponent();

            XMLWriteBtn.Click += new RoutedEventHandler(doWrite);
            XMLReadBtn.Click += new RoutedEventHandler(doRead);
        }

        void doWrite(object sender, RoutedEventArgs e)
        {
            StringBuilder xmlData = new StringBuilder();
            XmlWriterSettings wSettings = new XmlWriterSettings();
            wSettings.Indent = true;
            XmlWriter writer = XmlWriter.Create(xmlData, wSettings);

            writer.WriteStartElement("Contact");
            writer.WriteStartElement("FullName");
            writer.WriteString(NameText.Text);
            writer.WriteEndElement();
            writer.WriteStartElement("Phone");
            writer.WriteStartAttribute("Type");

            if((bool)HomeBtn.IsChecked)
                writer.WriteString("Home");
            else if ((bool)OfficeBtn.IsChecked)
```

```
                writer.WriteString("Office");
            else if ((bool)CellBtn.IsChecked)
                writer.WriteString("Cell");

            writer.WriteEndAttribute();
            writer.WriteString(PhoneText.Text);
            writer.WriteEndElement();
            writer.Close();
            myText.Text = xmlData.ToString();
        }

        void doRead(object sender, RoutedEventArgs e)
        {
            StringBuilder textData = new StringBuilder();
            StringReader sReader = new StringReader(myText.Text);
            XmlReader reader = XmlReader.Create(sReader);
            while (reader.Read())
            {
                switch (reader.NodeType)
                {
                    case XmlNodeType.Element:
                        textData.Append("Element: " +
                                        reader.Name + "\r\n");
                        if (reader.Name == "Phone")
                        {
                            string type = reader.GetAttribute("Type");
                            textData.Append("Attribute: Type = " +
                                            type + "\r\n");
                        }
                        break;
                    case XmlNodeType.Text:
                        textData.Append("Value: " +
                                        reader.Value + "\r\n");
                        break;
                    case XmlNodeType.XmlDeclaration:
                        textData.Append("Declaration Name: " +
                                        reader.Name + "\r\n");
                        textData.Append("Declaration Value: " +
                                        reader.Value + "\r\n");
                        break;
                    case XmlNodeType.EndElement:
                        break;
                }
            }
            reader.Close();
            myText.Text = textData.ToString();
        }
    }
}
```

FIGURE 15.1

Silverlight application that reads data from `TextBox` and `RadioButton` controls, writes it to XML form in a `TextBlock`, and then parses the XML

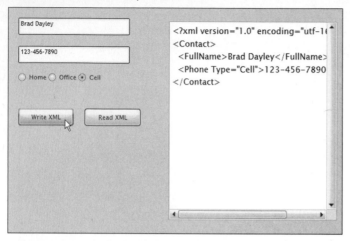

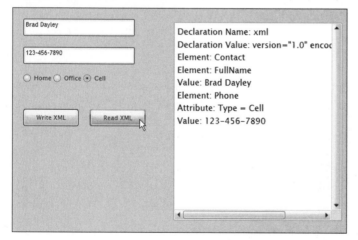

Serializing a Data Object into XML

Silverlight also provides a `System.Xml.Serialization` library that can be used to serialize objects into XML data and then deserialize the XML data back into an object. This provides you with the ability to quickly convert an object into XML data, send it to a destination, and quickly convert the XML back into object form at the destination. This is extremely useful if you are sending an object to and from a Web service.

The XmlSerializer class, which is part of the Systm.XmlSerialization library exposes Serialize() and Deserialize() functions that allow you to quickly convert objects to XML and then back inside your Silverlight applications.

Serializing objects into XML

The first step in serializing objects into XML is to create an object that can be serialized. This is done by creating a simple class and then implementing XML tag decorators that are exposed by the System.Xml.Serialization library to define the XML properties of the class.

The following is a list of the XML tag decorators that you can use to define XML properties of a class:

- XmlAttribute: Defines a member as an XML attribute
- XmlElement: Defines a member as an XML element
- XmlIgnore: Specifies that this member should be ignored when serializing or deserializing an object
- XmlRoot: Defines a member or the class itself as an XML root

The following code snippet defines a simple class named Movie that contains a single string member named MovieTitle. The class Movie is set as the XmlRoot tag Movies, and the MovieTitle member is defined as an XMLElement tag named MovieTitle:

```
[XmlRoot("Movies")]
public class Movie
{
    private string MovieTitle = "";
    [XmlElement("MovieTitle")]
    public string Title
    {
        get { return this.MovieTitle; }
        set { this.MovieTitle = value; }
    }
}
```

After the class is defined with XML properties, the instance of the class can be serialized using an XmlSerializer object. You need to create an instance of the XmlSerializer that maps to your object. This is done by calling the XmlSerializer constructor and passing in the type of the object you want to serialize. For example, the following code creates an instance of the Movie class and then uses the GetType() function to generate an XmlSerializer object:

```
Movie m = new Movie();
m.Title = "New Movie";
XmlSerializer serializer = new XmlSerializer(m.GetType());
```

To serialize the object into XML, use the `Serialize()` function of the `XmlSerializer` object. The `Serialize` function requires at least two arguments: the first argument points to a destination that the XML data can be written, and the second argument is the object to be serialized.

The destination argument can be a `Stream`, `TextWriter`, or `XmlWriter` object. For example, the following code serializes the `Movie` object m to a `StringBuilder` object xmlData:

```
StringBuilder xmlData = new StringBuilder();
serializer.Serialize(xmlData, m);
```

The `Serialize()` function takes care of implementing the XML tagging structure and writes a well-formed XML file to the destination.

Deserializing objects from serialized XML

Objects that have been serialized using the `XmlSerializer.Serialize()` function can easily be deserialized using the `XmlSerializer.Deserialize()` function. To deserialize an object, you need to create an instance of the `XmlSerializer` that maps to your object.

This is done by calling the `XmlSerializer` constructor and passing in the type of the object you want to deserialize. For example, the following code creates an instance of the `Movie` class and then uses the `GetType()` function to generate an `XmlSerializer` object:

```
Movie m = new Movie();
XmlSerializer serializer = new XmlSerializer(m.GetType());
```

To deserialize the object from XML, use the `Deserialize()` function of the `XmlSerializer` object. The `Deserialize` function requires a destination argument that points to the XML source of the object to be deserialized.

The source argument can be a `Stream`, `TextReader`, or `XmlReader` object. For example, the following code deserializes a `Movie` object m from a `StringReader` object xmlSource:

```
StringReader xmlSource = new StringReader(xmlText);
serializer.Deserialize(xmlSource);
```

The `Deserialize()` function takes care of parsing the XML tagging structure of the serialized object based on the XML decorators defined in the object's class definition and sets the value of the appropriate properties of the object.

Example: Serializing and deserializing XML data in isolated storage

The code in Listings 15.3 and 15.4 shows an example Silverlight application that accepts data from `TextBox` and `RadioButton` controls and writes that data to an object. The example code serializes the object into XML format and stores it in the isolated local file system. Then the code reads the XML file from the isolated local file system and deserializes the XML data back into an object.

The code in Listing 15.3 implements a simple form with two TextBox controls — NameText and EmailText. The code also implements two Button controls — SerializeBtn and DeserializeBtn — that are used to initiate an XmlSerializer to serialize and deserialize an object. A TextBlock control — myText — is nested inside a ScrollViewer control to display the results of the serialized and deserialized object.

LISTING 15.3

XAML Code That Implements Form and Button Controls to Collect Data That Will Be Used to Create an Object That Will Be Serialized and Then Deserialized

```
<UserControl x:Class="SerializationApp.Page"
    xmlns="http://schemas.microsoft.com/client/2007"
    xmlns:x="http://schemas.microsoft.com/winfx/2006/xaml"
    Width="600" Height="300">
    <Grid x:Name="LayoutRoot" Background="LightBlue">
        <TextBox x:Name = "NameText" Text="Full Name"
                            VerticalAlignment="Top"
                            HorizontalAlignment="Left"
                            Margin="20,20"
                            Width="200" Height="30"/>
        <TextBox x:Name = "EmailText" Text="Email Address"
                            VerticalAlignment="Top"
                            HorizontalAlignment="Left"
                            Margin="20,70"
                            Width="200" Height="30"/>
        <Button x:Name="SerializeBtn" Content="Serialize"
                VerticalAlignment="Top" HorizontalAlignment="Left"
                Margin="20,130"
                Height="30" Width="100" />
        <Button x:Name="DeSerializeBtn" Content="Deserialize"
                VerticalAlignment="Top" HorizontalAlignment="Left"
                Margin="140,130"
                Height="30" Width="100" />
        <ScrollViewer Background="White"
                    HorizontalScrollBarVisibility="Auto"
                    HorizontalAlignment="Right"
                    Margin="10" Width="300" Height="250">
            <TextBlock x:Name="myText"/>
        </ScrollViewer>
    </Grid>
</UserControl>
```

The code in Listing 15.4 adds a reference to the `System.Xml.Serialization` library that includes the Silverlight `XmlSerializer` class. It also adds references to the `System.IO` and `System.IO.IsolatedStorage` libraries to provide access to the `StringReader` and `IsolatedStorageFile` classes.

The code defines an `IsolatedStorageFile` named `localStore` as well as an `IsolatedStorageFileStream` named `localStream` that is used to store and retrieve an XML file.

At the bottom of the code in Listing 15.4, a `ContactData` class is defined with the `XmlRoot` decorator. The `ContactData` class contains two `string` members — `FullName` and `EmailAddr` — which are defined with the `XmlElement` decorator.

Inside the `Page()` constructor, the code initializes the `localStore` object to the current application's isolated local file system. Then the code attaches the `doSerialize()` and `doDeserialize()` Click event handlers to the `SerializeBtn` and `DeserializeBtn` controls, respectively.

Inside the `doSerialize()` event handler, the code first initializes the `localStream` object by creating a file named contact.xml in the isolated file system using the `FileMode.Create` argument. Then the code creates an instance of the `ContactData` class named `contact` from the values of `NameText.Text` and `EmailText.Text`.

Then the code creates an `XmlSerializer` object — serialize — using the `GetType()` function of the `contact` object using the following line of code:

```
XmlSerializer serializer = new XmlSerializer(contact.GetType());
```

Then the `Serialize()` function of the `serialize` object is used to write the `contact` data object to the `contact.xml` file using the `localStream` object, as shown in the following line of code:

```
serializer.Serialize(localStream, contact);
```

The code then closes the `localStream` and reopens it in `Open` mode. The contents of the file are written to the `Text` property of the `myText` `TextBlock` to be displayed.

Inside the `doDeserialize()` event handler, the code first initializes the `localStream` object by opening a file named contact.xml in the isolated file system using the `FileMode.Open` argument. Then the code creates a blank instance of the `ContactData` class named `contact`.

Then the code creates an `XmlSerializer` object — serialize — using the `GetType()` function of the `contact` object using the following line of code:

```
XmlSerializer serializer = new XmlSerializer(contact.GetType());
```

The `Deserialize()` function of the `serialize` object is then used to read the `contact.xml` file using the `localStream` object and sets the value of the `contact` data object as shown in the following code:

```
contact = serializer.Deserialize(localStream);
```

The code closes the localStream and writes a formatted version of the contact object to the Text property of the myText TextBlock to be displayed.

The results of the code in Listings 15.3 and 15.4 are shown in Figure 15.2. The user types a name and e-mail address in the text boxes. When the Serialize button is clicked, the data that is input by the user is written to an object that is serialized into XML, stored in the local file system, and displayed in the scroll viewer. When the user clicks Deserialize, the XML file is read from the local file system and deserialized into an object that is displayed in the scroll viewer.

LISTING 15.4

C# Code That Implements an XmlReader and XmlWriter to Read and Write XML Data

```csharp
using System;
using System.Collections.Generic;
using System.Windows;
using System.Windows.Controls;
using System.Windows.Documents;
using System.Windows.Input;

using System.Xml.Serialization;
using System.IO.IsolatedStorage;
using System.IO;

namespace SerializationApp
{
    public partial class Page : UserControl
    {
        IsolatedStorageFile localStore;
        IsolatedStorageFileStream localStream;

        public Page()
        {
            InitializeComponent();

            localStore  = IsolatedStorageFile.GetUserStoreForApplication();

            SerializeBtn.Click += new RoutedEventHandler(doSerialize);
            DeSerializeBtn.Click += new RoutedEventHandler(doDeSerialize
);
        }

        void doSerialize(object sender, RoutedEventArgs e)
        {
            localStream = new IsolatedStorageFileStream("contact.xml",
```
continued

497

LISTING 15.4 *(continued)*

```
                                          FileMode.Create,
                                          localStore);

        ContactData contact = new ContactData();
        contact.Name = NameText.Text;
        contact.Email = EmailText.Text;
        XmlSerializer serializer = new XmlSerializer(contact.GetType());
        serializer.Serialize(localStream, contact);
        localStream.Close();

        localStream = new IsolatedStorageFileStream("contact.xml",
                                                    FileMode.Open,
                                                    localStore);
        StreamReader sReader = new StreamReader(localStream);
        myText.Text = sReader.ReadToEnd();
        sReader.Close();
        localStream.Close();
    }

    void doDeSerialize(object sender, RoutedEventArgs e)
    {
        localStream = new IsolatedStorageFileStream("contact.dat",
                                                    FileMode.Open,
                                                    localStore);

        ContactData contact = new ContactData();
        XmlSerializer serializer = new XmlSerializer(contact.GetType());
        contact = serializer.Deserialize(localStream) as ContactData;
        localStream.Close();

        myText.Text = String.Format("Full Name: {0}\r\nEmail: {1}",
                                    contact.Name, contact.Email);
    }
}

[XmlRoot("ContactsXml")]
public class ContactData
{

    public ContactData()
    {
    }

    private string FullName = "";
    [XmlElement("FullName")]
    public string Name
    {
```

```
            get { return this.FullName; }
            set { this.FullName = value; }
        }

        private string EmailAddr = "";
        [XmlElement("Email")]
        public string Email
        {
            get { return this.EmailAddr; }
            set { this.EmailAddr = value; }
        }
    }
}
```

FIGURE 15.2

Silverlight application that serializes data from `TextBox` and `RadioButton` controls, writes the XML in a `TextBlock`, and then deserializes the XML

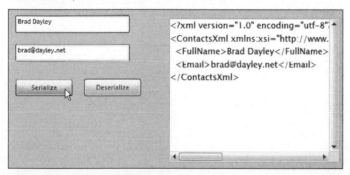

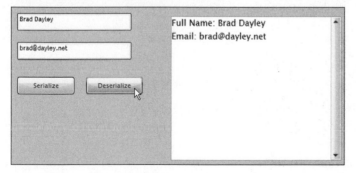

Implementing Data Binding in Silverlight Applications

An extremely useful feature of Silverlight is the ability to bind properties of Silverlight controls to data sources. When the values of the data sources change, the property values of the controls change as well. The `System.Windows.Data` library provides most of the functionality for data binding.

Data binding can be implemented as one-time, one-way, or two-way. One-way data binding only changes the value of the control based on the data source. In two-way binding, if either the control value or the source value changes, the other is updated as well.

To implement data binding in XAML code, you first need to implement a `Binding` statement encased in `{ }` brackets in place of the property value. The `Binding` statement uses the following syntax:

```
{Binding <value>, <options>}
```

The `value` setting in the `Binding` statement is the property of the data source that is used to fill in the value for the control property. You can also specify the following options in the `Binding` statement:

- `Converter`: Specifies the converter object that is called by the binding engine to modify the data as it is passed between the data source and target property
- `ConverterCulture`: Specifies the culture used by the converter to implement conversion of data
- `ConverterParamter`: Specifies a parameter that can be passed to the converter
- `Mode`: Specifies whether the data flow in the binding is one-way or two-way.
- `Source`: Specifies the source object for the binding

For example, the following code creates a two-way binding between the `Title` property of a data source to the `Text` property of a `TextBox` control:

```
<TextBox x:Name="nameBox" Text="{Binding Title, Mode=TwoWay}" />
```

The `Binding` statement tells the control only what property of the data source the value is bound to. You also need to set the value of the `DataContext` property of the control to assign a specific object as the data source. The `DataContext` property can be set in XAML; however, it is typically set in managed code.

For example, the following code creates a `Movie` object — m — and then sets the `DataContext` of the `nameBox` `TextBox` control to the movie object:

```
Movie mv = new Movie();
m.Title = "New Movie";
nameBox.DataContext = m;
```

To implement a class as a data source, the class must implement the INotifyProperty
Changed interface and have an event of type PropertyChangedEventHandler named
PropertyChanged.

For example, the following code defines a simple class named Movie that can serve as a data
source for data binding:

```
public class Movie : INotifyPropertyChanged
{
    private string MovieTitle;
    public event PropertyChangedEventHandler PropertyChanged;

    public string Title
    {
        get { return MovieTitle; }
        set
        {
            MovieTitle = value;
            PropertyChanged(this,
                        new PropertyChangedEventArgs("Title")
        );
        }
    }
}
```

> **NOTE** There are numerous implementations of data binding. Each of them is different
> based on the controls used, the data sources, and the functionality of the code. This
> section discusses only one of those methods.

To help you understand this method of data binding, consider the code in Listings 15.5 and 15.6
that is part of a Silverlight application that uses data binding to set and retrieve values of controls.

The code in Listing 15.5 implements a TextBlock, nameTitle, TextBox, nameBox, and a
ListBox, numberList control that implements Binding statements.

The nameTitle control implements a one-way binding to the Name property of the data source.
The nameBox control implements a two-way binding to the Name property. The numberList
property implements a one-way binding to the Numbers property.

The code in Listing 15.5 also implements two Button controls — UpdateBtn and SwitchBtn —
which are used to update and change the data binding.

LISTING 15.5

XAML Code That Implements a Data Binding to a TextBlock, TextBox, and ListBox Control as Well as Button Controls to Update and Switch Data Contexts

```
<UserControl x:Class="DataBindingApp.Page"
    xmlns="http://schemas.microsoft.com/client/2007"
    xmlns:x="http://schemas.microsoft.com/winfx/2006/xaml"
    Width="350" Height="300">
    <Grid x:Name="LayoutRoot" Background="LightBlue">
        <TextBlock x:Name="nameTitle"
                Text="{Binding Name, Mode=OneWay}"
                FontSize="30"
                VerticalAlignment="Top"
                HorizontalAlignment="Left"
                Margin="10,10,0,0"
                Height="50" Width="300" />
        <TextBox x:Name="nameBox"
                Text="{Binding Name, Mode=TwoWay}"
                VerticalAlignment="Top"
                HorizontalAlignment="Left"
                Margin="10,80,0,0"
                Height="30" Width="300" />
        <ListBox x:Name="numberList"
                ItemsSource="{Binding Numbers, Mode=OneWay}"
                VerticalAlignment="Top"
                HorizontalAlignment="Left"
                Margin="10,120,0,0"
                Height="120" Width="300" />
        <Button x:Name="UpdateBtn" Content="Update"
                VerticalAlignment="Bottom"
                Margin="-120,0,0,10"
                Height="30" Width="100" />
        <Button x:Name="SwitchBtn" Content="Switch"
                VerticalAlignment="Bottom"
                Margin="120,0,0,10"
                Height="30" Width="100" />
    </Grid>
</UserControl>
```

The code in Listing 15.6 adds a reference to the `System.ComponentModel` library to expose the `INotifyPropertyChanged` interface and `PropertyChangedEventHandler` class. At the bottom of Listing 15.6, a class named `Contact` is defined that implements the `INotifyPropertyChanged` interface and a `PropertyChangedEventHandler` handler.

The Contact class defines a string member — Name — and a List member — Numbers. The code also defines a function NotifyPropertyChanged() that triggers the PropertyChanged() event handler for the class. Both the Name and Numbers implement the NotifyPropertyChanged() function in their set handler. This is necessary so that the binding can be updated when these properties are modified.

The code in Listing 15.6 defines three Contact objects — personA, personB, and current. These objects are initialized in the initData() function to set up a data source to bind to the Silverlight controls.

The setContext() function accepts a Contact object as an argument and sets the Data Context of the LayoutRoot object to the Contact object using the following line of code. The DataContext property flows down to the nameTitle, nameBox, and numberList controls:

```
LayoutRoot.DataContext = c;
```

> **NOTE** The DataContext property is inheritable by child elements in the Silverlight application. If you have several controls that are bound to the same data source, then you can group those controls in a parent container such as a Canvas or Grid and then set the DataContext property of the parent. The data context flows down to the children without the need to set the property for each child.

Inside the Page() constructor, the doUpdate() and doSwitch() event handlers are attached to the UpdateBtn and SwitchBtn controls. Inside the doUpdate() handler, the name of the current Contact object is set to the value of nameBox.Text. When this value is set, the binding is updated by the PropertyChanged() event handler in the class, and the controls are updated.

Inside the doSwitch() handler, the current DataContext is switched between the personA and personB objects allowing you to see how changes to the context affect the value of control properties.

The results of the code in Listings 15.5 and 15.6 are shown in Figure 15.3. When you change the name in the text box and click Update, the title is changed as well. When you click Switch, the data context is switched between the two Contact objects and the controls are updated accordingly.

LISTING 15.6

C# Code That Implements a Contact Class That Is Used as a Data Source and Provides Functionality to Update and Switch the DataContext of Controls

```
using System;
using System.Collections.Generic;
using System.Windows;
using System.Windows.Controls;
```

continued

LISTING 15.6   *(continued)*

```csharp
using System.ComponentModel;

namespace DataBindingApp
{
    public partial class Page : UserControl
    {
        Contact personA, personB, current;
        Boolean isCurrentA;
        public Page()
        {
            InitializeComponent();

            initData();
            setContext(personA);
            isCurrentA = true;

            UpdateBtn.Click += new RoutedEventHandler(doUpdate);
            SwitchBtn.Click += new RoutedEventHandler(doSwitch);
        }

        void initData()
        {
            personA = new Contact();
            personA.Name = "Mike";
            personA.Numbers =
                new List<string>() { "111-222-333", "444-555-6666" };
            personB = new Contact();
            personB.Name = "Ted";
            personB.Numbers =
                new List<string>() { "123-456-7890", "098-765-4321" };
        }

        void setContext(Contact c)
        {
            current = c;
            LayoutRoot.DataContext = c;
        }

        void doUpdate(object sender, RoutedEventArgs e)
        {
            current.Name = nameBox.Text;
        }

        void doSwitch(object sender, RoutedEventArgs e)
        {
            if (isCurrentA)
            {
                setContext(personB);
                isCurrentA = false;
            }
```

```csharp
            else
            {
                setContext(personA);
                isCurrentA = true;
            }
        }
    }

    public class Contact : INotifyPropertyChanged
    {
        private string ContactName;
        private List<string> ContactNumbers;
        public event PropertyChangedEventHandler PropertyChanged;

        public Contact()
        {
        }

        public void NotifyPropertyChanged(string property)
        {
            if (PropertyChanged != null)
            {
                PropertyChanged(this,
                            new PropertyChangedEventArgs(property));
            }
        }

        public string Name
        {
            get { return ContactName; }
            set
            {
                ContactName = value;
                NotifyPropertyChanged("Name");
            }
        }

        public List<string> Numbers
        {
            get { return ContactNumbers; }
            set
            {
                ContactNumbers = value;
                NotifyPropertyChanged("Numbers");
            }
        }
    }
}
```

FIGURE 15.3

Silverlight application that binds data from an object to a `TextBlock`, `TextBox`, and `List` control

 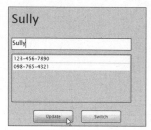 

Implementing a DataGrid Control

The `DataGrid` Silverlight control is extremely powerful and dynamic. It provides you with the ability to display a list of objects in tabular form in your Silverlight applications. The `DataGrid` control can handle setting up columns and rows and presentation of the data. It also provides a rich set of event handlers and properties that allow you to interact with the control from managed code.

To add a `DataGrid` control to your Silverlight applications, add the following namespace to the XAML file that will host the control:

```
xmlns:my="clr-namespace:System.Windows.Controls;
assembly=System.Windows.Controls.Data"
```

After you add the `Data` namespace to your application, you can add a `DataGrid` control to the XAML file. This is done by adding a definition for the `DataGrid` control in the XAML file and setting the properties necessary for the functionality you desire.

For example, the following code defines a `DataGrid` that sets the `AutoGenerateColumns`, `RowBackground`, `AlternateRowBackground`, `GridlinesVisiblity`, `HeadersVisibility`, `Height`, and `Width` properties.

```
<my:DataGrid x:Name="dGrid"
             AutoGenerateColumns="True"
             RowBackground="White"
             AlternatingRowBackground="LightGray"
             GridlinesVisibility="Horizontal"
             HeadersVisibility="Column"
             Height="180" Width="380"/>
```

Data is added to the DataGrid by setting the ItemsSource of the control to an object that implements the Innumerable interface, such as a List or other collection. For example, the following code sets the ItemsSource property of a DataGrid control named grid to a List of integers resulting in a DataGrid similar to the one in Figure 15.4:

```
List<int> nums = new List<int>() { 100, 1234, 54321, 111 };
dGrid.ItemsSource = nums;
```

FIGURE 15.4

A DataGrid displaying a list of numbers

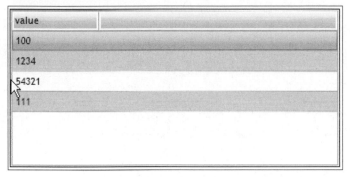

The DataGrid control also provides numerous event handlers in addition to the standard mouse, keyboard, and element handlers. For example, editing a cell in the data grid triggers the BeginCellEdit and CommitCellEdit events. This provides a means to interact with the DataGrid from managed code as users make changes in the data.

For example, to attach a BeginCellEdit event handler to a DataGrid control, you can use the following code:

```
dGrid.BeginningCellEdit += new
    EventHandler<DataGridCellEditingCancelEventArgs>(
    dGrid_BeginningCellEdit);
```

The code in Listings 15.7 and 15.8 shows an example Silverlight application that implements a DataGrid control that displays a list of movies. The code in Listing 15.7 adds the my namespace to the UserControl and defines a DataGrid named dGrid.

The code also sets the AutoGenerateColumns, RowBackground, AlternateRowBackground, GridlinesVisiblity, HeadersVisibility, Height, and Width properties of dGrid.

LISTING 15.7

XAML Code That Implements a DataGrid

```
<UserControl x:Class="DataGridApp.Page"
        xmlns:my="clr-
namespace:System.Windows.Controls;assembly=System.Windows.Controls.Data"
            xmlns="http://schemas.microsoft.com/client/2007"
            xmlns:x="http://schemas.microsoft.com/winfx/2006/xaml"
            Width="400" Height="200">
    <Grid x:Name="LayoutRoot" Background="White">
        <my:DataGrid x:Name="dGrid"
                    AutoGenerateColumns="True"
                    RowBackground="White"
                    AlternatingRowBackground="LightGray"
                    GridlinesVisibility="Horizontal"
                    HeadersVisibility="Column"
                    Height="180" Width="380"/>
    </Grid>
</UserControl>
```

The code in Listing 15.8 defines a simple class named Movie at the bottom. A List — movieList — is defined as a member of the Page class and the initData() function manually generates three Movie objects to populate movieList.

After the movieList List is populated, the code inserts the ItemsSource property of the dGrid control to movieList. The results are shown in Figure 15.5.

LISTING 15.8

C# Code That Generates a List of Objects and Populates a DataGrid

```
using System;
using System.Collections.Generic;
using System.Windows;
using System.Windows.Controls;

namespace DataGridApp
{
```

```csharp
public partial class Page : UserControl
{
    List<Movie> movieList = new List<Movie>();
    public Page()
    {
        InitializeComponent();
        initData();
        dGrid.ItemsSource = movieList;
    }

    private void initData()
    {
        movieList.Add(new Movie()
        {
            Title = "Star Wars", Rating = "PG",
            Year = 1977, Available = true
        });
        movieList.Add(new Movie()
        {
            Title = "Empire Strikes Back",
            Rating = "PG", Year = 1980,
            Available = true
        });
        movieList.Add(new Movie()
        {
            Title = "Return of the Jedi",
            Rating = "PG", Year = 1983,
            Available = false
        });
    }
}

public class Movie
{
    public string Title { get; set; }
    public int Year { get; set; }
    public string Rating { get; set; }
    public bool Available { get; set; }
}
}
```

FIGURE 15.5

A Silverlight application that displays a list of movies in a `DataGrid` control

Using LINQ in Silverlight to Query SQL Databases

Silverlight 2 introduced the ability to use LINQ queries to access SQL data. LINQ provides a language-based method of querying data. This allows you to write a query in C# or Visual Basic that can be used against any LINQ provider such as LINQ to SQL, LINQ to XML, LINQ to TerraServer, and many others.

 If you are considering accessing a lot of data from your Silverlight applications, we strongly recommend using LINQ queries.

LINQ queries are basically SQL-type queries that conform to the structure and syntax of the .NET language in which they are being implemented. For example, the following is a simple LINQ query in C#:

```
var movies = from m in db.Movies
            where m.Date == aDate
            select m;
```

The following is the same LINQ query in Visual Basic:

```
Dim query = From m In db.Movies _
            Where m.Date = aDate _
            Select m
```

The LINQ language itself is out of the scope of this book; however, we want to spend some time discussing how to implement it in your Silverlight applications. The following sections take you through the process of implementing the LINQ-to-SQL interface in a Silverlight application using a Web service in Visual Studio.

Creating a Web server Silverlight application project that accesses SQL using LINQ

The first step is to create a Silverlight application project in Visual Studio. You need to select the option Add a new Web to the solution for hosting the control and set the project type to Web Application Project, as shown in Figure 15.6. This is necessary so that you can create a WCF Web service to connect to the database.

FIGURE 15.6

Creating a Web server Silverlight application in Visual Studio

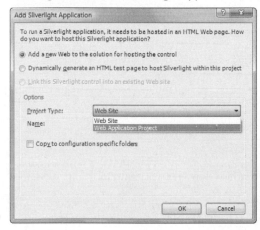

Two projects will be created in the Solution Explorer of Visual Studio, a Silverlight application project, and a Web server project.

Adding an SQL Server Database to the project

If you have not already created a database, you can add one to the project by right-clicking on the App_Data folder in the Web server project and choosing Add ➪ New Item from the pop-up menu. Then select SQL Server Database from the Templates list, as shown in Figure 15.7.

FIGURE 15.7

Adding an SQL Server Database to a Silverlight Web server project in Visual Studio

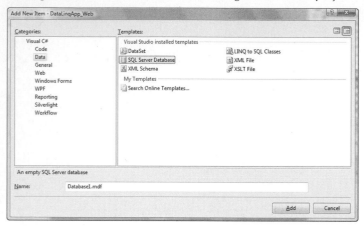

You can then use the Solution Explorer to add the necessary tables to the Database. In this example, we created a table named `Movie` and added columns for a `Title`, `Rating`, `Year`, and `Available`, as shown in Figure 15.8.

FIGURE 15.8

Defining a movie table in an SQL database

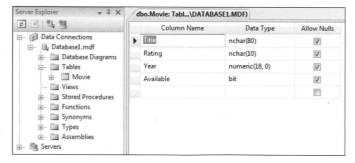

Adding a LinqToSql DataClass to the project

After the SQL database you want to use for you application is in place, you need to add a `LinqToSql DataClass` object to the project. Right-click on the Web server project and choose Add ⇨ New Item from the pop-up menu. Then select LINQ to SQL Classes from the Templates list, as shown in Figure 15.9.

FIGURE 15.9

Adding a LinqToSQL class to a Silverlight Web server project in Visual Studio

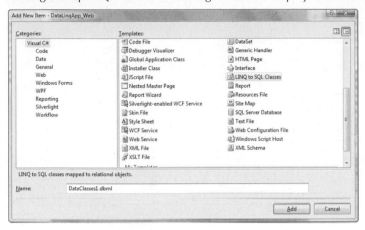

This creates a file named `DataClasses1.dbml` in the project and displays the Designer for that project. Click the Server Explorer link in the `DataClasses1.dbml` Designer view to display a list of data connections, as shown on the left in Figure 15.10. Select the table from the database with which you want to interface from the list of data connections and drag it onto the designer, as shown on the right in Figure 15.10.

FIGURE 15.10

Dragging a database table onto the Design pane of a data class in Visual Studio

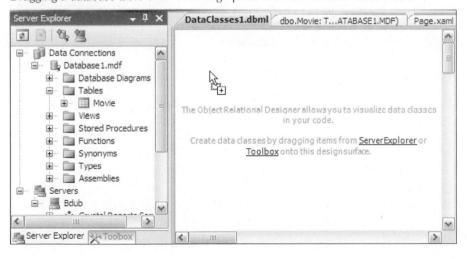

Set the LinqToSql class serialization to unidirectional

You will need to set the LinqToSql class to be serializable before you can use it in the Web service. To make the class serializable, click on the Design pane of the DataClasses1.dbl file and select properties from the drop-down list to display the Properties pane, as shown in Figure 15.11. Set the Serialization Mode property from None to Unidirectional.

Setting the Serialization Mode property of a data class in Visual Studio

Create a Web service to access the database

Now that the LinqToSql class is created and wired up, you need to create a database to access the database. Right-click on the Web server project and choose Add ⇨ New Item from the drop-down menu. Then select WCF Service from the Templates list. Leave the default name. This creates three new files in your project — IService1.cs, Service1.sfc, and Service1.svc.cs.

Open the IService1.cs file in Visual Studio and replace the basic DoWork() contract with the following code (or your own contract if you are implementing a different database), as shown in Listing 15.9:

```
[ServiceContract]
public interface IService1
{
    [OperationContract]
    List<Movie> GetMoviesByTitle(string mTitle);
}
```

This implements a contract that returns a List object using a method. Now you need to implement that method in the `Service1.svc.cs` file. There is a shortcut to this in Visual Studio.

Open the `Service1.svc.cs` file in Visual Studio, right-click on the `IService1` interface, and choose Implement Interface ➪ Implement Interface from the drop-down menu, as shown in Figure 15.12. This should create skeleton code similar to the following:

```
public List<Movie> GetMoviesByTitle(string mTitle)
{
    throw new NotImplementedException();
}
```

FIGURE 15.12

Implementing a service interface for a service contract in Visual Studio

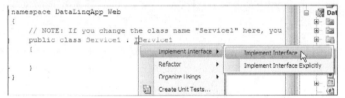

This is where the LINQ query needs to be added to access the database. Replace the throw statement in the function with the following code — or your own code — that implements a LINQ query, as shown in Listing 15.10:

```
DataClasses1DataContext db = new DataClasses1DataContext();
var movies = from m in db.Movies
             where m.Title.Contains(mTitle)
             select m;
return movies.ToList();
```

Fix up the Web.config file

For some reason, Visual Studio insists on binding Silverlight applications using `wsHttpBinding`; however, Silverlight only supports using `basicHttpBinding`. Open the `Web.config` file for the project and replace the following code:

```
<endpoint address="" binding="wsHttpBinding"
    contract-"DataLinqApp_Web.IService1">
```

with this code:

```
<endpoint address="" binding="basicHttpBinding"
    contract="DataLinqApp_Web.IService1">
```

Setting up the Silverlight project to use the LINQ service

When the Web server side of the Silverlight project is wired, configure the Silverlight application itself to consume the data exposed by the `LinqToSql` service. The following sections take you through the process of referencing the WCF service and binding the SQL data to a `DataGrid` control.

Add a reference to the data service

The first step in accessing the SQL data from a Silverlight application is to add a reference to the `IService1` Web service. This is done by right-clicking the References folder in the Silverlight project and selecting Add Service Reference from the drop-down list to display the Add Service Reference dialog box, as shown in Figure 15.13.

Click Discover to find the `Service 1.svc` service. Expand the link, as shown in Figure 15.13. The `Contract` you defined in the `IService.cs` file should be listed in the Operations list. Select the `IService1` service and click OK to add the `ServiceReference1` reference.

FIGURE 15.13

Adding a service reference to a Silverlight application project in Visual Studio

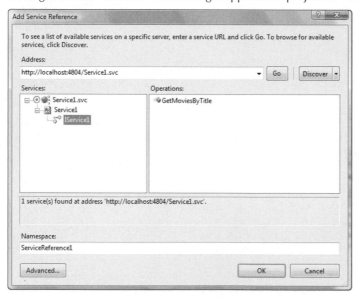

The SQL data source is now accessible to your Silverlight application.

Add a DataGrid to the Silverlight application

Now you need to create a Silverlight control that can consume the data from the LINQ query. One of the best options is a `DataGrid` because it naturally conforms to database-style data.

Add the following code to the `UserControl` of the `Page.xaml` file shown in Listing 15.11 to add the Data namespace:

```
xmlns:my="clr-namespace:System.Windows.Controls;assembly=
System.Windows.Controls.Data"
```

Then add a `DataGrid` contol with the appropriate settings for your application, as shown in Listing 15.11. Implement a `TextBox` and `Button` control that are used to send the string to query against the database to the data service, as shown in Listing 15.11.

Add managed code to access the data service

The code in Listing 15.12 implements managed code that attaches an event handler to the `Button` control to initiate access to the data service. First, attach a `Click` event handler to the `Button` control using code similar to the following:

```
SearchBtn.Click += new RoutedEventHandler(doSearch);
```

Then, inside the Click event handler `doSearch()`, create a `ServiceClient` object — `wSer-vice` — using the `ServiceReference1` service reference as shown in the following code:

```
ServiceReference1.Service1Client wService =
    new DataLinqApp.ServiceReference1.Service1Client();
```

The communication between the Silverlight application and the data service needs to be asynchronous so that the Silverlight interface is still responsive while waiting for the Web service to respond. This is done by attaching a completed event handler to the `ServiceClient` object.

Use the following code, shown in Listing 15.12, to attach a `GetMoviesByTitleCompleted` event handler to the `wService` object. This event is triggered when the `GetMoviesByTitle` request is completed:

```
wService.GetMoviesByTitleCompleted +=
    new EventHandler<DataLinqApp.ServiceReference1.
        GetMoviesByTitleCompletedEventArgs>(getMoviesDone);
```

When the completed event handler is attached, you can add an asynchronous call to the `GetMoviesByTitle` operation of the data service using the following code:

```
wService.GetMoviesByTitleAsync(titleSearch.Text);
```

The value of the `titleSearch` Textbox is passed in as the search parameter to the service. The last thing you need to do is add the completed event handler for the `GetMoviesByTitleCompleted` event as shown in the following code:

```
void getMoviesDone(object sender,
  DataLinqApp.ServiceReference1.GetMoviesByTitleCompletedEventArgs e)
{
    movieGrid.ItemsSource = e.Result;
}
```

Inside the `getMoviesDone()` event handler, shown in Listing 15.12, the result from the `GetMoviesByTitleAsync` request is bound to the `movieGrid` control using the `ItemsSource` attribute.

The results of the code in Listings 15.9, 15.10, 15.11, and 15.12 of the `DataLinqApp` are shown in Figure 15.14. When the user types a string in Search text box and clicks Search, the database is queried using a LINQ query and the results appear in the `DataGrid` control.

FIGURE 15.14

Silverlight application that Implements a LINQ SQL query to search a movie database

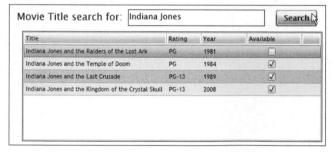

LISTING 15.9

IService1.cs Code of the DataLinqApp

```
using System;
using System.Collections.Generic;
using System.Linq;
using System.Runtime.Serialization;
using System.ServiceModel;
```

```
using System.Text;

namespace DataLinqApp_Web
{
    [ServiceContract]
    public interface IService1
    {
        [OperationContract]
        List<Movie> GetMoviesByTitle(string mTitle);
    }

}
```

LISTING 15.10

IService1.cs Code of the DataLinqApp

```
using System;
using System.Collections.Generic;
using System.Linq;
using System.Runtime.Serialization;
using System.ServiceModel;
using System.Text;

namespace DataLinqApp_Web
{
    public class Service1 : IService1
    {
        public List<Movie> GetMoviesByTitle(string mTitle)
        {
            DataClasses1DataContext db = new DataClasses1DataContext();
            var movies = from m in db.Movies
                         where m.Title.Contains(mTitle)
                         select m;
            return movies.ToList();
        }
    }
}
```

LISTING 15.11

Page.xaml Code of the DataLinqApp

```xml
<UserControl x:Class="DataLinqApp.Page"
    xmlns:my="clr-namespace:System.Windows.Controls;assembly=System.
   Windows.Controls.Data"
    xmlns="http://schemas.microsoft.com/client/2007"
    xmlns:x="http://schemas.microsoft.com/winfx/2006/xaml"
    Width="600" Height="300">
    <Grid x:Name="LayoutRoot" Background="White">
        <StackPanel Orientation="Horizontal">
            <TextBlock Text="Movie Title search for: "
                       FontSize="18"
                       Margin="15,10,0,0"
                       VerticalAlignment="Top" />
              <TextBox x:Name="titleSearch"
                       Width="250" Height="30"
                       Margin="5,10,0,0"
                       VerticalAlignment="Top"/>
              <Button x:Name="SearchBtn" Content="Search"
                       Background="Blue"
                       FontWeight="Bold" FontSize="14"
                       Width="75" Height="30"
                       Margin="20,10,0,0"
                       VerticalAlignment="Top"/>
        </StackPanel>
        <my:DataGrid x:Name="movieGrid"
                     RowBackground="LightBlue"
                     AlternatingRowBackground="Beige"
                     AutoGenerateColumns="True"
                     CanUserResizeColumns="True"
                     GridlinesVisibility="Horizontal"
                     HeadersVisibility="Column"
                     Width="550" Height="200" />
    </Grid>
</UserControl>
```

LISTING 15.12

Page.cs Code of the DataLinqApp

```csharp
using System;
using System.Collections.Generic;
using System.Linq;
using System.Windows;
using System.Windows.Controls;
using System.Windows.Input;


namespace DataLinqApp
{
    public partial class Page : UserControl
    {
        public Page()
        {
            InitializeComponent();
            SearchBtn.Click += new RoutedEventHandler(doSearch);
        }

        void doSearch(object sender, RoutedEventArgs e)
        {
            ServiceReference1.Service1Client wService =
                new DataLinqApp.ServiceReference1.Service1Client();
                wService.GetMoviesByTitleCompleted +=
                    new EventHandler<DataLinqApp.ServiceReference1.
                        GetMoviesByTitleCompletedEventArgs>(getMoviesDone);
            wService.GetMoviesByTitleAsync(titleSearch.Text);
        }

        void getMoviesDone(object sender,
         DataLinqApp.ServiceReference1.GetMoviesByTitleCompletedEventArgs e)
        {
            movieGrid.ItemsSource = e.Result;
        }
    }
}
```

Summary

This chapter focused on implementing aspects of the Silverlight data framework to implement data from various sources in Silverlight applications. The XmlReader and XmlWriter classes provide a simple interface to read XML data into Silverlight applications and write XML data that can be sent to other services.

The XmlSerializer class provides a simple interface to serialize an object in your Silverlight applications into XML and then later deserialize the XML back into an object. Implementing data binding makes it simple to update controls with value by binding data sources to target properties. Silverlight supports LINQ queries to SQL databases making it easier to provide queried data to your applications.

In this chapter, you learned how to:

- Write XML data using the XmlWriter class
- Read XML data using the XmlReader class
- Serialize an object into an XML file and store it in the local file system
- Retrieve a serialized object from an XML file stored in the local file system
- Implement one-way and two-way data binding to properties of Silverlight controls
- Implement a DataGrid control using a list
- Access an SQL database from a Silverlight application using a WCF service
- Implement LINQ queries in Silverlight applications

Part V

Appendixes

Appendix A

Silverlight Resources

The purpose of this appendix is to provide links to resources that may be helpful when learning and developing Silverlight applications. The list is not comprehensive, but we hope it provides a good place to start.

www.Silverlight.net
Silverlight community page. You will find the most current information about Silverlight as well as links to learning resources. This is the Web site to use to find out what files need to be downloaded to begin developing Silverlight applications.

http://msdn2.microsoft.com/en-us/library/bb871518.aspx
Silverlight documentation on MSDN. You will find an overview of Silverlight, technical documentation on Silverlight, and articles on implementing some specific functionality such as Web media.

www.microsoft.com/silverlight/resources/
Microsoft's Silverlight home page. You will find helpful links to Silverlight development tools, communities, news, and other information.

http://silverlight.net/learn/tutorials.aspx
Silverlight tutorials on the Silverlight project site. You should review these tutorials if you get a chance; they give you a quick perspective into Silverlight.

http://silverlight.net/learn/tutorials.aspx
Silverlight hands-on labs on the Silverlight project site. You should also review the hands-on labs if you get a chance. They provide all of the code necessary to build Silverlight applications in a step-by-step method.

http://weblogs.asp.net/scottgu/

Scott Guthrie's blog. If you are looking for news on what is coming up with Silverlight, this is the place to look.

http://silverlight.net/blogs/jesseliberty/

Jesse Liberty's blog. Jesse does most of the tutorials for Silverlight, and his blog is a great place to get answers to tough questions.

http://timheuer.com/blog/

Tim Heuer's blog. Tim has posted some great videos that will help you quickly pick up on Silverlight development methods.

http://blogs.msdn.com/brada/archive/2008/03/16/silverlight-2-developer-poster.aspx

A printable poster that shows a quick view of the Silverlight 2.0 architecture. This poster can help you put the different frameworks that are involved in Silverlight development in perspective.

www.codeplex.com/sdlsdk

The Silverlight dynamical languages SDK. This Web site contains the links you need to begin building DLR Silverlight applications using Python, Ruby, and managed JavaScript.

www.go-mon.com/moonlight

The Moonlight plug-in from the Mono team at Novell. The moonlight plug-in allows you to design the XAML elements of the Silverlight applications on Linux. The plug-in currently supports Silverlight 1.0 applications only.

www.mono-project.com/Moonlight

The project page for the Moonlight project of the Mono team at Novell. This page shows the current project status and includes links to several downloads. They also post some news and other information here.

http://anonsvn.mono-project.com/source/trunk/lunareclipse

The Moonlight IDE called lunareclipse from the Mono team at Novell. The moonlight plug-in allows you to design the XAML elements of the Silverlight applications on Linux workstations.

www.mono-project.com/MoonlightNotes

The development notes page for the Moonlight project. This page includes critical development information that you will want to monitor if you are trying to develop Silverlight applications on Linux.

Appendix B

Silverlight Control Reference

The purpose of this appendix is to provide you with a list of the available methods, properties, and events for the most commonly used Silverlight controls. Implementing these controls is discussed throughout the book; however, there are far too many members of each control to discuss them all.

You should be fairly familiar with the controls and how to implement them in XAML and managed code by now. This appendix is intended as a simple reference where you can quickly look up what members are available for different controls.

> **NOTE** The controls in this chapter are based on the Silverlight 2 Beta 2 release. Microsoft has a tendency to "update" these controls to add and sometimes remove functionality. If one of the properties, methods, or events is giving you fits, or if you are looking for additional functionality for a control that you believe should be there, check the MSDN Web site at the following address to see if something has changed:
> http://msdn.microsoft.com/en-us/library/cc303041.aspx.

Border

Properties
ActualHeight, ActualWidth, Background, BorderBrush, BorderThickness, Child, Clip, CornerRadius, Cursor, DataContext, DesiredSize, Dispatcher, Height, HorizontalAlignment, IsHitTestVisible, Language, Margin, MaxHeight, MaxWidth, MinHeight, MinWidth, Name, Opacity, OpacityMask, Padding, Parent, RenderSize, RenderTransform, RenderTransformOrigin, Resources, Style, Tag, Triggers, VerticalAlignment, Visibility, Width

Methods

Arrange, ArrangeOverride, CaptureMouse, CheckAccess, Equals, Finalize, FindName,
GetAnimationBaseValue, GetHashCode, GetType, GetValue, HitTest, InvalidateArrange,
InvalidateMeasure, Measure, MeasureOverride, MemberwiseClone, ReleaseMouseCapture,
SetBinding, SetValue, ToString, TransformToVisual, UpdateLayout

Events

GotFocus, KeyDown, KeyUp, LayoutUpdated, Loaded, LostFocus, MouseEnter, MouseLeave,
MouseLeftButtonDown, MouseLeftButtonUp, MouseMove, SizeChanged

Button

Properties

ActualHeight, ActualWidth, Background, ClickMode, Clip, Content, ContentTemplate, Cursor,
DataContext, DesiredSize, Dispatcher, FontFamily, FontSize, FontStretch, FontStyle, FontWeight,
Foreground, Height, HorizontalAlignment, HorizontalContentAlignment, IsEnabled, IsFocused,
IsHitTestVisible, IsMouseOver, IsPressed, IsTabStop, Language, Margin, MaxHeight, MaxWidth,
MinHeight, MinWidth, Name, Opacity, OpacityMask, Padding, Parent, RenderSize,
RenderTransform, RenderTransformOrigin, Resources, Style, TabIndex, TabNavigation, Tag,
Template, TextAlignment, TextDecorations, TextWrapping, ToolTip, Triggers, VerticalAlignment,
VerticalContentAlignment, Visibility, Width

Methods

ApplyTemplate, Arrange, ArrangeOverride, CaptureMouse, CheckAccess, Equals, Finalize,
FindName, Focus, GetAnimationBaseValue, GetHashCode, GetTemplateChild, GetType, GetValue,
HitTest, InitializeFromXaml, InvalidateArrange, InvalidateMeasure, Measure, MeasureOverride,
MemberwiseClone, OnApplyTemplate, OnClick, OnContentChanged,
OnContentTemplateChanged, OnGotFocus, OnIsEnabledChanged, OnIsPressedChanged,
OnKeyDown, OnKeyUp, OnLostFocus, OnMouseEnter, OnMouseLeave,
OnMouseLeftButtonDown, OnMouseLeftButtonUp, OnMouseMove, ReleaseMouseCapture,
SetBinding, SetValue, ToString, TransformToVisual, UpdateLayout

Events

Click, GotFocus, KeyDown, KeyUp, LayoutUpdated, Loaded, LostFocus, MouseEnter,
MouseLeave, MouseLeftButtonDown, MouseLeftButtonUp, MouseMove, SizeChanged

Calendar

Properties

ActualHeight, ActualWidth, AreDatesInPastSelectable, Clip, Cursor, DataContext, DayStyle,
DesiredSize, Dispatcher, DisplayDate, DisplayDateEnd, DisplayDateStart, DisplayMode,
FirstDayOfWeek, Height, HorizontalAlignment, HorizontalContentAlignment, IsEnabled,
IsHitTestVisible, IsTabStop, IsTodayHighlighted, Language, Margin, MaxHeight, MaxWidth,

MinHeight, MinWidth, MonthStyle, Name, Opacity, OpacityMask, Padding, Parent, RenderSize, RenderTransform, RenderTransformOrigin, Resources, SelectableDateEnd, SelectableDateStart, SelectedDate, Style, TabIndex, TabNavigation, Tag, Template, Triggers, VerticalAlignment, VerticalContentAlignment, Visibility, Width

Methods

ApplyTemplate, Arrange, ArrangeOverride, CaptureMouse, CheckAccess, Equals, Finalize, FindName, Focus, GetAnimationBaseValue, GetHashCode, GetTemplateChild, GetType, GetValue, HitTest, InitializeFromXaml, InvalidateArrange, InvalidateMeasure, Measure, MeasureOverride, MemberwiseClone, OnApplyTemplate, ReleaseMouseCapture, SetBinding, SetValue, ToString, TransformToVisual, UpdateLayout

Events

DateSelected, DisplayDateChanged, DisplayModeChanged, GotFocus, KeyDown, KeyUp, LayoutUpdated, Loaded, LostFocus, MouseEnter, MouseLeave, MouseLeftButtonDown, MouseLeftButtonUp, MouseMove, SizeChanged

Canvas

Properties

ActualHeight, ActualWidth, Background, Children, Clip, Cursor, DataContext, DesiredSize, Dispatcher, Height, HorizontalAlignment, IsHitTestVisible, Language, Margin, MaxHeight, MaxWidth, MinHeight, MinWidth, Name, Opacity, OpacityMask, Parent, RenderSize, RenderTransform, RenderTransformOrigin, Resources, Style, Tag, Triggers, VerticalAlignment, Visibility, Width

Methods

Arrange, ArrangeOverride, CaptureMouse, CheckAccess, Equals, Finalize, FindName, GetAnimationBaseValue, GetHashCode, GetLeft, GetTop, GetType, GetValue, GetZIndex, HitTest, InvalidateArrange, InvalidateMeasure, Measure, MeasureOverride, MemberwiseClone, ReleaseMouseCapture, SetBinding, SetLeft, SetTop, SetValue, SetZIndex, ToString, TransformToVisual, UpdateLayout

Events

GotFocus, KeyDown, KeyUp, LayoutUpdated, Loaded, LostFocus, MouseEnter, MouseLeave, MouseLeftButtonDown, MouseLeftButtonUp, MouseMove, SizeChanged

CheckBox

Properties

ActualHeight, ActualWidth, Background, ClickMode, Clip, Content, ContentTemplate, Cursor, DataContext, DesiredSize, Dispatcher, FontFamily, FontSize, FontStretch, FontStyle, FontWeight, Foreground, Height, HorizontalAlignment, HorizontalContentAlignment, IsChecked, IsEnabled,

IsFocused, IsHitTestVisible, IsMouseOver, IsPressed, IsTabStop, IsThreeState, Language, Margin, MaxHeight, MaxWidth, MinHeight, MinWidth, Name, Opacity, OpacityMask, Padding, Parent, RenderSize, RenderTransform, RenderTransformOrigin, Resources, Style, TabIndex, TabNavigation, Tag, Template, TextAlignment, TextDecorations, TextWrapping, ToolTip, Triggers, VerticalAlignment, VerticalContentAlignment, Visibility, Width

Methods

ApplyTemplate, Arrange, ArrangeOverride, CaptureMouse, CheckAccess, Equals, Finalize, FindName, Focus, GetAnimationBaseValue, GetHashCode, GetTemplateChild, GetType, GetValue, HitTest, InitializeFromXaml, InvalidateArrange, InvalidateMeasure, Measure, MeasureOverride, MemberwiseClone, OnApplyTemplate, OnChecked, OnClick, OnContentChanged, OnContentTemplateChanged, OnGotFocus, OnIndeterminate, OnIsEnabledChanged, OnIsPressedChanged, OnKeyDown, OnKeyUp, OnLostFocus, OnMouseEnter, OnMouseLeave, OnMouseLeftButtonDown, OnMouseLeftButtonUp, OnMouseMove, OnToggle, OnUnchecked, ReleaseMouseCapture, SetBinding, SetValue, ToString, TransformToVisual, UpdateLayout

Events

Checked, Click, GotFocus, Indeterminate, KeyDown, KeyUp, LayoutUpdated, Loaded, LostFocus, MouseEnter, MouseLeave, MouseLeftButtonDown, MouseLeftButtonUp, MouseMove, SizeChanged, Unchecked

DataGrid

Properties

ActualHeight, ActualWidth, AlternatingRowBackground, AutoGenerateColumns, CanUserResizeColumns, Clip, ColumnHeadersHeight, ColumnHeaderStyle, Columns, ColumnWidth, CornerHeaderStyle, CurrentColumn, CurrentItem, Cursor, DataContext, DesiredSize, Dispatcher, GridlinesVisibility, HeadersVisibility, HeaderTemplate, Height, HorizontalAlignment, HorizontalContentAlignment, HorizontalGridlinesBrush, HorizontalScrollBarVisibility, IsHitTestVisible, IsReadOnly, IsTabStop, ItemsSource, Language, Margin, MaxHeight, MaxWidth, MinHeight, MinWidth, Name, Opacity, OpacityMask, OverrideRowDetailsScrolling, Padding, Parent, RenderSize, RenderTransform, RenderTransformOrigin, Resources, RowBackground, RowDetailsTemplate, RowDetailsVisibility, RowHeaderStyle, RowHeadersWidth, RowHeight, RowStyle, SelectedItem, SelectedItems, SelectionMode, Style, TabIndex, TabNavigation, Tag, Template, Triggers, VerticalAlignment, VerticalContentAlignment, VerticalGridlinesBrush, VerticalScrollBarVisibility, Visibility, Width

Methods

ApplyTemplate, Arrange, ArrangeOverride, BeginEdit, CaptureMouse, CheckAccess, EndEdit, Equals, Finalize, FindName, Focus, GetAnimationBaseValue, GetHashCode, GetRowDetailsVisibility, GetTemplateChild, GetType, GetValue, HitTest, InitializeFromXaml, InvalidateArrange, InvalidateMeasure, Measure, MeasureOverride, MemberwiseClone,

OnApplyTemplate, OnAutoGeneratingColumn, OnBeginningCellEdit, OnCleaningRow, OnCleaningRowDetails, OnColumnDisplayIndexChanged, OnCommitCellEdit, OnCommittingCellEdit, OnCommittingRowEdit, OnCurrentCellChanged, OnDataError, OnPrepareCellEdit, OnPreparingRow, OnPreparingRowDetails, OnSelectionChanged, ReleaseMouseCapture, SetBinding, SetValue, ToString, TransformToVisual, UpdateLayout

Events

AutoGeneratingColumn, BeginningCellEdit, CleaningRow, CleaningRowDetails, ColumnDisplayIndexChanged, CommitCellEdit, CommittingCellEdit, CommittingRowEdit, CurrentCellChanged, DataError, GotFocus, KeyDown, KeyUp, LayoutUpdated, Loaded, LostFocus, MouseEnter, MouseLeave, MouseLeftButtonDown, MouseLeftButtonUp, MouseMove, PrepareCellEdit, PreparingRow, PreparingRowDetails, SelectionChanged, SizeChanged

DatePicker

Properties

ActualHeight, ActualWidth, AreDatesInPastSelectable, CalendarStyle, Clip, Cursor, DataContext, DesiredSize, Dispatcher, DisplayDate, DisplayDateEnd, DisplayDateStart, FirstDayOfWeek, Height, HorizontalAlignment, HorizontalContentAlignment, IsDropDownOpen, IsEnabled, IsHitTestVisible, IsTabStop, IsTodayHighlighted, Language, Margin, MaxHeight, MaxWidth, MinHeight, MinWidth, Name, Opacity, OpacityMask, Padding, Parent, RenderSize, RenderTransform, RenderTransformOrigin, Resources, SelectableDateEnd, SelectableDateStart, SelectedDate, SelectedDateFormat, Style, TabIndex, TabNavigation, Tag, Template, Text, ToolTip, Triggers, VerticalAlignment, VerticalContentAlignment, Visibility, Width

Methods

ApplyTemplate, Arrange, ArrangeOverride, CaptureMouse, CheckAccess, Equals, Finalize, FindName, Focus, GetAnimationBaseValue, GetHashCode, GetTemplateChild, GetType, GetValue, HitTest, InitializeFromXaml, InvalidateArrange, InvalidateMeasure, Measure, MeasureOverride, MemberwiseClone, OnApplyTemplate, OnTextParseError, ReleaseMouseCapture, SetBinding, SetValue, ToString, TransformToVisual, UpdateLayout

Events

CalendarClosed, CalendarOpened, DateSelected, GotFocus, KeyDown, KeyUp, LayoutUpdated, Loaded, LostFocus, MouseEnter, MouseLeave, MouseLeftButtonDown, MouseLeftButtonUp, MouseMove, SizeChanged, TextParseError

DoubleAnimation

Properties

Dispatcher, KeyTime, Value

Methods

CheckAccess, Equals, Finalize, GetAnimationBaseValue, GetHashCode, GetType, GetValue, MemberwiseClone, SetValue, ToString

Events

Completed

DoubleAnimationUsingKeyFrames

Properties

AutoReverse, BeginTime, Dispatcher, Duration, FillBehavior, KeyFrames, RepeatBehavior, SpeedRatio

Methods

CheckAccess, Equals, Finalize, GetAnimationBaseValue, GetHashCode, GetType, GetValue, MemberwiseClone, ReadLocalValue, SetValue, ToString

Events

Completed

DoubleKeyFrame

Properties

Dispatcher, KeyTime, KeyValue

Methods

CheckAccess, Equals, Finalize, GetAnimationBaseValue, GetHashCode, GetType, GetValue, MemberwiseClone, SetValue, ToString

Ellipse

Properties

ActualHeight, ActualWidth, Clip, Cursor, DataContext, DesiredSize, Dispatcher, Fill, GeometryTransform, Height, HorizontalAlignment, IsHitTestVisible, Language, Margin, MaxHeight, MaxWidth, MinHeight, MinWidth, Name, Opacity, OpacityMask, Parent, RenderSize, RenderTransform, RenderTransformOrigin, Resources, Stretch, Stroke, StrokeDashArray, StrokeDashCap, StrokeDashOffset, StrokeEndLineCap, StrokeLineJoin, StrokeMiterLimit, StrokeStartLineCap, StrokeThickness, Style, Tag, Triggers, VerticalAlignment, Visibility, Width

Methods

Arrange, ArrangeOverride, CaptureMouse, CheckAccess, Equals, Finalize, FindName, GetAnimationBaseValue, GetHashCode, GetType, GetValue, HitTest, InvalidateArrange, InvalidateMeasure, Measure, MeasureOverride, MemberwiseClone, ReleaseMouseCapture, SetBinding, SetValue, ToString, TransformToVisual, UpdateLayout

Events

GotFocus, KeyDown, KeyUp, LayoutUpdated, Loaded, LostFocus, MouseEnter, MouseLeave, MouseLeftButtonDown, MouseLeftButtonUp, MouseMove, SizeChanged

Grid

Properties

ActualHeight, ActualWidth, Background, Children, Clip, ColumnDefinitions, Cursor, DataContext, DesiredSize, Dispatcher, Height, HorizontalAlignment, IsHitTestVisible, Language, Margin, MaxHeight, MaxWidth, MinHeight, MinWidth, Name, Opacity, OpacityMask, Parent, RenderSize, RenderTransform, RenderTransformOrigin, Resources, RowDefinitions, ShowGridLines, Style, Tag, Triggers, VerticalAlignment, Visibility, Width

Methods

Arrange, ArrangeOverride, CaptureMouse, CheckAccess, Equals, Finalize, FindName, GetAnimationBaseValue, GetColumn, GetColumnSpan, GetHashCode, GetRow, GetRowSpan, GetType, GetValue, HitTest, InvalidateArrange, InvalidateMeasure, Measure, MeasureOverride, MemberwiseClone, ReleaseMouseCapture, SetBinding, SetColumn, SetColumnSpan, SetRow, SetRowSpan, SetValue, ToString, TransformToVisual, UpdateLayout

Events

GotFocus, KeyDown, KeyUp, LayoutUpdated, Loaded, LostFocus, MouseEnter, MouseLeave, MouseLeftButtonDown, MouseLeftButtonUp, MouseMove, SizeChanged

GridSplitter

Properties

ActualHeight, ActualWidth, Background, Clip, Cursor, DataContext, DesiredSize, Dispatcher, Height, HorizontalAlignment, HorizontalContentAlignment, IsEnabled, IsHitTestVisible, IsTabStop, Language, Margin, MaxHeight, MaxWidth, MinHeight, MinWidth, Name, Opacity, OpacityMask, Padding, Parent, PreviewStyle, RenderSize, RenderTransform, RenderTransformOrigin, Resources, ShowsPreview, Style, TabIndex, TabNavigation, Tag, Template, Triggers, VerticalAlignment, VerticalContentAlignment, Visibility, Width

Methods

ApplyTemplate, Arrange, ArrangeOverride, CaptureMouse, CheckAccess, Equals, Finalize, FindName, Focus, GetAnimationBaseValue, GetHashCode, GetTemplateChild, GetType, GetValue, HitTest, InitializeFromXaml, InvalidateArrange, InvalidateMeasure, Measure, MeasureOverride, MemberwiseClone, OnApplyTemplate, ReleaseMouseCapture, SetBinding, SetValue, ToString, TransformToVisual, UpdateLayout

Events

GotFocus, KeyDown, KeyUp, LayoutUpdated, Loaded, LostFocus, MouseEnter, MouseLeave, MouseLeftButtonDown, MouseLeftButtonUp, MouseMove, SizeChanged

HyperlinkButton

Properties

ActualHeight, ActualWidth, Background, ClickMode, Clip, Content, ContentTemplate, Cursor, DataContext, DesiredSize, Dispatcher, FontFamily, FontSize, FontStretch, FontStyle, FontWeight, Foreground, Height, HorizontalAlignment, HorizontalContentAlignment, IsEnabled, IsFocused, IsHitTestVisible, IsMouseOver, IsPressed, IsTabStop, Language, Margin, MaxHeight, MaxWidth, MinHeight, MinWidth, Name, NavigateUri, Opacity, OpacityMask, Padding, Parent, RenderSize, RenderTransform, RenderTransformOrigin, Resources, Style, TabIndex, TabNavigation, Tag, TargetName, Template, TextAlignment, TextDecorations, TextWrapping, ToolTip, Triggers, VerticalAlignment, VerticalContentAlignment, Visibility, Width

Methods

ApplyTemplate, Arrange, ArrangeOverride, CaptureMouse, CheckAccess, Equals, Finalize, FindName, Focus, GetAnimationBaseValue, GetHashCode, GetTemplateChild, GetType, GetValue, HitTest, InitializeFromXaml, InvalidateArrange, InvalidateMeasure, Measure, MeasureOverride, MemberwiseClone, OnApplyTemplate, OnClick, OnContentChanged, OnContentTemplateChanged, OnGotFocus, OnIsEnabledChanged, OnIsPressedChanged, OnKeyDown, OnKeyUp, OnLostFocus, OnMouseEnter, OnMouseLeave, OnMouseLeftButtonDown, OnMouseLeftButtonUp, OnMouseMove, ReleaseMouseCapture, SetBinding, SetValue, ToString, TransformToVisual, UpdateLayout

Events

Click, GotFocus, KeyDown, KeyUp, LayoutUpdated, Loaded, LostFocus, MouseEnter, MouseLeave, MouseLeftButtonDown, MouseLeftButtonUp, MouseMove, SizeChanged

Image

Properties

ActualHeight, ActualWidth, Clip, Cursor, DataContext, DesiredSize, Dispatcher, DownloadProgress, Height, HorizontalAlignment, IsHitTestVisible, Language, Margin, MaxHeight, MaxWidth, MinHeight, MinWidth, Name, Opacity, OpacityMask, Parent, RenderSize,

RenderTransform, RenderTransformOrigin, Resources, Source, Stretch, Style, Tag, Triggers, VerticalAlignment, Visibility, Width

Methods

Arrange, ArrangeOverride, CaptureMouse, CheckAccess, Equals, Finalize, FindName, GetAnimationBaseValue, GetHashCode, GetType, GetValue, HitTest, InvalidateArrange, InvalidateMeasure, Measure, MeasureOverride, MemberwiseClone, ReleaseMouseCapture, SetBinding, SetValue, ToString, TransformToVisual, UpdateLayout

Events

Arrange, ArrangeOverride, CaptureMouse, CheckAccess, Equals, Finalize, FindName, GetAnimationBaseValue, GetHashCode, GetType, GetValue, HitTest, InvalidateArrange, InvalidateMeasure, Measure, MeasureOverride, MemberwiseClone, ReleaseMouseCapture, SetBinding, SetValue, ToString, TransformToVisual, UpdateLayout

Line

Properties

ActualHeight, ActualWidth, Clip, Cursor, DataContext, DesiredSize, Dispatcher, Fill, GeometryTransform, Height, HorizontalAlignment, IsHitTestVisible, Language, Margin, MaxHeight, MaxWidth, MinHeight, MinWidth, Name, Opacity, OpacityMask, Parent, RenderSize, RenderTransform, RenderTransformOrigin, Resources, Stretch, Stroke, StrokeDashArray, StrokeDashCap, StrokeDashOffset, StrokeEndLineCap, StrokeLineJoin, StrokeMiterLimit, StrokeStartLineCap, StrokeThickness, Style, Tag, Triggers, VerticalAlignment, Visibility, Width, X1, X2, Y1, Y2

Methods

Arrange, ArrangeOverride, CaptureMouse, CheckAccess, Equals, Finalize, FindName, GetAnimationBaseValue, GetHashCode, GetType, GetValue, HitTest, InvalidateArrange, InvalidateMeasure, Measure, MeasureOverride, MemberwiseClone, ReleaseMouseCapture, SetBinding, SetValue, ToString, TransformToVisual, UpdateLayout

Events

GotFocus, KeyDown, KeyUp, LayoutUpdated, Loaded, LostFocus, MouseEnter, MouseLeave, MouseLeftButtonDown, MouseLeftButtonUp, MouseMove, SizeChanged

ListBox

Properties

ActualHeight, ActualWidth, Clip, Cursor, DataContext, DesiredSize, Dispatcher, DisplayMemberPath, Height, HorizontalAlignment, HorizontalContentAlignment, IsHitTestVisible, IsTabStop, ItemContainerStyle, Items, ItemsHost, ItemsPanel, ItemsSource, ItemTemplate, Language, Margin, MaxHeight, MaxWidth, MinHeight, MinWidth, Name, Opacity, OpacityMask,

Padding, Parent, RenderSize, RenderTransform, RenderTransformOrigin, Resources, SelectedIndex, SelectedItem, SelectedItems, SelectionMode, Style, TabIndex, TabNavigation, Tag, Template, Triggers, VerticalAlignment, VerticalContentAlignment, Visibility, Width

Methods

ApplyTemplate, Arrange, ArrangeOverride, CaptureMouse, CheckAccess, ClearContainerForItemOverride, Equals, Finalize, FindName, Focus, GetAnimationBaseValue, GetContainerForItemOverride, GetHashCode, GetIsSelectionActive, GetTemplateChild, GetType, GetValue, HitTest, InitializeFromXaml, InvalidateArrange, InvalidateMeasure, IsItemItsOwnContainerOverride, Measure, MeasureOverride, MemberwiseClone, OnApplyTemplate, OnGotFocus, OnIsSelectionActiveChanged, OnItemContainerStyleChanged, OnKeyDown, OnLostFocus, OnSelectedIndexChanged, OnSelectedItemChanged, OnSelectedItemsChanged, OnSelectionChanged, OnSelectionModeChanged, PrepareContainerForItemOverride, ReleaseMouseCapture, ScrollIntoView, SetBinding, SetValue, ToString, TransformToVisual, UpdateLayout

Events

GotFocus, KeyDown, KeyUp, LayoutUpdated, Loaded, LostFocus, MouseEnter, MouseLeave, MouseLeftButtonDown, MouseLeftButtonUp, MouseMove, SelectionChanged, SizeChanged

MediaElement

Properties

ActualHeight, ActualWidth, Attributes, AudioStreamCount, AudioStreamIndex, AutoPlay, Balance, BufferingProgress, BufferingTime, CanPause, CanSeek, Clip, CurrentState, Cursor, DataContext, DesiredSize, Dispatcher, DownloadProgress, DownloadProgressOffset, Height, HorizontalAlignment, IsHitTestVisible, IsMuted, Language, Margin, Markers, MaxHeight, MaxWidth, MinHeight, MinWidth, Name, NaturalDuration, NaturalVideoHeight, NaturalVideoWidth, Opacity, OpacityMask, Parent, Position, RenderSize, RenderTransform, RenderTransformOrigin, Resources, Source, Stretch, Style, Tag, Triggers, VerticalAlignment, Visibility, Volume, Width

Methods

Arrange, ArrangeOverride, CaptureMouse, CheckAccess, Equals, Finalize, FindName, GetAnimationBaseValue, GetHashCode, GetType, GetValue, HitTest, InvalidateArrange, InvalidateMeasure, Measure, MeasureOverride, MemberwiseClone, Pause, Play, ReleaseMouseCapture, SetBinding, SetSource, SetValue, Stop, ToString, TransformToVisual, UpdateLayout

Events

BufferingProgressChanged, CurrentStateChanged, DownloadProgressChanged, GotFocus, KeyDown, KeyUp, LayoutUpdated, Loaded, LostFocus, MarkerReached, MediaEnded, MediaFailed, MediaOpened, MouseEnter, MouseLeave, MouseLeftButtonDown, MouseLeftButtonUp, MouseMove, SizeChanged

MultiScaleImage

Properties

ActualHeight, ActualWidth, AspectRatio, Clip, Cursor, DataContext, DesiredSize, Dispatcher, Height, HorizontalAlignment, IsHitTestVisible, Language, Margin, MaxHeight, MaxWidth, MinHeight, MinWidth, Name, Opacity, OpacityMask, Parent, RenderSize, RenderTransform, RenderTransformOrigin, Resources, Source, Style, SubImages, Tag, Triggers, UseSprings, VerticalAlignment, ViewportOrigin, ViewportWidth, Visibility, Width

Methods

Arrange, ArrangeOverride, CaptureMouse, CheckAccess, ElementToLogicalPoint, Equals, Finalize, FindName, GetAnimationBaseValue, GetHashCode, GetType, GetValue, HitTest, InvalidateArrange, InvalidateMeasure, LogicalToElementPoint, Measure, MeasureOverride, MemberwiseClone, ReleaseMouseCapture, SetBinding, SetValue, ToString, TransformToVisual, UpdateLayout, ZoomAboutLogicalPoint

Events

GotFocus, ImageFailed, ImageOpenFailed, ImageOpenSucceeded, KeyDown, KeyUp, LayoutUpdated, Loaded, LostFocus, MotionFinished, MouseEnter, MouseLeave, MouseLeftButtonDown, MouseLeftButtonUp, MouseMove, SizeChanged

Path

Properties

ActualHeight, ActualWidth, Clip, Cursor, Data, DataContext, DesiredSize, Dispatcher, Fill, GeometryTransform, Height, HorizontalAlignment, IsHitTestVisible, Language, Margin, MaxHeight, MaxWidth, MinHeight, MinWidth, Name, Opacity, OpacityMask, Parent, RenderSize, RenderTransform, RenderTransformOrigin, Resources, Stretch, Stroke, StrokeDashArray, StrokeDashCap, StrokeDashOffset, StrokeEndLineCap, StrokeLineJoin, StrokeMiterLimit, StrokeStartLineCap, StrokeThickness, Style, Tag, Triggers, VerticalAlignment, Visibility, Width

Methods

Arrange, ArrangeOverride, CaptureMouse, CheckAccess, Equals, Finalize, FindName, GetAnimationBaseValue, GetHashCode, GetType, GetValue, HitTest, InvalidateArrange, InvalidateMeasure, Measure, MeasureOverride, MemberwiseClone, ReleaseMouseCapture, SetBinding, SetValue, ToString, TransformToVisual, UpdateLayout

Events

GotFocus, KeyDown, KeyUp, LayoutUpdated, Loaded, LostFocus, MouseEnter, MouseLeave, MouseLeftButtonDown, MouseLeftButtonUp, MouseMove, SizeChanged

RadioButton

Properties

ActualHeight, ActualWidth, Background, ClickMode, Clip, Content, ContentTemplate, Cursor, DataContext, DesiredSize, Dispatcher, FontFamily, FontSize, FontStretch, FontStyle, FontWeight, Foreground, GroupName, Height, HorizontalAlignment, HorizontalContentAlignment, IsChecked, IsEnabled, IsFocused, IsHitTestVisible, IsMouseOver, IsPressed, IsTabStop, IsThreeState, Language, Margin, MaxHeight, MaxWidth, MinHeight, MinWidth, Name, Opacity, OpacityMask, Padding, Parent, RenderSize, RenderTransform, RenderTransformOrigin, Resources, Style, TabIndex, TabNavigation, Tag, Template, TextAlignment, TextDecorations, TextWrapping, ToolTip, Triggers, VerticalAlignment, VerticalContentAlignment, Visibility, Width

Methods

ApplyTemplate, Arrange, ArrangeOverride, CaptureMouse, CheckAccess, Equals, Finalize, FindName, Focus, GetAnimationBaseValue, GetHashCode, GetTemplateChild, GetType, GetValue, HitTest, InitializeFromXaml, InvalidateArrange, InvalidateMeasure, Measure, MeasureOverride, MemberwiseClone, OnApplyTemplate, OnChecked, OnClick, OnContentChanged, OnContentTemplateChanged, OnGotFocus, OnIndeterminate, OnIsEnabledChanged, OnIsPressedChanged, OnKeyDown, OnKeyUp, OnLostFocus, OnMouseEnter, OnMouseLeave, OnMouseLeftButtonDown, OnMouseLeftButtonUp, OnMouseMove, OnToggle, OnUnchecked, ReleaseMouseCapture, SetBinding, SetValue, ToString, TransformToVisual, UpdateLayout

Events

Checked, Click, GotFocus, Indeterminate, KeyDown, KeyUp, LayoutUpdated, Loaded, LostFocus, MouseEnter, MouseLeave, MouseLeftButtonDown, MouseLeftButtonUp, MouseMove, SizeChanged, Unchecked

Rectangle

Properties

ActualHeight, ActualWidth, Clip, Cursor, DataContext, DesiredSize, Dispatcher, Fill, GeometryTransform, Height, HorizontalAlignment, IsHitTestVisible, Language, Margin, MaxHeight, MaxWidth, MinHeight, MinWidth, Name, Opacity, OpacityMask, Parent, RadiusX, RadiusY, RenderSize, RenderTransform, RenderTransformOrigin, Resources, Stretch, Stroke, StrokeDashArray, StrokeDashCap, StrokeDashOffset, StrokeEndLineCap, StrokeLineJoin, StrokeMiterLimit, StrokeStartLineCap, StrokeThickness, Style, Tag, Triggers, VerticalAlignment, Visibility, Width

Methods

Arrange, ArrangeOverride, CaptureMouse, CheckAccess, Equals, Finalize, FindName, GetAnimationBaseValue, GetHashCode, GetType, GetValue, HitTest, InvalidateArrange, InvalidateMeasure, Measure, MeasureOverride, MemberwiseClone, ReleaseMouseCapture, SetBinding, SetValue, ToString, TransformToVisual, UpdateLayout

Events

GotFocus, KeyDown, KeyUp, LayoutUpdated, Loaded, LostFocus, MouseEnter, MouseLeave, MouseLeftButtonDown, MouseLeftButtonUp, MouseMove, SizeChanged

RepeatButton

Properties

ActualHeight, ActualWidth, Background, ClickMode, Clip, Content, ContentTemplate, Cursor, DataContext, Delay, DesiredSize, Dispatcher, FontFamily, FontSize, FontStretch, FontStyle, FontWeight, Foreground, Height, HorizontalAlignment, HorizontalContentAlignment, Interval, IsEnabled, IsFocused, IsHitTestVisible, IsMouseOver, IsPressed, IsTabStop, Language, Margin, MaxHeight, MaxWidth, MinHeight, MinWidth, Name, Opacity, OpacityMask, Padding, Parent, RenderSize, RenderTransform, RenderTransformOrigin, Resources, Style, TabIndex, TabNavigation, Tag, Template, TextAlignment, TextDecorations, TextWrapping, ToolTip, Triggers, VerticalAlignment, VerticalContentAlignment, Visibility, Width

Methods

ApplyTemplate, Arrange, ArrangeOverride, CaptureMouse, CheckAccess, Equals, Finalize, FindName, Focus, GetAnimationBaseValue, GetHashCode, GetTemplateChild, GetType, GetValue, HitTest, InitializeFromXaml, InvalidateArrange, InvalidateMeasure, Measure, MeasureOverride, MemberwiseClone, OnApplyTemplate, OnClick, OnContentChanged, OnContentTemplateChanged, OnGotFocus, OnIsEnabledChanged, OnIsPressedChanged, OnKeyDown, OnKeyUp, OnLostFocus, OnMouseEnter, OnMouseLeave, OnMouseLeftButtonDown, OnMouseLeftButtonUp, OnMouseMove, ReleaseMouseCapture, SetBinding, SetValue, ToString, TransformToVisual, UpdateLayout

Events

Click, GotFocus, KeyDown, KeyUp, LayoutUpdated, Loaded, LostFocus, MouseEnter, MouseLeave, MouseLeftButtonDown, MouseLeftButtonUp, MouseMove, SizeChanged

ScrollBar

Properties

ActualHeight, ActualWidth, Clip, Cursor, DataContext, DesiredSize, Dispatcher, Height, HorizontalAlignment, HorizontalContentAlignment, IsEnabled, IsHitTestVisible, IsTabStop, Language, LargeChange, Margin, MaxHeight, Maximum, MaxWidth, MinHeight, Minimum, MinWidth, Name, Opacity, OpacityMask, Orientation, Padding, Parent, RenderSize, RenderTransform, RenderTransformOrigin, Resources, SmallChange, Style, TabIndex, TabNavigation, Tag, Template, ToolTip, Triggers, Value, VerticalAlignment, VerticalContentAlignment, ViewportSize, Visibility, Width

Methods

ApplyTemplate, Arrange, ArrangeOverride, CaptureMouse, CheckAccess, Equals, Finalize, FindName, Focus, GetAnimationBaseValue, GetHashCode, GetTemplateChild, GetType, GetValue, HitTest, InitializeFromXaml, InvalidateArrange, InvalidateMeasure, Measure, MeasureOverride, MemberwiseClone, OnApplyTemplate, OnMaximumChanged, OnMinimumChanged, OnValueChanged, ReleaseMouseCapture, SetBinding, SetValue, ToString, TransformToVisual, UpdateLayout

Events

GotFocus, KeyDown, KeyUp, LayoutUpdated, Loaded, LostFocus, MouseEnter, MouseLeave, MouseLeftButtonDown, MouseLeftButtonUp, MouseMove, Scroll, SizeChanged, ValueChanged

ScrollViewer

Properties

ActualHeight, ActualWidth, Background, Clip, ComputedHorizontalScrollBarVisibility, ComputedVerticalScrollBarVisibility, Content, ContentTemplate, Cursor, DataContext, DesiredSize, Dispatcher, FontFamily, FontSize, FontStretch, FontStyle, FontWeight, Foreground, Height, HorizontalAlignment, HorizontalContentAlignment, HorizontalOffset, HorizontalScrollBarVisibility, IsEnabled, IsHitTestVisible, IsTabStop, Language, Margin, MaxHeight, MaxWidth, MinHeight, MinWidth, Name, Opacity, OpacityMask, Padding, Parent, RenderSize, RenderTransform, RenderTransformOrigin, Resources, ScrollableHeight, ScrollableWidth, Style, TabIndex, TabNavigation, Tag, Template, TextAlignment, TextDecorations, TextWrapping, ToolTip, Triggers, VerticalAlignment, VerticalContentAlignment, VerticalOffset, VerticalScrollBarVisibility, ViewportHeight, ViewportWidth, Visibility, Width

Methods

ApplyTemplate, Arrange, ArrangeOverride, CaptureMouse, CheckAccess, Equals, Finalize, FindName, Focus, GetAnimationBaseValue, GetHashCode, GetHorizontalScrollBarVisibility, GetTemplateChild, GetType, GetValue, GetVerticalScrollBarVisibility, HitTest, InitializeFromXaml, InvalidateArrange, InvalidateMeasure, Measure, MeasureOverride, MemberwiseClone, OnApplyTemplate, OnContentChanged, OnContentTemplateChanged, OnIsEnabledChanged, ReleaseMouseCapture, ScrollToHorizontalOffset, ScrollToVerticalOffset, SetBinding, SetHorizontalScrollBarVisibility, SetValue, SetVerticalScrollBarVisibility, ToString, TransformToVisual, UpdateLayout

Events

GotFocus, KeyDown, KeyUp, LayoutUpdated, Loaded, LostFocus, MouseEnter, MouseLeave, MouseLeftButtonDown, MouseLeftButtonUp, MouseMove, SizeChanged

Slider

Properties

ActualHeight, ActualWidth, Clip, Cursor, DataContext, DesiredSize, Dispatcher, Height, HorizontalAlignment, HorizontalContentAlignment, IsDirectionReversed, IsEnabled, IsFocused, IsHitTestVisible, IsTabStop, Language, LargeChange, Margin, MaxHeight, Maximum, MaxWidth, MinHeight, Minimum, MinWidth, Name, Opacity, OpacityMask, Orientation, Padding, Parent, RenderSize, RenderTransform, RenderTransformOrigin, Resources, SmallChange, Style, TabIndex, TabNavigation, Tag, Template, ToolTip, Triggers, Value, VerticalAlignment, VerticalContentAlignment, Visibility, Width

Methods

ApplyTemplate, Arrange, ArrangeOverride, CaptureMouse, CheckAccess, Equals, Finalize, FindName, Focus, GetAnimationBaseValue, GetHashCode, GetTemplateChild, GetType, GetValue, HitTest, InitializeFromXaml, InvalidateArrange, InvalidateMeasure, Measure, MeasureOverride, MemberwiseClone, OnApplyTemplate, OnIsEnabledChanged, OnIsFocusChanged, OnMaximumChanged, OnMinimumChanged, OnOrientationChanged, OnValueChanged, ReleaseMouseCapture, SetBinding, SetValue, ToString, TransformToVisual, UpdateLayout, UpdateTrackLayout

Events

GotFocus, KeyDown, KeyUp, LayoutUpdated, Loaded, LostFocus, MouseEnter, MouseLeave, MouseLeftButtonDown, MouseLeftButtonUp, MouseMove, SizeChanged, ValueChanged

SplineDoubleKeyFrame

Properties

Dispatcher, KeySpline, KeyTime, Value

Methods

CheckAccess, Equals, Finalize, GetAnimationBaseValue, GetHashCode, GetType, GetValue, MemberwiseClone, SetValue, ToString

Storyboard

Properties

AutoReverse, BeginTime, Children, Dispatcher, Duration, FillBehavior, RepeatBehavior, SpeedRatio

Methods

Begin, CheckAccess, Equals, Finalize, GetAnimationBaseValue, GetClockState, GetCurrentTime, GetHashCode, GetTargetName, GetTargetProperty, GetType, GetValue, MemberwiseClone, Pause, Resume, Seek, SeekAlignedToLastTick, SetTarget, SetTargetName, SetTargetProperty, SetValue, SkipToFill, Stop, ToString

Events

Completed

StackPanel

Properties

ActualHeight, ActualWidth, Background, Children, Clip, Cursor, DataContext, DesiredSize, Dispatcher, Height, HorizontalAlignment, IsHitTestVisible, Language, Margin, MaxHeight, MaxWidth, MinHeight, MinWidth, Name, Opacity, OpacityMask, Orientation, Parent, RenderSize, RenderTransform, RenderTransformOrigin, Resources, Style, Tag, Triggers, VerticalAlignment, Visibility, Width

Methods

Arrange, ArrangeOverride, CaptureMouse, CheckAccess, Equals, Finalize, FindName, GetAnimationBaseValue, GetHashCode, GetType, GetValue, HitTest, InvalidateArrange, InvalidateMeasure, Measure, MeasureOverride, MemberwiseClone, ReleaseMouseCapture, SetBinding, SetValue, ToString, TransformToVisual, UpdateLayout

Events

GotFocus, KeyDown, KeyUp, LayoutUpdated, Loaded, LostFocus, MouseEnter, MouseLeave, MouseLeftButtonDown, MouseLeftButtonUp, MouseMove, SizeChanged

TextBlock

Properties

ActualHeight, ActualWidth, Clip, Cursor, DataContext, DesiredSize, Dispatcher, FontFamily, FontSize, FontSource, FontStretch, FontStyle, FontWeight, Foreground, Height, HorizontalAlignment, Inlines, IsHitTestVisible, Language, LineHeight, LineStackingStrategy, Margin, MaxHeight, MaxWidth, MinHeight, MinWidth, Name, Opacity, OpacityMask, Padding, Parent, RenderSize, RenderTransform, RenderTransformOrigin, Resources, Style, Tag, Text, TextAlignment, TextDecorations, TextWrapping, Triggers, VerticalAlignment, Visibility, Width

Methods

Arrange, ArrangeOverride, CaptureMouse, CheckAccess, Equals, Finalize, FindName, GetAnimationBaseValue, GetHashCode, GetType, GetValue, HitTest, InvalidateArrange, InvalidateMeasure, Measure, MeasureOverride, MemberwiseClone, ReleaseMouseCapture, SetBinding, SetValue, ToString, TransformToVisual, UpdateLayout

Events

GotFocus, KeyDown, KeyUp, LayoutUpdated, Loaded, LostFocus, MouseEnter, MouseLeave, MouseLeftButtonDown, MouseLeftButtonUp, MouseMove, SizeChanged

TextBox

Properties

AcceptsReturn, ActualHeight, ActualWidth, Background, BorderBrush, BorderThickness, Clip, Cursor, DataContext, DesiredSize, Dispatcher, FontFamily, FontSize, FontSource, FontStretch, FontStyle, FontWeight, Foreground, Height, HorizontalAlignment, HorizontalContentAlignment, IsHitTestVisible, IsReadOnly, IsTabStop, Language, Margin, MaxHeight, MaxLength, MaxWidth, MinHeight, MinWidth, Name, Opacity, OpacityMask, Padding, Parent, RenderSize, RenderTransform, RenderTransformOrigin, Resources, SelectedText, SelectionBackground, SelectionForeground, SelectionLength, SelectionStart, Style, TabIndex, TabNavigation, Tag, Template, Text, TextAlignment, Triggers, VerticalAlignment, VerticalContentAlignment, Visibility, Width

Methods

ApplyTemplate, Arrange, ArrangeOverride, CaptureMouse, CheckAccess, Equals, Finalize, FindName, Focus, GetAnimationBaseValue, GetHashCode, GetTemplateChild, GetType, GetValue, HitTest, InitializeFromXaml, InvalidateArrange, InvalidateMeasure, Measure, MeasureOverride, MemberwiseClone, OnApplyTemplate, ReleaseMouseCapture, Select, SetBinding, SetValue, ToString, TransformToVisual, UpdateLayout

Events

GotFocus, KeyDown, KeyUp, LayoutUpdated, Loaded, LostFocus, MouseEnter, MouseLeave, MouseLeftButtonDown, MouseLeftButtonUp, MouseMove, SelectionChanged, SizeChanged, TextChanged

ToggleButton

Properties

ActualHeight, ActualWidth, Background, ClickMode, Clip, Content, ContentTemplate, Cursor, DataContext, DesiredSize, Dispatcher, FontFamily, FontSize, FontStretch, FontStyle, FontWeight, Foreground, Height, HorizontalAlignment, HorizontalContentAlignment, IsChecked, IsEnabled, IsFocused, IsHitTestVisible, IsMouseOver, IsPressed, IsTabStop, IsThreeState, Language, Margin, MaxHeight, MaxWidth, MinHeight, MinWidth, Name, Opacity, OpacityMask, Padding, Parent, RenderSize, RenderTransform, RenderTransformOrigin, Resources, Style, TabIndex, TabNavigation, Tag, Template, TextAlignment, TextDecorations, TextWrapping, ToolTip, Triggers, VerticalAlignment, VerticalContentAlignment, Visibility, Width

Methods

ApplyTemplate, Arrange, ArrangeOverride, CaptureMouse, CheckAccess, Equals, Finalize, FindName, Focus, GetAnimationBaseValue, GetHashCode, GetTemplateChild, GetType, GetValue, HitTest, InitializeFromXaml, InvalidateArrange, InvalidateMeasure, Measure, MeasureOverride, MemberwiseClone, OnApplyTemplate, OnChecked, OnClick, OnContentChanged, OnContentTemplateChanged, OnGotFocus, OnIndeterminate, OnIsEnabledChanged, OnIsPressedChanged, OnKeyDown, OnKeyUp, OnLostFocus, OnMouseEnter, OnMouseLeave, OnMouseLeftButtonDown, OnMouseLeftButtonUp, OnMouseMove, OnToggle, OnUnchecked, ReleaseMouseCapture, SetBinding, SetValue, ToString, TransformToVisual, UpdateLayout

Events

Checked, Click, GotFocus, Indeterminate, KeyDown, KeyUp, LayoutUpdated, Loaded, LostFocus, MouseEnter, MouseLeave, MouseLeftButtonDown, MouseLeftButtonUp, MouseMove, SizeChanged, Unchecked

Index